Security Yearbook 2020

A History and Directory of the IT Security Industry

RICHARD STIENNON

IT Harvest Press | Birmingham, Michigan

Cover image: Stellar Cyber
Cover and interior design: Val d'Orito
Copyright 2019 by IT-Harvest Press.
All rights reserved. Published 2019.

IT-Harvest Press is an imprint of IT-Harvest, LLC, Birmingham, Michigan, USA

Supplementary material for Security Yearbook 2020 and subsequent editions are available at www.security-yearbook.com

Security Yearbook 2020: A History and Directory of the IT Security Industry
ISBN 978-1-945254-04-8

1st Printing
Printed in the United States of America

Thank You to Our Sponsors

Premier Sponsor

Spirent Communications offers innovative test, measurement, analytics, and assurance solutions for next-generation devices and networks. Spirent's security validation solutions and consulting services are used by organizations worldwide to meet compliance requirements, validate content-aware device performance, prioritize infrastructure and security investments, and gain consolidated intelligence required to support risk management policies. For more information visit spirent.com.

Silver Sponsors

Qualys, Inc. (Nasdaq: QLYS) is a pioneer and leading provider of cloud-based security and compliance solutions with over 10,300 customers in more than 130 countries, including a majority of each of the Forbes Global 100 and Fortune 100. Qualys helps organizations streamline and consolidate their security and compliance solutions in a single platform and build security into digital transformation initiatives for greater agility, better business outcomes, and substantial cost savings.

Skybox provides the industry's broadest cybersecurity management platform to address security challenges within large, complex networks. By integrating with 130 networking and security technologies, the Skybox® Security Suite gives comprehensive attack surface visibility and the context needed for informed action. Our analytics, automation, and intelligence improve the efficiency and performance of security operations in vulnerability and threat management and firewall and security policy management for the world's largest organizations.

Advertisers

Threat Intelligence

Compliance Automation

Groupsense.io
Managed Threat Intelligence

Phosphorus

IoT Device Management

STELLAR
C Y B E R

Unified Security Analytics

Micro-Segmentation for IoT

Mobile Threat Defense

Event Sponsors

T.E.N. – Tech Exec Networks

CISOCentric

Security Current

Acknowledgments

I have learned that creating a book is an arduous process, especially topical non-fiction, which has to be written, fact checked, cited, and formatted in a short period of time. This first edition of Security Yearbook was started in July 2019 and went to press in December. Gathering the data for the directory would have been impossible without the help of Sambath Ramesh and his team. Processing the data into a suitable form was done with assistance of the masterful coding skills of Bek Khaitbaev, who is also creating the online version of the database as well as supporting the website (security-yearbook.com). I am forever grateful to my writing mentor and editor Joe Ponepinto, editor of *Orca, A Literary Journal*, (orcalit.com), for editing all of my writing, starting with my first book in 2010. Creating academically rigorous citations is the bane of any student's or author's writing. Without the help of Sarah Stiennon I could not have completed this book on time. Courtney Feldman is the best proofreader I know. She catches all of my mistakes, even structural ones. Finally, Val d'Orito has been a lifesaver on more than one occasion, as she applies her design skills to both the graphics and layout of my books.

I also want to thank the community of security industry leaders and pioneers who have been so supportive of the idea of a history, and so generous with their time.

Contents

Introduction 11

Chapter 1: Getting to Know the IT Security Industry 15
Chapter 2: A Brief History of the IT Security Industry 27
Chapter 3: Network Security History 33
     Story: Gil Shwed 47
     Story: Chris Blask 57
Chapter 4: DDoS Defense 61
Chapter 5: Endpoint Protection from AV to EDR 65
     Story: Ron Moritz 75
Chapter 6: Identity and Access Management 79
     Story: Barry Schrager 83
Chapter 7: Data Security 87
     Story: David Cowan 93
     Story: Sandra Toms 103
     Story: Deborah Taylor Moore 107
Chapter 8: Governance Risk Compliance 111
Chapter 9: Failures 117
Chapter 10: Research Methodology 121

The 2019 Security Directory 125

Alphabetical Listings by Company Name 127
Listings By Country 197
US Listings By State 227
Listings By Category 267

Introduction

This is the history of the IT security industry. And like many good histories it must begin with an apology. Winston Churchill, in writing the preface to his *History of the Second World War*, was not exactly apologetic as he took credit for being in a position of one who "bore the chief responsibility for the war and policy of the British Commonwealth and Empire." Yet he declined to call his Nobel Prize winning work a history so much as a "contribution to history." John Lewis Gaddis, in the original preface to *The United States and the Origins of the Cold War*, claimed it is impractical to attempt a "definitive study of the origins of the Cold War," in light of the fact that the inner workings of the Kremlin were unavailable to him at the time. The self-effacing Gandhi wrote in the preface to his autobiography: "I hope and pray that no one will regard the advice interspersed in the following chapters as authoritative." Machiavelli practically groveled before his benefactor in the opening words of his *Discourses on the First Ten Books of Livy* by saying, "You may well complain of the poverty of my endeavor since these narrations of mine are poor, and of the fallacy of (my) judgment when I deceive myself in many parts of my discussion." So this author must be doubly apologetic, first for this attempt at conveying the breadth and depth of the lives and experiences of so many founders, inventors, and builders of IT security, and second for even mentioning the monumental works of these historians.

With that said, this history is meant to redress something that is missing from our world: a concise recounting of what has gone before in an entire industry that has arisen alongside the information age. When an industry has surpassed 25 years of existence, and experienced tremendous growth in size and relevance, there are participants who are oblivious to the past. Founders, marketers, salespeople, researchers, admins, policy makers, and students just beginning their journeys, who stumble into security through various paths, have a view of the industry that is a snapshot in time. Only through understanding the continuum of what has come before and has led to the present can they begin to understand what the future holds.

Twenty-five years is a very short time span and in the perspective of the 800-year history of the Roman empire, or even the 243-year history of the United States, it may be considered too soon to write a history of the IT security industry. By all measures the industry continues to grow at a rate of 25% each year. In addition to the spending on IT security that means that every year there are 25% more people who make their living practicing security. They are threat hunters, researchers, reverse engineers, developers, system administrators, network architects, data privacy professionals, cryptographers, and their managers and executives. In addition there are the marketing, sales, legal, product managers, and finance people who build products, take them to market, and grow the companies that provide the technology to counter the looming threat of bad actors.

The participants in this industry are on a mission. Yes, they are building careers, striving to get ahead, showing up to work, just as anyone does. But they are also fighting a battle. They are white hats fighting the black hats. They are driving toward a better world, one where data, privacy, and the future are sacrosanct. This is their story.

Students of history have learned to question the perspective of the historian. Are they from the school of liberalism? Neoliberals? Are they Realists? Constructivists? Which events do they choose to relate? And from what perspective? This history of the IT security industry is from the perspective of an industry analyst.

What is an industry analyst? It's someone whose job is to make sense of industry trends. They are tasked with predicting the technology future accurately and providing guidance that buyers of technology can use to make their purchasing decisions. An analyst has biases and their own experiences that color their perspective. One who comes from the financial world may focus on the numbers. A geek at heart is going to focus on the technology. A practitioner may even have an animosity towards vendors. But every analyst in every industry acquires a broad perspective, and like them, a security industry analyst must have a very wide purview. There are over 2,336 vendors of IT security products in over 200 separate categories. Grasping the entirety of that industry is a challenge *Security Yearbook 2020* hopes to achieve.

This analyst is a technologist at heart. An aerospace engineer by training and a structural engineer by experience, I jumped into security in 1995. It was the advent of the internet that led me to networking, as I launched an internet service provider for the automotive industry, appropriately named Rustnet, and then security as I joined Netrex, the managed security service provider (MSSP) acquired by ISS and now part of IBM's managed security service. My experience of stumbling into security is not uncommon. In the early days people did not study security in school. There were no cybersecurity programs. They came from all walks of life. Some may have had computer science backgrounds, but many were just caught up in the excitement of countering hackers, or perhaps they were hackers themselves. Like all entrepreneurs, they recognized a problem, thought of a solution, and attempted to build it. Thus, Gil Shwed, Shlomo Kramer, and Marius Nacht, the founders of Check Point Software, saw the problem with network access and invented the stateful firewall. John McAfee, Dr. Solomon, Eugene Kaspersky, and Roger Thomas tackled the problem of viruses spread though shared floppy disks. As the industry grew to incorporate more and more defensive components there were inventors and pioneers of each new category.

I played some small part in this industry. While at Netrex I introduced Shlomo Kramer to Robert Moskowitz, who convinced Check Point to pivot from SWAN to IPSec as the basis for what became VPN-1. I attended the first IPSec bakeoffs in Andover, Massachusetts, and Plano, Texas. I went on to PricewaterhouseCoopers where I conducted risk assessments and penetration tests of large technology, transportation, and financial services companies. I was drafted into Gartner as their second analyst covering security. I served stints at Webroot Software, Fortinet, and Blancco Technology Group. Some of my writing and research has influenced the direction of some of the largest players.

There are thousands of books on security and they are predominantly how-to guides. There are also hundreds of books that could be considered histories, but they are histories of incidents. I have written two such books, one on the history of state sponsored attacks (*Surviving Cyberwar*) and one on network warfare (*There Will be Cyberwar*). But there is no history of the people and companies who comprise the IT security industry. This book is an attempt at compiling that history.

CHAPTER 1

Getting to Know the IT Security Industry

The IT security industry is comprised today of over 2,336 vendors and an estimated 365,000 people working at those vendors. Of course there are many, many more people who work in IT security, from level one analysts in a Security Operations Center (SOC), to systems administrators who ensure that the servers under their purview are configured as optimally as possible, to the directors, VPs, and Chief Information Security Officers (CISOs) who lead the way in both the meticulous effort of maintaining a defensible posture and warding off an ever-growing number of threat actors.

The architecture of security lends itself to a simple way to approach the industry. A layered defense at the levels of network, endpoint, identity, and data security provide an appropriate way to think about the industry as a whole. While large, mature vendors of security products may seek to encompass all of the sectors, it is rare for them to dominate a market in more than one major category. There is a reason for that, which derives from the way IT security staff are specialized in these categories. Network security professionals have obtained their expertise studying network protocols, routing, DNS, and at least in the early days, the intricacies of telecom architectures. In the meantime, those in endpoint security have grown into their professions either from a system-centric focus on operating systems and applications, or from fighting the daily battle to ensure that virus signatures are up-to-date and systems properly patched. Data security practitioners are familiar with encryption, data governance, key management, and privacy concerns, while those who manage identities are expert in directory services, and myriad means of authentication.

In the modern enterprise with large security teams, this specialization has evolved over twenty years and purchasing decisions are made independently, with each team responsible for choosing the best solution for their areas of expertise.

It's no wonder then that a firewall vendor that grew to success through a relentless pursuit of enterprise customers, enhancing their product to stay competitive, seeking always to claim the fastest throughput, the largest number of connections per second, the lowest latency, and the best management, would be well-versed in competing for the attention of network security teams, but completely lacking in the connections, messaging, or evolved products needed to sell an endpoint security solution to completely different teams. Cisco has tried and failed to get on the endpoint, even though it has had moments when it dominated in both networking and firewalls. Fortinet, a company that relentlessly introduces products of its own making into every hot segment of security, has never succeeded at gaining success on the endpoint. Only the still unproven strategy of attempting to be the single source of security products for large customers justifies a network security company like Fortinet investing in the research and development of its Forticlient software.

The endpoint security vendors have even more trouble trying to cross boundaries into network security. They have teams of hundreds if not thousands of developers who are expert in reverse engineering, malware capture and analysis, and deployment to endpoints. Because they have to continuously enhance their endpoint protections, their client software tends to get bloated and it consumes more and more of a desktop's resources. Most end users of traditional endpoint security products have no great love for the products themselves. Frequent AV updates slow systems down and AV products are prone to false positives and generate continuous alerts. The AV admins have no great loyalty to the products they use and are always ready to listen to a vendor who promises a smaller footprint, fewer false positives, and better catch rates.

If a vendor like Symantec, the largest AV company with a market cap hovering around $14 billion on August 1, 2019 (with a jump to $16 billion after the announcement that Chinese chip maker Broadcom plans to acquire them), were to introduce a gateway security product, it would be met with derision by the network security teams within the enterprise. Network people are interested in avoiding slowdowns and false positives, and AV products are things that slow down performance. Symantec is a good example because it has tried many times to enter the network security space. The merger with Blue Coat was only the latest, and last, such attempt.

Network Associates is another example. The company was formed as a roll-up of a swath of security products and desktop management tools. One of those products, the Gauntlet Firewall acquired from Trusted Information Systems, was eventually end-of-lifed. It had only managed to penetrate the market to the tune of 3,000 customers by 2003 when NAI stopped support and turned those customers over to Secure Computing.

Identity and Access Management is a separate major category that resists efforts of vendors to include other products in their portfolios. This space had the additional burden of Microsoft entering the directory services market with Active Directory, a move that pretty much ended the opportunity for IAM vendors until recently, when a new crop of cloud services came about.

Finally encryption. From the vibrant days of competition between RSA, SafeNet, Entrust, Gemalto, and hundreds of others, the space has consolidated somewhat and the products commoditized. Yet there are still 321 vendors in this major category, and each addresses the need for protecting data and making encryption ubiquitous.

It is this striation of security vendors into categories that follow the overall IT security defense posture of layered defense that assists the understanding of the space. Most vendors fall into one of the major categories.

Category	Company Count
Network	373
Data Security	321
IAM	309
GRC	303
Endpoint	215
Operations	123
IoT Security	118
MSSP	113
Application Security	113
Security Analytics	101
Fraud Prevention	71
Threat Intelligence	69
Email Security	61
Training	19
Deception	15
Testing	13

Network Security

Network security vendors make up 16% of the total. Companies include Cisco, Palo Alto Networks, Check Point Software, Fortinet, SonicWall, and WatchGuard in the firewall space. There are numerous vendors that provide IPS, VPN, and network scanning solutions.

Data Security

This category is so large because it includes all of the data encryption vendors and the technologies needed for encryption, like certificate creation, key management, and the SSL Certificate Authorities (CAs). It also includes Information Rights Management (IRM).

Identity and Access Management

IAM is such a big category—309 companies—because in addition to directory services such as Microsoft Azure, Okta, and Ping Identity, it includes all the password managers and the multitude of solutions for strong authentication. These can be a simple mobile device token, or biometrics of fingerprints, retinas, irises, or keystrokes.

GRC

Governance Risk and Compliance (GRC) is the category that comprises all the tools used to ensure compliance with either security frameworks such as ITIL, NIST, or COBIT, or regulations such as GLBA, SOX, HIPAA, or GDPR. For the purposes of this Yearbook, technologies like risk scoring, posture analysis, and logging are lumped into this major category.

Endpoint Security

This category comprises 215 vendors that provide anti-virus, anti-malware, physical device security, server or endpoint hardening, and VM and container security. There are even some mainframe security vendors.

In addition to these categories there are several technologies that deserve their own classification because they are still new, and their buying centers (the team within the enterprises that makes the purchasing decision) and their usage prevent them from fitting into one of the other categories. These are:

Security Operations

A simple way to think of this category is anything needed by a Security Operations Center (SOC) to improve its operations. It could be a malware analysis tool for reverse engineering, or an incident handling tool.

Security Orchestration is part of Operations. It's simple in concept: identify the repetitive tasks that sap the efficacy of security operations and automate them. Account suspension and recovery, password resets, firewall policy changes, TCP resets, and routing changes are all examples of things a security orchestration solution is designed to do.

Security Orchestration and Response (SOAR) is becoming the term for orchestration solutions that take measures to respond to a discovered breach. This may be isolating infected machines, installing new policies in network security devices, or shunning an attack source through TCP resets. As attackers automate, these SOAR solutions will evolve to provide a response in minutes rather than the multi-day time frames which are currently considered best practice.

IoT Security

The Internet of Things (IoT) is the newest broad category of products that have been found lacking in security controls. Closed-circuit TV cameras, like those used at traffic intersections, and even baby monitors, thermostats, mobile devices like bar code scanners, and industrial control systems (ICS) all fall into this category. Add in the sensors and controls for ships, trains, bridges, and medical devices, all built and deployed with little thought of the way hackers would attack them, and you have a recipe for future disasters. Thus a new category of vendors has cropped up just in the past five years to address the problem with IoT security. Because of the special requirements for different segments, these vendors tend to focus on specific categories: consumer IoT, medical devices, automobiles, maritime, and industrial controls systems (ICS).

Managed Security Service Providers

Most organizations are not prepared to invest in all the product categories listed here, and even if they did, would not have the resources to manage them. Managed Security Service Providers (MSSPs) offer a broad range of products that they will deploy and remotely manage for their customers. The 113 listed in the directory are primarily MSSPs. There are thousands more that may be consulting firms that offer managed services as a sideline, or resellers that manage the products they sell. MSSPs invest in monitoring automation, security analytics, and finding and retaining staff that thrive in the stressful environment of dealing with continuous attacks against all of their customers.

Managed services are evolving into a category called Managed Detection and Response. Companies like eSentire deploy network monitoring sensors on a customer's network and endpoint detection and response (EDR) such as Carbon Black or CrowdStrike on desktops and servers. If an attack is detected, they use network defenses to shut it down or quarantine the misbehaving endpoint for remediation.

Application Security

Application security encompasses code scanning, containerization, application hardening, and mobile app analysis and protection. In academic circles and the US military this is often called software assurance, but the category has become very broad with 113 solution providers.

Security Analytics

One dramatic change in the makeup of the IT security industry over the last three years is the rise of security analytics. Most Security Information and Event Management (SIEM) solutions have morphed from aggregators of security alerts with a few algorithms meant to highlight the important

events, to full-fledged threat hunting and breach detection platforms. In 2019 Microsoft, Google, and AT&T made major announcements in this space. Microsoft and Google hoped that their ability to monitor and collect information from vast swaths of the internet would power something new. Google's Chronicle, announced with great fanfare and high expectations, stumbled out of the gate and has been reabsorbed into Google. AT&T acquired cloud SIEM vendor AlienVault and appointed its CEO, Barmak Meftah, as CEO of its newly formed AT&T Cybersecurity, which includes AT&T's managed services along with AlienVault's SIEM solution.

Detection has an interesting history. Clifford Stoll in *The Cuckoo's Egg* describes his archaic technique of hooking up a thermal printer to his network at Berkeley Labs and pouring through the printouts to see connection attempts that eventually led him to attackers in Eastern Europe. In the late '90s products from ISS and the open source Snort were deployed on network taps to log network events triggered by rules meant to detect hacking attempts through regular expression or signature matches. The problem with Intrusion Detection Systems (IDS) is that they generated far too many alerts to be dealt with. The question was raised: raised: If you could truly detect an attack, why would you generate an alert if you could block the attack before it did anything bad? One response was the creation of Intrusion Prevention (IPS), which eventually became a feature in firewalls. A limited number of things, such as worms, direct attacks over vulnerable protocols like

Telnet, and other attacks against known vulnerabilities, were simply blocked at the gateway.

But managing alerts from firewall logs, system logs, and IDS systems stayed with us and gave rise to two separate industry segments. One was Security Information and Event Management solutions like QRadar (now owned by IBM) and ArcSight (now part of Micro Focus). The other was Managed Security Service Providers (MSSPs). Because most organizations could not staff a 24x7x365 operation to monitor thousands of alerts a day, outsourcing to an MSSP became the preferred solution. MSSPs would also offer to manage the firewall and IDS devices to maintain their configurations and tune them.

But as major breaches at Target and SONY Entertainment made clear, simply logging and monitoring such events was not effective. In retrospect it was found that Target's deployment of FireEye products had seen the original attacks against their point of sale systems, yet the alert got lost in the shuffle.

So the latest trend in cyber defense is Breach Detection and Response. The idea is that network and endpoint agents are deployed that capture suspicious behavior either from network traffic or endpoint activity. Vendors like Cybereason, Ensilo (acquired by Fortinet in 2019), and Stellar Cyber attempt to turn all of that data into strong indicators that an attack is underway. The goal is early detection and fast response. It is the automation of what is called threat hunting, usually a manual process of digging through all the data by an expert analyst assisted by tools such as Sqrrl

(now part of AWS), or Arbor Networks for network data.

Fraud Prevention

Fraud prevention solutions have a lot of overlap with identity and access management, but instead of a community of employees they address the wider world of customers. Banks and online retailers are the usual buyers of fraud prevention products. These products may verify or assign risk scores to customers during the on-boarding process, or they may monitor for unusual behavior. There are products to detect account takeover attempts and products that will check against a database of breached accounts to alert a user to change their password.

Threat Intelligence

Countering targeted attacks has become the most pressing requirement for cyber defense. Long the domain of firewalls, anti-virus, and access controls, the cybersecurity industry began a reinvention that dates to the release of the now famous APT1 report by Mandiant[1], which was primarily a breach response forensics company and is now a significant part of FireEye. As always the industry is driven by threat actors: hackers, cyber criminals, hacktivists, and now nation-states. However, for years the industry's driving philosophy was to ignore the threat actors and focus on the actual attacks. Firewalls were deployed to limit access to corporate networks. Intrusion Prevention Systems (IPS) were deployed to block known worms and network exploits. Frequently updated anti-virus on the endpoint helped control the spread of malicious software such as Trojans, spyware, and worms. Defenders did not worry about who was attacking them, only the signature of the attack.

The rise of targeted attacks, specifically from nation-state actors, can be traced to the 2003–2004 Titan Rain incidents, where a lone analyst at Sandia Labs, Shawn Carpenter, discovered widespread infiltration of many government research labs and military bases.[2] While well-known inside the defense industrial base (DIB), it was not until Mandiant published its APT1 report in 2013 that the industry started to respond to the devastating impact of targeted attacks with new tools and services. That report, published the week before the RSA Conference in San Francisco, caused an entire industry to pivot. One vendor, Cyphort, scrapped its product and re-tooled to become a breach detection vendor in the weeks following. Breach detection, sandbox analysis of target-specific malware, network monitoring, packet capture, and threat intelligence services became the fastest growing sectors in the IT security industry.

Types of threat intelligence vendors

The threat intelligence category can be broken into several sub-categories: Reputation Services, Malware Analysis, Threat Actor Research, and DarkWeb Research. The vendors provide feeds and reports that, once consumed by their customers, can identify ongoing attacks, infections, and exfiltration activity.

Reputation services have long been a differentiator for IPS vendors. Identifying and blocking attack traffic at the gateway based on signatures is compute intensive because it requires full packet analysis. It is much easier to block all connection attempts from a particular IP address or internet domain. Thus Cisco, TippingPoint (HP), Corero, McAfee, and small vendors like Sentinel IPS, have incorporated IP reputation into their products.

In the meantime, standalone IP reputation services have sprung up to offer raw feeds of IP addresses scored on a risk scale. These services can scan IP addresses and websites looking for the presence of malware, or lay traps that identify attacks from particular IP addresses. The now essentially defunct Norse Corporation had over 35 such honey nets deployed around the world to attract attack traffic. They claimed to have records of over 5 million IP addresses (out of 4 billion) that they considered malicious. Of course, IP reputation is a fluid quality. An IP address of a server associated with a particular Denial of Service (DoS) attack could become completely benign if the administrator cleans the machine. So IP reputation services have to be updated continuously, creating the business model for a subscription service.

MSSPs such as SecureWorks, Symantec, NTT, AT&T, and TrustWave collect security event information from all their customers. They are able to correlate and scrub that data and often provide those feeds to customers, although they have yet to break these feeds out as separate service offerings.

Threat feeds based on malware analysis mirror the types of infrastructure that every AV firm has built to inform their own signature update ability. Providers like ThreatGRID (acquired by Cisco) and LastLine spin up thousands of virtual machines (sandboxes) and instrument them to extract Indicators of Compromise (IoC), which can include source IP addresses, Command and Control (C&C) IP addresses, MD5 hashes of the payload and its constituent parts, and other data. Team Cyrmu is perhaps the firm with the longest history, founded in 1998.

Threat actor research firms such as Accenture's iDefense, Intel 471, and iSIGHT Partners (now part of FireEye) have processes that require much greater human resources to provide. In addition to automated systems, these vendors rely on analysts to track particular cyber criminals, hacktivist groups, or teams associated with nation-state cyber espionage. Their products are primarily in the form of research reports that contain detailed descriptions of the threat actors, including their Tactics, Techniques, and Procedures (TTP). This type of report does not lend itself to a feed but most vendors are building APIs so that their data can be queried. Intel 471 has based its offering on a dashboard and feed of the activities of over nine million separate threat actor identifiers.

Another category of threat research service is that provided for purposes of brand protection or early alerting. Vendors such as GroupSense, Flashpoint Security, BrandProtect, Digital Shadows, and Recorded Future (acquired by Insight Partners in 2019 for $780 million) attempt to identify when a customer is being targeted or even the early planning stages of an attack. They use so-called Open Source Intelligence (OSINT) and tools for mining pastebin, chat channels, and anonymous sites hidden within the Tor network to gather their intelligence—the so-called Deep Web.

Deep & Dark Web Defined: While the Deep Web is that vast portion of the Internet that is not indexed by search engines, estimated at over 90% of the entire web, the Dark Web is accessed by Tor (The Onion Router) or I2P (Invisible Internet Project). In this way the anonymity of participants is protected. Researchers at many vendors and law enforcement agencies infiltrate these Deep & Dark corners of the internet to collect intelligence on threat actor intentions, tools, capabilities, and methods.

Most organizations track mentions of their key executives, products, and company via Google News alerts and frequent searches of social media and various paste and data dump sites where cybercriminals often share known exploits or pilfered material. But by the time this material is publicly available, it has already been discussed, shared, and exploited by the communities active in the Deep & Dark Web. Monitoring public paste sites is not sufficient for effective research and the data that shows up there is often out of date.

Though extremely valuable to both cyber and physical security teams, gathering data and gleaning intelligence from the Deep & Dark Web is extraordinarily difficult. Thus subscribing to a service that provides that monitoring is called for.

Email Security

Email security comes in many flavors. Because email-born malware does not detonate until it lands on the desktop it could be considered a form of endpoint security, but because most protections are deployed somewhere in the network it could as easily fall in the network security bucket. It is easier to give email security its own category. When email was primarily managed on-prem, typically on a Microsoft Exchange server, solutions like Brightmail, Trend Micro, and IronPort were delivered as an appliance. As email moves to the cloud, primarily Office 365, email security has followed. There are 61 vendors of email security products. Because most breaches are credited to some sort of email delivery of a malicious payload or URL, these solutions attempt to identify and block these attacks before a user can open an attachment or click on a link.

Training

When all else fails, perhaps security awareness training can provide the last line of defense. Product vendors in the category produce training tools delivered over the network. Many compliance programs require some sort of security awareness training. Unfortunately most of these vendors report success rates, when measured by people clicking on links or opening attachments, of around 95%. If an attacker can count on their own success rate of 5% they will continue to use email as one of their primary attack vectors.

Another training sector that is growing is providers of cyber ranges: virtual environments where defenders can square off against attackers.

Deception

Deception as a means of defense is as old as physical conflict. Massive engineering works were deployed in World War II to trick bomber squadrons into targeting decoys built from timber and tarps to look like factories. In IT security the first commercial concept of deception was separate servers that were instrumented to detect changes to files, login attempts, and exfiltration of data. These were often deployed in the internet-facing DMZ with the hope that attackers would waste time poking around in this honeypot and also identify themselves and the techniques and tools they had at their disposal. These early commercial products did not fare well because targeted attacks were not very sophisticated and the primary defenses of firewalls, IPS, and privileged user management could address most of the attack methodologies. But today, attackers have gained that sophistication, and discovering them on the corporate network has become a critical component of breach discovery and response.

A modern deception solution has these four components.

1. Many honeypots are distributed throughout the network as tempting VMs. A solution from the likes of Attivo or TrapX will manage the deployment of such virtual honeypots and monitor them continuously. An alert that an attack is underway is usually a good indi-

cator that some security control has failed or a sophisticated attack is actually occurring.

2. Honeynets. A complete network of endpoint honeypots is configured to look like a real network. In this way attackers can be monitored as they encroach on one server, escalate privileges, and traverse towards a goal.

3. Tainted data. Files with tempting data in them are spread through the network, even the production network. They are configured with technology that will phone home if they are opened, thus giving the organization a heads-up that a breach has occurred and possibly identifying where the attacker is.

4. Credential deception is more rare. The idea is to seed social networks, especially LinkedIn, with fake identities of employees. If a security team sees attempted logins using variants of these fake identities it would be an early warning that reconnaissance was occurring. This, and early warning from mining the dark web, are two of the few ways that recon can be detected.

Security Testing

With such a complex collection of security technology deployed it is becoming necessary to test frequently. One method is automated attack and penetration testing. These tools attempt to mimic the capabilities of a Red Team. In addition to vulnerability scanning, the tools will attempt exploits. This can be a scary prospect for a CISO. A safer way is security instrumentation.

The overall philosophy of layered defense, in addition to providing a framework for breaking out the history of each layer, also leads to a complicated range of solutions deployed in most organizations. Breach detection and response in particular crosses over several boundaries as network, endpoint, and identity systems are mined for indications of an attack underway. Just as in other complex systems it is becoming necessary to test and optimize the entire system of security controls that are in place. Infrastructures are complex and simple misconfigurations can dramatically undercut efforts to secure them, as we are learning from recent cloud breaches. Security Instrumentation addresses the blind spots that will inevitably develop in multi-layer defenses. Vendors such as Verodin (now part of FireEye), Spirent, and AttackIQ are leading in the space.

The concept of security instrumentation is straightforward. Deploy sensors, generally as virtual machines in a cloud, or on small dedicated hardware devices across your network zones such as partner, desktop and server networks, DMZs, and internet. These sensors, which live in your production environment, measure the efficacy of your security tools across network, endpoint, email, and cloud.

The sensors run a large and growing library of test behaviors against other sensors, thus operating safely and ensuring that your assets aren't targeted while validating whether the security tools you purchased to protect those assets are working.

Security instrumentation also requires integration with security management solutions such as firewall managers, endpoint security managers, log managers, SIEMs, and other devices. These control points are instrumented to measure the response to the attacks generated by all the sensors.

For example, not only was a test not blocked, but perhaps it wasn't detected. Or a test was detected on a firewall manager, but the events never made it to the SIEM. And all too often, events that do make it to the SIEM don't result in a notable or correlated event because of faulty configurations as well as problems around alerting, parsing, time stamping, routing, etc., meaning the likelihood of a human seeing and responding to the event is very low.

Security Instrumentation automatically identifies these issues and provides actionable, prescriptive information on how to mitigate them. Best of all, once you apply a fix such as a signature, firewall rule change, endpoint security adjustment, or SIEM correlation rule, you can revalidate to ensure the changes work and then continuously validate to ensure there isn't drift from a known good state. This automated, continuous validation results in end-to-end security measurement and improvement across your entire security stack.

Summary

Think of the overall IT security industry in terms of the layers of defense. Thus, network, endpoint, data, identity, and GRC are the major buckets with several new categories included at the high-

er level: threat intelligence, testing, deception, breach detection and response, and IoT.

The task for a CISO is to choose the products that, when combined, provide the most effective defense. The best product for any one organization depends on many factors. While cost is usually the top concern, that has to be weighed against efficacy, ease of management, available support, and even the skill sets of existing personnel. There are also regional considerations. In what appears to be a trend towards digital mercantilism, many countries are encouraging the purchase of home-grown solutions. The suspicions raised about Huawei, Kaspersky, or Lenovo can be just as easily applied to US companies. If this trend continues it will only serve to increase the number of vendors in the space. If corporate ownership becomes a deciding factor in whether a security product can be trusted, then each country will need at least one vendor in each of the above categories.

It is often claimed that there are too many vendors and the IT security industry is ripe for consolidation. Yet, each of the vendors listed in this book has demonstrated viability and growth, indicating that customers have decided that they need their products. Despite the temptation to call it consolidation when a big vendor acquires a smaller vendor, it is not consolidation. It is the market process at work. A large vendor like Cisco, Symantec, or McAfee cannot rely on their teams to invent the next product that will develop into significant revenue for them. They look out into the market and choose the startups that are experiencing rapid growth and acquire them to add their people and products to their portfolios. In this way they stay relevant and often take future competitors off the table.

Startups get funded thanks in large part to the lucrative exits to these large acquirers. There are spectacular stories of such success. Aorata, an Israeli startup, developed technology to detect attacks that took advantage of weaknesses in Microsoft Active Directory. They had barely gotten off the ground before Microsoft snapped them up for a rumored $200 million.[3] Another startup, Demisto, which developed orchestration capabilities, was acquired by Palo Alto Networks in early 2019 for $560 million after only four years.[4]

One way for an established vendor to adjust to major market changes is to acquire. Gateway hardware security vendors are facing such a challenge from cloud security solutions. As computer workloads move to the cloud and employees become increasingly mobile there is less need for stacks of appliances protecting the data center. How is a Cisco, Palo Alto Networks, or Fortinet going to protect their market share? Look to each

of these to continue to acquire cloud security vendors to fill out the gaps in their offerings and provide a path to transition away from hardware.

1. "Exposing One of China's Cyber Espionage Units," *Mandiant*, https://www.fireeye.com/content/dam/fireeye-www/services/pdfs/mandiant-apt1-report.pdf

2. Richard Stiennon, *Surviving Cyberwar* (Government Institutes, 2010, pp 1-10.

3. Ingrid Lunden, "Microsoft Buys Israeli Hybrid Cloud Security Startup," *Tech Crunch*, November 13, 2014, https://techcrunch.com/2014/11/13/microsoft-buys-israeli-hybrid-cloud-security-startup-aorato-in-200m-deal/

4. "Palo Alto Networks Announces Intent to Acquire Demisto," *Palo Alto Networks*, February 19, 2019, https://www.paloaltonetworks.com/company/press/2019/palo-alto-networks-announces-intent-to-acquire-demisto

CHAPTER 2
A Brief History of the IT Security Industry

The IT security industry is different from all technology sectors in a fundamental way—there is an outside driver.

If one were to write the history of data storage from the early days of magnetic grids, acoustic coils, and huge platter arrays the size of washing machines to the present day of Solid State Drives (SSD), you would have a history of how vendors strove to create ever more denser storage capability at ever-higher reliability and lower cost. The only driver for that industry segment was the competitive market.

The outside driver for the IT security industry is threat actors. Early viruses and worms were created with no more nefarious purpose than to demonstrate vulnerabilities. Over time, as the internet became ubiquitous, criminal threat actors evolved to steal account credentials for banking, or steal clicks for affiliate networks, or deface websites to promulgate some hacktivist's agenda. Although nation-state threat actors were busy behind the scenes from the very beginning, it was not until 2003 and Titan Rain that we learned just how mature cyber espionage was. The AP1 report

of 2013 began the shift in the industry to countering targeted attacks. Destructive nation-state attacks, such as Stuxnet and the 2015 attacks on Ukraine's power grid, demonstrated the need for defenses for industrial control systems.

The dual revelations from Edward Snowden and a still-unknown leaker to Der Spiegel of the TAO ANT catalog have identified the intelligence community (IC) as a category of threat actor that is better funded, better organized, and more targeted than any before. For vendors, the IC is a worrisome threat because they often target the products of firewall, network, and endpoint vendors. Take, for example, the FLAME virus, identified by Kaspersky Labs, which used a tool that spoofed Microsoft's update service to gain a foothold in the target.

While the history of threat actors and their attacks is a fascinating study, tracking the history of the industry itself has value as well. That history is the story of the people, products, and companies that counter this outside driver. Within each company there were the usual drivers to create products that were faster, easier to manage, and profitable, but also each vendor is under the constant threat of becoming obsolete as a better solution arrives to counter the latest threat.

A new vendor can start with a new technology to address the latest attack methodology and then expand its capability to encompass the features offered by legacy vendors. A great example of a missed opportunity was the nascent market for anti-spyware solutions. In the early 2000s there were thousands of spyware products that fit into a confusing spectrum of maliciousness. A free tool like WeatherBug could be downloaded to a PC to give real-time updates on the weather. It would then generate pop-up ads or jigger search results to provide revenue for the creator and the thousands of affiliates they worked with. Because these tools were installed with the user's permission, the anti-virus vendors of the day decided that they would not include them in their anti-malware solutions. This opened the door for specialist anti-spyware products like SpySweeper from Webroot Software in Boulder, Colorado.

Webroot, which in 2004 had ten different products from MacCleaner to SpySweeper, took in $108 million from Technology Crossover Ventures and doubled down on its anti-spyware business. Within three months of launching an enterprise solution, it was selling $1 million each month in business anti-spyware and began the move to incorporate anti-virus, too. It had a very short window to gain market share based on its new feature. But by 2005, all the major AV vendors, led by McAfee, simply added anti-spyware features to their AV products. It was a rare instance of established vendors recognizing a market trend and responding effectively. It would be 15 years before Webroot could effectively pivot into a different space and ultimately be sold to Carbonite for $615 million in 2019.

The lesson learned from Webroot's experience is the danger of an entrenched vendor recognizing a competitive threat early enough to fend it off by developing its own product.

An arena that experienced better results was that of email security gateways. The driving feature for Brightmail, IronPort, and CipherTrust was anti-spam. Brightmail was acquired by Symantec for $370 million in 2004.[1] IronPort was acquired by Cisco for $830 million.[2] And CipherTrust was acquired by Secure Computing for $274 million in 2006.[3]

The history of network security has seen successful entrants leveraging a defining feature to become major players. Fortinet built a platform to deliver in-line anti-virus while Palo Alto went to market with an "application aware" feature. Both quickly evolved into full-function firewalls to compete successfully with Check Point Software, Cisco, and Juniper in the enterprise.

Acquisition replaces R&D in the security space

Market success in the security industry has two paths. Both require fast growth. One path leads to an acquisition, and the other to independence and usually an IPO.

The dynamic for the industry was, for much of the 2000s, a feeder system of venture-backed startups being acquired by the big vendors Symantec, Network Associates (McAfee), Cisco, and even CA. Each acquisition, at attractive multiples of 10X revenue and more, encouraged more investment on the part of venture capital and would launch a new batch of wealthy founders back into the ecosystem to try their hand at serial entrepreneurship.

This ecosystem made sense for large companies in a fast-paced industry. Innovation, engineering and going to market, require a combination of luck, ingenuity, and most importantly, timing. Having the latest product to counter the latest threat is one thing. Having it ready for market when the threat arises is another. The idea that a Network Associates or Symantec could lead such innovation from the top down and continue to succeed is unlikely compared to the ability to recognize when a particular product is doing well and fills a gap in their product portfolio. Thus, since its inception Symantec has acquired over 80 companies.[4] McAfee started during the frenzied '90s as a roll up of several disparate businesses.

While this churn of startups feeding the big players is still part of the IT security industry dynamic, something happened in the late 2000s to disrupt the success of the big players. Instead of being happy with steady growth in an industry that apparently books higher revenue each year, the large vendors often get spooked by big moves by their competition.

In September 2006 EMC, the storage giant, made a move into the security space when it acquired RSA Security,[5] which included the SecurID product line. RSA Security was formed when publicly-traded Security Dynamics acquired RSA, the encryption company, in 1996.[6] EMC may have been reacting to Symantec's oversize investment in Veritas, an EMC competitor, in 2004. Symantec paid $13.5 billion for Veritas, effectively turning it into a holding company with two major business units. This move began the slow decline of Symantec as a driving force in security. Spinning Veritas back out in 2015 after 11 years of a failed effort left Symantec thrashing around to regain its position of leadership.[7] A desultory merger with Blue Coat in 2016 did not re-inject growth and ultimately Symantec was put on the blocks for sale. Chinese chip maker Broadcom, on its own path to enter the security industry, had already acquired CA for $18.9 billion in 2018 and paid $10.7 billion for Symantec's enterprise business in a deal announced in August 2019.

Meanwhile Network Associates had its own issues. Like all tech companies in the early 2000s it was reeling from the drop off in sales and valuations after the dot com bust. Network Associates had several leadership changes and decided to remake itself by first divesting most of its product line, including the Gauntlet Firewall. It then went on a buying binge, quickly acquiring Foundstone, a vulnerability management company, Intruvert, an early IPS vendor, and Entercept, an endpoint intrusion prevention company. It then made the ill-fated decision to rebrand itself as McAfee, after its flagship product. This rebranding proved to be ill-fated because John McAfee, the highly erratic figure who had originally combined his AV company with Network General to form Network Associates, rose seemingly from the dead to leverage the name recognition for his own purposes.

In 2010, McAfee's new CEO, Dave DeWalt, negotiated an astounding deal. Intel, a chip manufacturer, bought into the idea that an AV company would be synergistic with a silicon company. McAfee was sold to Intel for $7.68 billion. Intel attempted to repair the brand by renaming the company as Intel Security. It would be five years of stagnation and new management at Intel before Intel Security was spun off again, and re-rebranded as McAfee.

There are other games played at the top of the security industry food chain. As the center of focus shifted to defense against nation-state adversaries and the Pentagon stood up US Cyber Command on May 21, 2010, it seemed to make sense that defense contractors would start to make acquisitions. In fact, Raytheon entered the market with its acquisition majority stake in Websense in 2015. It combined its other cyber products in the newly branded Forcepoint in 2016. Lockheed Martin acquired Industrial Defender, one of the first industrial control systems security plays, in 2014. But no defense contractor made a strategic decision to lead in cyber security, leaving Symantec, McAfee, and Cisco to continue to play their own part in the industry. The Defense Industrial Base is primarily a customer, not a vendor, of security products.

Which leads to today. There are at least 2,336 vendors of IT security products. This number includes the managed security services providers and the new realm of cloud-delivered services.

Of 2,336 vendors, 1,316 are based in the United States, with Israel second (218) and the UK third (178). Within the US the center of the industry is based in California with 448 vendors, most of those in the Bay Area. The second major concentration is around Washington, DC with 166. These proportions have not changed very much over the last decade. The only force at work appears to be a form of digital mercantilism that is driving each country to favor homegrown vendors over foreign.

Digital mercantilism began after Edward Snowden revealed the deep relationship between the NSA and US technology vendors. European countries were the loudest protestors and the EU has taken measures to protect the privacy of its member states' data with the General Data Protection Regulation (GDPR) enacted in 2018 to impose fines on companies that did not take extraordinary measures to protect the data entrusted to them. By mid-2019 there were 12 enforcement actions, with the largest targeting Facebook.[8]

Ironically, the United States is fueling digital mercantilism by singling out Huawei, a network gear manufacturer. The intelligence community (IC) has been waging a campaign to keep Huawei out of the US, backed now by the administration with Secretary of State Pompeo making strong demands on US trading partners. One view would be that blocking Chinese manufacturers from competing with US network gear companies would be "protective," but in actuality, accusing a vendor of having insecure products is a tactic that could easily backfire. If every vulnerability is deemed a backdoor, then US vendors can be tarred with the same brush. Digital mercantilism will spread and each country will push a buy-local message, leading to more security vendors, or at least the continued success of the existing local vendor: Panda Security in Spain, AVG in Germany, Kaspersky in Eastern Europe, and AhnLab in South Korea. Look for each category of vendor, from threat intelligence to deception to security analytics, to have its own participant in each country.

The IT security industry ecosystem has been decapitated by the wayward path of Symantec and McAfee. Luckily, Cisco, Palo Alto Networks, and even Microsoft, are filling the gap.

1. Todd Weiss, "Symantec to Acquire Brightmail," *Computerworld*, May 19, 2004, https://www.computerworld.com/article/2565099/symantec-to-acquire-brightmail.html

2. Nancy Gohring, "Cisco to Acquire Ironport for $830M," *Computerworld*, January 4, 2007, https://www.computerworld.com/article/2548788/cisco-to-acquire-ironport-for--830m.html

3. Robert McMilla, "Secure Computing to Buy CipherTrust," *Computerworld*, July 12, 2006, https://www.computerworld.com/article/2545639/secure-computing-to-buy-ciphertrust.html

4. "List of Mergers and Acquisitions by Symantec," *Wikipedia*, accessed November 27, 2019, https://en.wikipedia.org/wiki/List_of_mergers_and_acquisitions_bySymantec

5. "EMC Completes RSA Security Acquisition," *Dell Technologies*, September 18, 2006, https://corporate.delltechnologies.com/eus/newsroom/announcements/2006/09/09182006-4605.htm

6. David Einstein, "Online Security Company to Buy RSA," *SF Gate*, April 16, 1996, https://www.sfgate.com/business/article/Online-Security-Company-to-Buy-RSA-2986043.php

7. "Symantec to Acquire Veritas," *Information Week*, December 16, 2004, https://www.informationweek.com/update-symantec-to-acquire-veritas-for-$135-billion/d/d-id/1029104

8. "Major GDPR Fine Tracker," *Alpin*, accessed November 27, 2019, https://alpin.io/blog/gdpr-fines-list/

CHAPTER 3

Network Security History

Among the many threads that weave together to form the history of the IT security industry, one stands out in sharp contrast: the addition of Check Point's Firewall-1 to Sun Microsystem's catalog of software products. The origin story of Check Point always points to this seminal event in its early history. Founded by Gil Shwed, Shlomo Kramer, and Marius Nacht in 1993, Check Point not only gave rise to the network security industry, it was the spark that fueled what is today a booming startup eco-system in Israel.

Gil Shwed holds the patent for the stateful inspection firewall, a critical innovation that simplified and dramatically improved the performance of gateway firewalls. He, like so many cyber security startup founders coming out of Israel, spent four years within Unit 8200, a division of the Israeli Defense Force often compared to the US's NSA. Shwed joined the Unit at age 18 in 1986. He and his co-founders launched Check Point Software Technologies Ltd. in 1993.

Firewall-1 was the first stateful inspection firewall. It was all software and could run on most flavors of Unix, eventually including IRIX from Silicon Graphics, HPUX from HP, AIX from IBM, and most importantly, Solaris from Sun Microsystems. The mid-'90s, before Microsoft introduced Windows NT to disrupt the market, were notable for the battles between microcomputer vendors to win the enterprise market. They each encouraged software developers to port their products to their platforms and, like Sun, published an ever expanding catalog of available software solutions. Much like a listing in the AWS Marketplace today will generate a flow of new revenue, being in Sun's catalog meant low friction sales for the software company.

Soon after launching, Firewall-1 was listed in Sun's catalog, immediately turning on the spigot of sales driven by Sun's large professional sales organization and its myriad resellers. Check Point was selling products in the US before it had hired its first US salesperson. The timing was perfect. The internet was booming, Sun was the leader in internet-facing servers, and it quickly became apparent that to connect an organization to the internet you needed a firewall.

Check Point turned in phenomenal growth numbers in those early years at tremendous gross margins, as to be expected from a software-only company. 1995 revenue was $9.5 million, followed by $31.9 million in 1996.

Check Point orchestrated a masterful IPO on Nasdaq. It opened an office for its US headquarters in Redwood City, California, recruited Deb Triant away from Adobe to be its US CEO, and went to market with the story that operations would be led from the US while R&D would reside in Israel.

By 2001 CHKP clocked $528 million in revenue. It had the largest share of the firewall market but was starting to see weakness in its software-only strategy. It has never been explained why Check Point did not try to enforce its patent for stateful inspection, a technology incorporated in all of its successful competitors, most notably the Cisco PIX line of firewalls.

Cisco had acquired the PIX technology from a team of developers at Network Translation, Inc. in November 1995. The software was incorporated in a series of appliances dramatically improving the form factor and purchasing ease for a standalone gateway firewall. Check Point still required a customer to purchase and configure a server from Sun, HP, or Microsoft, then install the software separately. Much of that configuration and integration was carried out by the reseller channel eventually dominated by Nokia, which developed a set of purpose-built appliances to primarily run Firewall-1. Check Point leadership was probably influenced by the previous decade's war between

the two go-to-market models: that of Apple Computer, which controlled all of its own software running on its own hardware platform, and the much more successful model of Microsoft, which stuck to software that would run on any PC hardware. But endpoint models rarely translate to networking models where throughput, low latency, and reliability are paramount.

Check Point eventually addressed the appliance model by acquiring Nokia's hardware business. But by that time it had given up market share to Cisco, which far outsold Check Point with its multi-purpose ASA appliance that incorporated networking, a PIX firewall, and VPN capability.

Check Point was also late in recognizing that firewalls were evolving rapidly.

Nir Zuk was a Check Point engineer who moved to the US in 1997, where he created a WAN optimization product for Check Point that he claims was never rolled out because of jealousy from the Israeli development team.[1] He left Check Point in 1999 and soon after started OneSecure with the initial goal of creating a managed VPN service, but quickly pivoted to one of the first Intrusion Prevention solutions (IPS). IPS must have been an idea whose time had come because there were actually four other vendors that all introduced IPS products in the same time frame of 2002-2003: IntruVert, TippingPoint, ISS, and Sourcefire.

IntruVert Networks was founded in San Jose in the fall of 2000 by Parveen Jain. IntruVert used the term Intrusion Prevention in its original marketing, although in a press release in which they announced $15 million in Series B funding in 2012 they referred to themselves as "IntruVert Networks, a developer of next generation intrusion detection systems (IDS)." IntruVert was acquired by Network Associates in April of 2003 for a reported $100 million. It gave NAI (soon to be re-branded to match its flagship product, McAfee) a network security component that fared much better than the Gauntlet Firewall, which was end-of-lifed that year and its customers turned over to Secure Computing for support.

Another of these vendors was TippingPoint, which began life as a network appliance vendor in January 1999 called Shbang!. It experienced a rocky few years, which included an IPO as Netpliance in 2000 in which it raised $144 million.[2] In 2002 it discontinued the appliance operations and re-started as a network security vendor selling an intrusion prevention appliance. Under CEO John McHale it raised additional funds through a PIPE (Private Investment in a Public Company). It was then acquired by networking company 3Com in late 2004 for an announced $430 million. At the time quarterly revenue was $9.7 million.

By April 2010 3Com itself was acquired by HP for $2.7 billion.[3] And finally, the TippingPoint division was spun off to Trend Micro in 2015 for $300 million.[4]

ISS (Internet Security Systems) also pivoted into the IPS space. It was founded in 1993 by Chris Klaus, who had developed the first version of its flagship vulnerability scanner while working for the Department of Energy on an internship. While he was enrolled at Georgia Institute of Technology he released the first version of Internet Security Scanner as freeware. While Chris served as CTO he brought in Tom Noonan to be CEO in 1995. Venture backing was provided by Greylock Ventures and Sigma Partners, with further rounds coming from Ted Schlein at Kleiner Perkins, and AT&T Ventures. The first product was Internet Security Scanner, one of the first vulnerability scanners. They continued to roll out additional assessment tools, including System Scanner for servers. In 1998 ISS formed X-Force, a professional service arm, as well as one of the first research teams that led the way for future research arms at major security vendors. ISS went public on Nasdaq on March 23, 1998.[5]

In 1999 ISS acquired Netrex Security Solutions, a Southfield, Michigan, based reseller that had been one of the first resellers of Check Point Software. Netrex had developed the back-end systems to allow a Security Operations Center to manage the firewalls and security for many of its customers, becoming one of the first to introduce what became known as Managed Security Services.

In 2001 ISS acquired BlackICE, an endpoint protection platform created by Rob Graham, and in 2002 it launched its own managed security service.

In 2003 ISS introduced Proventia, a line of gateway security appliances that, with the addition of German web filtering company Cobion, became one of the first UTM solutions.

In 2004 Klaus stepped down as CTO to be replaced by Chris Rouland (later founder of Endgame Systems, Bastille Networks, and Phosphorus, an IoT security startup).

In 2006, ISS was acquired by IBM for $1.93 billion. IBM X-Force and managed services are still major components of ISS in use today. Many of the alumni of what was a tight-knit community can be found at an annual get-together at the RSA Conference in San Francisco.

Sourcefire was founded by Marty (Martin) Roesch in 2001. In his own words he is, "A computer-building, Neuromancer-reading, software-writing, hardware-hacking, hopelessly passionate geek."[6] Roesch was the developer of Snort, an open source IDS. He believed firmly in a business model, much like Red Hat's for Linux, of supporting an open source product to generate a community of users, then creating a for-profit venture to support those users that needed enterprise class features and capabilities. He wrote in his popular blog, "The value of an open source technology to the company that develops and supports it is the community that grows around it."[7]

Roesch, a technologist at heart, recruited Wayne Jackson as CEO to run Sourcefire. Jackson took the company public in 2007 and stepped down in 2008 to be replaced by John Burris, who passed away in 2012. Roesch was acting CEO until John Becker was brought in to lead the company to its eventual sale to Cisco in July 2013. Roesch stayed on until 2019 to guide Cisco's security strategy.

The idea behind IPS was to look deeper into every session and look for signature matches with known attacks. It was primarily a defense against network-born worms, but there were hundreds of attacks over various protocols that could be identified and blocked. Unlike IDS, an IPS device would be inline and able to do that blocking.

In 2003 Gartner made the unusual move of removing all firewall vendors from the Leaders Quadrant of the Magic Quadrant for Enterprise Firewalls, with the challenge put forth that a vendor would not be put back into the Leaders Quadrant until IPS functionality was incorporated into its firewall product.*

Netscreen Technology was one of the fastest growing hardware appliance firewall vendors in 2003. It had been started by Ken Xie, Yun Ke, and Feng Deng. Its form factor and throughput were competitive with the Cisco PIX products at a lower total cost of ownership than a Nokia/Check Point firewall. When Netscreen acquired Nir Zuk's OneSecure in 2002 it quickly incorporated IPS into its appliances and became the only firewall in the Leaders Quadrant. Soon after, Juniper Networks acquired Netscreen for $4.5 billion.

Multifunction to UTM to Next-Gen Firewall

A pattern was beginning to emerge following the dictate articulated by Gartner analyst John Pescatore: *what can be done in the network should be done in the network*. Entrepreneurs began to bundle multiple security functions into one appliance. Fortinet was one of those.

Ken Xie, one of the founders of Netscreen, left in 2000 to form Fortinet. The initial idea behind Fortinet was to perform anti-virus filtering with a network appliance. This was particularly challenging because a virus signature could be a snippet of code embedded anywhere in a relatively large package, not just in the headers where firewalls looked, or the early packets of an attack where IPS looked. It required massive amounts of memory and specialized chipsets to do AV inline. Thus, Fortinet spent years and millions of dollars creating Application-Specific Integrated Circuits (ASICs) to handle the inspection and memory requirements.

As it turned out, doing AV inline was not the killer feature of this next generation of firewalls. The killer feature, arguably still driving firewall innovation today, was not initially even considered to be a security function. It was content URL filtering.

Content URL filtering, or web filtering, addressed a completely different requirement than security. As enterprises became more and more dependent on the internet for productivity, they began to recognize that their employees were either wasting time or exposing other employees to what was termed a hostile work environment by their browsing behavior. In the first instance it was watching movies or browsing to sports sites. In the second, it was viewing pornography or other objectionable material from their work computers. Companies like Websense and Blue Coat saw this and introduced products that sat behind the firewall and proxied all web traffic. They

scrambled to classify all the websites and content on the internet and provide a policy engine that would allow administrators to decide what kind of content was appropriate for the work environment. It was only much later that websites began to deliver malware and pose a security threat. Eventually the web filter evolved into the Secure Web Gateway. But in the meantime Blue Coat and Websense sold their products to most large enterprises at costs that were often as high or higher than the primary firewall: $50,000 or more.

So Fortinet simply took advantage of all of its processing power in its appliances to add URL content filtering as a feature. This paved the way for what became known as Unified Threat Management (UTM), the concept of incorporating many security functions in a single appliance. A Fortinet salesperson could now target companies that were simultaneously looking to refresh their firewalls and were approaching contract renewal time for its web filtering solution.

Meanwhile Nir Zuk left Juniper to found Palo Alto Networks, now the largest firewall vendor by market cap. The PAN firewalls were also appliance-based, but used off-the-shelf network processing silicon instead of developing ASICs. Palo Alto Networks quickly rose to the Leaders Quadrant in the Gartner Magic Quadrant and went public July 20, 2012, to great fanfare. Palo Alto wisely came up with a new term for its multi-function security gateway, calling it a NextGen Firewall. It was truly Nir Zuk's next generation of security appliance after Netscreen. Gartner had discounted the term UTM, which was coined by Charles Kolodgy at IDC, and in a rare move adopted Palo Alto Networks' term.

Local Internet Breakouts

One other aspect of the industry that has driven the success of multi-function firewalls is a long term trend away from corporate networks to local internet breakouts. This is simply an architecture that uses the internet as a means of transporting corporate traffic instead of a traditional hub-and-spoke MPLS network. This trend is accelerating dramatically thanks to cloud transformation.

Organizations with many locations, such as retail stores and chain restaurants, may have hundreds if not thousands of locations. Their architecture choice is to backhaul all traffic to the corporate data center over expensive leased lines and apply firewall, IPS, anti-malware, sandboxing, and content URL filtering there, or deploy lower cost UTM devices to each location and purchase broadband access from a local provider. There is no way they can deploy the expensive stack of equipment for all these functions that they have in their data center, so they are driven to lower-cost standalone appliances that provide all these protections. This provides an efficient use of bandwidth because traffic destined for the internet goes directly to the desired websites and traffic for the corporate data center can be connected via authenticated VPN.

But note that the primary feature that drove the transition to UTM was content URL filtering.

Over time there are innovations in network security that could give rise to new products. Startups with such new ideas should be aware of just how quickly a UTM vendor can add their features to their existing products, usually with a software update. One such feature was bot detection, basically monitoring outbound traffic for signs of infected hosts. That feature is already incorporated in most UTM products today.

The idea of combining multiple security functions in a single appliance is so common that it is surprising that some analysts give credit to a particular vendor for inventing it. All firewall vendors eventually migrate to this multi-function model. WatchGuard, SonicWall, Untangle, Clavister, and the startup Red Piranha in Perth Australia, are just a few of the gateway security appliances that combine functionality. They each target different market segments or bring a different twist to their approach. WatchGuard, SonicWall, and even Fortinet do well in the distributed enterprise companies that have hundreds or thousands of locations. Think restaurant and retail chains.

If any company deserves credit for approaching network security with a revolutionary innovation it is iPolicy. Founded in 1997, it billed itself as the first Intrusion Prevention firewall. Its technology was based on the concept of single pass inspection of all packets. Then policies would be applied based on traditional factors like source, destination, and protocol, but also on the content of the packets. But iPolicy was early with this concept and eventually ran out of funds and was sold to Tech Mahindra in 2007.[8]

Palo Alto Networks

Palo Alto Networks is the largest firewall vendor, based on a market cap of $24 billion as of November 2019. Compare that to Check Point's $18.2 billion and Fortinet's $17.7 billion.

Zuk is a driven entrepreneur and was well known for his outspoken criticism of Check Point, where he was an early employee. He joined in 1994, only a year after it was founded, and moved to the US in 1997, the year Check Point went public.

When asked in an interview what he found difficult about working at Check Point, he said, "We started a small engineering group here in the United States and we built a product called Floodgate, a quality-of-service product Check Point started serving, and then in 1998 we had a complete implementation of a bandwidth optimization product. The product was ready to be released, and then Check Point decided not to release it. The reason given to me for not releasing it was that the engineers in Israel were really angry that someone in the US was having fun building new products. I'm not kidding you, that was the reason! Then I said, okay, this is an organization that I don't want to work for, and I left that day."[9]

With initial funding of $9.4 million and 25 engineers from Netscreen/Juniper, he was able to quickly create a viable product. Launched in 2005, PAN introduced its first product in 2007. The go-to-market message for PAN was that traditional firewalls could not distinguish between applications delivered over port 80 and 443 and therefore could not apply firewall policies based on application. In this case an "application" would be software-as-a-service such as Salesforce or Netsuite. It could also be an application within an application, such as a game within Facebook.

One of the strategic successes of PAN was to raid the vaunted Check Point reseller network. Check Point is famous for protecting its channel jealously, although also famous for reducing the points (percentage of a sale) it shares with its channel over time. A newcomer wishing to sell through those channel partners would offer much higher margins, but would also have to disguise the fact that they were selling a firewall or Check Point could cut the reseller off from a lucrative renewal business. PAN went to market as a device that could sit behind a Check Point or Cisco firewall and merely provide visibility into what applications were in use. Once in place it was just a matter of time before they could demonstrate there was no need for the legacy firewall since it was redundant.

By the time PAN went public in 2012 it reported having 6,500 customers compared to the 125,000 enterprise customers claimed by Fortinet. Check Point probably had twice as many. But PAN had won the hearts and minds of its customers and the authors of the Gartner Magic Quadrant granted it Leader status in the 2011 Magic Quadrant for Enterprise Firewalls, a fact made clear in PAN's S-1 filing.[10]

The other UTM vendors

There are many other UTM vendors around the world. Like the endpoint security space there are often local vendors that established a market foothold in their own country or region with products that fit the local demand, like AhnLab in South Korea, or Astaro in Germany and Cyberoam in India, both acquired by Sophos.

SonicWall was founded in 1991 by two brothers, Sreekanth and Sudhakar Ravi to build ethernet cards for Apple products. In the late '90s they pivoted to hardware firewall and VPN appliances. They addressed the small-to-medium business market segment, but eventually built larger appliances that at times were challengers for the fastest feeds and speeds in the firewall segment measured in connections per second and throughput. They also built a graphical management interface that was competitive with Firewall-1. SonicWall continued to add features to become a full-fledged UTM, and even predated Fortinet with many features. Remote offices and retail outlets had special demands for the appliances they wanted, including Wifi access points, multiple ports for network segmentation, and eventually slots for cellular access cards that would allow a store to have a backup wireless connection in case its broadband connection failed.

SonicWall went public in 1999 with only 54 employees and a run rate of $10 million in annual revenue.[11] By the time SonicWall was acquired by Dell in March 2012, it had 950 employees. Valuation was estimated between $1 billion and $1.5 billion.[12]

Dell spun SonicWall out to Francisco Partners, a private equity firm that also owns WatchGuard and Elliot Management. Bill Conner was appointed as CEO. Conner was the founding CEO of encryption company Entrust, which he first took public, then managed when it was taken private by Thoma Bravo, another private equity firm, until it was sold to what is now Entrust Datacard.

WatchGuard is a UTM vendor based in Seattle, Washington. It was founded as Seattle Software Labs in 1996, but changed its name to WatchGuard Technology a year later and went public on Nasdaq in July 1999, when it reported having 134 employees.[13] It was then taken private by Francisco Partners and Vulcan Capital in a deal announced in July 2006 for $151 million. WatchGuard's CEO, Prakash Panjwani, is an experienced IT security executive who led SafeNet to a successful sale to Gemalto in January 2015.

Sophos, primarily an anti-virus vendor, has made two acquisitions in the UTM space. The first was Germany's Astaro, acquired in 2011.[14] At the time of the announcement Astaro was doing $56 million in revenue for its small appliances and had 200 employees around the world. It had recently introduced a unique product, Astaro RED, which was a simple little box that acted as an ethernet bridge back to the home office. Even after the Sophos acquisition, this was a volume leader in shipments for the company. Astaro also sold a "virtual UTM," a set of security capabilities that could be installed in a VM on the customer's premises, much like Untangle sells today.

Sophos then acquired Cyberoam, a UTM vendor based in India, in February 2014. Cyberoam sold mid-range UTM devices throughout India, the Middle East, and Africa and was beginning to move into the US, where its CEO, Hemal Patel, resided half of the time. When acquired it had 550 employees. Cyberoam's unique approach was to focus firewall policy enforcement on user identities instead of network and protocol designators. This was a harbinger of the modern Identity Defined Perimeter.

Sophos has re-branded the Astaro UTM products as Sophos SG and maintains a separate brand for Cyberoam. It was a public company traded on the London Exchange and its market cap was $2.6 billion as of mid-2019. Thoma Bravo announced an acquisition of Sophos in October 2019 for $3.9 billion.[15]

AhnLab was created by Ahn Cheol-soo in 1995 as an anti-virus vendor. It has since added UTM products under the product name TrusGuard. It went public on the KOSDAQ exchange in 2001. It is valued at $480 million.

From Hardware Sales to Subscription Model

Tom Noonan, CEO of ISS, once related a conversation he had with John Thomson, CEO of Symantec: "Tom, I have booked 85% of my quarterly revenue on the first day of the quarter." This is very enticing, especially to the CEO of a publicly traded firm. Wall Street watches quarter over quarter growth and will punish any company that misses on expectations. A company that starts each quarter with zero revenue and has to meet or beat its previous quarter is under constant pressure, and the CEO faces diminished bonuses or even termination if he or she misses. So John Thomson at Symantec was in the enviable position of having most of his revenue already committed and often already collected thanks to the subscription model prevalent in the AV world, something Tom Noonan was very cognizant of as ISS pivoted into subscription services for its Preventia line of security appliances.

The introduction of IPS and later content URL filtering and anti-malware functions into UTM devices opened the door to subscription models for hardware and software vendors. In the past, the model was an upfront fee for the hardware and software and several tiers of annual support fees, from 10-25% of the license cost. But with these new features that needed constant updates, they were able to charge for subscriptions. Those updates were pre-sold for one to three years. The vendor would collect the subscriptions up front but not recognize the revenue on their bottom line until the time had passed.

Mobile devices side-step firewall controls

The UTM vendors took advantage of the need for smaller all-in-one security appliances at remote offices to displace the large pieces of equipment that resided in the data center. But how are controls to be applied to the browsing activity of employees on their mobile devices? Most productivity tools have mobile apps and every web page is available from a mobile device. Or an employee could simply tether their mobile device to their laptop and bypass all the security on the office network.

The solution is to redirect all web and app connections from mobile devices to the cloud, where filters and controls can be applied. Blue Coat attempted to leapfrog the competition it faced from UTM vendors with just such a solution, but as is so often the case, it is hard for an entrenched vendor to introduce a product that will compete with its core offering. On top of that, an effective cloud-delivered service requires specialized architectures and faces technological challenges that are hard to overcome.

The Zscaler Story

In 2008 Jay Chaudhry was looking for his next venture. Chaudhry is arguably one of the most successful company founders in the security space. His first security company, SecureIT, in Atlanta, Georgia, provided professional services and integration for security solutions. He sold it to Verisign in 1998 for $69 million in Verisign stock, which was trading at $43 at the time.[16] Chaudhry went on to found several other companies, which resided in the same office building in Atlanta and shared a cafeteria. Air2Web was a wireless application company and AirDefense was a wireless security solution sold eventually to Motorola. His next venture was extremely well timed.

CipherTrust was one of the first secure email gateway solutions. They went to market with the concept that any two CipherTrust email appliances would use SSL to talk to each other, guaranteeing that all email between two servers would be encrypted all the time. But that feature was a non-starter. Typically, people just don't care about data security. What's the point of encrypting email in transit when an attacker can just retrieve it from the victim's inbox? The feature that led to CipherTrust becoming a runaway success was anti-spam. At the time Chaudhry described customers who would not relinquish Proof of Concept devices that CipherTrust would loan them because they reported immediate 85% reductions in email volumes thanks to the spam filtering.

Chaudhry accepted outside investment from Greylock Ventures and Asheem Chandna (another Check Point alumnus). CipherTrust eventually sold to Secure Computing in 2006 for $185 million.[17] But that valuation was far below the $370 million that Symantec paid for competitor Brightmail or the $830 million that Cisco paid for IronPort, both email gateway devices that caught spam.

After a stint at Secure Computing, Chaudhry left to work on his next venture. He wanted to address two megatrends that were becoming apparent in 2008. He saw the combination of mobility, where devices were no longer under corporate control, and cloud computing, where apps were moving out of the data center, as two trends that would challenge the security status quo.

He envisioned a born-in-the-cloud security solution that would replace all of the functionality of the security stack in a traditional data center: Firewall, IPS, anti-malware, and yes, content URL filtering. He recruited a team of developers with security, OS, and network expertise and they built out a series of their own data centers around the world to essentially create a reverse content delivery network (CDN). Zscaler looks like an Akamai that has edge servers to push cached copies of content to users with as few hops as possible between them and the YouTube videos they want to watch. But in Zscaler's case the distributed edge network provides network access. Any user on any device can connect to any cloud app through these edge nodes.

The Zscaler cloud runs on specialized hardware that is built for multi-tenancy. There is a policy control plane that sits on top of the whole infrastructure, which allows a customer company to define granular policies for every user and every app they want to use. There is an enforcement engine that applies filters to decrypted traffic to prevent malware and attacks from spreading. Unknown executables can be sequestered while they are detonated in a sandbox and observed to determine if they pose a threat. Finally there is a logging component that either stores all the logs per customer or directs them to a destination of the customer's choice. The network infrastructure requires peering relationships with the major cloud and app providers that gets a user's traffic to its destination as efficiently as possible. The move to Office365 by most large enterprises has driven many customers to either sign up for Microsoft's ExpressRoute service, or take advantage of Zscaler's established routes to Microsoft's data centers.

One final aspect that Zscaler has brought to market is an implementation of Zero Trust networking. Zscaler Private Access (ZPA) is a separate product designed to allow corporate users to gain access to internal applications whether they reside in the cloud or the corporate data center. It uses much of the same infrastructure for access to the Zscaler edge but does not require the security filters because authorized users accessing corporate apps are not exposed to the threats of the untrustworthy internet. ZPA acts as a broker for access to corporate apps. No IP address is needed for the app, as only Zscaler needs to know where the app resides. A user authenticates to the corporate directory service, be it Active Directory, AzureAD, Okta, or Ping Identity, and Zscaler makes the connection to the app. This zero trust networking connects users to apps. The apps are not visible at all to the internet as a whole, thus they are "stealthed" from attackers.

Zscaler went public on Nasdaq at $26 in March 2018. As of November 2019 it is trading at $52 with a market cap of $6.6 billion and 1,700 employees.

You can see that Zscaler completes the story of network security evolution that started as standalone software running on generic servers, grew to specialized hardware appliances, and now has migrated to the cloud. All of the traditional vendors have also recognized the importance of cloud architectures and are scrambling to evolve. Most simply virtualize their software and ask customers to run their software in the cloud in front of their apps. Palo Alto has acquired cloud capabilities by acquiring Evident.io for cloud configuration monitoring, Twistlock for container security, PureSec for serverless security, and RedLock for cloud compliance. Meanwhile Check Point has acquired Dome9, a cloud firewall. Look to 2020 for more acquisitions by these vendors as they adopt to the new world of cloud.

As is so often the case, and as Chris Blask points out, technology finds solutions when they are needed. The flurry of network security startups in the 1993-1995 timeframe is just one example, as is the simultaneous invention of IPS, the rapid move to all-in-one appliances in the mid-2000s, and now the rush to cloud offerings.

---

* The author of that Gartner MQ is the author of *Security Yearbook 2020*.

1. Dan Blacharski, "How I Got Here: Nir Zuk," *IT World*, April 5, 2010, https://www.itworld.com/article/2756415/how-i-got-here--nir-zuk--cto--palo-alto-networks.html?page=2

2. "TippingPoint Technologies," *Nasdaq*, accessed November 27, 2019, https://www.nasdaq.com/market-activity/ipos/overview?dealId=70388-3143

3. "HP Completes Acquisition of 3Com Corporation," *HP*, April 12, 2010, https://www8.hp.com/us/en/hp-news/press-release.html?id=342187

4. Sarah Kuranda, "Trend Micro to Acquire HP TippingPoint," *CRN*, October 25, 2015, https://www.crn.com/news/security/300078537/trend-micro-to-acquire-hp-tippingpoint-for-300m.htm

5. "Company Timeline," *IBM Internet Security Systems* (web archive), accessed November 27, 2019, https://web.archive.org/web/20070420103923/http:/www.iss.net/about/timeline/index.html

6. Martin Roesch, "Charting a New Course," *Noteworthy* (blog), January 22, 2019, https://blog.usejournal.com/charting-a-new-course-7bfb41dedd54

7. Martin Roesch, "Kawasaki Interviews MySQL CEO," *Security Sauce* (blog), August 28, 2006, http://securitysauce.blogspot.com/2006/08/

8. "Tech Mahindra Corporate Overview," *Tech Mahindra Limited*, 2010, http://docshare01.docshare.tips/files/3863/38630501.pdf

9. Dan Blacharski, "How I Got Here: Nir Zuk," *IT World*, April 5, 2010, https://www.itworld.com/article/2756415/how-i-got-here--nir-zuk--cto--palo-alto-networks.html?page=2

10. "Palo Alto Networks, Inc," *US Secretaries and Exchange Commission* (form), April 6, 2012, https://www.sec.gov/Archives/edgar/data/1327567/ 000119312512153764/d318373ds1.htm

11. "IPO Calendar," *Nasdaq,* accessed November 27, 2019, https://www.nasdaq.com/market-activity/ipos

12. "Dell Buys SonicWall," *eSecurity Planet*, March 14, 2012, https://www.esecurityplanet.com/network-security/dell-buys-sonicwall.html

13. "WatchGuard Technologies, Inc," *Nasdaq*, accessed November 27, 2019, https://www.nasdaq.com/market-activity/ipos/overview?dealId=4327-5039

14. "Sophos Acquires Internet Security Appliance Maker Astaro," *Tech Crunch*, May 6, 2011, https://techcrunch.com/2011/05/06/sophos-acquires-internet-security-appliance-maker-astaro/

15. Joe Panettieri, "Sophos to be Acquired by Private Equity," *MSSP Alert*, October 14, 2019, https://www.msspalert.com/investments/sophos-acquired-by-private-equity/

16. "Verisign Buys SecureIT," *Wired*, July 6, 1998, https://www.wired.com/1998 /07/verisign-buys-secureit/

17. Antony Savaas, "Secure Computing Completes CipherTrust Acquisition," *Computer Weekly*, September 1, 2006, https://www.computerweekly.com/news /2240078284/Secure-Computing-completes-CipherTrust-acquisition

STORY

Gil Shwed

Gil Shwed is the co-founder and CEO of Check Point Software Technology in Israel.

I founded Check Point with my good friends Marius Nacht and Shlomo Kramer. I met Shlomo during my military service in Israel. We served in the same unit and we always knew that we wanted to develop a product, to be entrepreneurs. I don't think we used the term entrepreneurs, but we wanted to develop our own product and do something, and throughout our army service we shared many ideas and many thoughts about what we could do together and what products we could develop.

I left the army at the age of 22, in 1991, after four years of service. Then I started consulting for several companies and my main job quickly became one in which I worked for Marius Nacht, in a company called, back then, Optrotech, which became Orbotech (Orbotech Ltd. is an Israeli technology company used in the manufacturing of consumer and industrial products throughout the electronics and adjacent industries). We also thought about entrepreneurship and technologies

and things we could develop together. That was 1987–1989 with Shlomo, and 1991 with Marius. And around the end of '92 or the beginning of '93, I realized that it was time to start what became Check Point.

The idea for Check Point was actually based on an idea that I'd had since about 1990: technology for securing networks, for screening traffic that runs on the network. The challenge was to connect two classified networks and make sure that only the things that should pass between these two networks actually passed. I looked at commercial solutions but didn't find anything adequate. I came up with the simple idea of defining a language that allowed you to describe the characteristics of the communication protocol.

Based on that language, I created a virtual machine code and then I had a virtual machine which scanned every IP packet to determine whether it should pass or not. But I did some market research, and my conclusion was that it wasn't the right time for that idea. Most of the market was not ready for the concept that their networks needed to be compartmentalized and that they needed to separate between different departments. It was doable, but just not very exciting. It was a niche market that would require us to do a lot of work, and we weren't sure there would be an adequate return. It was too early.

At the end of '92, the US changed its regulations regarding the internet and suddenly the internet became, instead of a purely academic network, a network that could be open to everyone. Dozens of companies started to connect. In 1993 I suddenly saw that the internet was going to have a big impact. And the first question for everyone was, "Okay, we connect to the internet but how do we keep our network separate from the 15,000 universities and students that are out there?" Two things came to me. First, the technology that I had in mind was the right technology to solve this problem, and second, that the internet is going to be something very, very exciting and important because it can really open the world, especially for me sitting in Israel. I actually worked with companies in the US, and the fact that I could instantly send my code or an email looked like a revolution that would change the world.

That was actually a year before the Web was invented, so it wasn't even about surfing or things like that. Just the fact that we could communicate in real-time with low cost with everyone around the world looked to me very, very revolutionary. And that's when I went to Marius and Shlomo and asked them if they remembered the idea that I had discussed with them a few years before. I said it's time to take that idea and try to bring it to market and develop a product.

We then asked ourselves okay, how do we go to customers? The first channel that we thought would take us to market were the ISPs, because they were pretty much the only people who saw the potential of the internet. The IT community didn't really see the potential.

So the first people we tried to convince to become our partners were the ISPs.

We debated the right approach to developing this idea. Should we work at night, wait until we had a product, and then start to sell it? We were thinking about going to some big organizations here in Israel, maybe offer them our idea and develop the first few versions for them. We considered many different alternatives. In the end, our analysis and our brainstorming suggested that if the market was moving really, really fast we couldn't do it as a side job or at night; we needed to dedicate all our time to the new idea. Today it sounds obvious. But then it wasn't obvious, because up to that point I was doing three, four things in parallel at any given time.

We began to look for investors. Back then there wasn't a big venture capital industry in Israel. There were a few, but we didn't approach them. We didn't think they would even listen to us. Instead, we took a systematic approach. We looked at some people with financial backgrounds, and we contacted some software companies that we knew in Israel. And a few organizations. We presented the idea to all of them, based on a basic plan that said that we needed around $100,000 to bootstrap our company, to buy computers for $20,000, for travel expenses to the US, and so on.

Finally we had two competing companies that wanted to invest with us. One of them was BRM, which was a small anti-virus software company from Jerusalem. They actually OEMed their product to a company called Fifth Generation Systems that was acquired around then by Symantec. So they had a great OEM contract to develop a new backup system for Symantec. The other was Aladdin Knowledge Systems. To us they both looked like giant software companies. But I think BRM had 30 employees. Aladdin had a few more. We ended up choosing BRM as an investor and actually they gave us $250,000.

From that point, we worked night and day to develop a product and to find a go-to-market strategy. That all happened between February and June of 1993.

In February of '93 the first internet security conference was held in San Diego. I spent most of my savings buying an airline ticket, and Marius and I flew to San Diego to figure out what was going on in the industry and whether other people had the same idea.

At first BRM gave us a lot of support and pushed us in many good directions. We also had some disagreements because, for example, they didn't always believe that we could make it, and they also weren't a huge believer in the internet. They believed in networks and security, but they weren't sure whether the internet was going to be the right thing. For example, they were developing a network product for a Novell environment, and they really wanted us to develop a Novell version of our software, which we felt was not the right direction.

Around a year and a half later, in early or mid-1995, BRM felt that they wanted to sell some of their shares and maybe even raise more money for Check Point. We didn't really want to raise money because we didn't need to. It was a year and a half since we'd started working with them and we were already profitable and didn't need any money. But BRM hired a small boutique investment firm called Broadview, an M&A high-tech company based in New Jersey.

That led to a parade of venture capitalists to come see us, which was a very strange experience, because usually entrepreneurs run after investors and convince them to invest. In our case, we didn't want any money and we looked at the process as a nuisance. I mean, we were ready to help and assist BRM, but conversations with investors took time from our running the business—and we simply didn't need the money.

When BRM started the process they felt Check Point would be valued at around $12 million.

A few months later, after speaking to almost every possible VC, BRM sold their share at $50 million. They tried to convince Marius, Shlomo, and me to sell some shares too, but we didn't want to, because we didn't feel it was the right time. Only six months later, Check Point went public at a valuation of $500 million and after the first day on the market it rose to $800 million. So obviously BRM didn't have the right timing. But it was a very valuable experience. I spoke to almost every major VC firm in Silicon Valley, and the winners ended up being Venrock and US Venture Partners.

We went from nearly zero sales in '93 to a little bit less than $1 million in '94—that was the first year we started selling—to almost $10 million in '95. And $32 million in 1996. So we moved from 1 to 10 to $32 million in three years. And the next year, 1997, revenue was $80 million.

We developed our go-to-market strategy along the way. In the spring of 1994 we understood that we were three guys sitting in Tel Aviv. If we wanted to be successful we needed to do it in the US, because technology products that are successful in the US can succeed all over the world. It doesn't work the other way around. If you're successful in any other country, it doesn't translate to a worldwide success or to success in the US

We defined the US as our primary market, and the marketing strategy was to find partners: resellers, distributors, ISPs, OEMs, and so on. OEMing to a big company was one of them. Even though that wasn't the only thing we tried—quite the contrary—we looked at five companies in the market that could be a major OEM for us. Sun Microsystems was number one on our list. But we said we couldn't build the business plan based on the fact that one out of five would decide to work with us. So we actually started by recruiting resellers, like ISPs and other software resellers. Since at the time there weren't really software resellers that specialized in internet products, we looked at different people who sold, for example, Unix soft-

ware, and were resellers of Sun Microsystems—people who were selling networking equipment, and a few others.

Early on I had a good relationship with Sun in Israel. Actually, I worked for the Sun Microsystems distributor in Tel Aviv as a consultant for many years, so every time someone came to visit Tel Aviv from Sun, they helped me get a meeting. One of these people was in the CIO organization of Sun. When he came to Tel Aviv in early '94 I showed him our product. I explained to him why I thought it was interesting, and he said, "You know what? I think we can use something like that at Sun because we are connected to the internet and we have a lot of networks. I want to evaluate the product. And if we become a user, maybe I can also recommend to our business development people that they meet with you and consider distributing the software."

At that point we had about twenty beta sites of the product around the world and we were getting good feedback on the product. Nineteen out of those twenty beta sites told us they would like to buy the product, but we didn't have any distribution. We hadn't found anyone that would sell the software and support it. In April of '94 Marius and Shlomo sent me to the US, telling me, "Gil, you need to go to there. Your task is very simple. Don't come back home without a million dollar check."

The guy from the CIO's office at Sun had arranged a meeting with Sunsoft, the software arm of Sun, which was looking at ways to distribute their software to the internet. When I went to the

US one of my first meetings was in Silicon Valley with the business development people at Sun.

But we didn't rely just on Sun. The major effort was signing small resellers in different states in the US to become our initial resellers. These things worked in parallel really, really fast. By June of '94 I had become a very good friend of the Sun people. I spent almost every weekend with them. But in April my first meeting was actually with a company called JVNC Network, that was the spinoff ISP from Princeton University. They were in charge of the network of the states of New York and New Jersey. They told me, "Gil, there's a big trade show next week in Las Vegas, Interop. Why don't you come and show your product in the trade show?"

That was a very important moment for us. But it was probably the longest night for me. I came to the US in the morning, had a bunch of meetings with JVNC in New Jersey, then I went almost all the way to DC to meet with TIS, Trusted Information Systems. They were offering a proxy server as a free toolkit. I wanted to see if we could get some sort of cooperation agreement with them. I finished the day again in Princeton. I spent the whole night talking to Marius and Shlomo on the phone and convincing them that we could put up a part of the Interop booth of JVNC Network within ten days. And we ended up doing that. We won the best of show award as a new network product. Plus, at Interop we found some business development guys at the Digital booth and the Cisco booth, and we invited them to our booth around the same time as the Sun team was com-

ing by. So when the Sun people came to see our product they saw the buzz we were building.

That was the beginning of May in '94. By June, the people from Sun told us, "We've got all the opinions. We want to do business with you." We were still clueless about what the business terms would be. They said, "Okay, let's meet and start discussing business. We can even fly to Tel Aviv and see your business and meet there."

We consulted our lawyer, a very good friend of mine and a very smart person. He said "No way. Don't make them come to Tel Aviv. If they come to Tel Aviv and see that you are sitting in the rooming house and that you are three people, even though they know all of that, they will know that you are a small company. If they see that, you won't get a good deal. Also don't go to Mountain View and sit with them at their office, because there they don't have any motivation to close the deal. They can put you off. They'll say, 'Whatever we disagree on, let's continue tomorrow,' and weeks and months can pass like that."

So we ended up meeting in New York, in the offices of a big law firm. Sun sent three people to the meeting, a product marketing person, the business development person, and a lawyer. From Check Point we brought ten people to the meeting. Yes, we were only three employees at the company, so we got two lawyers from Israel, a lawyer from the US, a business consultant from the US, and two of our board members. So when the Sun people came into the room they felt that they were meeting with a big company. They came with jeans and t-shirts; we came with suits and ties. By the end of the week we had agreed on the business terms. We still had nothing written, but over the weekend I sat in the hotel room with the business development person from Sun, and we documented what we agreed on. And a few weeks later, we had that letter of intent signed, and I was able to go back home with a million dollar deal—actually more than that. Over the next three years the deal was for $3 to 5 million.

From there we had to do two things. First we needed to build the company, because to scale up and work with Sun we needed to recruit people. Second, we needed to find more distribution channels, not to compete with Sun, but to augment that. We had to develop our own independent channel in parallel to Sun. Our strategy was to look at people who were not in the Sun reseller network.

By the way, one of the things that helped us in negotiations was that many Sun resellers were already interested, so we showed that interest to Sun and it told them there was potential. They understood that their resellers wanted it, and if they didn't sign the deal with us, we'd work directly with the resellers. Basically that started Check Point as a company. What we understood very quickly was that the number one priority was a sales and marketing organization to support all the resellers, to grow the business, and to support Sun. So Marius, Shlomo, and I knew that we would have to become a virtual sales and marketing organization. We had to recruit people and resellers.

Marius spent almost all his time with his suitcase in the US, traveling from one city to another every day. He didn't have a house, he didn't have an office. He literally had a carry-on bag and a beeper. No cell phones back then. He would collect messages every few hours, and based on the messages, decide which city to go to the next day. He became our sales, marketing, and support organization. Shlomo took responsibility for Europe. He had a family, so he said, "I'll be in charge of development and Europe so I can leave early in the morning and be back late at night. My wife won't even pay attention that I traveled." That was his theory, at least.

My first tasks were to recruit a head of Check Point sales and marketing in the US and to start an R&D organization in Israel. So the first few recruitments that we did in Israel were R&D people, the first three, four, and five developers who would keep developing the Firewall-1 product. The product itself was pretty good in the first version, but you can't be in technology without devoting most of your resources to improving the technology. So that's what we did.

About six or seven months later we recruited our head of sales and marketing, Deb Triant. She had been the VP of Marketing for Adobe in Silicon Valley. And that was the first major sales and marketing person we had. And then I worked with her very closely to build a sales team and recruit more resellers to support Sun, and really build the company around that idea. When we were three people, we were spending, I don't know, $10,000 to $20,000 a month. Now we had a million dollar contract from Sun Microsystems, which allowed us to do everything we needed to. It gave us a secure future for the next few years, which we used smartly to develop a business. We could have just sat back in Israel and developed the software and enjoyed the benefit of that business, and that would have been a pretty good business for the three of us. But we really insisted on building an entire company, sales and marketing and so on, so we could be independent and not 100% reliant on Sun.

One of the first people who showed interest in Check Point was a salesperson at BBN, a big government contractor, a research firm, in Boston. They were running the network for all the Boston educational institutions: Harvard, MIT, Boston University, and probably 50 others. He took us to many big Boston-area accounts like Digital, Gillette, and State Street Bank. They all showed interest in the product. I remember going to Gillette, a very conservative company. But they wanted to connect to the internet and because they saw our product, and they switched from Digital to Sun, because they were excited about that potential.

That sales guy demonstrated the potential. He tried to convince the bosses at BBN to become a Check Point reseller, but they didn't want to. Our experience with ISPs at that point was that most of them had plenty of business selling connectivity. The ones that came from academia didn't have much interest in doing more business. They liked the product, but they didn't want to become a reseller. And so this guy decided that he would quit

his job and become the first Check Point reseller. And that's what he did. The name of that business was Internet Security Corporation. They even owned the domain security.com, by the way.

Here's one example of how we started the channel for network security products:

BRM tried to convince me to go public in the summer of '95, when we were forecasted to have sales of around $10 million that year. I remember that very vividly because Deb Triant reminded me over the years about it. She came to Tel Aviv. The investors called us in to a big meeting with all our accountants and lawyers and shareholders, and told me, "Gil, we see you have a nice business—$10 million." Back then $10 million was actually enough to go public. And they said, "You should go public now."

I was the youngest person in the room, maybe 27 years old. All the other people were grayer and older than me, and very authoritative, all of them running big businesses. And I told them, "No way, guys. We are building a business here. We are not here to sell it, we are not here to be involved in financing. That will distract us from the main goal, which is to develop the best security and the best business around it." Deb was shocked at how I could sit there as the kid in the room and tell them, "No way." Which by the way, I think maybe that's what also triggered them to sell part of their share to our VCs later in '95.

At that point, I didn't want to go public. But at the beginning of '96, around February or March, I pretty much had no choice because we already had a subsidiary in the US with sales and marketing, we had already built a development organization, and we already had several offices around the world. The investors came to me again and said, "Gil, it's time to go public." By then the US investors had also joined us. Just to be clear, they closed the share purchase from BRM around November of '95, and by February they were already convincing me to go public. We went public at the end of June of 1996 on Nasdaq. So less than three years after we started we had an IPO. For me it was too early, for the investors it was too late.

Doing an IPO is like doing basic training in the Army. It's a very difficult process that tests your abilities. It took two or three months to get all the documents done and to select the bankers. And then we did a three week road show around the world. We started in Switzerland, on my 28th birthday, and moved to London, then the US We visited 35 cities in three weeks, and it was completely crazy. It's one of the most intense experiences that I have had.

We were in New York for the opening of trading. Both the New York Stock Exchange and Nasdaq were customers by then.

I remember the morning of the IPO because I met with Deb and with our head of sales in the US, who had been with us only three or six months. They were both excited by our stock's performance. We priced the IPO at $14 a share. The trading opened at $24 a share, so everybody was very happy. But I gave them a very hard time. I told them, "You see, it's now June 29 or June 30. We're lucky because we are public and the quar-

ter is going to be great. But you didn't make your numbers. The quarter is great from all the previous business that you had. Your goal was to bring new resellers and new customers, but sales are coming from the old channels, not from you."

I think they were completely shocked that I was obsessed with the challenges that we had in the quarter. The next quarter was much better for them, and for the whole company.

I think it's amazing to see where the industry has gone, because for most high-tech industries after ten, or definitely twenty years, you see that demand stabilizes. We had a period like that, between the years of 2002 to 2007 or 2008. The industry flattened out. But still, if you look at our industry for the last 26 years, it's amazing to see how much the market has grown well beyond our expectations. In the early days I said the internet was going to be big, it's going to change the world, but I couldn't imagine how big it would become. I couldn't imagine how big of an impact it would have on our lives.

And I think we see the same thing in terms of the security and the cyber requirements. In the early days of cyber a firewall was a simple thing to protect your network from students and universities. Today your overall cyber strategy is critical for running your business. It's critical for infrastructure. It's an important element in the relationships between countries and particularly for modern militaries. Even more important, every small business and every large business needs to protect themselves from the same powers that superpowers need to deal with. Our industry has evolved, both in terms of size and also in terms of the complexities. If in the early days you needed to have a firewall and anti-virus software, you were pretty secure. Today there's probably 18 major categories of technologies. Out of these 18 categories, there's probably three or four subcategories in each one. That's why today there are close to 3,000 cyber companies around the world.

It creates a huge challenge for everyone, because whether you're a small company or a big company, if you are coming up with a new idea you need to fight for mindshare with 2,000 other companies, not to mention the 1,000 or so that are still in stealth mode.

We need to have products that actually work together. So if I recognize an attack with a malicious file, I can block that file on the network, and I can block that file on the cloud, as well as on the mobile device. If I recognize a new malicious website, I need to be able to block its access in all the posts and all the vectors. There can be at least 16 different attack vectors, and we now have several dozen technologies to combat them.

The main focus for Check Point today is on what we call Threat Cloud. It's a unified cloud that connects all the security elements and makes sure that every threat is recognized by all elements in real-time.

STORY

Chris Blask

Chris Blask contributed to the invention of the gateway firewall and Network Address Translation (NAT) while he was at BorderWare. He is the Global Director Industrial and IoT Security at Unisys. He is also chair of the industrial control system ISAC.

A lot of folks take an odd path to a security career. I was just another odd-pather. I didn't finish high school, I was running a baling room, making huge bales out of strips of paper and dust, into my early 20s. After getting married I took some classes and got a computer job and one thing led to another.

My first job was a little company called Enterprise Computer Systems, which was a Data General VAR building systems for lumberyards. Soon after I joined my bosses left. I was left holding the technical bag and spent a year or two doing that.

When I left that job I was teaching landscaping, Unix, and C at Greenville Tech. I ended up being a Kelly girl at General Electric, a full-time contract role. My job was to take care of the networks for these plants making 150-ton turbines for power generation in a building one quarter of a mile long. Sixty percent of the computer terminals were down when I got there. So, I took a clipboard and a pencil and I walked all of the cables to map out the network and take inventory.

I did that for a few weeks until they were all working. About that time they were installing a video conference center. I wanted to have mobile video conferencing. So I got some catalogs and ordered RF modulators and things. I connected the industrial control network, the plant floor network with the machine tools and terminals and data to the internet via the IT network. I stacked up various pieces of equipment and ran cables between them so that I could have a rolling box of video gear and I could plug in to the network anywhere and be part of a global GE video conferencing network.

This is ironic in that, of course I worry about OT security now and in 1990 I was the guy that connected IT to OT, for what seemed like a really good purpose. And it was effective. We had a German-made machine go down, so we got the supplier's engineers to a GE video conference location and I crawled around underneath the machine holding a camera to troubleshoot it. I was wearing a headset and would point the camera where the engineer said to resolve the problem. The economic and functional reasons for doing it were perfect but of course, I hadn't thought of security.

After GE I moved to Toronto and got a job with a little company called C Change. The two founders were former NCR guys that had figured out how to basically hack the drivers on NCR disk drives. I needed the job so I came on as a sales guy.

We were selling internet connections and the gear for connecting. As one of the first ISPs in Canada we were housing Livingston Portmaseters in a closet at 1 Young Street in Toronto. Each Portmaster had 32 ports for dial-up modems. We also became a reseller for Livingston.

We also sold Rockwell NetHoppers. These neat little boxes had ethernet on the one side and a phone port on the other side with a modem and a little router in it. They were selling like hotcakes. Which is fantastic, but every time we sold a Rockwell NetHopper the customer would call us back and say it doesn't work.

Every time we sold a NetHopper we would have problems associated with people using the same IP addresses on both ends. I remember sitting in a Chinese restaurant in Mississauga, Ontario near the Meadowview GO station with the other sales guys, Clyde Stephens and Paul Hunt, and going over and over and over this. I had a Mac and I drew a little cloud: that's C-NET and the line down here is our customer's network.

We're selling this little box in the middle. What we need to do is build a box that will solve their problems.

The web wasn't popular at that time. We had DNS and mail and FTP and Gopher. I stared at the picture and thought we have to do security because the one thing between our customers and the internet is this little box. So we'll sell that too. Now everyone just calls that the Firewall. So the BorderWare firewall server was invented. This put me in a weird situation when I first met Marcus Ranum and the other people who had been writing the history before me, because at that point you did not put servers by definition on a firewall. You stripped code out, you did less, and you examined it and you had the best people in the world read the code.

I went to one of the first security conferences. Dennis Richie was up on stage with Marcus Ranum of firewall toolkit fame. I stood up and asked whether it was possible to have a firewall without reading all the code yourself. Marcus being Marcus said, "No. There's no way I would trust anything," and everybody agreed. I said, "You have it all wrong. My mom needs a firewall and she's not reading the code." And a big debate began about *well then we can't have security*. Maybe, but my mom still needs a firewall.

And tens and tens of thousands and millions and millions of companies need firewalls. So everything we've done to this point is fine, great, that's how you do it, but it doesn't address this next issue. I found myself coming back to that over and over again. The war story is that me and the two guys stayed up for three days and I bought the Mountain Dew and we just got it done in time.

As we went down this path of creating the BorderWare Firewall, I had a conversation with an older guy from a big tech company who told me my sales plan for selling millions of firewalls was all wrong. I could only sell to the Fortune 1000 and then I would be done. The reason he gave? That there were not enough IP addresses!

I freaked out. I got off the phone and I ran into my boss John Alsop's office I told him, "Look there are not enough IP addresses, the world is going to end, the whole thing's a bad idea." And he didn't even blink an eye. He just sat there with his hands folded and said, "Look, I realize when there is enough demand for something technical solutions are a challenge, so don't worry about it, it will work out."

And over the next fifteen minutes in a little conference room with our one whiteboard, we got Omaya Algundi, who was our technical lead engineer, and Andrew Flint, who was the first hired engineer building BorderWare. We stood at the whiteboard and drew a little box in the center and a line on each side and then a little Gopher server.

I put 10 dot on the left hand side and said "Okay, we're building a physical box with two-way network interfaces. We have to have a real IP address on the outside, even if it's only one or two. And on the inside is our class C that says that 10 dot can't be used anywhere else, so all of our customers can have 15 million addresses on the inside. If we can figure out some way to just build

a table or something." And we invented network address translation right there. But that's not the point. The point is that John Mayes also invented NAT at the same time, as did others. To John Alsop's point: it had to be done.

And it was, and now not only does my mom have a firewall in several of her rooms, but they all do NAT. And we're not out of IP addresses even though we're out of IP addresses. And IPV6 isn't taking over the world because we continue to hack our way through things well enough.

Later I ran into John Mayes at one of the early Internet World conferences. We had chili dogs. We weren't competing because PIX wasn't a firewall; yes, it sort of did NAT, but it did other things, too.

As far as I can tell he went home and added security to PIX.

In fact, Check Point launched with Sun at Interop in Atlanta and I relaunched BorderWare at the same place, right across the hall. I had a 10' x10' booth with nobody but me, and I was up till 4 a.m. at Kinko's getting documentation, while Check Point had banners all up and down the escalators. BorderWare was number two in the early days before it got bought by Secure Computing.

When BorderWare was sold I joined TIS for a year or so before they got pulled into McAfee and then in June of '98 I joined Cisco to take over the Century firewall product line, which was put into end-of-life in the first month. I was also given the PIX, which was end-of-life in the next month as well. PIX was supposed to die in late '98.

To my point, everybody on the earth needs firewalls. At a certain point in the market somebody like Cisco needs to come along and sell billion of dollars worth and millions of individual units. So I took over project management for the PIX team just as Cisco had determined to announce the end-of-life of the product.

We got really black ops about it. Intel stopped making parts for the PIX 510 so we now only had the 520 and we engineered the 515 sort of in secret. We announced it late '98 or '99, and then the gold series that lived there for 515, 525, 535.

The thing worth taking out of this is that at that point the security market thought it was really grown up. That was 1998 and look at the industry today!

CHAPTER 4

DDoS Defense

One of the clearest segmentations of the IT security industry is that of Distributed Denial of Service defense, or DDoS defense. Traditional network security is concerned with blocking attacks meant to breach a network, whereas DDoS is an attempt by attackers to disable a network-attached service. In its most direct form, attackers merely overwhelm a server by initiating more requests than it can handle, causing it to crash, reboot, or simply be too busy to respond to legitimate requests. Or, even more difficult to counter, the network pipes connecting to the service can be flooded with traffic as simple as a UDP Ping request.

Place a firewall or other network defense in front of a server and it bears the brunt of the DDoS attack. But the firewall often fails, which accomplishes the attacker's aim. Thus specialized equipment evolved to handle those attacks.

One of the first and more elegant denial of service attacks took advantage of a weakness in TCP/IP. A SYN flood is a stream of connection requests to establish a TCP connection. The TCP socket on a server becomes overwhelmed be-

cause the short SYN requests, often from spoofed sources, are never acknowledged, leaving all available sockets open waiting for a response. Check Point Software quickly added SYN flood defense to Firewall-1. Later, as more DDoS methodologies were devised by attackers, specialized equipment was developed. Hardware appliances from Top Layer (rebranded Corero), Arbor Networks, and Radware would be deployed in front of the rest of the security stack. Often multiple DDoS defense devices with load balancers to multiply their power were required to squelch the flood of requests targeting the servers behind them.

But an appliance cannot stop an attack that fills the pipes in front of it. For that you need to build something special, something that Barrett Lyon was one of the first to create.

Lyon was working at an IT consulting firm when one of their clients, Don Best Sports, came under fire from DDoS extortionists in Eastern Europe. Don Best provided a sports data service to Las Vegas casinos. Lyon deployed a sufficient number of proxies in a data center and contracted with carriers to have large enough available bandwidth to counter the impending attacks and successfully warded them off.

Another type of attack, the GET flood, mimics thousands of web browsers requesting pages. This type of attack makes the web server work at maximum capacity, serving up its pages and effectively preventing legitimate traffic from getting through.

Flood attacks using SYN and GET can be blocked if the source is known. Just block all traffic from a specific IP address.

It did not take long for hackers to develop techniques for distributing their attacks among hundreds, thousands, and potentially millions of attacking hosts. One of the largest, the Mirai botnet, was comprised of one hundred thousand compromised IoT devices.[1] Another, attributed to North Korea, was a botnet recruited from compromised PCs by a worm. It was used to attack dozens of websites associated with the US and South Korea, including whitehouse.gov, cia.gov, and Korean banks. Recruiting hundreds of thousands of devices makes the task of identifying and blocking the sources almost impossible. These are the most effective attack techniques known, and can be very expensive to counter. The winner is usually the one with the most available bandwidth.

Barrett Lyon, after demonstrating that there are effective counter measures to DDoS, began to get requests from a very specific niche industry: online gaming sites. In 2003 millions of US citizens participated in poker, slot machines, craps, and sports betting online. There were dozens of companies providing such services, most of them hosted offshore in the Caribbean, Costa Rica, or Gibraltar. These were very lucrative businesses. One small operation consisting of tele-operators and a closet of servers in an office in Costa Rica claimed to do $2 billion in annual revenue. At that level of turnover it is easy to understand why they were prime targets for extortion threats that targeted their online presence. Being down for even a day meant millions in lost gaming revenue.

The biggest day of the year for sports betting sites that serve the US is Super Bowl Sunday. Leading up to Super Bowl XXXVIII in 2004 the gaming sites began to receive extortion emails from Eastern Europe. The letters said in effect: pay us $30,000 via Western Union by a set date or we will take you offline. The owners of the gaming sites began to call on Barrett Lyon to replicate the defenses he had created for Don Best Sports.

It was then that Lyon invented DDoS defense as a service. He took funding from one of the Costa Rican gambling operations. The new company was named Prolexic Technologies. Within a year Prolexic hosted 80% of the online gaming websites in the world and succeeded in putting a stop to the nascent extortion racket emanating from Eastern Europe.[2]

The architecture designed by Lyon and his team of network security engineers used three primary elements to defend against DDoS, elements that are worth studying.

First, Prolexic would proxy a customer's web servers in their own data centers placed strategically around the world. A proxy is just a server that mimics the original site. A request for a web page would go to the Prolexic server, which would in turn retrieve the relevant web page from the original server in Costa Rica and serve it back to the requestor. By positioning a proxy server in between all transactions Prolexic could apply various defenses. These included hardened operating systems that would not be vulnerable to common exploits found in off-the-shelf operating systems. Lyon called on the expertise of one of the world's top BSD developers based in Hawaii. BSD is an open source version of Unix. The community of BSD developers has focused on creating as secure an operating system as possible. Prolexic customized BSD by removing all the components not needed by a web server. Then they enhanced its ability to thwart the type of resource restrictions (memory, open ports, etc.) that usually caused servers to fail when they received too many connections. They also developed load balancing technology so that an attack of millions of requests could be served across multiple servers.

The next investment Prolexic made was in off-the-shelf network gear from the likes of Arbor Networks and Top Layer. These devices could detect attacks, send alerts, and throttle attack packets. The cost for such devices can exceed $100K and the special security knowledge to run them is not readily available to a typical organization. Prolexic could make that investment because they were protecting multiple paying clients.

The final component of Prolexic's defense was bandwidth. The typical heavily trafficked website of the day used 10-20 megabits per second of bandwidth. Through its relationships with major backbone Internet providers, Prolexic could use up to 18 gigabits per second of bandwidth, an unprecedented amount. Most Internet services see the largest amount of bandwidth for outward bound traffic. YouTube, Google's video hosting service, has to supply terabits of data to its consumers of streaming video. So negotiating contracts with carriers for large amounts of incoming traffic is relatively easy and inexpensive. The largest attack Prolexic experienced was 11 gigs of traffic. These measures: hardened, load-balanced servers, defensive devices, and massive amounts of available bandwidth are the core of DDoS defense.

Lyon, the technical founder, lost control of Prolexic, which was eventually sold to an operation in the Philippines, and then acquired by the large Content Delivery Network (CDN) company Akamai, and is still the core of their security offering. Lyon has since founded several network delivery companies. He worked with David Cowan at Bessemer to launch Defense.net, which was acquired by F5 in 2014.[3]

Meanwhile, CDNs like Cloudflare provide DDoS defense for the masses just by dispersing websites to its edge. An attack from Eastern Europe would hit Cloudflare's European data center. Visitors to the attacked website would just experience slowdown as their requests are served from another data center.

As web hosting in general moves to cloud services like Google Cloud Platform, Amazon Web Services, or Microsoft Azure, customers get automatic DDoS defense because these providers have massive bandwidth available to them. Elasticity, the concept of spinning up servers in response to demand, also serves as a DDoS defense. David Cowan believes the opportunity for new DDoS defense vendors is limited, yet companies like Link11 in Germany are experiencing growth.

1. "What is the Mirai Botnet?" *Cloudflare*, accessed November 27, 2019, https://www.cloudflare.com/learning/ddos/glossary/mirai-botnet/

2. Joseph Menn, *Fatal System Error*, (NY: PublicAffairs: 2010).

3. "F5 Networks Acquires Defense.Net Inc," *Business Wire*, May 22, 2014, https://www.businesswire.com/news/home/20140522006599/en/F5-Networks-Acquires-Defense.Net

CHAPTER 5

Endpoint Protection from AV to EDR

Anti-virus products predated the internet. The 1980s were a time when viruses were transferred from machine to machine via floppy disks. The original anti-virus vendors grew from companies that provided a variety of utilities for the nascent PC industry. File storage, system optimization, disk cleaning, data erasure, backup and recovery, and anti-virus made up bundles sold by software companies that primarily addressed the consumer market. As PCs invaded the workplace, so did viruses, and as networks became predominant in the '90s viruses began to spread over the wire instead of through dirty diskettes. As viruses became more and more virulent, the importance of AV grew, as did the AV market.

Symantec

Symantec has always been a company in search of an identity. 2019 marked, if not the demise of Symantec, perhaps the end of its market relevance. It's worth reviewing the twisted path it took over 25 years.

The Symantec name came from a small software company founded in 1982 by Stanford grads to create a database program for the new IBM PC. It was acquired by a smaller competitor, C&E Software, in 1984. The combined company retained the Symantec name and shipped its first major product called Q&A in 1985. Sales that year were $1.4 million.[1]

Under its CEO at the time, Gordon Eubanks, Symantec embarked on a strategy of acquiring niche products and taking them to market. In 1987 Symantec acquired tools for project management (TimeLine), presentations (ThinkTank) and compilers for the Macintosh (THINK C and THINK Pascal), and an email system called InBox.

Symantec went public in 1989 and its stock took off, giving it the currency to continue to acquire companies including Peter Norton's PC software company, Norton Utilities, for $60 million in stock. Symantec also acquired a C++ compiler and pcAnywhere for remote desktop management. By 1993 Symantec even got into the contact management business when it acquired the makers of Act!, from Contact Software International.

In October 1993 Symantec finally entered the AV market when it acquired Cleveland-based

Certus International Corp. Five years later, it acquired the AV products of both Intel and IBM. Symantec also acquired Fifth Generation Systems, which had a contract with a small company in Jerusalem called BRM for anti-virus software. That acquisition gave BRM the capital to invest in Check Point Software.

Eubanks stepped down from Symantec in 1999 to be replaced by John W. Thompson, an executive from IBM. Thompson had a 28-year career at IBM, rising to the role of General Manager of the Americas. He had little experience with security products, but was tasked with growing the enterprise security business. He embarked on divesting the company of non-security products like the Internet Tools division and the Visual Café product line, as well as Act! He then started acquiring security companies such as firewall vendor Axent Technologies, L-3 Network Security for vulnerability management[2], and Seagate's Network Storage Management Group. He also looked briefly at Finjan Software. He passed on that investment, but was so impressed with Finjan's CTO, Ron Moritz, that he later hired him as Symantec's CTO. Moritz defined Symantec's acquisition strategy, which he termed the NSSSM strategy: networks, systems, storage, and security management.

Very early in his tenure, Thompson relates, Symantec suffered a breach on a Friday. He asked, "Who's our CISO?" They did not have one. By the following Monday morning Symantec had appointed its first CISO.

Under pressure to keep Symantec's stock price up, Thompson continued an aggressive acquisition strategy, culminating in 2004 with the largest acquisition in the software industry for the time: the $13.5 billion purchase of Veritas, a data center software and storage company. The best evidence that this was a major blunder for Symantec is the valuation for the Veritas division when it was spun out to investors led by the Carlyle Group in 2015 for $8 billion.[3]

Under John Thompson, Symantec continued to grow through acquisitions. It played an important role in the overall industry, offering an alternative to an IPO to many high-flying startups with good technology. The big paydays for investors and founders fueled more startups and more investments.

Sygate, acquired on August 16, 2005, had a series of desktop tools including a popular PC firewall that Symantec discontinued after the acquisition. It also gave Symantec a Network Access Control (NAC) product.[4]

Altiris was acquired on April 6, 2007, for $830 million. It produced system and asset management software. At the time Thompson told analysts, "Added to our portfolio, (Altiris) makes us infinitely more competitive with the likes of a Microsoft."[5]

Vontu, a data loss prevention (DLP) company, was acquired November 5, 2007 for $350 million.[6]

PC Tools, another PC utility company focused on security, was acquired August 18, 2008. PC Tools was run as a separate company until Symantec killed it in May 2013.[7]

AppStream, a provider of application virtualization software was acquired on April 18, 2008.[8]

MessageLabs was one of Symantec's larger acquisitions. It paid $695 million in November 2008 for the online messaging and web filtering company.[9]

PGP was acquired June 4, 2010, for $300 million.[10] The Pretty Good Privacy software was originally a free encryption solution that mirrored RSA's encryption algorithms. It was created by Phil Zimmermann. The technology was acquired by Network Associates and then spun out to PGP Corporation, formed by Phil Dunkelberger and Jon Callas. The acquisition, along with Guardian Edge which was announced at the same time (for an additional $70 million), gave Symantec an endpoint encryption solution.

The Verisign certificate business was acquired August 9, 2010 for $1.28 billion.[11] It was the end of an era for the first certificate authority to sell SSL certs recognized by the major browsers. Verisign, which eventually got out of the security business, had decided to focus on its remarkable cash cow of maintaining the top level domain servers and collecting a fee for every .com, .net, and .name domain. Symantec later spun this business off to DigiCert in November, 2017 for $1 billion.[12]

RuleSpace, acquired in January 2010, provided content URL filtering services for many ISPs.[13]

Clearwell Systems was acquired May 19, 2011, for $390 million. It provided e-discovery solutions for legal firms.[14]

LiveOffice, a cloud email and messaging archiving company, was acquired on January 17, 2012. Price: $115 million. The products were already integrated with Clearwell's discovery solutions.[15]

Odyssey Software for device management including mobile devices was acquired March 2, 2012. It was followed by Nukona, acquired April 2, 2012, which was a mobile application management solution.[16]

NitroDesk, a nine-person shop with application container technology for Android devices, was acquired May 2014.[17]

Then came the divestiture of Veritas. Splitting off Veritas in 2015 was the first acknowledgement that Symantec was suffering and was in need of restructuring. The following year Symantec acquired Blue Coat, the manufacturer of secure web gateway appliances, for $4.65 billion. It was almost a reverse merger as the CEO of Blue Coat, Greg Clark, became the CEO of the merged companies.

Blue Coat had had its own troubles over the years. It was initially launched as CacheFlow in 1996. In early 2002 CacheFlow's CEO Brian NeSmith took the company public. Its stock jumped almost five fold on opening day.[18] NeSmith then pivoted the company into secure gateway appliances and renamed it Blue Coat.

Blue Coat quickly became the largest vendor of content URL filtering appliances. Every large organization needed a way to block employee access to inappropriate or time wasting websites. Adding a category for malicious websites made these devices security products and gave rise to the category of secure web gateways. Blue Coat had a problem though. A gateway appliance that sits in the data center is very expensive. It has to handle tens of thousands of simultaneous sessions.

In the early 2000s, large distributed enterprises like retail stores, distribution centers, car dealerships, and restaurants were moving to local internet breakouts. Instead of back-hauling all the traffic from the remote location to HQ over very expensive MPLS circuits, each location would go directly to the internet over low-cost broadband. To provide security they needed to replicate the stack of security gear found at HQ, but without the million dollar price tag associated with data center grade equipment.

This gave rise to the inexpensive, all-in-one security appliance industry led by WatchGuard, SonicWall, and Fortinet. They each added content URL filtering as a subscription service to these devices. At price points of $1,000 or less, Blue Coat could not compete.

Blue Coat stopped growing, and in February 2012 was taken private by Thoma Bravo for $1.3 billion. Considering the $4.65 billion Symantec paid for Blue Coat, this was a good outcome for Thoma Bravo. But not so good for Symantec.

Shortly after Greg Clark took the reins in November 2016, Symantec acquired consumer credit protection company LifeLock for $2.3 billion. Combined with the Norton consumer AV business, this represented $2.2 billion in annual revenue for the consumer division.[19]

But growth was lackluster under Greg Clark and he stepped down in May 2019. The an-

nouncement caused a 15% tumble in Symantec's stock price.[20]

The newly appointed interim CEO, Richard Hill, soon announced a sale of the company to Broadcom, but it fell apart in July. It was later restructured and on November 5, 2019, Symantec's enterprise security business was acquired by Broadcom, while its consumer business remained a public company called NortonLifeLock.[21] This spelled the end of Symantec as a security behemoth. It is likely that it will not play the same role in the industry as it has in the past.

Network Associates

Network Associates was formed from the combination of McAfee Associates with Network General and its Sniffer product. This was one of the early attempts to create a security company that would cover both endpoint and network security, a combination that continues to fail as a strategy. Back then the goal was to dominate the enterprise software space. Security had not become a big enough sector to inspire pure play roll-ups. That would change.

Aryeh Goretsky, now Distinguished Researcher at ESET, was the first employee of John McAfee. He conducted a reddit AMA (Ask Me Anything) in 2019.[22] During the AMA he also provided this short summary of his experience in the AV industry:

Heady days, indeed. When I entered the field in 1989, the number of computer viruses was in the tens, with slightly more of them targeted at the

Classic Mac OS than for DOS. That flipped in a year or so to DOS, and hasn't changed back since.

We used to advise customers to update their software once a quarter, and monthly for high-risk computers like those belonging to secretaries and technicians who might be accessing floppy diskettes from untrusted sources. That recommendation changed to two months and then a single month as the number of new viruses being seen increased. When I left McAfee in 1995, there was already work underway to automate the download of updates by dialing into a dedicated BBS system. These days, anti-malware programs update themselves hourly with continuous checking between that for additional types of telemetry, which might mean a threat was detected.

At the beginning, we might have received 2-3 floppy diskettes a month with new viruses on them. That increased to weekly, and uploads of suspect files were occurring multiple times a day to our BBS.

Computer viruses were initially spread mostly through floppy diskettes at the speed at which they could be couriered around the globe, and sometimes through BBS (intentionally or otherwise). Worms like the Morris Worm were not really thought about in the same way as computer viruses, and would not be for years until internet access started to become ubiquitous, and consumer desktop operating systems started to come with TCP/IP stacks, and dial-up networking began to replace BBS.

Dozens became hundreds and hundreds became a couple of thousand by the time I left McAfee Associates in 1995. That was a steep hockey curve back then, but a blip by today's standards, where

you might see 250,000-300,000 malware samples arrive on a daily basis.

In his AMA Goretsky credits John McAfee with the successful growth of one of the first AV vendors, going from one employee to an IPO in three years. McAfee formed McAfee Associates in 1989 and raised $42 million in its IPO in 1992. McAfee's AV software was one of the first to be distributed over a network rather than shrink-wrapped boxes of instruction manuals and floppy disks (later CDs).

In 1993 John McAfee suffered a mild heart attack and turned the reins of McAfee Associates over to Bill Larson, who became CEO. Larson had been VP of Sales and Marketing for Sun Microsystems. He proceeded on an acquisition binge. He acquired Brightwork Development in 1994 and Saber Software in 1995, both LAN management companies. In 1997 he acquired Jade KK, a Japanese AV company for $21 million. Finally he merged the company with Network General later that year. The company was renamed Network Associates.

Network Associates continued to operate as a collection of endpoint and network solutions until 2003, when the newly appointed president, Gene Hodges, embarked on a major restructuring. The plan was to double down on security and divest the desktop management, LAN management, and other tools. The Gauntlet Firewall product line was handed over to Secure Computing and the other divisions spun out. Left with only the AV product, the company was re-branded as simply McAfee, which seemed like a logical move until John McAfee reemerged from Belize and came into the spotlight.

McAfee, the company, focused on security. It acquired Foundstone, the vulnerability scanning software company along with its founders, Kevin Mandia, Stuart McClure, and George Kurz. Mandia later left to form FireEye, where he is CEO. Mandia later left to form Mandiant, now part of FireEye, where Mandia is CEO. McClure left McAfee to found Cylance, which sold to BlackBerry in late 2018 for $1.4 billion. Kurtz left to found CrowdStrike. After an IPO in 2019 CrowdStrike's market cap hit $21.7 billion before settling down to $12 billion. CrowdStrike found itself caught up in the news in 2019 as the US President and Republican leadership promulgated a Russian disinformation narrative that somehow CrowdStrike was a Ukrainian company and it had transferred a server containing hacked Democratic National Committee emails to Ukraine.

Hodges also acquired an endpoint intrusion prevention company, Entercept, and a network intrusion prevention company, IntruVert in 2003, led by Parveen Jain.

In 2007 Dave DeWalt took over at McAfee. Gene Hodges moved on from McAfee to become CEO of Websense, a content URL filtering company where he acquired PortAuthority, one of the leading Data Leak Prevention companies. Gene retired in 2013 and passed away in 2018 at the age of 67.[23]

Dave DeWalt had been president of Documentum before joining McAfee, where he acquired Secure Computing, bringing the Gauntlet Firewall back into the fold in addition to multiple other firewall brands that Secure Computing had consolidated. He then went on to sell McAfee to Intel for $7.68 billion, where for a short time it was branded Intel Security.

The Intel acquisition made no sense at all, although all of the executives involved spun a story of how Intel would somehow embed security into its chips. The last year before the acquisition, McAfee reported just over $2 billion in revenue. Even four years later the Intel Software and Services Group was reporting $2.216 billion in revenue. McAfee sales completely stalled out while it was part of Intel.[24]

In 2016 Intel spun out McAfee to TPG, a private equity firm, at a valuation of $4.2 billion, a $3.48 billion dollar loss from when it acquired McAfee in 2011. Intel maintained a 49% ownership and continued to finance $2 billion in debt from the acquisition.[25]

Today McAfee is still privately held, led by Chris Young. It has over 9,000 employees and claims 97 million corporate endpoints and 522 million consumer endpoints protected by its software. According to LinkedIn, total employment has dropped 2% in two years, indicating that growth still eludes it despite its large footprint on endpoints.

Trend Micro

Founder-led companies like Trend Micro tend to have less complicated histories than those that pass through the hands of multiple CEOs and investors. Trend Micro never succumbed to the temptation to develop or acquire a firewall vendor. They stuck to their mission of countering malware. Thus, endpoint protection, email protection, and server protection have been Trend's focus from its founding, with recent incursions into cloud security.

Trend was founded in 1988 by successful entrepreneur Steve Chang, his wife, Jenny Chang, and his wife's sister Eva Chen. The company soon moved its headquarters to Taipei, Taiwan, from Los Angeles. In 1992 Trend developed an OEM agreement with Intel whereby Intel sold a LAN AV product produced by Trend. In 1998 it went public on the Tokyo stock exchange, where it is still listed.

Eva Chen served as Trend's CTO until taking over from Steve as CEO in January 2005.

Although focused, Trend has made several strategic acquisitions over the years.

InterMute anti-spyware was acquired May 2005, for $15 million, and incorporated into Trend's AV products by the end of the year. Incidentally, this was the same timeframe in which McAfee decided to write spyware signatures for its products. These moves put an end to Webroot Software's grand plans for its Spy Sweeper product line. Until that point all the anti-virus vendors treated spyware as applications that the end user wanted to install, therefore as "potentially unwanted," not as malware.[26]

Kelkea, acquired in June 2005, was an anti-spam vendor with 20 employees. Major ISPs such as AOL used their IP blacklists.[27]

Provilla was a data leak prevention company that employed 22 people. It was acquired October 2007.[28]

Identum, an identity-based encryption company, was acquired in February 2008.[29]

Third Brigade, a Canadian endpoint intrusion prevention solution, was a transformative acquisition for Trend in April 2009. Many of the Third Brigade executives joined Trend in senior roles. The product formed the basis of Trend's cloud workload protection suite.[30]

TippingPoint, the Intrusion Prevention pioneer that had been acquired by HP, was acquired by Trend in October 2015 for $300 million. IPS from Tippingpoint is still supported by Trend.[31]

Immunio, a container and application scanning tool, was acquired in November 2017.[32]

Part of the reason Trend Micro has been able to resist non-strategic acquisitions is the more sober environment of the Japanese stock market. It is not subject to the same pressures that a Nasdaq-listed company is under to increase revenue each quarter at the risk of increasing costs and confusing the customer base. Trend dominates the market for AV in Japan and continues to evolve as computing infrastructure moves to the cloud.

Kaspersky Lab

Kaspersky Lab is the AV company founded in 1997 by husband and wife Eugene and Natalya Kaspersky, and Alexey De-Monderik, who now serves as an advisor. Eugene and Natalya divorced in 2007, and by 2011 Natalya was bought out by Eugene. Kaspersky Lab, still private, reports that its revenue has exceeded $1 billion annually. Its research team is well regarded and responsible for uncovering many samples of nation-state malware, including Stuxnet and Flame (attributed to the Equation Group, which is thought to be part of the NSA's Tailored Access Operation).

Endpoint Detection and Response

Anti-virus solutions are the best depiction of the arms race that occurs between threat actors and defenders. From the early days of a handful of new viruses every month to today, when AV companies have to analyze over half a million variants a day, there has been a steady increase in threats targeting endpoints. This has led to new approaches that leverage machine learning, such as that employed by Cylance, to memory inspection, alerting, and blocking such as that of CrowdStrike and others. These new solutions are termed Endpoint Detection and Response (EDR). The response part means isolating an infected machine and cleaning it before an attack can spread to do damage.

There are 255 endpoint security vendors listed in the directory. They run the gamut from anti-virus, to encryption, to the control of physical devices and their ports. These histories of the major endpoint product vendors are just a small part of many transactions, investments, and startups that have occurred, with many more to come.

1. "Symantec Corporation," *Advameg Inc*, accessed November 27, 2019, https://www.referenceforbusiness.com/history2/11/Symantec-Corporation.html.

2. "Symantec Acquires L3," *Norton LifeLock Inc*, accessed February 14, 2019, https://www.symantec.com/about/newsroom/pressreleases/2000/symantec_0214_01

3. Chad Bray, "Carlyle Group and Other Investors to Acquire Vertias Technologies for $8 Billion," *New York Times*, August 12, 2015, https://www.nytimes.com/2015/08/12/business/dealbook/carlyle-group-veritas-technologies symantec-deal.html

4. Paul Roberts, "Symantec Acquires Endpoint-Security Company Sygate," *eWeek*, August 16, 2005, https://www.eweek.com/security/symantec-acquires-endpoint-security-company-sygate

5. Jim Finkle, "Symantec to Acquire Altris in $830 Mln Deal," *Reuters*, January 29, 2007, https://www.reuters.com/article/us-symantec-altiris idUSN2947872520070129

6. "Symantec to Acquire Vontu," *CIO*, November 6, 2007, https://www.cio.com.au/article/195068/symantec_acquire_vontu/

7. Amanda Conroy, "Symantec Buys PC Tools," *PCWorld*, August 23, 2008, https://www.pcworld.com/article/150227/acquisition.html

8. David Marshall, "Symantec Finally Acquires AppStream," *InfoWorld*, April 9, 2008, https://www.infoworld.com/article/2637561/symantec-finally-acquires-appstream-to-complete-the-virtualization-package.html

9. "Symantec Completes Acquisition of MessageLabs," *Dark Reading*, November 17, 2008, https://www.darkreading.com/cloud/symantec-completes-acquisition-of-messagelabs/d/d-id/1129860

10. Anuradha Shukla, "Symantec to Acquire PGP and GuardianEdge," *Network World,* May 12, 2010, https://www.networkworld.com/article/2209366/symantec-to-acquire-pgp-and-guardianedge.html

11. DealBook, "Symantec Acquires VeriSign for $1.82 Billion," *New York Times*, August 10, 2019, https://dealbook.nytimes.com/2010/08/10/symantec-acquires-verisign-for-1-28billion/

12. Zeus Kerravala, "DigiCert's Acquisition of Symantec's Security Business," *CSO*, November 7, 2017, https://www.csoonline.com/article/3236188/digicert-s-acquisition-of-symantec-s-security-business-is-good-news-for-customers.html

13. Mike Rogoway, "Symantec Buys RuleSpace," *Oregonian*, July 10, 2019, https://www.oregonlive.com/siliconforest/2010/10/symantec_buys_rulespace.html

14. Forrester Research, "Symantec to Acquire Clearwell Systems," *CSO*, May 20, 2011, https://www.csoonline.com/article/2136098/symantec-to-acquire-clearwell-systems-to-bolster-ediscovery.html

15. Jeremy Kirk, "Symantec Acquires LiveOffice," *CIO*, January 16, 2012, https://www.cio.com/article/2400460/symantec-acquires-liveoffice-cloud-based-archiving-company.html

16. "Symantec Completes Acquisition of Nukona," *Dark Reading*, April 16, 2012, https://www.darkreading.com/mobile/symantec-completes-acquisition-of-nukona/d/d-id/1137495

17. Jeremy Kirk, "Symantec Acquires NitroDesk," *PCWorld*, May 28, 2014, https://www.pcworld.com/article/2248060/symantec-acquires-nitrodesk-for-email-security-on-android.html

18. Dawn Kawamoto, "CacheFlow Jumps Fivefold Following IPO," *Cnet*, January 2, 2002, https://www.cnet.com/news/cacheflow-jumps-fivefold-following-ipo/

19. "Symantec to Acquire Lifelock for $2.3 Billion," *Norton LifeLock Inc*, November 20, 2016, https://www.nortonlifelock.com/about/newsroom/press-releases/2016/symantec_1120_01

20. Jordan Novet, "Symantec CEO Greg Clark Steps Down," *CNBC*, May 9, 2019, https://www.cnbc.com/2019/05/09/symantec-ceo-greg-clark-steps-down-stock-drops-.html

21. Jane Edwards, "Broadcom Closes $10.7B buy of Symantec's Enterprise," *GovConWire*, November 5, 2019, https://www.govconwire.com/2019/11/broadcom-closes-107b-buy-of-symantecs-enterprise-security-assets-rick-hill-hock-tan-quoted/

22. u/goretsky, "IamA Aryeh Goretsky," r/IamA, *Reddit*, September 20, 2019, https://www.reddit.com/r/IAmA/comments/d6z3km/iama_aryeh_goretsky_today_im_the_distinguished/

23. "Gene Hodges," *Forever Missed*, accessed November 27, 2019, https://www.forevermissed.com/gene-hodges/#about

24. Richard Stiennon, "Five Reasons Intel Should Spin Off McAfee," *Forbes*, July 21, 2015, https://www.forbes.com/sites/richardstiennon/2015/07/21/five-reasons-intel-should-spin-off-mcafee

25. John Mannes, "Intel Spins Out Intel Security," *Tech Crunch*, September 7, 2016, https://techcrunch.com/2016/09/07/intel-spins-out-intel-security-with-tpg-to-form-new-mcafee-valued-at-4-2b/

26. Ellen Messmer, "Trend Micro to Buy Anti-Spyware Firm InterMute," *Network World*, May 10, 2005, https://www.networkworld.com/article/2320853/trend-micro-to-buy-anti-spyware-firm-intermute.html

27. Cath Everett, "Trend Micro Tackles Spam with Kelkea Buy," *ZDNet*, June 14, 2005, https://www.zdnet.com/article/trend-micro-tackles-spam-with-kelkea-buy/

28. Ellen Messmer, "Trend Micro Buys Data-Leak Specialist Provilla," *Network World*, October 29, 2007, https://www.pcworld.idg.com.au/article/195920/trend_micro_buys_data-leak_specialist_provilla/

29. Mathew Humphries, "Trend Micro Buys Into Encryption," *geek.com*, February 27, 2008, https://www.geek.com/news/trend-micro-buys-into-encryption-with-identum-purchase-573095/

30. Ellen Messmer, "Update: Trend Micro Acquiring Third Brigade," *Network World*, April 29, 2009, https://www.networkworld.com/article/2254079/update--trend-micro-acquiring-third-brigade-as-part-of-data-center-security-strategy.html

31. "Intrusion Prevention System," *TippingPoint*, accessed November 27, 2019, http://docs.trendmicro.com/en-us/tippingpoint/intrusion-prevention-system.aspx

32. "Trend Micro Buys Immunio," *Dark Reading*, November 28, 2017, https://www.darkreading.com/application-security/trend-micro-buys-immunio/d/d-id/1330502

STORY

Ron Moritz

Ron Moritz is a partner in OurCrowd, one of the biggest seed investment funds in Israel. His career has spanned roles at Finjan Software, Symantec, Computer Associates, and Microsoft. He also helped create the CISSP (Certified Information Systems Security Professional) certification and was one of the first to earn it.

I think my very first exposure to security was dealing with Unix boxes, PDP-11s, and other tech equipment that were pervasive in universities. I was taking a class and we all had access to a minicomputer, some PDP-11 or similar. There was one username and password that was given to everybody. It was the superuser account. Just out of curiosity, I started playing around with the security one day when I was supposed to be coding something, and realized I could change the password and ended up locking everybody out, including the people who were supposed to be managing this system. As a result of that, I started to realize how fragile the systems were.

I carried this security awareness into my first job as a coder at the university. Eventually I mi-grated into sysadmin roles and took responsibility for the nuts and bolts of security in the Data General world. That led me to an auditor role. At the time an auditor of the IT organization also took on the role of security guy because there wasn't an IT security department. There were people who were tasked with configuring various mainframe security tools like RACF and Top Secret, but not necessarily anyone tasked with the role of making sure that the IT organization and the data they were responsible for was secure. So the auditors did that.

We saw a lot of different types of creative attacks at the university. Some of them were combinations of cyber and IT attacks. All the systems were fragile. Once we discovered that a student in one of the dormitories had set up a series of modems and created his own ISP. He had a telco line brought into his dorm. He basically created a commercial offering to the community to get internet access in the days before AOL Online. He had several hundred modems piggybacking off of the university's big data line.

In the mid-'90s I realized that it was a good time to begin to look at the other side. Instead of being a security practitioner, I could get into the commercial side of security tools. It was time to go off and build some products. I was looking in two directions. One was in the direction of Silicon Valley. The other was called the Silicon Wadi, wadi being a dry riverbed. There were maybe a dozen cybersecurity companies in Israel in the mid-'90s, Check Point obviously being one of them. That is when I connected with Finjan Software.

With the introduction of Java and Java code, and ActiveX, which was the Microsoft alternative to Sun's Java, code was starting to move across the internet in the same way that data content was moving. The founder of Finjan (Shlomo Touboul) had an idea about how to protect computers from potentially malicious code transmitted over the network, but he had very little technical background in security, so we ended up being a good match. He had a vision for the problem he wanted to solve, and I had some of the experience on the technical side. So that's how I got involved with Finjan Software. That's when I moved from one side of the table to the other.

Finjan introduced me to the other side of the world: the marketing, the analyst firms, all the people that help you position yourself in the market and help you with visibility. I learned all about the marketing side of security. You learn a lot when you're creating technology and trying to bring it to life and bring it to the market.

I also learned how to deal with investors, how companies get funded. The investors and the

Board of Directors of Finjan agreed that it was time to start talking about selling the company. They also convinced me at that point to return to Silicon Valley, which would be a better place from which to visit possible acquirers.

With the help of an external banker we identified a bunch of different target companies, mostly in the anti-virus and firewall spaces. I remember sitting across a table from the Computer Associates team out in Long Island at one point, thinking how challenging it was to be in that position across the table from them, only to find myself years later on the same side as the CA negotiators and thinking how much easier it was to be on their side as the acquirer than the seller.

One of the companies we talked to was Symantec, the leader in the industry, the biggest of the cybersecurity companies at the time. They were tracking toward $1 billion in annual revenue, which made them the biggest standalone security vendor.

I remember walking in to make our presentation along with the CEO of Finjan and our banker. I was there with my CTO hat on. We were surprised that we were meeting directly with John Thompson, who had just taken over the reins of Symantec a few months earlier. He was looking to sponge up knowledge about the security industry because that wasn't his background. He had been running a huge part of IBM's software business, perhaps some of their services as well. After a 28-year career with IBM he became the CEO of Symantec, which had basically stalled, so the investors, the shareholders, and the board were looking to make some changes. He was not skilled in the art of computer security. The meeting turned into a professor-student discussion where he asked a lot of questions and I shared a lot of data. A lot of the things that we talked about weren't related to Finjan software. We got our pitch in, but we went well beyond that. The meeting time ran very long.

The fact that we were meeting with the CEO, the CFO, and the head of sales of the largest computer security company at the time was impressive because usually you meet with the people who are closer to the business, mid-level managers. But in this particular case it was John Thompson himself who led the meeting. The two of us ended up having a great relationship. It was summer of '99, and they began a diligence process.

During the process of reviewing Finjan, there were some changes in management, including the long-time CTO of Symantec, and at some point toward Q4 of '99, they concluded that they didn't want to acquire Finjan.

But the very next day, I got a call from John's office. We had a quick conversation. He said, "Listen, I have a long laundry list of things that I need." He rattled through those, and being the great sales guy that he was, I couldn't say no. We ended up meeting and he invited me to be the Global CTO for Symantec. Professionally and personally, I felt I couldn't reject that opportunity.

I helped create a strategy for Symantec that they ended up executing on for the next decade, from 2000 to 2010, a strategy that helped inform many of the acquisitions they did over those years, and really helped John build the company out.

By the time that Veritas acquisition happened, I had already left Symantec and joined CA.

I called the strategy I helped create for Symantec the NSSSM strategy: networks, systems, storage, and security management. Only three companies, HP, IBM, and CA, could execute on such a strategy of combining all the parts. But it was certainly part of the vision that we drew up for Symantec when we looked at driving Symantec from the consumer side of the business to making it an enterprise cybersecurity powerhouse. We realized the need to manage everything was part of that story. So storage management did fit into that narrative, but there were a lot of other parts that Symantec needed before the Veritas acquisition could "sing." So the timing was off. Veritas didn't quite fit in at the time that they did it, but it certainly was part of the macro thinking. If you really believe that management needs to be controlled across all the components of IT, all of the data services they use, this is perfectly reasonable.

That's where the Veritas acquisition was supposed to take Symantec, but I think just the timing of it didn't allow it to fully capitalize on the capabilities that Veritas brought to the table.

CHAPTER 6

Identity and Access Management

Identity and Access Management (IAM) is the sector devoted to on–boarding users, assigning unique credentials, defining and enforcing what systems, networks, and applications they are authorized to use, and revoking that access when they depart as employees or customers. There are 309 vendors that fit in this classification, primarily because there are so many ways to authenticate users, from one-time password (OTP) tokens to grids displayed on screen (a user remembers the coordinates and in response to a challenge, fills in the corresponding numbers and letters they see in the grid), to biometrics and location.

Strong authentication relies on requiring at least two of three things:

1. Something you know, like your username/ password.
2. Something you have, like a one-time password generator, or a digital certificate.
3. Something you are, such as your face, fingerprint, voice, gait, or even the way you type.

This is often called two-factor or multi-factor authentication.

The largest vendors of IAM products provide directory services, a specialized database usually based on the Lightweight Directory Access Protocol.[1] LDAP was first created in 1993. In the late '90s and early 2000s there was significant competition between CA, IBM, Oracle, and Novell for directory services. But then Microsoft entered the market with Active Directory, which effectively dominated the industry, and Microsoft won the enterprise.

It all began with RACF.

Barry Schrager describes in the next story how he developed the idea of applying controls to every file and service on mainframe computers. He was working within a university IT department and attending the SHARE user group meetings for mainframe computers. He put together a presentation of his ideas meant to address a looming problem of students and staff messing with each other's files. Shortly after, IBM introduced RACF (Resource Access Control Facility) for their systems. But Schrager felt RACF did not even come close to implementing the controls he envisioned, so he commercialized his ideas with ACF2 (Access Control Facility 2). He saw rapid adoption by the US government, starting with the CIA, and General Motors. But then CA began giving away its product, Top Secret, bundled with its other software. While ACF2 and later versions of RACF were resource-centric (based on who can access each file or service), Top Secret was user-centric (based on what resources user can access). Schrager describes it as two approaches with the same result. He eventually sold ACF2 to a small company that was immediately snapped up by CA.

With the rise of the web came a handful of startups to address the need for what was called web access management, a type of single sign-on. Vendors included Netegrity with its SiteMinder product, Oblix COREid, and Novell iChain. CA acquired Netegrity in 2004 for $430 million.[2] Oracle acquired Oblix in 2005.[3] Novell, in the meantime, was eventually acquired by the Attachmate Group in 2011, which in turn was acquired by Micro Focus in 2014.

While Microsoft established a near monopoly in IAM through Active Directory, a new generation of IAM vendors arose to address a new opportunity: the cloud.

Okta was founded in 2009 by two former Salesforce executives. They saw that granular access controls for software-as-a-service and cloud resources would become needed. Most IAM solutions were hosted on legacy systems in the data center. If cloud services were taking off, there would be a need for a cloud-native IAM solution. The market proved them right. Okta raised $225 million in venture backing before going public in 2017. It had a market cap of $15 billion in November 2019.

ForgeRock was created in 2010 to fork and commercialize Sun Microsystem's identity platform after Oracle acquired what remained of the once high flying computer company. Founded by ex-Sun employees in Norway, ForgeRock is now headquartered in San Francisco.

Ping Identity was founded in 2002 by Andre Durand and Bryan Field-Elliot, and is often used for cloud identity services. It was acquired by Vista Equity Partners in 2016 and went public in 2019. With close to 1,000 employees and a market cap of $1.8 billion, it is growing quickly.

OneLogin was founded in 2009. It is one-fourth the size of Ping Identity. Although it grew rapidly over the last two years, the last six months of 2019 saw growth flatten out.

Polyrize is a good example that innovation in cloud IAM is still happening. Funded in 2019 with a $4 million seed round, the Israeli company is the youngest vendor to enter the space.

As Microsoft reacted to the cloud era and built its Azure cloud, it did not miss that along with moving Exchange servers from customer premises it would need to provide a cloud version of Active Directory. It announced Azure Active Directory for its developer community on July 12, 2012.[4] Azure AD is going to be the one to beat for all cloud IAM solutions. But differentiating on multi-cloud environments and messaging against vendor lock-in will give the Oktas and Pings a chance to succeed against Microsoft's messaging.

---

1. J. Sermersheim, "Lightweight Directory Access Protocol," *The Internet Society*, June, 2006, https://tools.ietf.org/html/rfc4511

2. Matt Hines, "CA to Buy Netegrity for $430 Million," *Cnet,* October 6, 2004, https://www.cnet.com/news/ca-to-buy-netegrity-for-430-million/

3. Stacy Cowley, "Update: Oracle buys Obix," *Infoworld*, March 28, 2005, https://www.infoworld.com/article/2668338/update--oracle-buys-oblix.html

4. Alex Simmons, "Announcing the Developer Preview," *Microsoft Azure*, https://azure.microsoft.com/en-us/blog/announcing-the-developer-preview-of-windows-azure-active-directory/

STORY

Barry Schrager

Barry Schrager is responsible for the work that led to the creation of RACF at IBM and ACF2 as a commercial product for mainframe access control. He was Assistant Director of the University of Illinois-Chicago Circle Computer Center from 1968 to 1978. He is currently employed by a large financial institution and still works with IBM mainframe security.

I first started going to SHARE, the first enterprise IT user group, in 1969. It was my first travel experience and SHARE was a great organization. We now look at social media for exchanging ideas and thoughts and plans and assistance with research. That usage didn't exist at the time. SHARE was a vehicle for this because you got mainframe people together in a room. Out of 600 to 800 people you found a bunch who shared your interest in certain issues. You were able to sit down with them and compare notes and come up with potential solutions. We eventually got to the point of trading code that we had written.

One of the issues that came up was that we were getting dinged on security by our organiza-

tions. I was working for the University of Illinois in Chicago, and we had students who were deleting other kids' data, graduate students' data, deleting the professors' sample data that the students were going to write programs against. Some other people were having similar issues where stuff would accidentally be deleted or, God forbid, somebody would do it on purpose. That started the whole issue of data security. Then, in 1972 I met Eldon Worley, who also had ideas about data security.

He and I and a guy from Boeing got together. I gave a SHARE presentation on our thoughts for data security, and where we thought the IBM community should go with it. Not much happened with it, but at that time I also formed the SHARE security and compliance project and we came up with a series of requirements. I gave a paper in 1974, a presentation about what was needed, and one of the main issues was system integrity. We still see that in the mini and desktop computers of today. We determined that nobody should be able to modify the operating system or bypass the standard interfaces. The operating system was a requirement because we felt that in a multi-user system, like OS/360, if you gave people the capability of bypassing the standard interfaces, they could do anything they wanted.

That was the system integrity part. And then we came up with a series of requirements for future security. Fast-forward two years later. IBM had announced RACF as a resource access control facility, but it didn't meet the crucial requirements we had described. It did not provide protection by default, which meant that everything was protected unless you gave permission

For example, in '78, the audit team at General Motors was complaining to me that they had a Delco division and a GM research group. Each had RACF installed for two years. One had 3% of their data protected, and the other had 5% of their data protected. One of the auditors said, "We don't really know what percentage of that data has to be protected, but we know 3% ain't it."

I sat down with a co-worker. We'd developed a prototype for ACF2. which we decided to develop into a commercial product. We attempted to get the University of Illinois to back the project but they declined. But then Rod Murray from London Life Insurance asked us to develop a commercial version of ACF.

We created a working version of ACF2 running at London Life. Then Jerry Lyons from Pontiac Motor Division came to look at it. London Life was raving about it. General Motors decided they were going to have Pontiac install it on a trial basis and see what happened. We went to Pontiac, Michigan, and installed it, and got it up

in production. Three months later Pontiac Motors was at 100% data protection. So here you have General Motors Research, and Delco at 5% data protection—and Pontiac at 100%. They asked us to go to Chevrolet. They were up and running and 100% protected in two months. After that ACF2 took off.

Through SHARE I became friendly with Barry Lewis from the Central Intelligence Agency. We set up a trial at the CIA, and a month later he called me and said, "Barry, got some good news and some bad news." I said, "Okay, give me the bad news." He said, "We found a way to bypass your products, the system integrity requirement." And I said, "Okay Barry, tell me how you did it and I'll fix it." He said, "Nah, it wasn't your fault. It was IBM's fault, but you could have blocked it." I said, "Okay, tell me how we block it." He said, "Nah, we may have to use it." In 1978 the CIA was already looking at hacking into computers.

What was the good news? He said, "We're going to buy it. We're going to recommend it to a hundred of our collaborators and subcontractors."

I said, "Great, give me their names and I'll call them." He said, "I can't give you the names; you'll just get calls." So out of that we got the NSA and MI-6 and the entire Australian government. But the nice thing was Barry Lewis was really supportive of us. Linda Vetter from General Motors was another big supporter. They both came to SHARE to present on their use of ACF2.

From then on our sales people could go to a prospect who objected to buying from a little bitty company instead of IBM and say, "First of all, our product is better. And second, it's being used by the CIA and General Motors."

When we started a perpetual license was $27,000 for the first CPU and $18,000 for subsequent CPUs. Maintenance was some percentage of that. General Motors negotiated a license of $18,000 plus maintenance. They eventually had over 100 systems.

We were doing about $17–$18 million a year, but over $12 million was going out the door in expenses.

Around '84, another company developed a product called Top Secret. They took a different approach, almost the opposite of that used by RACF and ACF2. Instead of assigning permissions based on a resource like ACF2 does, Top Secret assigned permissions to users.

If you think about it, it's a matrix. In the one way you're looking at it from the bottom. In the other you're looking at it from the side, but the answer is in the middle and they're both perfectly okay.

Top Secret never gained any traction against ACF2. In the meantime, IBM rewrote RACF in the early '80s to be what you see in use today. Then the company that developed Top Secret sold it to CA, and CA started giving it away with their other software. We could not compete with free, so we sold ours to University Computing in 1986. Little did we know, about eight or nine months later, University Computing was acquired by CA. So that's how ACF2 ended up at CA.

CHAPTER 7

Data Security

Data security, among all the aspects of IT security, has the distinction of having a history that is thousands of years old. Hiding the true meaning of written messages pre-dates all information technology. But, as an industry, encryption is much younger. Before the internet, encryption devices were the realm of defense and intelligence agencies. The commercial industry came about after Whitfield Diffie invented non-symmetric key exchange, paving the way for the first vendor of modern encryption tools, RSA.

Data security, as an industry, has a different set of drivers. Data security is foundational to all security. In a layered model it is the last, best defense against an attack. But data security is based on math and the attacks are against the algorithms and the way they are implemented. At any point in time the underlying cryptography is bulletproof, but all it takes is for a single demonstration of an attack methodology to render all the defenses ineffective and set off a rush of innovation to improve the algorithms and replace them wherever they are used. Attackers include the intelligence agencies that have waged a continuous battle to

be able to decrypt captured data and communications of their adversaries. Another major class of attackers is cryptanalysts, researchers who have an academic interest in finding ways to break the latest cryptography. Their frequent publication of these techniques drives the industry as a whole to constantly improve.

So to understand the history of data security some understanding of the history of cryptography is required. Just as Check Point Software ushered in the era of commercial network security, RSA and Verisign were the pioneers of commercial data security.

When Whitfield Diffie had his eureka moment that led to the invention of asymmetric key exchange, there were already many encryption algorithms, including DES, RC1, 2, 3, 4, etc. These were block cyphers that performed various operations on a block of clear text to create cypher text based on the input of a secret key. Simplifying the concept to its basic functionality: imagine a string of 1s and 0s that represent the clear text of a message. Take a secret key, another string of 1s and 0s, and munge it with the clear text in such a way that you can only reverse the process (decrypt) if you know the secret key. That is the basic concept of symmetric key encryption.

But how, over the internet, do you let someone know what the secret key is without exposing it to attackers? During World War II, secret key distribution required an out-of-band communications method. It could be embedded in the typewriter-like devices used on German U-boats. Or a spy behind enemy lines would have a code book he carried on his or her missions. On the internet, how do you let the recipient of an encrypted email or document know what the secret key is?

Ralph Merkle first proposed a key transmission method in general terms. He proposed distributing puzzles that would be easy for the intended recipient to solve but extremely difficult for an eavesdropper to solve.[1] It was Whitfield Diffie who struck upon the idea of using a property of exponential math, the discrete algorithm problem, to devise the first public key encryption scheme. A recipient could publish a key that anyone could use to encrypt a message while only the recipient had the key to decrypt the message. Public key distribution thus depends on a system that is easy to compute for the intended recipient but enormously difficult for an eavesdropper.

Ron Rivest, Adi Shamir, and Leonard Adleman, three computer scientists working at MIT in 1977, built on the Diffie-Hellman concept. It's reported that after a late night celebration of Passover at the house of an MIT student, Rivest came up with a one-way function that would serve as the basis of most modern public key cryptographic systems.[2] A one-way function is meant to be easy to compute in one direction, extremely difficult to compute in the other direction. Rivest's function was simply factoring the product of two large prime numbers. It is easy to multiply two large prime numbers (100+ digits long), while it is computationally close to impossible to factor that product back to its two prime numbers.

The RSA algorithm made commercial encryption possible. The three inventors went on to found RSA Data Security in 1982 and soon after Verisign, which was spun out and funded and chaired by David Cowan of Bessemer Venture Partners. Cowan is still at Bessemer today, a VC firm that manages a small portion of the Bessemer Trust set up by the Henry Phipps in 1907 to manage the investment of his wealth derived from the sale of Carnegie Steel. Cowan played a formative role in the IT security industry,[3] first with Verisign, then with many other investments, including LifeLock (acquired by Symantec), Good Technology (acquired by BlackBerry), Endgame (acquired by Elastic in 2019), iSight Partners (acquired by FireEye), Tripwire (now part of Belden), Auth0, Axonius, Claroty, Illusive Networks, Virtru, and Defense.net (one of Barrett Lyon's startups, which was another stab at DDoS defense, and that was sold to F5 in 2014).[4]

Data security requires Confidentiality, Integrity, and Authenticity, or CIA. Encryption addresses the confidentiality part, but what about integrity and authenticity? This is accomplished by encapsulating the plain text in an envelope along with a hash of the original and signing the envelope with a digital signature created from the author's private key. The one-way hash proves the text was not tampered with because any attempt at changing it would result in a different hash. Only the owner of the private key could have encrypted the message, thus providing authenticity.

RSA, which sold software libraries for encryption, was acquired by Security Dynamics in 1996 for stock that was valued at $251 million shortly after the announcement.[5] The combined companies were branded RSA Security in 1999. Security Dynamics had developed the widely used one-time password token, SecurID.

In 2006 EMC acquired RSA Security for $2.1 billion. It also acquired Network Intelligence, a network monitoring and alerting platform. The combination formed the basis of a separate division for EMC dubbed RSA, the security division of EMC. The division went on to acquire NetWitness in 2006, a packet capture and analysis vendor led by Amit Yoran, previously the founder of MSSP Riptech, and currently the CEO of Tenable.

RSA continued to be an acquirer of security vendors until Dell acquired EMC for $67 billion in 2016. In November 2019 Bloomberg reported that Dell was investigating selling RSA for $1 billion.[6]

Digital certificates

As David Cowan relates in the next story, Verisign was formed to issue SSL certificates "from the cloud." While it had a good run in the beginning, it eventually sold what was left of the digital certificate business to Symantec. In the meantime Verisign made the surprising move of acquiring Network Solutions. Now it oversees the operation of the biggest domain business in the world and is valued at $22 billion.

Entrust was founded as a spinoff from Nortel Networks in Ottawa, Canada, in 1994. It sold PKI software to banks and large enterprises that needed their own certificate authority. Public Key Infrastructure is the pyramid of trusted signers of digital certificates. At the top of the pyramid in the PKI model is a CA (Certificate Authority) that signs digital certificates for the next tier down. In its original design there was supposed to be a government agency or consortium that would sign the certificates of all the other CAs. This never happened, but there was still a market for CA software. As an enterprise software play, Entrust had the exact model that Verisign was created to counter. It went public in 1998 and had a market cap of $5 billion by 2000.[7] In 2001, after a drop in revenue, Bill Conner came on board as CEO. He had been an executive at Nortel, which still owned 25% of Entrust. Conner expanded the focus on authentication products. Entrust provided digital certificates embedded in passports and identity cards, often called smart cards.

In 2009 Conner oversaw the sale of Entrust to private equity firm Thoma Bravo for $125 million.[8] He continued to lead Entrust until it was acquired in 2013 by Datacard Group, a manufacturer of machines that made credit cards and identity cards. After paying $500 million for Entrust, the companies were combined to form Entrust Datacard.[9] Connor is now the CEO of SonicWall, which was spun out to Francisco Partners in 2016.

SafeNet started out as Industrial Resource Engineering in 1983. IRE went public in 1989 in the over-the-counter market. It raised $4 million. IRE produced one of the first VPN solutions that were rapidly adopted by banks, and was resold by MCI. In the 2000s SafeNet acquired many companies, including Cylink, Raqia Networks, SSH, and Datakey. Vector Capital took SafeNet private in 2007, paying $634 million. As a private company it continued to make acquisitions, including Ingrian Networks in 2008, which made appliances for their concept of "network attached encryption."[10] SafeNet was sold to Gemalto in 2014 for $890 million.

Gemalto was formed in 2006 by the merger of two smart card companies, Gemplus and Axalto. It employs close to 9,000 people. Gemalto was sold to Thales Group in 2017 for about $6 billion. To get regulatory approval for the sale, Gemalto had to spin off its hardware security module (HSM) business to Entrust.

Other Data Security Categories

There are many more products that fit into the data security category. Digital Rights Management (DRM) is copy protection for software and content. Information Rights Management (IRM) is similar, but usually deployed to control corporate documents.

There are many vendors, especially since the enactment of GDPR, which provide data discovery and tracking for personal information.

It is surprising how many vendors provide secure file transfer services, twenty-one at last count. There are also secure messaging platforms from Telegram to WhatsApp to Symphony. There are also secure data rooms where boards or investors can share the files needed for board meetings or due diligence for M&A.

Secure data erasure companies like Blancco and White Canyon, address the need to sanitize devices when they are sold or recycled.

As the root of security, data security will always be a major component of the overall industry. New means of communication, storage, and processing of data will lead to new products and new companies. The fear of quantum computing disrupting the industry is already being addressed by companies with post-quantum encryption stories.

---

1. Martin Hellman, "An Overview of Public Key Encryption," *IEEE Communications Society Magazine* 40, no. 5 (2002).

2. Michael Calderbank, "The RSA Cryptosystem: History, Algorithm, Primes," *University of Chicago*, August 20, 2007, http://www.math.uchicago.edu/~may/VIGRE/VIGRE2007/ REUPapers/FINALAPP/Calderbank.pdf

3. "David Cowen," *Bessemer Venture Partners* (website),

accessed November 27, 2019, https://www.bvp.com/team/
david-cowan

4. "F5 Networks Acquires Defense.Net Inc," *Dark Reading*,
March 23, 2014, https://www.darkreading.com/attacks-
breaches/f5-networks-acquires-defensenet-inc/d/d-
id/1269167

5. "RSA Security Inc," *Company Histories.com* (website),
accessed November 27, 2019, https://www.company-
histories.com/RSA-Security-Inc-Company-History.html

6. Michael Novinson, "Dell Investigating Sale of RSA," *CRN*,
November 26, 2019, https://www.crn.com/news/security/
dell-investigating-sale-of-rsa-security-for-at-least-1-billion-
repor

7. James Bagnall, "Seven Years After Going Private, Kanata
Firm Entrust is Hiring Again," *Ottawa Citizen*, February 24,
2016

8. "Thoma Bravo Completes $124M Acquisition of Entrust,"
Thoma Bravo, July 29, 2009, https://www.thomabravo.com/
media/thoma-bravo-completes-124m-acquisition-of-entrus

9. Brian Prince, "Entrust to Be Acquired by Datacard
Group," *Security Week*, December 17, 2013, https://www.
securityweek.com/entrust-be-acquired-datacard-group-
secure-identity-business

10. "SafeNet to Acquire Ingrian Networks Inc," *Business
Wire*, February 28, 2008, https://www.businesswire.com/
news/home/20080228005307/en/SafeNet-Acquire-Ingrian-
Networks

STORY

David Cowan

David Cowan is a Partner at Bessemer Ventures, one of the most prominent VC firms in technology and security. He founded Verisign and has made dozens of investments since.

When I was a kid, my father gave me a Scientific American article to read about public-key cryptography. It was the first public explanation, if you will, of the RSA invention. And I remember talking to him about the implications that it had for sharing secrets, but also for authenticating messages and authenticating people and providing nonrepudiation of communications, which was all mentioned in the article.

Fifteen years later, when I joined Bessemer Venture Partners and was thinking about where I could find big opportunities to build tech companies, I thought back on that Scientific American article. That was because in 1992, when I joined Bessemer, one of the first companies that I looked at was PSINet. PSINet was the first—an internet security provider in upstate New York that had spun out of the SUNY system. And I did the deal.

We funded it at Bessemer. It was the first venture-funded ISP.

And with this commercial ISP, I realized that for the first time there would be companies sharing networks. Until then, there were some companies sharing the ARPANET with the government, but now it would be companies sharing networks with each other. And I realized that this was the first time this network, this ARPANET, which was now being opened up to companies, meant that parties with different interests would be sharing the same networking infrastructure. So there had to be some rules in order to allow for privacy and to prevent parties from obstructing communications among other parties, and all the things that today we worry about in the cybersecurity realm.

I asked the PSI guys, particularly Marty Schoffstall, the CTO, how they planned to provide this to their clients. And he said, "That's all figured out. None of that is an issue. We put up something called a firewall, and we buy this little box from Morningstar, and it allows everyone to control exactly what traffic goes in and out of their networks."

Yes, the firewalls worked, but it seemed like there were other security issues going on. So I kept talking to some other smart people around at that time. In fact, I went on a three-month journey talking to smart people out there, like Eric Schmidt, who was at Sun at the time, and Al Lill, who was a Gartner analyst, and Rick Sherlund, who was a Goldman analyst, and various technologists. I went around asking them questions about where tech was going.

The only person I talked to who had any actual operational background in security was this guy who had been the CEO of Codex, which Motorola bought. Back then, being in cybersecurity meant you were building encryption/decryption boxes. This was before public-key encryption. So you put a secret key in at one end, and the same secret key had to be available at the other end so you could encrypt messages. Codex sold these boxes to the Navy and a few other government installations where they wanted to be able to send messages securely. But it was only within the military where the secret key was available at both sides.

So I went to the CEO and I said, "Now, it looks like there are going to be a lot of companies sharing this ARPANET thing, and it seems like security's now going to be a much more important issue." He literally put his arm around my shoulder and said, "Son, don't ever invest in security." That was something I remember pretty clearly. Which kind of made sense if you were looking backward at what you were able to do in security at the time.

But I thought, "Okay, it seems like we need to figure out how we're going to secure messages on the internet with all these different parties where they can't share secrets." And I remembered that article that my father had given me. I looked up this RSA and asked, "Is anybody doing this?" And I found this little company in Foster City. It had no venture backing because no investors would give them money, let alone even meet with them, because, of course, there was no security industry at the time.

I reached out to Jim Bidzos, who was the CEO of Verisign, and asked if I could talk to him. Here I was, a brand new associate at a venture firm without a very illustrious background or track record. But he took the meeting. At the time, they were doing two things with this RSA invention. They were selling tool kits to make it easy for developers to create symmetric keys and then use them for encryption/decryption.

They were also licensing apps on public-key cryptography to companies who wanted to embed it in their products. The big licensers of that were Lotus and IBM, which were probably the two largest customers of those patents. Novell might've been a customer, too. The company was doing a few million dollars of revenue a year between the two businesses, but wasn't growing very much. I thought, "This seems very important, and it seems like one day this has to be a ubiquitous technology."

Then I went back home to Boston. I used to host poker games with CEOs who would meet two or three times a year with various other

CEOs and founders. For the one in Boston, I invited Ron Rivest, to whom Jim Bidzos introduced me. I started talking to Ron about what RSA was doing. He pointed out something that Jim hadn't mentioned, which was this idea of using a certificate authority to issue certificates, which we could then use to authenticate servers and enable very, very easy encryption on the web.

A year later, when Netscape had come onto the scene, people thought nobody really trusts this, and nobody's going to want to enter their credit card information and things like that. Ron explained that you could build this certificate authority that would allow you to encrypt communications with unique keys. It was potentially a much bigger business. I thought maybe we could build a certificate authority. It would be something that would be much, much bigger than selling tool kits and licenses.

I went back to Jim, and suggested Bessemer should invest, with the goal of building a certificate authority.

Jim said, "I would love to build a certificate authority, but it would take a lot of money, and I don't have it. And I can't take your money because I don't control the company." At the time the company was 51% controlled by an eccentric billionaire who bought it from Rivest, Shamir, and Adleman. He told me the billionaire would need to agree to it.

I got on a plane, and flew to Miami, and then drove across Florida to the Everglades to this shack with a corrugated tin roof. And in that shack in the middle of the swamp was the office of Addison Fischer. He asked, "What are you doing here?" And I said, "I'm with Bessemer Venture Partners, and I want to invest in this company you control, RSA, in California." And he said, "This is a very valuable company because we hold these key patents." And I said, "Patent licensing is not really a great business. But we could build a certificate authority, and we could do something really big."

He said, "Well, I think these patents are really valuable, and I would not be willing to let you invest at any valuation below 20 million pre." 20 million pre in 1994 would be like saying $1 billion today.

Nobody invested in private companies at 20 million pre back then, so I left. In the next month or so I moved to California, and hosted my next poker game out in Los Altos. Jim Bidzos came to that one. I told him about my trip to the Everglades and the disappointing outcome. We thought it was too bad there was no way for Bessemer to invest." But then Jim had an idea. He said, "What if we created a spinout and we fund it to do the certificate authority?"

If Bessemer funded the spinout, then Addison had no dilution in his ownership of the patents because Bessemer would have no rights to those. It sounded like a good idea.

In January of '95, I hired a lawyer from Cooley, and I had him file incorporation papers for Digital Certificates International. At the time, I was the only officer on the documents. Bessemer put whatever we had to put into the entity to make it real. Then I went to Jim and said, "Now, let's negotiate an exchange of assets from RSA to this entity for equity."

We agreed that RSA would get a third of this new entity in exchange for everything that we needed from the company in order to build a certificate authority. It wasn't clear that legally or technically we really needed anything from RSA to do this, but it was important to be working amicably with them. They might've come after us for the patents. They did have a lot of technical expertise in how to build public-key software. I was okay giving up a third of the company in order to make RSA our ally instead of our competitor, which in retrospect was a good decision.

As part of that deal, we also agreed that we would take strategic investment from some companies who had been working closely with RSA. I approached Visa, Mitsubishi, Intel, and some others. They all said they wanted to participate. Bessemer led a series-A round into this entity along with Visa, Mitsubishi, and Intel. The remainder—whatever wasn't held by RSA—we set aside for an option pool. It was Jim's genius that when we did the original series-A deal, we gave 1% of the company to Netscape.

We closed that deal in March of 1995. Jim agreed to serve as interim CEO in addition to serving as CEO of RSA. We set up Digital Certificates International to collocate with RSA in Foster City. Jim took a bunch of people from RSA and hired them into DCI. He was running both and I was serving at the time as chairman and CFO of DCI. He got the team to start working on the software that we needed to stand up a certificate authority.

Jim and I hired Steve Combs to recruit a CEO. Steve started bringing us candidates. The first one was Chuck Boesenberg, who was a proven CEO. I thought he was great, and tried to hire him, but he would not join this little, weird thing. You have to understand that this company, DCI, wasn't a software company, and it wasn't a hardware company. At the time, those were the only two kinds of tech companies that existed. I remember trying to get the partners at Bessemer to even put in the initial money to seed this thing. It was very difficult because they kept asking me, "What does this company do?"

I told them, "We're going to sell integers, but they're really big integers." No wonder Chuck Boesenberg said no. We had a similar experience with some other potential execs. But then Steve brought us this young buck, Stratton Sclavos, who hadn't yet struck it big and had a little more appetite for risk. He seemed like a really smart, aggressive, well-regarded sales leader, who also had experience from his previous job dealing with joint ventures because he had worked in one between two big tech companies.

In June of 1995, we hired Stratton as CEO. He came in and started hiring a full team. The company moved out of the RSA office to another nearby in Foster City. He hired a whole bunch of people, including Dana Evans as CFO. He looked at this whole thing we were doing, and he really simplified it to focus on the biggest opportunity and make it more understandable to the world. He came up with this idea that a digital certificate was like a driver's license for the internet. He told the board it was about bringing trust to the web.

It was mid-1995. Netscape was going public. Everyone was excited about this new application of the internet. Dana said, "We're not going to do user authenticating. We're not going to do the nonrepudiation. We're not going to do all these things. We can bring trust to this by issuing certificates of servers that enable communications with the server in a secure way." It's what people today are looking to blockchain to do.

Thanks to their 1% ownership, Netscape put our public key into the Netscape browser. By late '95 we had it operational. Anyone with a Netscape browser who went to a server that had a certificate would see the little lock go on and would be able to have an encrypted session. And as soon as Microsoft saw Netscape doing that, they came to us and asked for the public key. We gave it to them, and they put it in Internet Explorer. But we didn't have to give them 1% of the company. They just did it because they needed to have parity with Netscape.

Stratton also hired a marketing firm to come up with a name. They came up with Verisign. We all agreed: great, great name. And we changed the name to Verisign a couple of months after he joined the company.

Within a year of starting the company we now had an effective monopoly on encrypted communications for the web. Anyone who wanted to have trust with users on the web had to come and get an SSL cert, for which we charged about $250 a year. That quickly turned into a phenome-

nal business. Eventually other people figured out how to set up certificate authorities, and certificates got cheaper.

This isn't really part of cybersecurity history, but the next brilliant thing that Stratton did was parlay the company's value into a much bigger success by acquiring Network Solutions, which was the SAIC spinout that manages .com, .net, and .org to this day and gets paid annual fees from every one of those domains every year for managing them, which is really the most profitable government-mandated monopoly in history.

By the time the SSL market lost most of its value it didn't really matter because Verisign was now running this even more valuable business. Ultimately they sold the SSL business to Symantec. So that's the history of Verisign.

Back in the early '90s bringing trust to the web didn't seem like the most important thing because there really was no web. When I funded PSINet there was no web. It didn't exist. What companies were doing on the internet primarily was file transfer and email.

But you could see email was the fastest-growing traffic. The question was, how are we going to provide security around email to know that they're encrypted and authenticated and all of that?

So the first security investment I made was in Worldtalk. Worldtalk built a mime gateway for email servers in order to encrypt and decrypt messages using enterprise-level keys that were certified by CAs like Verisign. Obviously they weren't relying on Verisign in 1993, when certificate authorities didn't exist. But that's ultimately what Worldtalk evolved into. It was one of the first email security companies.

Then I invested in Tumbleweed, which was another similar email security company. After Verisign, I invested in Valicert, which was Chini Krishnan's company, and was the first to provide certificate revocation abilities on top of certificate authorities.

Ultimately all three of those companies went public: Worldtalk, Tumbleweed, and Valicert. As a public company, Tumbleweed acquired the other two, and they all ultimately were acquired by Axway. The other early investment Bessemer made back then was in Altiga, which was one of the first VPN boxes. That was in 1996, I think. Cisco bought that, and it turned into the Cisco VPN product.

After I met with the PSI guys and they explained to me what a firewall was, I took a meeting from Gil Shwed, who was raising a round for his startup, Check Point. He told me that he was going to make a firewall that would compete with Morningstar. He was going to compete with them by getting distribution through partners. That sounded to me like a terrible idea. Selling something that was effectively commoditized and relying on big partners to sell it for you never really seemed to work for startups. But he did it. He cut a deal with Sun. And Sun ended up selling the shit out of those Check Point firewalls.

Gil built one of the most valuable security companies ever. I admit I missed that one. It wasn't because I didn't appreciate the importance of firewalls early on. It was because I had underestimated the ability to work with Sun as a distributor.

One other thing worth mentioning is that there was another source of certificates at the time—Entrust. Entrust was the company run by Alberto Perez, and basically was a certificate authority software that people could use to make their own certificates. Without all the nomenclature we have today about cloud computing, it just seemed pretty obvious that it was a lot better for one person to build a certificate authority and then sell the certs than to expect everyone out there who wants a cert to build their own certificate authority and then somehow get their public keys out there.

Verisign was actually in some ways the first cloud company because it took this on-premise model of Entrust and said, "We're going to do the exact same thing they're doing, but we're going to do it ourselves in this multi-tenant way, and then give access to everybody." Within a year we saw that Verisign was really taking off. At Bessemer, I started looking for other examples of that where we could take on-premise software and host it and sell access to it.

Keynote was basically Mercury Interactive in the cloud. Flycast competed with the prevailing ad software company, moving that aspect to the cloud. I met with Marc Benioff in 1999 because he was moving Siebel into the cloud, but he wanted $100 million pre—money, which was in 1999 pretty much like the $20 million Addison Fischer wanted. I said, "That's crazy," which was another terrible, terrible, terrible decision.

I got off the board of Verisign in I think 2003, when my day job at Bessemer required that I free up time.

What's next? The good news for the security industry is bad news: things are getting worse, not better. There's still a lot to be fixed and all kinds of new problems cropping up. I've always felt that the cybersecurity industry is unlike other tech industries, because in those other technology matures. In microprocessors, you get an Intel. In networking, you get a Cisco. In databases, you get an Oracle. In search, you get a Google. In cybersecurity, though, there's no such thing as mature technology because you have so many people constantly working to render your technology obsolete all the time.

And there's no such thing as a mature product. The ones that become mature are soon obsolete. There's a constant need for reinvention in cyber. I don't see how it ever ends. As long as technology is dynamic and there are new ways to hack it, the cyber industry is always going to need startups and reinvention and innovation.

I think that the major problem facing enterprises today is the historical artifact of the SIEM model, where security products throw alerts into a SIEM to be resolved by network professionals there. This was fine early on in the industry when you were truly just sending exceptions because you had some kind of perimeter defense, which was basically deterministic like a firewall. If some-

thing weird happened, you sent it off to a human being to investigate. But in today's world, where there's no perimeter, enterprise is just drowning underneath these alerts. SOC analysts are unable to deal with them to the point where most alerts don't ever get dealt with. It leads to a situation where people say, "Target knew there was an attacker in the system and didn't do anything about it." That's a very simplistic way of saying there were just too many alerts to get to.

The other issue I see, which I blame on stupid venture capitalists, is that one-third to half of the money that's been invested in cyber has been wasted because of singular mistakes. That is the idea that a bunch of extremely smart engineers— and they are all extremely smart engineers—have found a way to identify an attack in the system due to some anomaly that points to an adversarial presence in your network. The thinking is that by baselining your network and finding anomalies, we can find intruders. This has been, in my opinion, disastrous because any anomaly-based system creates false positives. If you have false positives in a product, then you cannot operationalize the product. All you can do is create an alert and just add more and more alerts onto the SIEM.

And more alerts are not what people need. You're not solving a problem by saying something suspicious is going on. Every analyst sees thousands of suspicious things every day. They don't need to be told that there's two more on the list. There's no value in that. Where there is a lot of value in helping enterprises somehow tame this monster. I put all of those technologies roughly into the category of orchestration—how you make an SOC effective. There are different ways of doing it. You can do it by using machine learning to reduce alerts by discounting those common to the whole internet, like what GrayNoise does. You can do it by realizing an alert is basically the same as these twelve other alerts, so let's put them together into a single alert. You can take an alert that suggests there's an attack going on, but it is not a severe attack. Or you can take an alert that suggests a severe attack, but it's not against a system in your company that has any crown jewels or is near any system with crown jewels. So don't worry about it, or don't worry about it as much. In other words, don't prioritize it.

That kind of alert management technology is great. Technology that focuses on the productivity of the analysts, kind of like what call center software does. Technology that automates responses to alerts, like what Phantom and Demisto do, are great. Anything that's allowing you to tame that monster I think is really solving the biggest problem that enterprises have.

There are two other technologies that I really like that qualify as new categories, which I think are under-appreciated today, but am very confident will be important for deterministic defenses. One of them is the idea of simulated attack. We all know that pen testing is silly. You pay somebody to get into your network. Big deal. They show you one path in. You block that path, but so what? There's like a thousand other paths. But a simulated attack, which I think of as 24/7 pen testing, is where you do what Verodin and AttackIQ do.

I think SafeBreach is really powerful, better than pen testing.

The other area that I love is deception technology. I have an investment in that space in Illusive Networks, because deception is the only way out there to deterministically catch human intruders on your network. If you're trying to track somebody who's traversing your network with an APT that's going after your crown jewels, all the anomaly-based systems are just going to throw off alerts that you have to investigate. A deception product is going to give you a 100% certain alarm that there is a human intruder. Operationally, it's much more valuable.

I know a lot of people talk about IoT as being the next big area for security. But I've never been able to get that excited about it because it's such a broad thing that encompasses so many different kinds of devices. If you're talking about the security issues of an RFID tag-like sensor and you're comparing that to nuclear reactor equipment in a SCADA environment, lumping them all into one word like "IoT" is just meaningless.

For example, with a baby monitor in your home the only thing you're scared of is somebody looking at videos of your home. That's it. Whereas if you're looking at a nuclear reactor, you're mostly worried about somebody sabotaging your nuclear plant and causing a meltdown. The threats are different. The vectors are different. And the solutions are different. So IoT is just too general a term.

I invested in Claroty because I think SCADA systems represent an enormous vulnerability. But

SCADA systems are SCADA systems. To call it IoT is not very helpful.

I've spent a lot of time in the last two years studying quantum computing, so I believe I'm as up-to-date as anyone on the cyber implications of quantum computers. The panic is a little bit premature on the impact of quantum on encryption. Undoubtedly there will come a time where quantum computers can break conventional RSA encryption. And there will be some period of time where some nation-states and not others have access to quantum computers with that capability.

However, there are other algorithms out there that are quantum-proof. And like Y2K, there will be a retooling of encryption using these other algorithms. There will be a period of time where people claim the sky is falling just like we did in 1999. But then the retooling will happen, and it will be over. So to me, it's a one-time thing that does not present opportunities for entrepreneurs and venture investors to build new companies.

I think DDoS is done because it's one of the many, many markets that are being steamrolled by the major cloud providers. When you put your application onto Amazon, you pretty much don't have to worry about DDoS anymore. As everything moves into the cloud, either Google or Amazon or Azure, DDoS just becomes less and less of an issue.

I spend no time on blockchain. Back in the '90s, when we started Verisign, we looked at using public key for doing nonrepudiation, and nobody wanted it. Then there was this company started by Stuart Haber, something with a V, I can't remember the name. But it was a brilliant idea. He said, "Look, we provide nonrepudiation. You give us any data. We'll hash it. We'll hash all our hashes together. And every week, we'll publish the hash within the *New York Times*. And then we can prove nonrepudiation for anybody who wants it."

It was a perfect solution, but nobody wanted it. Blockchain is basically the same concept: it's nonrepudiation using public keys, which is then married with a decentralized infrastructure. Doing those two things for Bitcoin is great. For currency that you want to be decentralized without regulation by any governments, it's perfect. But while there may be a few other things where you need decentralization, for almost every other application that anybody has ever come to me involving blockchain, I asked them, "Why do you need decentralization to do this? Why can't the organizing company behind this simply use public keys to sign data and then publish the hashes?"

Nobody's ever been able to say why that's not good enough and why they have to go through this whole blockchain thing. It's kind of bizarre.

STORY

Sandra Toms

Sandra Toms recently joined Absolute Software as Chief Marketing Officer. Her career at RSA, the security division of EMC, now part of Dell, spanned twenty years.

The first year, '91, the RSA Conference was a bunch of cryptographers talking about the science behind cryptography. It was totally different than today. There were a lot of concerns about what was happening with the key escrow debates, Skipjack algorithm, all these things that were happening with the government, and it felt like at that time RSA was definitely poking a stick in the eye of the NSA.

There were posters when I joined that were still up and had to do with "NSA is listening to your calls" and all that kind of stuff. Kurt Stammberger and his team had created those. But then those wars subsided a bit. It became all about controlling the export of strong encryption, which was another way the RSA Conference was able to grow and pull the industry along with it.

We were all in it together. We all wanted to ship products with strong encryption. So the thinking was, let's get together and do something about it. It was a pretty incredible way to draw competitors in, where they could lay down their arms because we all had bigger issues to tackle. It was incredible to be a part of that.

My first conference in '98: it was cryptographers, it was standards, and it was developers. At that point, I realized that there was a bigger audience of people who were using security, the enterprise and information security professionals. So at that point in time, I took a look at the agenda. I was largely left to my own devices, so I just experimented.

At my first RSA conference I thought, "This event's going to go away because we're going to solve the security issue. It's going to be easy." Little did I know what I was really getting into, as it just kept growing.

As I looked at the agenda I realized, "We don't have anything that's called hackers and threats. That would be an interesting talk." It would be an interesting track and could play throughout the years and add more tracks. At the first RSA Conference there were six tracks. One of them was called an RSA products track, talking about the SDKs (Software Development Kits). It was part of security dynamics. There was a little bit about SecureID and I realized that the only people who sat through those sessions were other RSA employees. I thought, "Okay, so maybe this isn't the most useful track in the world. Let me change things up."

As information security became more commonplace among consumers the conference grew organically, and we were always thinking, "Okay, what's next? What do we need to do? What are the tracks that'll be most interesting and continue to grow the event?"

In '98 we said it was 2000 attendees, but I do believe that was a lie. It was probably that 2000 people registered. That doesn't mean they showed up.

For the latest event, RSAC 2019, we had over 42,000 people show up. We don't get the number of registrations anymore. It's just who shows up, because that's the most telling number.

The very first RSA conferences were at the Hotel Sofitel. Then it went to the top of Knob Hill and multiple hotels there, and then it moved to San Jose. We were always trying to get space at Moscone, but we were always such a small event that they could not fit us in to the schedule.

We jumped back and forth between San Francisco and San Jose, and then eventually landed in San Francisco because we were finally big enough.

If we had 42,000 last year, of that about 10,000 to 12,000 were full conference attendees. That number could fluctuate based on various things. During the SARS scare we saw our numbers go down. Definitely after 9/11 the numbers went down. No one wanted to travel. One thing that can impact it too is the hotel room prices in San Francisco. It's really hard to justify to your boss that you are staying in San Francisco and the hotel room is going to cost $700 a night. The price of the ticket to attend a conference is dwarfed in comparison to the hotel room prices.

The RSA Conference didn't start off as an exhibition. It started off as a meeting and then started to become important to people, and they wanted to have some kind of presence there. Managing was always outsourced. LKE is probably a name you have seen. They came on pretty early. One of the first people who wanted a presence there was Bruce Schneier, who was interested in getting his book, *Applied Cryptography*, out in the marketplace and thought that it was a good place to sell books.

The core team of the RSA conference when I was there was five people. They focused on content, and different special programming like Innovation Sandbox and the student program and diversity programming. There were one-day events as well, such as the executive security option forum and the fraud-related meeting. We also partnered with a board of directors group to train board members.

Britta Glade is now responsible for working with a program committee 40-plus people to select the program each year. The 40 people are volunteers, which is amazing. It shows you how much people in the industry really like the conference.

We've developed a very fair and open approach to content. If you're not selected, you can ask why. The program committee provides feedback to help you in future years to try to hit the mark with a proposal to speak.

But if people need more technical training, I would say RSA Conference is not for them. You could instead do a SANS package, which is two days of SANS training, and then roll into RSA Conference. I think it's best to approach the conference as a team, as an organization within information security, to figure out what you're looking to do differently over the next year, and which vendors you'll need to evaluate. And then visit those vendors among the 700 different booths on the show floor.

The conference content itself is broad. It's not deep. It gives you a nice survey of what's happening in different areas, from law to hackers and threats to anything, endpoints, etc.

Art Coviello was the CEO for RSA for many, many years. When he called me I said, "Hey, I'm thinking about leaving. I feel like I've run my course with RSA Conference. I love the program, I love the team, but it just feels like I'm ready for a different challenge."

He suggested that I talk to Christy Wyatt, who's the CEO of Absolute. Christy's focused on delivering value through our OEM partners like Dell, HP, and Lenovo. She had just started. She was very strong, very technical. I felt like I could learn a lot from her and that's what you want in a new job: someone who's going to help people with different skills. I've been here seven weeks, and it's been an incredible ride. Really great people throughout the organization.

Deborah Taylor Moore

Deborah Taylor Moore is an independent advisor to security startups and investors. Her career began at Microsoft in the early 2000s. As the security industry grew she joined one of the fastest growing IT security consultancies, NetSec, which was acquired by MCI, which in turn was acquired by Verizon.

I got started selling secure messaging at IBM and was one of the most successful sellers in that line of business. I was the top person worldwide.

I was recruited by Microsoft to help them with their customer satisfaction and to pull more customers onto the Outlook Exchange platform, as well as the whole portfolio of products: SharePoint, their BI Tools, BizTalk, and a bunch of other solutions that they were including as part of their enterprise agreement.

It was apparent to me right away as we started to get customers who were being hit by SQL Slammer, Code Red, Nimda—all of the worms and viruses—that security was the next big thing. They would be down for days, and there was no partner in our Microsoft ecosystem that handled security, and Microsoft didn't really have a plan.

This was before they embarked on the Trusted Computing Initiative, where they took all of the developers out of the field and brought them in to learn secure coding.

Because of the all security issues I rarely got a chance or the opportunity to do what I was brought in for—talk about the products and solutions—because the customers were so angry about the downtime associated with security. I thought, wow, Microsoft has deployed this ubiquitous software and everyone's experiencing these problems. And then I realized Microsoft was creating a new industry in security.

So I tried to figure out who could solve these problems; what kind of company had people who could help? For that I had to go outside Microsoft, and I found these two guys from NetSec, who had started a managed security service, but also were doing professional services for the intel community and federal government and also some commercial services like pen testing for the private sector. They had started their company in 1998 and it was about 2003 when I met them. They needed someone to do the business translation, to talk to people about security and why NetSec's solutions were necessary.

This predated incident response services. People were interested in security only because the government started to pay attention. They had put some security standards into law in about 2001 but the government agencies were kind of slow to react, putting the burden of compliance on the private sector. Some of them had experienced the same problems that my commercial customers at Microsoft had experienced. And they were mandated now to put together a security program.

So I sent the capabilities that we had, and I just mapped them to the requirements that NIST had established and went in and started to sell our programs and services to the Federal government.

That's how I got started. I wrote incident response plans for government, I helped agencies with the certification and accreditation of their systems—all following the NIST guidance for the most part. But more importantly, there were a lot of products that we were starting to use on the managed services side for our commercial customers. Governments always want you to build a SOC specifically for them. Kind of similar to private clouds today: it's our servers, our stuff, we don't trust you securing our infrastructure as a third party. We need to secure it.

So I frequently put people on site to run these SOCs and in some cases we ran the SOC independent of the customer facility, but we were still protecting the customer's environments.

We were a small coterie of about 150 consultants in the beginning, probably some of the brightest people that you could imagine. Our only competitor at that time was ISS. They were doing the exact same thing. We also acted almost as a VAR (Value Added Reseller) because we would sell solutions to folks through our partnerships.

We used to recommend signing up with Foundstone for vulnerability scanning. Those early products were kind of like asset management—they were the early point protection solutions. So many people spawned out of this company who went on to be the engineers who created some of the next security tools. They took important roles inside companies like Sourcefire, Check Point and others.

We sold firewalls, IDS, IPS, and we had put together a SIEM that was homegrown, and we also worked a bit with Qualys. We had a group that did secure coding for secure software development. And we did a vulnerability assessments. We would have a crack team of ethical hackers go into a bank and transfer $10 million to their accounts to prove that the banks weren't secure.

Back then we would get deals through wild practices like war dialing and picking up conversations from mobile phones outside federal agencies. Then we would communicate what we had learned to the vulnerable customers. It's a style of selling and cybersecurity that has changed dramatically. You can't do that sort of thing anymore. But we had to get people's attention in the beginning.

So we started to do a bit of education. We brought 40 CIOs into one place and they were so compelled by what we were doing that they all came. We went from about $1.5 million run rate to about $14.5 million in just my department in 18 to 20 months. That was the beginning of security, at least for me.

We sold NetSec to MCI, which had our company for about three months before Verizon bought them. So technically we all went to Verizon Business, and to celebrate we had a Martini Bowling party. Everyone had to be driven home afterwards.

After that I started to work as a VP to help them with a few of their acquisitions of additional cybersecurity companies before I left and started to do it full time on my own.

Clients I worked with were early stage companies that wanted to make sure they were developing viable products and solutions to bring to market. But mostly they (a) needed help bringing them to market, (b) usually needed to get some assistance with getting funded, and (c) needed to grow the business and have a go-to-market business development plan.

I worked with an incubator funded by Ireland to help their startups. I also worked with the predecessor to Tivoli.

As the center of gravity of the cybersecurity industry began to shift to the DC area, especially after the government announced $7.2 billion in spending in 2009, I was well placed. Since 2009 Sourcefire has been acquired by Cisco and Mandiant by FireEye. I expect to play a role in many more mergers and acquisitions coming from this area.

CHAPTER 8

Governance Risk Compliance

Security professionals like to point out that compliance does not equal security, yet there are 303 vendors of products that fit in this category. While compliance is not security, the responsibilities of oversight by auditors and stake holders creates the need for tools to measure and report on security controls.

Governance Risk and Compliance (GRC) takes many forms. It can be the sets of policies, controls, and checks of these controls required by a particular government regulation, or it can be the set of practices meant to ensure that an organization is fulfilling its own internal mandate.

Risk Management, a significant component on the GRC space, is poorly defined. An over-reliance on risk management detracts from other approaches to establishing security practices. The problem with Risk Management is that it relies on nearly impossible methodologies, as described in the following article excerpt, originally published in *Network World*, October 15, 2012.[1]

Why risk management fails in IT

It is frustrating to see the amount of budget allocated to compliance when you consider that most of the money goes to documenting security controls, not improving defenses. One of the biggest reasons is that risk management, a carry-over from the bigger world of business, does not work in IT security.

While few small businesses have formal risk management programs, most large businesses do. They even have risk committees that are drawn from the board of directors, often headed up by the CFO. The goal is to identify risks and either reduce their potential impact with compensating controls or purchase insurance to further reduce the business risk.

For example, a large airline, thanks to its risk management program, may recognize rising fuel prices could hurt its competitiveness and decide to hedge fuel on the open market, or a car manufacturer that has gone too far down the path of Just-In-Time supply may start to warehouse critical components in case a supplier in Thailand is wiped out by a flood.

But try to translate risk management theories to IT and you run into troubles. Every risk management program starts with the dictate to identify all IT assets and weight them based on their criticality to business operations. That leads to the first big problem.

1. It is expensive and almost impossible to identify all IT assets.

While at first glance identifying assets appears to be a simple problem, it is actually extremely complex; almost fractally complex. IT assets include every computer (desktop, laptop, server, print server), every application (database, email, ERP), every dataset (customer lists, earth resources data, product pricing guide), all email, all documents in all versions, all identities, and all communications.

As companies increasingly turn to cloud computing, they need strategies to protect and recover data stored in multiple places.

Now, add in the proliferation of devices coming in with consumerization—smartphones, iPads, even e-readers—and the data that reside on them. Then add in the dynamic nature of the cloud, where servers can be in a constant state of flux as load is elastically met with more or fewer virtual machines. Like I said, it's complicated.

The next big problem?

2. It is impossible to assign value to IT assets.

The concept behind risk management is that you assign a value to each asset. There are many algorithms for doing so. It usually involves a cross-functional team meeting and making at least high-level determinations. But it is obviously impossible to assign a dollar value to each IT asset. Is it the cost of replacing the asset? That might work for a lumberyard, but an email server might have a replacement value of $2,000 while the potential damage to a company from losing access to email for an extended period could be millions of dollars in terms of lost productivity.

What about the value of each email? How much is one email worth? Ten cents? Zero? What about the internal email between the CFO and the CEO on the last day of the fiscal year warning that they missed their targets? Its dollar value is zero, but the risk from that email getting into the wrong hands could be the loss of billions in market capitalization.

Most organizations give up on the dollar value asset ranking and come up with low-medium-high valuations. Try to picture a team of IT asset managers in a room and one of them agreeing that his job is to manage servers that have little or no value. If there is no value to an IT asset, it has long since been replaced or eliminated. Every IT asset is of high value. So why bother classifying them all?

3. Risk management methods invariably fail to predict the actual disasters.

In the late '90s the automotive industry attempted to apply risk management techniques to product design. The method of choice was a huge spreadsheet template labeled Design Failure Mode Effects Analysis (DFMEA). The product engineers (me) would sit in a room for several days and look at every component—every fastener, every stamping, every piece of cloth in a car seat—and decide every possible way each component could fail in the federally mandated tests.

We would generate a huge list of possible failures—stripped bolt, fatigue crack, buckling, worn nap—and submit it to upper management who would never look at it. Of course, we failed to predict the failures that actually happened in production. You remember the recliner failures on the Saturn car seats?

Another example: A giant financial services data center located on the Gulf Coast of Florida used risk management techniques. Among the usual list—power failure, Internet outage, fire—was a line item for a hurricane with a storm surge of greater than 20 feet (the level above sea level of the data center). Because there had not been a single such storm in 100 years this received a risk rating of 9 out of 10, with 10 being the least likely. An FDIC auditor pointed out that in that particular year there had been four such storm surges to hit the Gulf Coast. The data center risk profile had never been revisited to reflect a changing environment.

It is the changing nature of risk that is impacting risk regimes today. IT assets that were not of interest to a pimple-faced 13-year-old hacker in Canada in 1999 can be of extreme interest to a cybercriminal operation in Eastern Europe or a nation-state looking to leapfrog a Western competitor. It is impossible to know beforehand which IT assets will be of interest to an attacker.

4. Risk management devolves to "protect everything."

For risk management to work it has to be comprehensive, so comprehensive protections are deployed. Firewalls, IPS, and AV everywhere, and vulnerability management (VM) systems deployed to check the exposure of every single device on the network. Vulnerability management has to be continuous because new vulnerabilities are announced every month for just about every application, OS, and device.

A patch management system is then used to ensure that every application has the latest patch. Risk management methodologies strive for that golden state when no vulnerabilities exist anywhere. And, failing that, the desire is to minimize the total exposure time to new vulnerabilities. Organizations spend an inordinate amount of time and money on these protections. Of course, they still succumb to targeted attacks that use previously unknown vulnerabilities.

Despite these arguments there is a thriving business in vulnerability and patch management.

One effective driver is that the Payment Card Industry Data Security Standard (PCI DSS) requires vulnerability scanning for every merchant that wants to accept credit cards.[2] PCI standards carry a lot of weight because compiling with them is a universal requirement and the standard has real measures that can be validated. It has given rise to offerings like those from Qualys, Trustwave (part of Singtel), and Beyond Security for automated monitoring and reporting of vulnerabilities. The Payment Card Industry certifies Qualified Security Assessors and lists 387 of them on its website.[3]

For internal operations, vulnerability management solutions can take two forms. One is to use that list of assets and the version numbers of the OS and all of the applications. Compare that list to known vulnerabilities and you can know which systems need to be patched or otherwise protected. An example of systems that cannot be patched regularly are high-end medical equipment. Because regulations may require re-certifying a piece of equipment when the software is changed, most medical equipment is not patched in a timely manner. Of course patching is disruptive to any production system that has to be scheduled for downtime and then tested before going back into production. So one way to avoid the risk of an unpatched system is to ensure it is not connected to a hostile network, like the internet. Unfortunately many organizations, especially hospitals, are not aware of all their network connections.

Internal scanning of IT assets for vulnerabilities is accomplished with tools that are deployed on the inside. These may be from Qualys, Tenable (which supports the open source Nessus scanner), or Rapid7, or any of the other 22 vendors in the space.

Risk Management

It is not an easy task but many vendors have attempted to provide risk scores for organizations. They use a formula based on the severity of a vulnerability and some measure of an asset's criticality to make it easier to identify high-risk vulnerabilities as well as roll up an overall risk score for the organization. While metrics are useful and can drive continuous improvement, they can be misleading because they do not take into account the determination of a threat actor. A full-fledged risk management system will identify assets, rank them based on criticality, invest vulnerability data, and track compliance with a host of security regulations and frameworks.

A new category that is seeing some traction, thanks to greater concern about supply chain risk, is vendors that provide third party risk scores. The idea is that a large organization may want to apply pressure to its suppliers to improve their own security profile. The third party risk scores generated by vendors like SecurityScorecard, RiskRecon, NormShield, and BitSight, are created by scanning from the outside. Other vendors take it much deeper by providing management tools for conducting full internal risk assessments with questionnaires and tests of security controls.

Frameworks

While PCI DSS is a proscriptive industry requirement, there are frameworks that provide the basis of many GRC programs. The ISO 27001 series specify the documentation of a complete Information Security Management System (ISMS). Within the ISO standards are requirements for establishing an ISMS, identifying roles, and documenting processes for incident response and reporting.

COBIT was created by ISACA, the Information Systems Audit and Control Association, in 1996. The name derived from "Control Objectives for IT." Many organizations that use COBIT require their security programs to fit within this general purpose framework.

ITIL is a large collection of IT management guidance produced by the UK government. Its name came from Information Technology Infrastructure Library.

NIST, the US National Institute for Standards and Testing, has produced a modern Cybersecurity Framework.[4] While not mandated, it is gaining traction in the US government and those that sell to government agencies.

Other GRC solutions

Because there are so many different frameworks and regulations that call for cyber security controls, several vendors create tools that map the controls so a customer can generate reports for audits from multiple parties.

Logging and log management are a requirement of Information Management Systems so tools that capture and store logs and make them easily readable are a sub-category of GRC.

The vendors of Data Leak Prevention (DLP) may not agree that they reside in the GRC category, but their products are often deployed to comply with requirements to protect PII (Personally Identifiable Information). While the vision for DLP is to prevent corporate intellectual property from being exfiltrated, most solutions are tuned to alert when credit card numbers, social security numbers, and other PII leak.

Another requirement of many GRC programs is regular security awareness training. Thus vendors like KnowBe4, PhishX, Secure Mentem, and Cofense create and deliver tools to not only train employees, but track the effectiveness of that training.

As more countries implement data privacy regulations, the EU's GDPR being the most impactful today, there will be more investment in GRC solutions to meet new requirements for tracking and reporting. Expect the number of vendors in this space to increase dramatically.

---

1. Richard Stiennon, "Why Risk Management Fails in IT," *Network World*, October 15, 2012, https://www.networkworld.com/article/2160724/why-risk-management-fails-in-it.html

2. "PCI Security Standards Overview," *PCI Security Standards Council*, accessed November 27, 2019, https://www.pcisecuritystandards.org/pci_security/standards_overview

3. "Qualified Security Assessors," *PCI Security Standards Council*, accessed November 27, 2019, https://pt.pcisecuritystandards.org/assessors_and_solutions/qualified_security_assessors

4. "Cybersecurity Framework," *National Institute of Standards and Technology*, Accessed November 27, 2019, https://www.nist.gov/cyberframework

CHAPTER 9

Failures

Learning from failure is one of the most valuable reasons to study history. Successes like Check Point Software in Israel lead to more investment, economic growth for a country, and innovation as the company invests in R&D. Failures tend to be forgotten by all but those who were part of the company. Attempting research into defunct companies will often turn up all the press mentions as it got several rounds of funding, won big deals, and made acquisitions, but once it begins to fail there is no one there to write the press releases or record its demise.

Complete failures in the IT security industry are rare. Unless one has insight into the internal operations it is often difficult to even determine if a company has failed. Was the sale of the company just an exit for the founders and investors, or was it a fire sale of intellectual property and key people? In recent history, the crash of Norse Corporation is one of the few admitted failures. Norse, based in Kansas City, raised it first seed round in 2011. It went on to raise $33 million total. It appeared to be a vibrant company hiring and marketing at a healthy pace when Brian

Krebs reported that there had been a major round of layoffs in January 2016.[1] With that revelation customers who were close to buying Norse's threat intelligence feeds canceled or put their orders on hold. That led to the CEO leaving, and eventually the company was disbanded.

Was the sale of Mirage Networks to Trustwave a failure?[2] Was Finjan?

One measure of failure when an acquisition occurs is whether the investors turned a profit or lost the value of their investment. Bruce Schneier's Counterpane, one of the original cohorts of MSSP, had $90 million in investment when it was sold to British Telecom in 2006 for a reported $90 million.[3] In such cases the founders rarely walk away with anything, a measure of failure.

Another failure attributed to the dot com boom was Vigilinx Digital Security Solutions, an attempt by investors to build a major player in the security consulting space to compete with PricewaterhouseCoopers, KPMG, Deloitte, and EY. Investors pledged $90 million to a venture of their own creation and hired Bruce Murphy from PricewaterhouseCoopers to lead it. It was only two years before it morphed into a reseller and managed security firm, and was eventually sold to TruSecure for an undisclosed amount.

Many failures are brought about by investors losing interest in supporting the companies they have funded. One of the largest failures was that of Nexi, an attempt to create the god-box of networking to compete with Cisco and Juniper in the carrier space. Benchmark Capital had poured $100 million into the development of Nexi's first product, a datacenter solution that in addition to being a switch, had a full-fledged firewall. A turnover in partners led Benchmark to pull the plug on Nexi before it had a chance to start delivering products.[4]

Cosine Communications, founded in 1998, was the last dot com company to go public. It too created a god-box for switching, networking, and security. It raised $230 million in its IPO in 2000 and its stock jumped 195%.[5] It employed over 400 hundred people when it ran out of money and shut down in a few short years. Its portfolio of 80 patent applications and its leftover gear and few remaining customers were handed off to Fortinet at fire sale prices.

Crossbeam Systems was another hardware venture deemed a failure. It had gone to market with what was, in retrospect, a failed strategy. Crossbeam invested $72.5 million to create and sell a multi-blade security appliance. Up to ten cards were load balanced to handle high throughput for security software products, primarily Check Point, and ISS. It was eventually sold to Thoma Bravo and then sold to Blue Coat.

In 2019 ThinAir shut down. It was a startup in the data discovery space. Its agent deployed to Windows desktops allowed a customer to discover what data was on each of its endpoints, a valuable capability for compliance with data privacy regulations. In late 2018, as it was burning through its remaining funding, it attempted to sell to a competitor that pulled out at the last minute. It had to lay off its employees and shutter operations.

Failures in the security space are remarkably rare considering the number of vendors. The reason is that most vendors that survive a couple of years actually provide products that customers value. The customers renew and companies continue to make headway as they take on investment, hire marketing and sales teams, and focus on a geographic region or an industry vertical.

---

1. Brian Krebs, "Sources: Security Firm Norse Corp. Imploding," *Krebs On Security* (website), January 16, 2016, https://krebsonsecurity.com/2016/01/sources-security-firm-norse-corp-imploding/

2. "Trustwave Acquires Mirage Networks," *Trustwave*, February 17, 2009, https://www.trustwave.com/en-us/company/newsroom/news/trustwave-acquires-mirage-networks/

3. Antony Savaas, "BT Acquires Counterpane," *ComputerWeekly.com*, October 26, 2006, https://www.computerweekly.com/news/2240078847/BT-acquires-Counterpane-for-managed-network-security

4. Randall E. Stross, *eBoys: The First Inside Account of Venture Capitalists at Work* (NY: Random House, 2000).

5. "Cosine Gaines 195 Percent in IPO," *Cnet*, January 2, 2002, https://www.cnet.com/news/cosine-gains-195-percent-in-ipo-shuffles-revenue/

CHAPTER 10
Research Methodology

Most tech industry analysts takes a top-down approach: follow what the big players are doing and keep an eye on the up-and-comers. Track the revenue of the big players and make some assumption about their market share to derive an overall number. The following directory is an attempt at bottom-up analysis: discover and track every vendor. Estimate each vendor's revenue based on what they report and colored by the number of people they employ. In this manner it is possible to have visibility into each sub-category and track its growth in revenue year to year.

What is a security vendor?

To be included in this directory a vendor must produce and sell its own IT security product. This is a simple determination for a firewall or endpoint security vendor, but what about service providers? MSSPs are included because they are an important part of the industry. They have to develop their own tools to collect, manage, and analyze security event data, although there are hundreds that use off the shelf products such as AlienVault,

now the anchor to AT&T's Cybersecurity business unit.

There are hundreds of consulting firms that provide pen testing, design, staff augmentation, and breach investigation services. While many of them eventually develop their own products and become vendors, as long as they are purely consulting providers they are not included in the directory.

Systems Integrators (SIs) and value added resellers (VARs) are also not included unless they have their own products. Thus Optiv, the biggest reseller of security products in the United States is listed as an MSSP because it also offers managed services.

There are over two hundred cyber insurance companies. This is a category outside the scope of the directory.

How to find vendors?

It is surprisingly difficult to discover all of the vendors in a particular category. Many startups steadfastly resist any effort to be pigeon-holed into a particular category. They would rather be the only vendor in a category of their own definition than a minor vendor in an existing category. Meanwhile the large analyst firms, Gartner, IDC, and Forrester, rush to label new categories as they evolve, creating confusion. Thus we have two categories for multi-function gateway appliances, UTM and Next-Gen Firewall. Or the new category of IRM from Gartner, which they decided stands for Integrated Risk Management, even though that three letter acronym was already in use for Information Rights Management.

It may not be possible to find every single vendor, especially those that have not built English language websites, but as a vendor grows it becomes visible by:

Funding announcements. Crunchbase, Pitch-Book, and Momentum Cyber are comprehensive researchers and archivists of venture funding.

Conference appearances. By the time a vendor has acquired customers and hired a marketing team it will begin to show up in the listing of vendors exhibiting at conferences such as InfoSec in Europe and RSA Conference in San Francisco and Asia.

The first steps for any startup today is to get a Twitter handle and create a LinkedIn page, both valuable tools for discovering new and small vendors.

Vendor briefings. As a vendor matures it starts to reach out to the analyst community in an effort to be noticed. While the Gartner Magic Quadrant tracks the largest vendors in a space, there is always the hope of being named a Cool Vendor, a designation reserved for new vendors

with technology that catches the eye of a Gartner analyst. Forrester Wave reports are another source of vendor information and smaller independent analyst firms may cover emerging vendor spaces.

Press coverage. A mention in an article at Dark Reading, CIO.com, or mainstream media helps a vendor get on the radar.

SEO. At one time there was an argument made that industry analysis was no longer needed thanks to Google search. But search has become less and less effective for enumerating a space. Each vendor strives to be on the first page of results for its space in the hope that customers will find them. Every category soon develops a number of Top Ten sites that list the top ten vendors, but inclusion in the top ten is a pay-to-play game so it is unreliable.

Once a vendor is identified, it is tracked as it grows, is acquired, becomes an acquirer, or in a very few rare cases, fails and goes out of business. This Security Yearbook series will be published each year with important updates covering the new vendors and those that have been acquired.

One difficult question is: When should a vendor be removed from the directory? A small vendor like Aorato, acquired by Microsoft in 2014 for its ability to defend Active Directory, will be included in the year it was acquired but removed the following year because the acquisition was a pure technology play. The product and its brand are absorbed into the mother ship. Similar acquisitions may be to acquire the team but the products are discontinued quickly. A company like SafeNet, acquired by Gemalto, which in turn was acquired by Thales, is listed in this first edition of the directory but will be removed in the next.

The key factor for keeping a vendor in the directory is the brand. Thus Lancope, Viptela, and OpenDNS are not in the directory although the products continue to be supported. Arbor Networks is in the directory because the brand has been preserved through the acquisition by a holding company and sale to NETSCOUT. Ownership is designated in the company name.

Once a vendor is identified, its headquarters address, URL, and LinkedIn profile are recorded in the database. The LinkedIn profile will report number of people who self-identify as an employee of the company. This number is good for companies that are growing. Generally, as people are let go from a company they do not update their employment status until they land a new role, so the fact that a company is shrinking may not be picked up immediately. Spot testing the LinkedIn data against data provided by vendors indicates that the LinkedIn number is surprisingly accurate.

Vendor briefings are required to understand a space. These hour-long sessions with an industry analyst reveal the company strategy and aspirations as well as the underlying technology and how they differentiate themselves from their competitors. It is up to the analyst to determine the validity of their claims for number of customers, growth, etc. Anecdotal evidence from end users and reference customers provide valuable confirmation. Magic Quadrants from Gartner, Forrester Wave Reports, and the vendor's own published research all help to make vendors stand out.

The Security Yearbook is put to bed in November to make it into print by February, so changes to the directory are frozen at that time. Updates are published throughout the year at www.security-yearbook.com.

The 2020
Security Directory

Alphabetical Listings by Company Name

0 Patch (10)
Endpoint / Micropatching
London, UK
0patch.com

1E (424)
Endpoint Detection and
Response (EDR)
London, UK
1e.com

1H (8)
Network / Security for
Webhosting
Sofia, Bulgaria
1h.com

1Password (67)
IAM / Password Management
Toronto, Canada
1password.com

2FA Inc. (11)
IAM / Authentication
Austin, TX, USA
2fa.com

2Keys (77)
MSSP / Managed Identity
Platform
Ottawa, Canada
2keys.ca

3ami Network Security (1)
GRC / Activity Auditing
Wigan, UK
3ami.com

3CM
GRC / Cloud Compliance
3cm.io

418 Intelligence (4)
Threat Intelligence Gamification
Reston, VA, USA
418intelligence.com

42Crunch (19)
Application Security / API
Security
Irvine, CA, USA
42crunch.com

4iQ (100)
Threat Intelligence / Stolen
Identities
Los Altos, CA, USA
4iQ.com

5Nine Software (46)
Operations / Hyper-V
Security
West Palm Beach, FL, USA
5nine.com

6Scan (1)
GRC / Vulnerability Management
Miami Beach, FL, USA
6scan.com

6WIND (76)
Network / IPSec VPN
Router
Montigny-le-Bretonneux,
France
6wind.com

802Secure (48)
IoT Security / IoT Network
Monitoring
Emeryville, CA, USA
802secure.com

8e14 Networks (5)
Network / Microsegmentation
San Francisco, CA, USA
8e14.net

9Star (19)
IAM / Managed Identity
Platform
Austin, TX, USA
9starinc.com

@RISK Technologies (61)
GRC / Risk Measurement
Dallas, TX, USA
atrisktech.com

10 Networks (821)
Network / DDoS Defense
Appliance
San Jose, CA, USA
a10networks.com

A1Logic (3)
Data Security / Memory
Protection
Bethesda, MD, USA
a1logic.com

AaDya Security (24)
MSSP / For SMB
Plymouth, MI, USA
aadyasecurity.com

Abatis UK Ltd. (3)
Endpoint Protection
Egham, UK
abatis-hdf.com

Abnormal Security (21)
Email Security / Anti-phishing
San Francisco, CA, USA
abnormalsecurity.com

Absio (8)
Data Security / Software-Defined Distributed
Key Cryptography (SDKC)
Denver, CO, USA
absio.com

Note: Numbers in parentheses indicate employee count

Absolute Software (578)
Endpoint / Mobile Device
Security
Vancouver, Canada
absolute.com/en

Abusix (19)
Threat Intelligence
San Jose, CA, USA
abusix.com

Acalvio Technologies (64)
Deception
Santa Clara, CA, USA
acalvio.com

Accellion (180)
Data Security / IRM
Palo Alto, CA, USA
accellion.com

Acceptto (33)
Fraud Prevention /
Behavior-Based Identity
Verification
Portland, OR, USA
acceptto.com

Access Data Corp. (250)
GRC / Forensics
Lindon, UT, USA
accessdata.com

Accolade Technology (10)
Network Appliance Se-
curity
Franklin, MA, USA
accoladetechnology.com

Accudata Systems, Inc.
(195)
Operations / Security
Management
Houston, TX, USA
accudatasystems.com

achelos GmbH (33)
Testing / TLS Testing
Paderborn, Germany
achelos.de

ACID Technologies (2)
Threat Intelligence
Tel Aviv-Yafo, Israel
acid-tech.co

Acreto Cloud (8)
IoT Security / IoT Mi-
crosegmentation
Jersey City, NJ, USA
acreto.io

Acsia (372)
Security Analytics / UEBA
Dublin, Ireland
acsia.io

Actifile (4)
GRC / DLP
Herzliya, Israel
actifile.com

Active Countermeasures
(16)
Security Analytics / Threat
Hunting
Spearfish, SD, USA
activecountermeasures.
com

Active Fortress
Endpoint Protection
Tampa, FL, USA
activefortress.com

**ActivIdentity Corp. (now
HIDGlobal)** (2,307)
IAM
Austin, TX, USA
hidglobal.com

Acuity Risk Management
(8)
GRC / Risk Management
London, UK
acuityrm.com

Acumera (32)
MSSP / Managed Firewalls
Austin, TX, USA
acumera.net

Acunetix (53)
GRC / Vunerability Scan-
ner (Web)
Mriehel, Malta
acunetix.com

Adaptiva (47)
Endpoint / Configuration
Management
Kirkland, WA, USA
adaptiva.com

Adaptive Mobile (133)
Endpoint / Mobile Device
Security
Dublin, Ireland
adaptivemobile.com

Adaware (51)
Endpoint / Anti-virus
Montreal, Canada
adaware.com

ADF Solutions (53)
GRC / Forensics
Bethesda, MD, USA
adfsolutions.com

Adjust (290)
Fraud Prevention / Bot
Detection
Berlin, Germany
adjust.com

AdNovum (1)
IAM
Zürich, Switzerland
adnovum.ch

Adtran Inc. (200)
Network / Firewalls
Huntsville, AL, USA
adtran.com

ADVA Optical Networking
(2,241)
Network / Secure Switch-
ing
Munich, Germany
advaoptical.com

Advenica (50)
Network / Air Gap
Malmö, Sweden
advenica.com

Aegify (19)
GRC / Risk Management
San Jose, CA, USA
aegify.com

Aerobyte (10)
Network / Zero-Trust
Networking
Boca Raton, FL, USA
aerobyte.com

Aerohive Networks (557)
IAM / Network Access
Control
Milpitas, CA, USA
aerohive.com

Agari (184)
Email Security
Foster City, CA, USA
agari.com

Agat Software (29)
Network / Security for
Unified Comms
Jerusalem, Israel
agatsoftware.com

Agora SecureWare (4)
Data Security / Secure
Collaboration
Bioggio, Switzerland
agora-secureware.com

**AHA Products Group
(part of Comtech EF Data
Corporation)** (1)
Data Security / Encryption
Hardware
Moscow, ID, USA
aha.com

Ahnlab (429)
Endpoint / Anti-virus
Gyeonggi-do, South Korea
ahnlab.com

Note: Numbers in parentheses indicate employee count

Ahope (21)
Application Security / Mobile
Seoul, South Korea
ahope.net/main

Aiculus (5)
Application Security / API Security
Melbourne, Australia
aiculus.co

AimBrain (16)
IAM / Biometrics
London, UK
aimbrain.com

Aircuve (1)
IAM / Authentication
Seoul, South Korea
aircuve.com/wp/en

Akamai Technologies (500)
Network / DDoS Defense
Cambridge, MA, USA
akamai.com

Aker (72)
Network / Web Filtering
Brasilia, Brazil
aker.com.br

Akheros (4)
Network / NBAD
Paris, France
akheros.fr

alcide (29)
Endpoint / Container Security
Tel Aviv, Israel
alcide.io

Alert Logic (659)
GRC / Log Management
Houston, TX, USA
alertlogic.com

AlertEnterprise (147)
IAM / Physical Identity & Access Management
Fremont, CA, USA
alertenterprise.com

alertsec (5)
GRC / Encryption Monitoring for Third Parties
Palo Alto, CA, USA
alertsec.com

Algosec (395)
Operations / Firewall Policy Management
Petah Tikva, Israel
algosec.com

AllClear ID (149)
Fraud Prevention / Identity Protection Service
Austin, TX, USA
allclearid.com

Allegro Software (6)
IoT Security / Embedded Device Security
Boxborough, MA, USA
allegrosoft.com

Allgeier IT (63)
MSSP / Managed Email Security
Bremen, Germany
Allgeier-it.de

Allgress (42)
GRC / Compliance
Livermore, CA, USA
allgress.com

Allot (926)
Network / Content URL Filtering
Hod HaSharon, Israel
allot.com

Allure Security (12)
Deception / Document Decoys, Anti-website Spoofing
New York, NY, USA
alluresecurity.com

Alpha Recon (14)
Threat Intelligence Platform
Colorado Springs, CO, USA
alpharecon.com

AlphaGuardian Networks (1)
IoT Security / ICS Monitoring
San Ramon, CA, USA
alphaguardian.net

Alsharq International Co. (6)
Data Security / Certificate Authority
Kuwait
alsharq.com.kw

Alsid (31)
Network / AD Defense
Paris, France
alsid.com

Altitude Networks (10)
Data Security / File Monitoring
San Francisco, CA, USA
altitudenetworks.com

Altr (53)
Data Security for Apps
Austin, TX, USA
altr.com

Alyne (34)
GRC / Risk Measurement
Munich, Germany
alyne.com

Ambitrace (3)
Data Security / Data Tracking and Logging
San Francisco, CA, USA
ambitrace.com

Amgine Securus (2)
Network and Endpoint Monitoring
South Korea
amgine.co.kr

Amtel, Inc. (52)
Endpoint / Mobile Device Security
Rockville, MD, USA
amtelnet.com

Analyst Platform (8)
Threat Intelligence Platform
Reston, VA, USA
analystplatform.com

Anchiva (10)
Network / UTM
Beijing, China
en.anchiva.com

Anchor ID (7)
IAM / Mobile Authentication
Kingston, NY, USA
anchorid.com

Anchorage (48)
Data Security / Secure Storage
San Francisco, CA, USA
anchorage.com

Anitian (31)
GRC / Compliance Automation
Portland, OR, USA
anitian.com

Anixis (1)
IAM / Password Management
Glenmore Park, Australia
anixis.com

Anjuna (10)
Data Security / Runtime Encryption
Palo Alto, CA, USA
anjuna.io

Anomali (301)
Threat Intelligence Platform
Redwood City, CA, USA
anomali.com

Anonyome Labs (76)
Data Security / Secure Communications
Salt Lake City, UT, USA
anonyome.com

Anqlave (10)
IAM / 2FA
Singapore, Singapore
anqlave.com

Antiy Labs (1)
Endpoint / Malware
Analysis
Beijing, China
antiy.net

**AnubisNetworks
(BitSight)** (35)
Email Security / Email
Protection
Lisbon, Portugal
anubisnetworks.com

Apcon (249)
Network / Packet Capture
and Analysis
Wilsonville, OR, USA
apcon.com

APERIO Systems
IoT Security / ICS
Haifa, Israel
aperio-systems.com

aPersona (7)
IAM / MFA Platform
Raleigh, NC, USA
apersona.com

**Apollo Information
Systems** (20)
MSSP / Managed Security
Services
Los Gatos, CA, USA
apollo-is.com

Aporeto (44)
Endpoint / Container
Security
San Jose, CA, USA
aporeto.com

Apozy (4)
Endpoint / Content URL
Filtering
San Francisco, CA, USA
apozy.com

AppDetex (102)
Threat Intelligence / Brand
Monitoring
Boise, ID, USA
appdetex.com

AppDome (62)
Application Security
Tel Aviv, Israel
appdome.com

Apperian (11)
Endpoint / Mobile App
Security
Boston, MA, USA
apperian.com

AppGuard (40)
Endpoint / Application
Containment
Chantilly, VA, USA
appguard.us

AppKnox (19)
Application Security / Mo-
bile Application Security
Testing
Singapore, Singapore
appknox.com

Applicure (7)
Network / Web Application
Firewall
Ramat Gan, Israel
applicure.com

AppMobi (14)
Endpoint / Mobile App
Protection
Poughkeepsie, NY, USA
appmobi.com

AppOmni (19)
Data Security / Cloud DLP
San Francisco, CA, USA
appomni.com

Appray (2)
Application Security /
Mobile App Scanning
Vienna, Austria
app-ray.co

AppRiver (221)
Email Security
Gulf Breeze, FL, USA
appriver.com

AppSec Labs (18)
Application Security / Mo-
bile Application Security
Testing
Kfar Saba, Israel
appsec-labs.com

AppsPicket (2)
IAM / Authentication
Hammersmith, UK
appspicket.com

Apptega (11)
GRC / Compliance Plat-
form
Atlanta, GA, USA
apptega.com

AppViewX (244)
Data Security / Encryption
and Key Management
Seattle, WA, USA
appviewx.com

AppVision (10)
Application Security /
Appsec Code Hardening
and Monitoring
San Francisco, CA, USA
appvision.net

Apricorn (23)
Data Security / Encrypted
Storage
Poway, CA, USA
apricorn.com

Aprivacy (5)
Data Security / Secure
Communications
Kitchener, Canada
aprivacy.com

Aptible (40)
GRC / Compliance Man-
agement
San Francisco, CA, USA
aptible.com

Apvera (12)
GRC / User Activity Mon-
itoring
Singapore, Singapore
apvera.com

**Aqua Security Software,
Inc.** (136)
Endpoint / Container
Security
Ramat Gan, Israel
aquasec.com

Aquila Technology (16)
Email Security / An-
ti-phishing
Burlington, MA, USA
aquilatc.com

AquilAI
Email Security / An-
ti-phishing
Cheltenham, UK
aquil.ai

Araali Networks (4)
Application Security /
Appsec for Containers
Fremont, CA, USA
araalinetworks.com

Arama Tech (4)
GRC / Compliance Con-
trols
Glostrop, Denmark
aramatech.com

Arbor Networks (554)
Network / DDoS Defense
Burlington, MA, USA
netscout.com

Arc4dia (5)
Security Analytics / Breach
Detection and Response
Montreal, Canada
arc4dia.com

Archimigo (7)
GRC / Compliance Man-
agement
Melbourne, Australia
archimigo.io

Note: Numbers in parentheses indicate employee count

ArcMail Technology (13)
GRC / Email Archiving
Shreveport, LA, USA
arcmail.com

Arcon (342)
GRC / Rights Management
Mumbai, India
arconnet.com

Arctic Security (20)
Threat Intelligence
Oulu, Finland
arcticsecurity.com

Arctic Wolf Networks (236)
Security Analytics / SIEM
Sunnyvale, CA, USA
arcticwolf.com

ArcusTeam
IoT Security / Vulnerability
Management
Tel Aviv-Yafo, Israel
arcusteam.com

Ardaco (27)
Data Security / Secure
Communications
Bratislava, Slovakia
ardaco.com

Area 1 Security (78)
Email Security / Anti-phishing
Redwood City, CA, USA
area1security.com

ArecaBay (6)
Application Security / API
Security
Los Altos, CA, USA
arecabay.com

Argus Cyber Security (139)
IoT Security / Automotive
Cybersecurity
Tel Aviv, Israel
argus-sec.com

Aries Security (12)
Training / Cyber Range
Wilmington, DE, USA
ariessecurity.com

Arilou Technologies (20)
IoT Security / Automotive
Security
Ramat Gan, Israel
ariloutech.com

AristotleInsight (24)
GRC / Discovery and
Analysis of Assets
Onalaska, WI, USA
aristotleinsight.com

Arkose Labs (59)
Fraud Prevention / Graduated Friction
San Francisco, CA, USA
arkoselabs.com

Armis (150)
IoT Security / Device Discovery and Protection
Palo Alto, CA, USA
armis.com

**Armjisoft Digital Rights
Management Systems,
Inc.** (1)
Data Security / DRM
New York, NY, USA
armjisoft.com

Armor (243)
MSSP Cloud Security
Richardson, TX, USA
armor.com

Armor Scientific (7)
IAM / Authentication
Newport Beach, CA, USA
armorsci.com

Armorblox (42)
Data Security / DLP
Cupertino, CA, USA
armorblox.com

ArQit (13)
Network / Post-quantum
Defense
London, UK
arqit.io

**Array Networks (OSS
Corp.)** (193)
Network / SSL VPN
Milpitas, CA, USA
arraynetworks.com

Articsoft Technologies (1)
Data Security / Encryption
PGP
Centennial, CO, USA
articsoft.com

**Aruba Networks, an HP
Company** (150)
Network / UEBA
Santa Clara, CA, USA
arubanetworks.com

Arxan Technology (153)
Application Security
San Francisco, CA, USA
arxan.com

Arxceo Corporation (3)
Network / Intrusion Prevention
Ponte Vedra Beach, FL,
USA
arxceo.com

ASPG (29)
Data Security / Encryption
for Mainframes
Naples, FL, USA
aspg.com

Assac Networks (1)
Endpoint / Mobile Device
Protection
Ramat HaSharon, Israel
assacnetworks.com

Assuria (20)
Security Analytics / SIEM
Reading, UK
assuria.com

AT&T Cybersecurity (297)
Security Analytics / SIEM
San Mateo, CA, USA
alienvault.com

Atar Labs (32)
Operations / Security
Orchestration
London, UK
atarlabs.io

Atomic Mole (2)
GRC / Risk Analytics &
Management
Rockville, MD, USA
atomicmole.com

Atomicorp (15)
Endpoint / Host Intrusion
Prevention
Chantilly, VA, USA
atomicorp.com

Atonomi (4)
IoT Security / Blockchain
Seattle, WA, USA
atonomi.io

Atos Group (450)
IAM
Bezons, France
atos.net/en

AttackFlow (5)
Application Security /
Appsec Code Scanning
San Francisco, CA, USA
attackflow.com

AttackIQ, Inc. (61)
Testing / Security Instrumentation
San Diego, CA, USA
attackiq.com

Attify (12)
Application Security /
Mobile App Security
Bangalore, India
attify.com

Attila Security (23)
IoT Security / IoT Firewall
Fulton, MD, USA
attilasec.com

Note: Numbers in parentheses indicate employee count

Attivo Networks (165)
Deception
Fremont, CA, USA
attivonetworks.com

Auconet (12)
IAM / Network Access
Control
Berlin, Germany
Auconet.com

Augur Systems (1)
Operations / SNMP Traps
Wakefield, MA, USA
augur.com

**Aunigma Network
Solutions** (5)
Network / Cloud Browser
Proxy
Atlanta, GA, USA
aunigma.com

Auth0 (480)
IAM / Single Sign-On APIs
Bellevue, WA, USA
auth0.com

AUTHADA (14)
Fraud Prevention / Using
Mobile Identity
Darmstadt, Germany
authada.de

Authen2cate (3)
IAM / Authentication
Rochester Hills, MI, USA
authen2cate.com

Authenex Inc. (13)
IAM / Authentication
Mountain View, CA, USA
authenex.com

Authentic8, Inc. (75)
Network / Cloud Browser
Isolation
Redwood City, CA, USA
authentic8.com

Authernative (2)
IAM / Authentication
Redwood City, CA, USA
authernative.com

Authlete (9)
IAM / OAuth Gateways
Tokyo, Japan
authlete.com

AuthLite (1)
IAM / Two-Factor Authen-
tication
Springfield, IL, USA
authlite.com

AuthLogics (6)
IAM / Authentication
Bracknell, UK
authlogics.com

Authomate (7)
IAM / 2FA (mobile)
Morganville, NJ, USA
authomate.com

AuthRocket
IAM / Authorization and
User Management
Denver, CO, USA
authrocket.com

Authshield Labs Pvt. Ltd.
(1)
IAM / Two-Factor Authen-
tication
Delhi, India
auth-shield.com

Authy (3)
IAM / 2FA for Consumers
San Francisco, CA, USA
authy.com

Automox (57)
GRC / Patch Management
Boulder, CO, USA
automox.com

Autonomic Software (13)
Endpoint / Patch Manage-
ment
Danville, CA, USA
autonomic-software.com

Avanan (55)
Operations / Security Tool
Deployment
New York, NY, USA
avanan.com

Avast Software (1,390)
Endpoint / Anti-virus
Prague, Czech Republic
avast.com

Avatier (35)
IAM / Identity Manage-
ment Platform
Pleasanton, CA, USA
avatier.com

Avaya (150)
Network / SSL VPN
Santa Clara, CA, USA
avaya.com

Avepoint (904)
Data Security / Cloud
Backup
Jersey City, NJ, USA
avepoint.com

Averon (30)
IAM / Mobile Authenti-
cation
San Francisco, CA, USA
averon.com

Avertium (108)
MSSP / Managed Services
Phoenix, AZ, USA
avertium.com

Aves Network Security (6)
Endpoint / Temporary
Patching
London, UK
avesnetsec.com

Avi Networks (330)
Network / Web Application
Firewall
Santa Clara, CA, USA
avinetworks.com

Aviatrix (90)
Network / Firewall Enablement in the Cloud
Palo Alto, CA, USA
aviatrix.com

Avira (454)
Endpoint / Anti-virus
Tettnang, Germany
avira.com

Avnos (27)
Endpoint / Application
Whitelisting
Singapore, Singapore
avnos.io

Avocado Systems, Inc. (10)
Application Security / App
Hardening
San Jose, CA, USA
avocadosys.com

Avoco Secure (6)
IAM / Cloud Authentica-
tion
London, UK
secure2trust.com

Awake Security (51)
Network Monitoring
Sunnyvale, CA, USA
awakesecurity.com

AwareHQ (43)
Network / Monitor Social
Networks
Columbus, OH, USA
awarehq.com

Awareness Technologies
(25)
Operations / Employee
Monitoring
Westport, CT, USA
awarenesstechnologies.com

Axiad IDS (26)
IAM / Authentication
Santa Clara, CA, USA
axiadids.com

Axiado (9)
Endpoint / Secure Hardware
San Jose, CA, USA
axiado.com

Axio (52)
GRC / Risk Management
New York, NY, USA
axio.com

Axiom Cyber Solutions (3)
GRC / Vulnerability
Scanner
Las Vegas, NV, USA
axiomcyber.com

Axiomatics (45)
IAM / Database Access
Control
Stockholm, Sweden
axiomatics.com

Axonius (33)
Operations / Orchestration
New York, NY, USA
axonius.com

Axuall (5)
IAM / Identity Verification
Cleveland, OH, USA
axuall.com

Axway (2,035)
GRC / Secure File Transfer
Phoenix, AZ, USA
axway.com

Ayehu (55)
Operations / Orchestration
San Jose, CA, USA
ayehu.com

Ayyeka (42)
IoT Security / Secure
Remote Monitoring
Jerusalem, Israel
ayyeka.com

B-Secur (37)
IAM / Biometrics (ECG)
Belfast, UK
b-secur.com

BAE Systems (150)
MSSP / Managed Services
Guildford, UK
baesystems.com

Baffin Bay Networking (34)
Network / Threat Detection & Network Forensics
Stockholm, Sweden
baffinbaynetworks.com

Baffle (30)
Data Security / Database
Encryption
Santa Clara, CA, USA
baffle.io

Balbix (52)
GRC / Asset Management
San Jose, CA, USA
balbix.com

Bandura Cyber (36)
Network / Reputation
Firewall
Columbia, MD, USA
banduracyber.com

Banff Cyber (1)
MSSP / Website Defacement Monitoring
Singapore, Singapore
banffcyber.com

Banyan Security (19)
Network / Zero-Trust
Networking
San Francisco, CA, USA
banyansecurity.io

Barac (11)
Network / NBAD
London, UK
barac.io

Baramundi Software (98)
GRC / Endpoint Management
Augsburg, Germany
baramundi.com

Barillet (24)
GRC / Manager of Managers
Be'er Sheva, Israel
barillet.co.il

Barracuda Networks
(1,427)
Network / Anti-spam
Campbell, CA, USA
barracuda.com

Barricade IT Security (2)
MSSP / Managed Services
Islip, NY, USA
barricadeitsecurity.com

Barrier1 (2)
Network / UTM
Minneapolis, MN, USA
thebarriergroup.com

Basil Security (4)
Operations / Policy Enforcement
Atlanta, GA, USA
basilsecurity.com

Basis Technology (131)
Operations / Forensics
(Text Analysis)
Cambridge, MA, USA
basistech.com

Bastille (1)
Network / Wireless Security
Atlanta, GA, USA
bastille.net

Bay Dynamics (79)
GRC / Information Risk
Intelligence
New York, NY, USA
baydynamics.com

Bayshore Networks, Inc.
(30)
IoT / ICS
Durham, NC, USA
bayshorenetworks.com

Be Strategic Solutions (7)
Training / Crisis Simulation
Tel Aviv, Israel
best.be-strategic.solutions

Beachhead Solutions, Inc.
(15)
Endpoint / MDM
San Jose, CA, USA
beachheadsolutions.com

Beame.io
IAM / Mobile Authenticator
Tel Aviv, Israel
beame.io

Beauceron (24)
GRC / Risk Measurement
Fredericton, Canada
beauceronsecurity.com

Becrypt (62)
Data Security / Encryption
London, UK
becrypt.com/uk

Behaviosec (41)
Fraud Prevention / Behavior Monitoring
San Francisco, CA, USA
behaviosec.com

Belarc Inc. (16)
GRC / IT Asset Management
Maynard, MA, USA
belarc.com

Belkasoft (19)
Operations / Mobile Device Forensics
Palo Alto, CA, USA
belkasoft.com

BeSafe (8)
Data Security / Cloud Key
Management
Yerevan, Armenia
besafe.io

Note: Numbers in parentheses indicate employee count

Beta Systems Software AG (222)
IAM
Berlin, Germany
betasystems.com

Better Mobile App Security (19)
Endpoint / Mobile App Security
New York, NY, USA
better.mobi

Bettercloud (256)
Network / Cloud Activity Monitoring
New York, NY, USA
bettercloud.com

Beyond Security (54)
GRC / Vulnerability Management
San Jose, CA, USA
beyondsecurity.com

BeyondTrust (628)
IAM / Privileged Access Management
Johns Creek, GA, USA
beyondtrust.com

BI.ZONE (81)
Threat Intelligence Aggregator
Moscow, Russia
bi.zone

Bibu Labs (3)
Deception / Decoys
Toronto, Canada
bibulabs.com

BicDroid (7)
Data Security / Encryption
Waterloo, Canada
bicdroid.com

Big Switch Networks (218)
Network / DDoS Defense
Santa Clara, CA, USA
bigswitch.com

BigID, Inc. (105)
Data Security / Data Discovery
Tel Aviv-Yafo, Israel
bigid.com

BIID (22)
IAM / Mobile Identity Platform
Sant Cugat del Vallès, Spain
biid.com

Binary Defense (55)
MSSP / SOC as a service
Stow, OH, USA
binarydefense.com

BinaryEdge (5)
Opertions / Internet Scanning
Zürich, Switzerland
binaryedge.io

BIO-key (67)
IAM / Biometrics, Fingerprint
Wall, NJ, USA
bio-key.com

BiObex (8)
IAM / 2FA
Reston, VA, USA
biobex.com

BioCatch (111)
Fraud Prevention / Authentication Through Behavior
Tel Aviv-Yafo, Israel
biocatch.com

BioConnect (64)
IAM / Biometrics
Toronto, Canada
bioconnect.com

BioEnable (84)
IAM / Access Control, Biometrics
Pune, India
bioenabletech.com

BioID (10)
IAM / Biometrics
Sachseln, Switzerland
bioid.com

BioWatch
IAM / Biometrics
Martigny, Switzerland
biowatchid.com

BIS Guard (1)
Application Security / Code Wrappers to Prevent Tampering
Ofra, Israel
bisguard.com

Biscom (169)
Data Security / Secure File Transfer
Chelmsford, MA, USA
biscom.com

BitDam (24)
Endpoint / Anti-malware
Tel Aviv, Israel
bitdam.com

BitDefender (1,600)
Endpoint / Anti-virus
Bucharest, Romania
bitdefender.com

BitGlass (123)
Security Analytics / Breach Discovery
Campbell, CA, USA
bitglass.com

BitLyft (6)
MSSP / Managed SIEM
Lansing, MI, USA
bitlyft.com

BitNinja (18)
Endpoint / Server Protection
London, UK
bitninja.io

BitSight (428)
GRC / Security Ratings
Boston, MA, USA
bitsight.com

Bittium (1,907)
Data Security / Secure Communications
Oulu, Finland
bittium.com

Bivio Networks (36)
Network / Gateway Security Platform
Pleasanton, CA, USA
bivio.net

BlackFog (5)
Endpoint / EDR
Cheyenne, WY, USA
blackfog.com

Blackpoint (26)
MSSP / MDR
Ellicott City, MD, USA
blackpointcyber.com

Blackridge (66)
IoT Security / ICS
Reno, NV, USA
Blackridge.us

Blacksands (13)
Network / Software Defined Perimeter
Ann Arbor, MI, USA
blacksandsinc.com

BlackStratus (57)
MSSP / Security Platform for MSPs
Piscataway, NJ, USA
blackstratus.com

Blancco (251)
Data Security / Erasure
Bishops Stortford, UK
blancco.com/en

BlastWave (16)
Network / Microsegmentation
Mountain View, CA, USA
blastwaveinc.com

Blind Hash (2)
IAM / Password Management
Boston, MA, USA
blindhash.com

Block Armour (6)
Network / Zero-Trust Networking
Mumbai, India
blockarmour.com

Bloombase (20)
Data Security / Network-Attached Encryption
Redwood City, CA, USA
bloombase.com

Blue Hexagon (32)
Security Analytics / Breach Detection
Sunnyvale, CA, USA
bluehexagon.ai

Blue Lance Inc. (12)
GRC / Asset Management
Houston, TX, USA
bluelance.com

Blue Planet-works (13)
Application Security / Isolation
Tokyo, Japan
blueplanet-works.com

Blue Ridge Networks (34)
Network / Microsegmentation via Tokens
Chantilly, VA, USA
blueridgenetworks.com

Bluecat Networks (10)
Network / DNS Security
Bracknell, UK
bluecatnetworks.com

BlueCedar (39)
Endpoint / Mobile Device Protection
San Francisco, CA, USA
bluecedar.com

BlueKaizen (5)
Training
Egypt
bluekaizen.org

Blueliv (67)
Threat Intelligence
Barcelona, Spain
blueliv.com

BlueRisc (7)
Endpoint / Binary Code Vulnerability Analysis
Amherst, MA, USA
bluerisc.com

BlueTalon (32)
Data Security / Database Policy Management
Redwood City, CA, USA
bluetalon.com

BlueVoyant (175)
MSSP / MDR
New York, NY, USA
bluevoyant.com

Bluink (16)
IAM / Mobile Authenticator
Ottawa, Canada
bluink.ca

Blumira (10)
Security Analytics / Threat Detection and Response
Ann Arbor, MI, USA
blumira.com

BluVector (Part of Comcast) (44)
Network / IDS
Arlington, VA, USA
bluvector.io

BMC Software (200)
Security Analytics / SIEM
Houston, TX, USA
bmc.com

Bob's Business (27)
GRC / Security Awareness Training
Barnsley, UK
bobsbusiness.co.uk

Boldon James (76)
GRC / DLP (Data Classification)
Farnborough, UK
boldonjames.com

Boole Server (22)
Data Security / Secure File Synch and Share
Milan, Italy
booleserver.com

BOSaNOVA (19)
Network / Secure Terminal Emulation
Phoenix, AZ, USA
bosanova.net

Botdoc (10)
Data Security / Secure File Transfer
Monument, CO, USA
botdoc.io

Bottomline (500)
Fraud Prevention / User Behavior Analytics
Portsmouth, NH, USA
bottomline.com

Boxcryptor (12)
Data Security / Cloud Encryption
Augsburg, Germany
boxcryptor.com

Brainloop (124)
Data Security / Secure Collaboration
Munich, Germany
brainloop.com/us

Braintrace (36)
MSSP / MDR
Salt Lake City, UT, USA
braintrace.com

BrandShield (18)
Fraud Prevention / Brand Abuse Discovery
Ramat HaSharon, Israel
brandshield.com

Bricata (34)
Network / IPS
Columbia, MD, USA
bricata.com

Brinqa (37)
GRC / Risk Analytics & Management
Austin, TX, USA
brinqa.com

British Telecom (300)
MSSP / Managed Services
London, UK
bt.com

Brivo (149)
IAM / Physical Identity & Access Management
Bethesda, MD, USA
brivo.com

BrixBits (3)
Application Security / Code Hardening
Houston, TX, USA
brixbits.com

BroadBridge Networks (3)
Security Analytics / Network Monitoring
Fremont, CA, USA
broadbridgenetworks.com

Broadcom (2,000)
Network / Security Hardware
San Jose, CA, USA
broadcom.com

Bromium (acquired by HP) (131)
Endpoint Sandbox
Cupertino, CA, USA
bromium.com

Note: Numbers in parentheses indicate employee count

BSI Group (50)
Training / Standards Certification
London, UK
bsigroup.com

Bufferzone (21)
Endpoint Sandbox
Giv'atayim, Israel
bufferzonesecurity.com

Bugcrowd (581)
Operations / Bug Reporting Platform
San Francisco, CA, USA
bugcrowd.com

Buglab (10)
Operations / Pen Testing Network
Casablanca, Morocco
buglab.io

Bugsec Group (87)
MSSP / Managed Security Services
Rishon LeZion, Israel
bugsec.com

Buguroo (45)
Fraud Prevention / Behavior Monitoring
Alcobendas, Spain
buguroo.com

Build38 (13)
Application Security / Mobile App Protection
Munich, Germany
build38.com

Bulletproof (23)
MSSP / Managed SIEM
Stevenage, UK
bulletproof.co.uk

BullGuard Ltd. (129)
Endpoint / Anti-virus
London, UK
bullguard.com

Bundesdruckerei (387)
IAM / Authentication PKI
Berlin, Germany
bundesdruckerei.de/en

ByStorm Software (1)
Data Security / IRM
Magnolia, TX, USA
bystorm.com

C1Secure (10)
GRC / Compliance Monitoring Platform
Atlanta, GA, USA
c1secure.com

C2A Security (17)
IoT Security / Automotive
Jerusalem, Israel
c2a-sec.com

C2SEC (6)
GRC / Risk Management
Redmond, WA, USA
c2sec.com

CA Technologies (part of Broadcom) (9,565)
IAM
New York, NY, USA
ca.com

CACI International Inc. (140)
MSSP / Managed Services
Arlington, VA, USA
caci.com

CalCom (28)
Endpoint / Server Hardening via MSFT System Center
Lod, Israel
calcomsoftware.com

Caligare (1)
Network Monitoring Netflow
Prague, Czech Republic
caligare.com

Callsign (129)
IAM / Authentication
London, UK
callsign.com

Calyptix Security Corporation (9)
Network / UTM
Charlotte, NC, USA
calyptix.com

Cambridge Intelligence (35)
Security Analytics / Data Visualization
Cambridge, UK
cambridge-intelligence.com

Camel Secure (7)
GRC
Santiago, Chile
camelsecure.com

Capgemini (250)
MSSP / Identity as a Service
Paris, France
capgemini.com

Caplinked (20)
Data Security / Secure Workflow File Sharing
Manhattan Beach, CA, USA
caplinked.com

Carbon Black (acquired by VMWare) (1,177)
Endpoint / EDR
Waltham, MA, USA
carbonblack.com

CardLab
IAM
Herlev, Denmark
cardlab.com

Carve Systems (22)
GRC / Risk Assessment
New York, NY, USA
carvesystems.com

Castle (51)
Fraud Prevention / User-Trained Account Access
San Francisco, CA, USA
castle.io

Cato Networks (118)
Network / Cloud Security Layer
Tel Aviv, Israel
catonetworks.com

Cavirin (69)
GRC / Cloud Compliance
Santa Clara, CA, USA
cavirin.com

CBL Data Recovery Technologies Inc. (36)
Data Security / Data Recovery and Data Destruction
Markham, Canada
cbldata.com

CD Networks (322)
Network / DDoS Defense
Diamond Bar, CA, USA
cdnetworks.com

Celestix (25)
IAM
Fremont, CA, USA
celestix.com

Cellcrypt (4)
Data Security / Secure Communications
London, UK
cellcrypt.com

Cellebrite (789)
Endpoint / Mobile Forensics
Petah Tikva, Israel
cellebrite.com

Cellrox (15)
Endpoint / Mobile Virtualization
Tel Aviv, Israel
cellrox.com

CensorNet (78)
Network / Content URL
Filtering
Basingstoke, UK
censornet.com

Censys (26)
GRC / Asset Management
Ann Arbor, MI, USA
censys.io

Centri (20)
IoT Security / For Mobile
Carriers
Seattle, WA, USA
centritechnology.com

Centrify (381)
IAM
Santa Clara, CA, USA
centrify.com

Centripetal (39)
Network / Reputation
Firewall
Herndon, VA, USA
centripetalnetworks.com

CenturyLink (2,000)
MSSP / Network Moni-
toring
Monroe, LA, USA
centurylink.com

Cequence Security (47)
Security Analytics / NBAD
Sunnyvale, CA, USA
cequence.ai

Cerdant (48)
MSSP / Managed Services
Dublin, OH, USA
cerdant.com

Certes Networks (49)
Network / VPN
Pittsburgh, PA, USA
certesnetworks.com

Certicom (167)
Data Security / Encryption,
PKI
Mississauga, Canada
certicom.com

CertiPath (33)
Data Security / Certificate
Authority Monitoring
Reston, VA, USA
certipath.com

Certisign Certificador
(754)
IAM
São Paulo, Brazil
certisign.com.br

Cervello (9)
IoT Security / Railway
Tel Aviv, Israel
cervellosec.com

CESPPA (13)
Operations / Bug Bounty
Manhattan Beach, CA,
USA
cesppa.com

Cezurity (9)
Endpoint / EDR
St. Petersburg, Russia
cezurity.com

CGS Tower Networks (12)
Network Taps
Rosh HaAyin, Israel
cgstowernetworks.com

ChameleonX (8)
Application Security /
Runtime Protection
Tel Aviv, Israel
chameleonx.com

Charismathics (4)
IoT Security / IoT
Munich, Germany
charismathics.com

Check Point Software
(5,604)
Network / UTM
Tel Aviv, Israel
checkpoint.com

Checkmarx (1)
Application Security / Software Development Security
Ramat Gan, Israel
checkmarx.com

Cheetah Mobile (1,948)
Endpoint / Android AV
Beijing, China
cmcm.com

Chronicle (part of Google)
(133)
Security Analytics / SIEM
Mountain View, CA, USA
chronicle.security

CI Security (68)
MSSP / MDR
Seattle, WA, USA
ci.security

**Cicada Security
Technology** (2)
Endpoint / Device Theft
Prevention
Montreal, Canada
cicadasecurity.com

Cienaga Systems (4)
Security Analytics / Cyber
Threat Management
Lakewood Ranch, FL, USA
cienagasystems.net

Cigent (16)
Network Monitoring
Fort Myers, FL, USA
cigent.com

Cimcor (13)
GRC / IT Asset Protection
Merrillville, IN, USA
cimcor.com

CIPHER Security (187)
MSSP / Managed Security
Services
Miami, FL, USA
cipher.com

CipherCloud (309)
Data Security / Cloud Visibility & Data Protection
San Jose, CA, USA
ciphercloud.com

CipherMail (1)
Email Security / Secure
Email
Amsterdam, Netherlands
ciphermail.com

CipherSiP (7)
IoT Security / Automotive
Haifa, Israel
ciphersip.com

ciphertrace (28)
Fraud Prevention / An-
ti-money Laudering
Menlo Park, CA, USA
ciphertrace.com

Circadence (175)
Training / Cyber Range
Boulder, CO, USA
circadence.com

Cisco (5,000)
Network / Firewall
San Jose, CA, USA
cisco.com

Citalid (6)
GRC
Versailles, France
citalid.com

Citicus (4)
GRC
London, UK
citicus.com

Citrix Systems, Inc. (1,000)
Network / Secure Remote
Access
Fort Lauderdale, FL, USA
citrix.com

Clarabyte (3)
Data Security / Erasure
Pittsburgh, PA, USA
clarabyte.com

Note: Numbers in parentheses indicate employee count

Claroty (145)
IoT Security / ICS
New York, NY, USA
claroty.com

Clavister (142)
Network / UTM
Örnsköldsvik, Sweden
clavister.com

Cleafy (21)
Fraud Prevention / Anti-fraud
Milan, Italy
cleafy.com

ClearDATA (191)
MSSP / HIPAA Cloud
Hosting
Austin, TX, USA
cleardata.com

ClearedIn (16)
Email Security / Anti-phishing
Los Altos, CA, USA
clearedin.com

Clearnetwork (8)
MSSP / SOC as a service
Hazlet, NJ, USA
clearnetwork.com

Clearswift (193)
Email Security
Theale, UK
clearswift.com

Clearwater (101)
GRC / Risk Management
Nashville, TN, USA
clearwatercompliance.com

Clone Systems (13)
MSSP / Security Monitoring
Philadelphia, PA, USA
clone-systems.com

Cloud Conformity (51)
GRC / AWS Compliance
Monitoring
Sydney, Australia
cloudconformity.com

Cloud Raxak (9)
GRC / Compliance
Los Gatos, CA, USA
cloudraxak.com

Cloud24X7 (18)
MSSP Enablement
Fort Lauderdale, FL, USA
cloud24x7.us

CloudCover (9)
GRC / Compliance as a
Service
Saint Paul, MN, USA
cloudcover.net

CloudeAssurance (5)
GRC / Risk Management
Atlanta, GA, USA
cloudeassurance.com

Cloudentity (33)
IAM / Cloud Identity
Management
Seattle, WA, USA
cloudentity.com

Cloudera (247)
Operations / Cloud Security
Palo Alto, CA, USA
cloudera.com

Cloudflare (951)
Network / CDN and DDoS
Defense
San Francisco, CA, USA
cloudflare.com

Cloudknox (19)
IAM / Cloud Identity
Management
Sunnyvale, CA, USA
cloudknox.io

Cloudmark Inc. (94)
Network / DNS Security
San Francisco, CA, USA
cloudmark.com/en

Cloudmask (10)
Email Security
Ottawa, Canada
cloudmask.com

Cloudneeti (34)
GRC / Compliance Management
Seattle, WA, USA
cloudneeti.com

CloudPassage (60)
Endpoint / Cloud Host
Security
San Francisco, CA, USA
cloudpassage.com

Cloudpurge (1)
Network / Virtualized
Remote Browsing
Sydney, Australia
cloudpurge.info

Cloudscreen (1)
Data Security / Discovery,
Classification
Yuhang District, China
cloudscreen.com

CloudSEK (42)
GRC / Risk Management
Bangalore, India
cloudsek.com

Cloudsploit (8)
Network / AWS Config
Testing and Monitoring
Silver Spring, MD, USA
cloudsploit.com

CMD (33)
Endpoint / Linux Security
Vancouver, Canada
cmd.com

Coalition (36)
GRC / Cyber Insurance
San Francisco, CA, USA
thecoalition.com

Cobalt (192)
Application Security / App
Testing for Security
San Francisco, CA, USA
cobalt.io

CODA Intelligence (6)
GRC / Vulnerability Management
Boston, MA, USA
codaintelligence.com

Code 42 Software (505)
Operations / Secure Backup and Recovery
Minneapolis, MN, USA
code42.com

Code Dx (10)
Application Security / Software Assurance Analytics
Northport, NY, USA
codedx.com

Code Intelligence (15)
Application Security /
Appsec
Bonn, Germany
code-intelligence.com

Codenomicon (15)
Application Security /
Code Analysis
Mountain View, CA, USA
codenomicon.com

CodeProof (8)
Application Security /
Mobile App Security
Bellevue, WA, USA
codeproof.com

Codified Security (5)
Application Security /
Code Scanning
London, UK
codifiedsecurity.com

Cofense (was PhishMe)
(393)
GRC / Anti-phishing
Training
Leesburg, VA, USA
cofense.com

Cog (127)
IoT Security / Microvirtualization Framework
Sydney, Australia
cog.systems

Cognigo (34)
GRC / Data Privacy Compliance for Cloud Storage
Jersey City, NJ, USA
cognigo.com

Cognito (6)
Fraud Prevention / Intelligence-Based Authentication
Palo Alto, CA, USA
cognitohq.com

Cohesive Networks (17)
Network / Cloud Tunnels over IPSec
Chicago, IL, USA
cohesive.net

Collective Software LLC (1)
IAM / AD Authentication
Springfield, IL, USA
collectivesoftware.com

ColorTokens (230)
Network / Zero-Trust Networking
Santa Clara, CA, USA
colortokens.com

Columbitech (12)
Network / Mobile VPN
Stockholm, Sweden
columbitech.com

Commugen (21)
GRC / Risk Management
Tel Aviv, Israel
commugen.com

Communication Devices, Inc. (7)
Operations / Secure Remote Management
Boonton, NJ, USA
commdevices.com

Communication Security Group (16)
Data Security / Secure Communications
London, UK
csghq.com

CommVault (2,532)
Operations / Backup and Recovery
Tinton Falls, NJ, USA
commvault.com

Comodo (1,411)
Data Security / SSL Certificates & PCI Compliance
Clifton, NJ, USA
comodo.com

Compass Security AG
Data Security / Secure File Transfer
Rapperswil-Jona, Switzerland
csnc.ch

Compelson Labs (Mobiledit) (17)
GRC / Forensics
Prague, Czech Republic
mobiledit.com/home

ComplyUp (5)
GRC / Compliance
Tampa, FL, USA
complyup.com

Compumatica (16)
Data Security / Secure Remote Access
Uden, Netherlands
compumatica.com

ComSignTrust (3)
Data Security / Digital Signatures for Data
Tel Aviv, Israel
comsigntrust.com

Confide (1)
Data Security / Private Messaging
New York, NY, USA
getconfide.com

Confident Technologies (3)
Fraud Prevention / Anti-fraud CAPTCHAS
Solana Beach, CA, USA
confidenttechnologies.com

Confluera (19)
Security Analytics / Autonomous Detection and Response
Palo Alto, CA, USA
confluera.com

ContentGuard (Pendrell Company) (5)
Data Security / IRM File Sharing for Mobile Phones
Kirkland, WA, USA
contentguard.com

ContentKeeper (37)
Network / Content URL Filtering
Braddon, Australia
contentkeeper.com

Continuum Security (30)
Application Security / Open Source Scanning
Huesca, Spain
continuumsecurity.net

Contrast Security (169)
Application Security
Los Altos, CA, USA
contrastsecurity.com

Control's Force (10)
Fraud Prevention / Insider Fraud Detection
Detroit, MI, USA
controlsforce.com

ControlGuard (8)
Endpoint / Device Control
Herzlia Pituach, Israel
atrog.com

ControlScan (137)
MSSP / Managed Security Services
Alpharetta, GA, USA
controlscan.com

Conventus (20)
GRC / Vulnerability Management
Chicago, IL, USA
conventus.com

Convercent (173)
GRC / Compliance Management
Denver, CO, USA
convercent.com

CopyNotify (1)
Data Security / Device Control for SMB
Pune, India
copynotify.com

Corax (31)
GRC / Security Ratings
London, UK
coraxcyber.com

Cord3 Innovation Inc. (15)
Data Security / Zero Knowledge File Encryption
Ottawa, Canada
cord3inc.com

Core Security (181)
GRC / Vulnerability Management
Roswell, GA, USA
coresecurity.com

Corelight (80)
Network / Traffic Analysis
San Francisco, CA, USA
corelight.com

Corero Network Security (90)
Network / DDoS Defense
Marlborough, MA, USA
corero.com

Coronet (85)
Network / Endpoint Radio Protection
Tel Aviv-Yafo, Israel
coro.net

Corsa (32)
Network / Zero-Trust Networking
Ottawa, Canada
corsa.com

Note: Numbers in parentheses indicate employee count

Cortex Insight (4)
Security Analytics / Vulnerability Measurement
London, UK
cortexinsight.com

Cosmian (8)
Data Security
Paris, France
cosmian.com

CoSoSys (63)
Network / DLP
Cluj-Napoca, Romania
endpointprotector.com

CounterCraft (26)
Deception
Donostia-San Sebastian, Spain
countercraft.eu

CounterFlow AI (14)
Network / Forensics
Crozet, VA, USA
counterflow.ai

Countersnipe Systems (11)
Network / IPS
Boston, MA, USA
countersnipe.com

CounterTack (57)
Security Analytics / Real-Time Attack Intelligence
Waltham, MA, USA
countertack.com

Covata (22)
Data Security / Secure File Sharing
Sydney, Australia
covata.com

Covisint (OpenText) (247)
IAM / Federated Identity Management
Southfield, MI, USA
covisent.com

CovR
IAM / Mobile Authenticator
Malmö, Sweden
covrsecurity.com

cPacket (60)
Network / Packet Capture
San Jose, CA, USA
cpacket.com

Crashtest Security (8)
Application Security / Appsec
Munich, Germany
crashtest-security.com

Criptext (12)
Email Security / Secure Email
New York, NY, USA
criptext.com

Critical Research Corporation (1)
Network / Endpoint Discovery
Austin, TX, USA
rumble.run

Critical Start (112)
MSSP / MDR
Plano, TX, USA
criticalstart.com

CriticalStack (12)
Threat Intelligence Aggregator
Cambridge, MA, USA
criticalstack.com

Critifence (6)
IoT Security / ICS
Herzliya, Israel
critifence.com

Cronus (17)
Testing / Attacker Simulation
Haifa, Israel
cronus-cyber.com

Crossmatch (259)
IAM
Palm Beach Gardens, FL, USA
crossmatch.com

CrowdStrike (1,513)
Endpoint / EDR
Sunnyvale, CA, USA
crowdstrike.com

Crown Sterling (17)
Data Security / Encryption
Newport Beach, CA, USA
crownsterling.io

Crusoe Security (6)
Network / Web Browsing Isolation
Neve Yarak, Israel
crusoesecurity.com

Crypho AS (5)
Data Security / Private Messaging
Tønsberg, Norway
crypho.com

Crypta Labs (13)
Data Security / Encryption (RNG)
London, UK
cryptalabs.com

Crypteia Networks (PCCW) (15)
Threat Intelligence Platform and Analytics
Neo Psychiko, Greece
crypteianetworks.com

Cryptelo (6)
Data Security / Secure Data Transfer
Prague, Czech Republic
cryptelo.com

Crypto International AG (1)
Data Security / Hardware for Crypto
Steinhausen, Switzerland
crypto.ch

Crypto Quantique (24)
IoT Security / Embedded Security
Egham, UK
cryptoquantique.com

Crypto4A Inc. (14)
Data Security / Entropy as a Service
Ottawa, Canada
crypto4a.com

Cryptomathic (67)
Data Security / Key Management, PKI
Aarhus, Denmark
cryptomathic.com

Cryptomill Cybersecurity Solutions (16)
Data Security
Toronto, Canada
cryptomill.com

CryptoMove, Inc. (23)
Data Security / Key Storage
Oakland, CA, USA
cryptomove.com

Cryptonite (6)
Network / Segmentation
Rockville, MD, USA
cryptonitenxt.com

CryptoPhoto (34)
IAM / 2FA Using Images
Australia
cryptophoto.com

Cryptosense (8)
GRC / VM for Cryptography
Paris, France
cryptosense.com

cryptovision (27)
IAM / Smart Card Solutions
Gelsenkirchen, Germany
cryptovision.com

Cryptshare (50)
Email Security / Encrypted
File and Email on Azure
Freiburg, Germany
cryptshare.com

Cryptsoft Pty Ltd. (10)
Data Security / PKI and
Identity
Greenslopes, Australia
cryptsoft.com

Cryptyk (17)
Data Security / Secure
Storage
Las Vegas, NV, USA
cryptyk.io

CSPi (143)
Network / Packet Capture
Lowell, MA, USA
cspi.com

CTF365 (8)
Training / Capture the Flag
Exercise
Cluj-Napoca, Romania
ctf365.com

CTM360 (34)
Security Analytics / Breach
Detection
Seef, Bahrain
ctm360.com

Cubro (64)
Network / Packet Capture
Vienna, Austria
cubro.com

Cujo AI (150)
Network / Home Security
for Carriers
El Segundo, CA, USA
getcujo.com

Culinda (2)
IoT Security / Medical
Devices
Irvine, CA, USA
culinda.io

Cupp Computing (9)
Endpoint Security
Palo Alto, CA, USA
cuppcomputing.com

Cura Software Solutions
(90)
GRC / Risk Management
Singapore, Singapore
curasoftware.com

Custodio Technologies (13)
Security Analytics / Breach
Detection and Response
Ubi, Singapore
custodio.com.sg

Cy-oT (12)
IoT Security / Wireless
Monitoring
Tel Aviv, Israel
Cy-ot.com

Cyabra (11)
Threat Intelligence / Fake
News Defense
Tel Aviv, Israel
cyabra.com

Cyan Forensics (9)
Operations / Endpoint
Forensics
Edinburgh, UK
cyanforensics.com

CYAN Network Security
(2)
Network / Secure Web
Gateway
Vienna, Austria
cyannetworks.com

Cybeats (12)
Operations / Incident
Response
Aurora, Canada
cybeats.com

CybelAngel (87)
GRC / OSINT Data Leak
Detection
Paris, France
cybelangel.com

Cybellum (9)
Endpoint / In-Memory
Prevention
Tel Aviv-Yafo, Israel
cybellum.com

Cyber 2.0 (16)
Endpoint / EDR
Tel Aviv, Israel
cyber20.com

Cyber 20/20 (11)
Operations / Behav-
ior-Based Malware
Detection
Herndon, VA, USA
cyber2020.com

Cyber adAPT (28)
Security Analytics / Net-
work Traffic Monitoring
Dallas, TX, USA
cyberadapt.com

**Cyber Advanced
Technology**
Network / IPS
Berkeley, CA, USA
www2.unhackablecloud.
com

Cyber Crucible (6)
Security Analytics / Breach
Detection
Severna Park, MD, USA
cybercrucible.com

Cyber Driveware
Network Malware Defense
Herzliya, Israel
cyberdriveware.com

Cyber Observer Ltd. (22)
GRC / Security Manage-
ment
Caesarea, Israel
cyber-observer.com

Cyber Operations, LLC (1)
Operations / ACL Man-
agement
Pelham, AL, USA
cyberoperations.com

Cyber Skyline (5)
Training / Continuous
Training for Cybersecurity
College Park, MD, USA
cyberskyline.com

Cyber Triage
Operations / Incident
Response Management
Herndon, VA, USA
cybertriage.com

Cyber-SIGN (1)
IAM / Biometrics Hand-
writing
Setagaya, Japan
witswell.com

Cybera (168)
Network / SDN Applica-
tion & Network Security
Franklin, TN, USA
cybera.net

CyberArk Software (1,228)
IAM / Privileged Access
Management
Petah Tikva, Israel
cyberark.com

Cyberbit (334)
Training / Cyber Range
Ra'anana, Israel
cyberbit.com

CyberCentric (2)
GRC / Data Access Mon-
itoring
New York, NY, USA
cybercentric.com

CyberCPR (1)
Operations / Secure Inci-
dent Response Manage-
ment
Cheltenham, UK
cybercpr.com

CyberCube (61)
GRC / Risk Management
San Francisco, CA, USA
cybcube.com

Note: Numbers in parentheses indicate employee count

Cyberready (16)
GRC / Anti-phishing
Training
Tel Aviv, Israel
cyberready.co.il

Cybereason (459)
Security Analytics / Breach
Detection
Boston, MA, USA
cybereason.com

**CyberEye Research Labs
& Security Solutions** (22)
GRC / Security Awareness
Training
Hyderabad, India
cybereyelabs.io

Cyberfense (5)
GRC / Risk Management
New York, NY, USA
cyberfense.com

CyberGhost (67)
Network / VPN
Bucharest, Romania
cyberghostvpn.com

CyberGRX (98)
GRC / Third Party Risk
Denver, CO, USA
cybergrx.com

Cybergym (47)
Training / Cyber Range
Hadera, Israel
cybergym.com

Cyberhat (47)
MSSP / Managed SOC
Tel Aviv, Israel
cyberhat.co.il

Cyberhaven (26)
Network Data Flow Mon-
itoring
Boston, MA, USA
cyberhaven.io

Cyberinc (43)
Network / Browser Isola-
tion
San Ramon, CA, USA
cyberinc.com

Cyberint (87)
Threat Intelligence
Petah Tikva, Israel
cyberint.com

Cyberkov (5)
GRC / Risk Assessment
Kuwait City, Kuwait
cyberkov.com

CyberMDX (36)
IoT Security / Medical
Devices
New York, NY, USA
cybermdx.com

Cybernance (9)
GRC / Risk Measurement
Austin, TX, USA
cybernance.com

Cybernet (1)
GRC / Security Manager
Ann Arbor, MI, USA
cybersecurity.cybernet.com

Cybernetiq (13)
GRC / Risk Measurement
Ottawa, Canada
cybernetiq.ca

CyberObserver (22)
Operations / Manager of
Managers
Caesarea, Israel
cyber-observer.com

CyberOne (5)
GRC / Policy Management
San Francisco, CA, USA
cb1security.com

CyberOwl (26)
GRC / Risk Measurement
Birmingham, UK
cyberowl.io

CyberPoint (2)
GRC
Baltimore, MD, USA
cyberpointllc.com

CyberPoint International
(54)
Endpoint / File Artifact
Detection (mostly PS)
Baltimore, MD, USA
cyberpointllc.com

CyberReef Solutions (2)
IoT Security / ICS
Shreveport, LA, USA
scadaaccess.com

CyberSafe Ltd. (7)
IAM / Access Control for
SAP
Longford, UK
cybersafe.com

CyberSafe Software (3)
Data Security / Full Disk
Encryption
Krasnodar, Russia
cybersafesoft.com

Cybersafe Solutions (16)
MSSP / MDR
Jericho, NY, USA
cybersafesolutions.com

CyberSaint (23)
GRC / Risk Management
Boston, MA, USA
cybersaint.io

CyberSeal (3)
Network / SIGINT Offen-
sive
Yehud, Israel
cyber-seal.net

CyberSecure IPS (11)
Network / IPS
Upper Marlboro, MD, USA
cybersecureips.com

**CyberSecurity
Corporation** (1)
IAM / Access Management
Kansas City, MO, USA
goldkey.com

Cyberseer (11)
MSSP / Threat Intel
London, UK
cyberseer.net

Cybersmart (18)
GRC / Compliance Auto-
mation
London, UK
cybersmart.co.uk

CyberSponse (67)
Operations / Incident
Response & Security Op-
erations
Arlington, VA, USA
cybersponse.com

CyberSprint (28)
GRC / Vulnerability
Scanner
The Hague, Netherlands
cybersprint.com

CYBERTRAP (20)
Deception
Wiener Neustadt, Austria
cybertrap.com

Cyberus Labs (12)
IAM / 2FA (mobile)
Kraków, Poland
cyberuslabs.com

Cyberwatch (15)
GRC
Paris, France
cyberwatch.fr

CyberX (97)
IoT Security / NBAD for
ICS
Waltham, MA, USA
cyberx-labs.com

Cybexer (12)
Opertions / Cyber Range
Tallinn, Estonia
cybexer.com

Cybonet (was PineApp)
(41)
Email Security / AV and
Sandboxing
Matam, Israel
cybonet.com/en

Cybraics (38)
Security Analytics
Atlanta, GA, USA
cybraics.com

Cybrary (297)
GRC / Training
College Park, MD, USA
cybrary.it

Cybrgen
Data Security / Distributed
Encrypted Storage
Las Vegas, NV, USA
cybrgendev.com

Cybriant (30)
MSSP / MDR
Alpharetta, GA, USA
cybriant.com

Cybric (19)
Operations / Security
Orchestration
Boston, MA, USA
cybric.io

CybSafe (39)
GRC / Security Awareness
Training
London, UK
cybsafe.com

Cycognito (43)
GRC / Vulnerability Man-
agement
Palo Alto, CA, USA
cycognito.com

Cycurity (45)
Security Analytics
Tel Aviv, Israel
cycurity.com

Cydarm (4)
Operations / Incident Re-
sponse Case Management
Docklands, Australia
cydarm.com

Cydome
IoT Security / ICS Mari-
time
Tel Aviv, Israel
cydome.io

cyel (5)
Network / IP Address
Morphing
Bern, Switzerland
cyel.ch

CyFIR (12)
GRC / Digital Forensics &
e-Discovery
Ashburn, VA, USA
cyfir.com

CYFIRMA (23)
Threat Intelligence
Oak Park, IL, USA
cyfirma.com

CYFORT Security (2)
Threat Intelligence
Herzliya, Israel
cyfort.com

Cygilant (110)
MSSP / MDR
Boston, MA, USA
cygilant.com

CyGlass (27)
Security Analytics / Cloud
SIEM
Littleton, MA, USA
cyglass.com

Cygna Labs Corp (8)
GRC / Audit of Azure
Environments
Miami Beach, FL, USA
cygnalabs.com

Cygov (13)
GRC / Compliance and
DLP
New York, NY, USA
cygov.co

Cyjax (10)
Threat Intelligence
London, UK
cyjax.com

**Cylance (part of
BlackBerry)** (888)
Endpoint / EDR
Irvine, CA, USA
cylance.com

Cylera (19)
IoT Security / Medical
Devices
New York, NY, USA
cylera.com

Cylus (23)
IoT Security / Railway
Tel Aviv, Israel
cylus.com

Cymatic (15)
Security Analytics / UEBA
Raleigh, NC, USA
cymatic.io

Cymmetria (23)
Deception (Honeypots)
Tel Aviv, Israel
cymmetria.com

Cymotive (75)
IoT Security / Automotive
Tel Aviv, Israel
cymotive.com

Cympire (12)
Training / Cyber Range
Tel Aviv, Israel
cympire.com

Cymulate (57)
Operations / Breach and
Attack Simulation
Rishon LeZion, Israel
cymulate.com

Cynash (13)
IoT Security / ICS
Wilmington, DE, USA
cynash.com

CyNation (14)
GRC / Third Party Risk
Assessment
London, UK
cynation.com

Cynerio (19)
IoT Security / Medical
Device Security
Ramat Gan, Israel
cynerio.co

Cynet (97)
Operations / APT Discov-
ery via Agentless Scan
Rishon LeZion, Israel
cynet.com

Cyph (2)
Data Security / Encrypted
Collaboration
McLean, VA, USA
cyph.com

Cyphercor – LoginTC (6)
IAM / Two-Factor Authen-
tication
Kanata, Canada
logintc.com

Cypherix Software (1)
Data Security / Encryption
Land O' Lakes, FL, USA
cypherix.com

Cypherpath (36)
Application Security /
Containers for Apps
Mountain View, CA, USA
cypherpath.com

Note: Numbers in parentheses indicate employee count

CYR3CON (55)
GRC / Vulnerability
Ranking
Tempe, AZ, USA
cyr3con.ai

CyRadar
Endpoint / EDR
Hanoi, Vietnam
cyradar.com

Cyrating (2)
GRC / Risk Scores
Paris, France
cyrating.com

Cyren (266)
Network / Web, Email &
Mobile Security
McLean, VA, USA
cyren.com

Cytegic (17)
GRC / Risk Profiling
Tel Aviv, Israel
cytegic.com

Cyware (89)
Operations / Alert Man-
agement
New York, NY, USA
cyware.com

Cyxtera Technologies
(982)
Network / Zero-Trust
Networking
Coral Gables, FL, USA
cyxtera.com

D-ID (25)
IAM / Anti-facial Recog-
nition
Tel Aviv, Israel
deidentification.co

D-Link Systems, Inc.
(1,000)
Network / UTM
Taipei City, Taiwan
us.dlink.com

D3 Security (101)
Operations / Incident
Management
Vancouver, Canada
d3security.com

Daon (148)
IAM / Identity Assurance
Reston, VA, USA
daon.com

Dark3 (20)
Network / SaaS Network
Monitoring
Alexandria, VA, USA
darkcubed.com

Darkbeam (5)
Threat Intelligence
London, UK
darkbeam.com

Dark Cubed (20)
Security Analytics / Net-
work Monitoring
Charlottesville, VA, USA
darkcubed.com

DarkLight.ai (20)
Security Analytics
Bellevue, WA, USA
darklight.ai

DarkOwl (25)
Threat Intelligence / Dark
Web Collection
Denver, CO, USA
darkowl.com

Darkscope (2)
Threat Intelligence
Wellington, New Zealand
darkscope.com

Darktrace (889)
Security Analytics / Breach
Detection
San Francisco, CA, USA
darktrace.com

Dash Solutions (7)
GRC / HIPAA Compliance
Management
Devon, PA, USA
dashsdk.com

Dashlane (179)
IAM / Password Manager
New York, NY, USA
dashlane.com

Data Encryption Systems
(4)
Data Security / Software
DRM
Taunton, UK
des.co.uk

**Data Security
Technologies**
Data Security / NoSQL
Policy Enforcement
Richardson, TX, USA
datasectech.com

Data Theorem (23)
Application Security /
Mobile App Scanner
Palo Alto, CA, USA
datatheorem.com

Datablink (26)
IAM / Authentication
McLean, VA, USA
datablink.com

DataDome (38)
Fraud Prevention / Bot
Detection
New York, NY, USA
datadome.co

DataGuise (125)
Data Security / Database
Security
Fremont, CA, USA
dataguise.com

**Datakey (ATEK Access
Technologies, LLC)** (31)
IAM / Authentication
Eden Prairie, MN, USA
datakey.com

DataLocker (39)
Data Security / Encrypted
Removable Memory
Overland Park, KS, USA
datalocker.com

DataMotion (44)
Email Security
Florham Park, NJ, USA
datamotion.com

DAtAnchor (13)
Data Security / Document
Security
Columbus, OH, USA
datanchor.net

DataPassports (3)
Data Security / IRM
Toronto, Canada
datapassports.com

DataResolve (82)
Security Analytics / UEBA
Noida, India
dataresolve.com

DATASHIELD (38)
MSSP / Managed Security
Services
Salt Lake City, UT, USA
datashieldprotect.com

**DataSunrise Database
Security** (285)
Data Security / Database
Security
Seattle, WA, USA
datasunrise.com

Datavisor (105)
Security Analytics
Mountain View, CA, USA
datavisor.com

Datex Inc. (29)
Data Security / Network
Data Masking
Mississauga, Canada
datex.ca

Dathena Science (51)
Data Security / Discovery
and Classification
Singapore, Singapore
dathena.io

Datiphy (15)
GRC / User Behavior
Monitoring
San Jose, CA, USA
datiphy.com

Dax Asparna Ltd. (11)
Data Security / Encrypted
File Sync and Social Con-
versations
Afula, Israel
asparna.com

DB Cybertech (34)
GRC / Data Discovery
San Diego, CA, USA
dbcybertech.com

DBApp Security (22)
Application Security / Web
Application & Database
Security
Hangzhou, China
dbappsecurity.com

Dcoya (7)
GRC / Anti-phishing
Training
Tel Aviv, Israel
dcoya.com

DealRoom (10)
Data Security / Deal Room
Chicago, IL, USA
dealroom.net

Debricked (17)
GRC / Vulnerability Man-
agement
Malmö, Sweden
debricked.com

Deceptive Bytes (3)
Deception
Holon, Israel
deceptivebytes.com

Deep Identity Pte Ltd. (85)
IAM / IAM
Singapore, Singapore
deepidentity.com

Deep-Secure (48)
Network / Air Gap (Data
Diodes)
Malvern, UK
deep-secure.com

Deepfence (8)
Network / IPS
Milpitas, CA, USA
deepfence.io

Deep Instinct (91)
Endpoint Machine Learn-
ing
Tel Aviv, Israel
deepinstinct.com

Deepnet Security (14)
IAM / Identity Manage-
ment
London, UK
deepnetsecurity.com

DeepSource (7)
Application Security /
Static Code Analysis for
Python and Go
San Francisco, CA, USA
deepsource.io

Deeptrace (7)
Data Security / Deep Fake
Detection
Amsterdam, Netherlands
deeptracelabs.com

DeepView (7)
Data Security / DL Detec-
tion Through Social Media
Monitoring
London, UK
deepview.com

deepwatch (133)
MSSP / MDR
Denver, CO, USA
deepwatch.com

Defence Intelligence (23)
Operations / Malware
Protection
Kanata, Canada
defintel.com

Defendify (19)
GRC
Portland, ME, USA
defendify.io

Defense Balance (13)
GRC / Security Awareness
Training
Cordoba, Argentina
smartfense.com

DefenseStorm (57)
GRC / Monitoring for
Compliance for Banks
Atlanta, GA, USA
defensestorm.com

Defentry (10)
Opertions / Web Scanning
Stockholm, Sweden
defentry.com

DefiniSec (1)
Email Security / Email
Encryption and Backup
El Cerrito, CA, USA
definisec.com

Dekart (1)
Data Security / Encryption
Chisinau, Republic of
Moldova
dekart.com

Dekko Secure (7)
Data Security / Encryption
Sydney, Australia
dekkosecure.com

Delfigo Security (5)
IAM / Mobile Device
Authentication
Boston, MA, USA
delfigosecurity.com

Dellfer (8)
IoT Security / Automotive
Novato, CA, USA
dellfer.com

Delta Risk (71)
MSSP / MDR
San Antonio, TX, USA
deltarisk.com

Delve Labs (21)
GRC / Vulnerability Man-
agement
Montreal, Canada
delve-labs.com

**Demisto (Palo Alto
Networks)** (158)
Operations / Incident
Response
Cupertino, CA, USA
demisto.com

Denim Group (94)
GRC / Vulnerability Man-
agement
San Antonio, TX, USA
denimgroup.com

Detectify (82)
Application Security / Web
Scanning
Stockholm, Sweden
detectify.com

Detexian (7)
Operations / Monitor
Cloud Configurations
San Diego, CA, USA
detexian.com

DeUmbra (3)
Security Analytics / Visualization
Austin, TX, USA
deumbra.com

DEVCON (14)
Fraud Prevention / Ad
Tech Security
Atlanta, GA, USA
devcondetect.com

Note: Numbers in parentheses indicate employee count

Device Authority (23)
IAM / Device Authentication
Reading, UK
deviceauthority.com

DeviceLock (25)
GRC / Endpoint Data Leak
Prevention
San Ramon, CA, USA
devicelock.com

Devo (184)
Security Analytics / Cloud
SIEM
Cambridge, MA, USA
devo.com

DFLabs (56)
Operations / Automated Incident & Breach
Response
Milan, Italy
dflabs.com

DH2i (8)
Network / Zero-Trust
Networking
Fort Collins, CO, USA
dh2i.com

Difenda Labs (37)
MSSP / MDR
Oakville, Canada
difenda.com

DigiCert (843)
Data Security / Certificate
Authority
Lehi, UT, USA
digicert.com

DigiPortal, Inc. (1)
Network / Anti-spam
Altamonte Springs, FL,
USA
digiportal.com

**Digital Authentication
Technologies** (6)
IAM / Location-Based
Authentication
Boca Raton, FL, USA
dathq.com

Digital Confidence Ltd. (1)
GRC / DLP
Tel Aviv, Israel
digitalconfidence.com

Digital Defense (110)
GRC / Vulnerability Management
San Antonio, TX, USA
digitaldefense.com

Digital Detective (3)
GRC / Forensics
Folkestone, UK
digital-detective.net

Digital Guardian (403)
GRC / DLP
Waltham, MA, USA
digitalguardian.com

Digital Hands (79)
MSSP / Managed Security
Services
Tampa, FL, USA
digitalhands.com

Digital Immunity (12)
Endpoint / System Hardening
Burlington, MA, USA
digitalimmunity.com

Digital Shadows (180)
Threat Intelligence /
OSINT Dark Web
San Francisco, CA, USA
digitalshadows.com

DigitalResolve (5)
Fraud Prevention / Activity
Auditing
Norcross, GA, USA
digitalresolve.com

DigitalShark (3)
Network / Web Defense
New York, NY, USA
digitalshark.org

DigitalStakeout (5)
Threat Intelligence Web
Alpharetta, GA, USA
digitalstakeout.com

DigitSec (7)
Application Security /
SFDC Scanner
Seattle, WA, USA
digitsec.com

**Diligent eSecurity
International** (8)
GRC / Asset Monitoring
Atlanta, GA, USA
desintl.com

Direct Risk Management
(2)
IAM / Authentication
Aliso Viejo, CA, USA
directrm.com

Disconnect (16)
Network / Consumer VPN
San Francisco, CA, USA
disconnect.me

Dispersive Networks, Inc.
(69)
Network / VPN
Alpharetta, GA, USA
dispersive.io

DisruptOps (15)
Operations / Monitor and
Fix Cloud Deployments
Kansas City, MO, USA
disruptops.com

Distil Networks (109)
Network / Bot Detection
San Francisco, CA, USA
distilnetworks.com

DISUK Limited (2)
Data Security / Encryption
Northampton, UK
disuk.com

Ditno (6)
Network / Cloud Firewall
Management and WAF
Sydney, Australia
ditno.com

Divvy Cloud Corp. (48)
Endpoint / Container
Security
Arlington, VA, USA
divvycloud.com

DNIF (6)
Security Analytics / SIEM
Mumbai, India
dnif.it

DocAuthority (34)
GRC / DLP
Ra'anana, Israel
docauthority.com

Dojo by BullGuard (1)
Network / Home Wifi
Security
Ra'anana, Israel
dojo.bullguard.com

DomainSkate (2)
Fraud Prevention / Brand
Abuse Discovery
New York, NY, USA
domainskate.com

DomainTools (102)
Threat Intelligence from
DNS
Seattle, WA, USA
domaintools.com

**Dome9 (acquired by
Check Point in 2018)** (82)
Network / Cloud Firewall
Policy Management
Tel Aviv, Israel
dome9.com

Dominode (3)
IAM / Identity Assertion
with Blockchain
Boca Raton, FL, USA
dominode.com

DOSarrest (26)
Network / DDoS Defense
Richmond, Canada
dosarrest.com

Dover Microsystems (23)
IoT Security / Firmware
Hardening
Waltham, MA, USA
dovermicrosystems.com

Dr. Web (1)
Endpoint / Android AV
Moscow, Russia
drweb.com

DRACOON (42)
Data Security / File Sharing
Regensburg, Germany
dracoon.com

DragonSoft (31)
Application Security WAF
and Scanning
New Taipei City, Taiwan
dragonsoft.com.tw

Dragos (164)
IoT Security / ICS
Hanover, MD, USA
dragos.com

DriveLock (47)
Endpoint Device Control,
DLP
Munich, Germany
drivelock.com

Drooms (116)
Data Security / Data
Rooms
Frankfurt am Main, Germany
drooms.com

Druva (643)
Endpoint Data Protection
& Governance
Sunnyvale, CA, USA
druva.com

DTEX Systems (87)
GRC / Insider Threat
Detection
San Jose, CA, USA
dtexsystems.com

Duality Technologies (18)
Data Security / Encrypted
Data Analysis
Newark, NJ, USA
duality.cloud

**DuoSecurity (now part of
Cisco)** (703)
IAM / Authentication
Ann Arbor, MI, USA
duo.com

Dynasec BV (20)
GRC / Compliance Management
Eindhoven, Netherlands
dynasec.org

E-Certify (2)
IAM
Wayville, Australia
ecertify.com

eAgency (10)
Endpoint / Mobile Security
Newport Beach, CA, USA
eagency.com

Early Warning (904)
Fraud Prevention / Identity
Assurance
Scottsdale, AZ, USA
earlywarning.com

east-tec (8)
Data Security / Erasure
Oradea, Romania
east-tec.com

Eastwind (5)
Network Monitoring for
Cloud
Salt Lake City, UT, USA
eastwindnetworks.com

Echosec (22)
Threat Intelligence / Intel
Gathering Tool
Victoria, Canada
echosec.net

EclecticIQ (110)
Threat Intelligence Platform
Amsterdam, Netherlands
eclecticiq.com

Eclypses (4)
Data Security / Encrypted
Storage
Colorado Springs, CO,
USA
certainsafe.com

Eclypsium (23)
Endpoint / Firmware
Protection
Beaverton, OR, USA
eclypsium.com

Ecora Software (24)
IAM / Authentication
Boston, MA, USA
ecora.com

edgescan (45)
GRC / Vulnerability Management
Dublin, Ireland
edgescan.com

Edgewave (62)
Email Security
La Jolla, CA, USA
edgewave.com

Edgewise Networks (34)
Network / Zero-Trust
Networking
Burlington, MA, USA
edgewise.net

EfficientIP (106)
Network / DNS Management
West Chester, PA, USA
efficientip.com

EFTsure (14)
Fraud Prevention / EFT
Protection
North Sydney, Australia
home.eftsure.com.au

Egis Technology (1)
IAM / Biometrics under
Display Fingerprint Sensor
Taipei, Taiwan
egistec.com

Egnyte (470)
Data Security / Secure File
Sharing
Mountain View, CA, USA
egnyte.com

EgoSecure (21)
Data Security / Data-at-
Rest Encryption
Ettlingen, Germany
egosecure.com

Egress (198)
Email Security
London, UK
egress.com

Elastic (200)
Security Analytics / SIEM
Amsterdam, Netherlands
elastic.co

Elcomsoft (16)
Operations / Forensics
Moscow, Russia
elcomsoft.com

Elemendar (4)
Threat Intelligence Analysis
Stourbridge, UK
elemendar.com

Elemental Cyber Security
(9)
GRC / Vulnerability Management
Dallas, TX, USA
elementalsecurity.com

Note: Numbers in parentheses indicate employee count

Elevate Security (21)
GRC / Security Awareness
Training
Berkeley, CA, USA
elevatesecurity.com

Emailage (174)
Email Security
Chandler, AZ, USA
emailage.com

Emergynt (16)
GRC / Risk Management
Cincinnati, OH, USA
emergynt.com

Empow (34)
Security Analytics / SIEM
Ramat Gan, Israel
empow.co

Emprise (35)
MSSP / Managed Services
Toledo, OH, USA
emptechllc.com

Emsisoft (27)
Endpoint / Android AV
Chicago, IL, USA
emsisoft.com

Encedo (2)
Data Security / Encrypted
Networks
London, UK
encedo.com

Encode (98)
Security Analytics
London, UK
encodegroup.com

Encryptics (24)
Data Security / IRM
Addison, TX, USA
encryptics.com

Endace (136)
Network / IDS
Ellerslie, New Zealand
endace.com

Endgame, Inc. (153)
Security Analytics /
Security Intelligence and
Analytics
Arlington, VA, USA
endgame.com

Endian (26)
Network / UTM
Bolzano, Italy
endian.com

Engage Black (7)
Data Security / Code
Signing
Aptos, CA, USA
engageblack.com

Engage Technologies
IoT Security / Code Auto-
mation
Kibbutz, Israel
engageiot.com

Enigmatos (5)
IoT Security / Automotive
Yavne, Israel
enigmatos.com

Enigmedia (17)
Data Security / Secure
Communications
San Sebastian, Spain
enigmedia.es

Ensign Infosecurity (255)
MSSP / Managed Services
Kuala Lumpur, Malaysia
ensigninfosecurity.com

**Ensilo (acquired by
Fortinet, 2019)** (86)
Security Analytics / Breach
Detection
San Francisco, CA, USA
ensilo.com

Ensure Technologies (26)
IAM
Ypsilanti, MI, USA
ensuretech.com

Ensurity (42)
IAM / 2FA
Hyderabad, India
ensurity.com

Entersekt (144)
IAM / Authentication &
Fraud Protection for Banks
Stellenbosch, South Africa
entersekt.com

Entreda (22)
Endpoint Monitoring and
Control
Santa Clara, CA, USA
entreda.com

Entrust Datacard (2,148)
Data Security / Key Man-
agement, CA
Minneapolis, MN, USA
entrustdatacard.com

Envault (3)
Data Security
Espoo, Finland
envaultcorp.com

Enveil (23)
Data Security / Encryption
of Data in Use
Washington, DC, USA
enveil.com

Envieta (84)
Data Security / Hardware
Security Modules
Columbia, MD, USA
envieta.com

eperi (26)
Data Security / Encryption
Pfungstadt, Germany
eperi.de/en

Equiinet (18)
Network / Firewall UTM
for Voice
Las Vegas, NV, USA
equiinet.com

Ericom (93)
Network / Browser Isola-
tion
Closter, NJ, USA
ericomshield.com

ERMES Cyber Security (11)
Data Security / DLP and
Web Browsing Protection
Turin, Italy
ermessecurity.com

ERMProtect (21)
GRC / Security Awareness
Training
Coral Gables, FL, USA
ermprotect.com

ERPScan (21)
GRC / Business Applica-
tion Security SAP
Amsterdam, Netherlands
erpscan.io

EScan (187)
Endpoint / AV
Mumbai, India
escanav.com

ESCOM (1)
Network / Anti-spam
Oakton, VA, USA
escom.com

eSentire (424)
MSSP / MDR
Cambridge, Canada
esentire.com

ESET (156)
Endpoint / Anti-virus
San Diego, CA, USA
eset.com

ESNC (4)
GRC / SAP Security
Grünwald, Germany
esnc.de

**eSphere Security
Solutions Pvt** (2)
Endpoint / Mobile Defense
Ahmedabad, India
espheresecurity.com

ESTsoft (402)
Endpoint / Android AV
Seoul, South Korea
estsoft.com

Ethoca (acquired by Mastercard) (221)
Fraud Prevention / Transaction Data
Toronto, Canada
ethoca.com

EventSentry (6)
Security Analytics / SIEM
Chicago, IL, USA
eventsentry.com

EventTracker (64)
MSSP / Managed Security Services
Fort Lauderdale, FL, USA
eventtracker.com

Evernym (56)
IAM / Identity Attestation
Herriman, UT, USA
evernym.com

Everspin (15)
Endpoint / Dynamic Image Replacement
Seoul, South Korea
everspin.global

Evident ID (51)
IAM / Identity Verification
Atlanta, GA, USA
evidentid.com

Exabeam (358)
Security Analytics / User Behavior Analytics
San Mateo, CA, USA
exabeam.com

Excelsecu (43)
Data Security / PKI and Data Encryption
Shenzhen, China
excelsecu.com/en/index.html

Exein (9)
IoT Security / IoT
Rome, Italy
exein.io

Exeon Analytics (10)
Security Analytics / Network Monitoring
Zürich, Switzerland
exeon.ch

Exonar (52)
Data Security / Data Discovery
Newbury, UK
exonar.com

Exosphere, Inc. (1)
Endpoint Protection
Campbell, CA, USA
exospheresecurity.com

Expanse (155)
GRC / Vulnerability Scanner
San Francisco, CA, USA
expanse.co

Expel (124)
MSSP / SOC as a Service
Herndon, VA, USA
expel.io

ExpressVPN (12)
Network / VPN
Tortola, British Virgin Islands
expressvpn.com

Extenua (4)
Data Security / Secure File Transfer
San Jose, CA, USA
extenua.com

ExtraHop Networks (451)
Security Analytics / Network Detection and Response
Seattle, WA, USA
extrahop.com

Extreme Networks (280)
IAM / Network Access Control
San Jose, CA, USA
extremenetworks.com

Extunda (8)
IoT Security / IoT Device Management
Istanbul, Turkey
extunda.com

Ezmcom (21)
Endpoint / Security Hardware
Santa Clara, CA, USA
ezmcom.com

EZShield (Sontiq) (39)
Fraud Prevention / Anti-fraud
Baltimore, MD, USA
ezshield.com

F-Secure (4,545)
Endpoint / AV
Helsinki, Finland
f-secure.com

F5 Networks (2,000)
Network / DDoS and Firewall
Seattle, WA, USA
f5.com

FairWarning (168)
Data Security / Cloud Data Security
Clearwater, FL, USA
fairwarning.com

Famoc (42)
Endpoint / MDM
Midleton, Ireland
fancyfon.com

Faraday (82)
Operations / Manager of Managers
Miami, FL, USA
faradaysec.com

Faronics Technologies Inc. (133)
Endpoint Security
Vancouver, Canada
faronics.com

Farsight Security (54)
Threat Intelligence Enrichment from DNS
San Mateo, CA, USA
farsightsecurity.com

Fasoo.com, Inc. (105)
GRC / Digital Rights Management
Seoul, South Korea
fasoo.com

Fast Orientation (5)
Security Analytics / UEBA
Washington, DC, USA
fastorientation.com

Fastly (567)
Network / DDoS Defense
San Francisco, CA, USA
fastly.com

FastpassCorp (106)
IAM / Password Management
Kongens Lyngby, Denmark
fastpasscorp.com

FastPath (49)
GRC / SaaS Authorizations
Des Moines, IA, USA
gofastpath.com

FCI Cyber (939)
MSSP / Device Management
Bloomfield, NJ, USA
fcicyber.com

Feedzai (368)
Fraud Prevention / Anti-fraud
San Mateo, CA, USA
feedzai.com

Note: Numbers in parentheses indicate employee count

Feitian Technologies (8)
IAM
Beijing, China
ftsafe.com

Fenror7 (6)
Operations / Lateral Movement Detection
Herzliya, Israel
fenror7.com

Fidelis Cybersecurity (282)
Security Analytics
Bethesda, MD, USA
fidelissecurity.com

Field Effect Software (28)
MSSP / MDR
Ottawa, Canada
fieldeffect.com

FileOpen Systems (8)
Data Security / DRM
Santa Cruz, CA, USA
fileopen.com

FinalCode (5)
Data Security / IRM
San Jose, CA, USA
finalcode.com

Fingerprint Cards AB (286)
IAM / Biometrics
Gothenburg, Sweden
fingerprints.com

Fingerprint-IT (1)
IAM / Biometrics
Vancouver, Canada
fingerprint-it.com

Finite State (22)
IoT Security / Firmware Monitoring
Columbus, OH, USA
finitestate.io

FireDome (19)
IoT Security / IoT for Device Manufacturers
Tel Aviv, Israel
firedome.io

FireEye (3,086)
Network / Malware Sandbox
Milpitas, CA, USA
fireeye.com

FireMon (224)
Operations / Firewall Policy Management
Overland Park, KS, USA
firemon.com

FirstPoint Mobile Guard (12)
Endpoint / Mobile Device Protection
Netanya, Israel
firstpoint-mg.com

Fischer International Identity (70)
IAM / IAM
Naples, FL, USA
fischerinternational.com

FixMeStick (17)
Endpoint / AV
Montreal, Canada
fixmestick.com

Fixnix (45)
GRC / SaaS for SMB
Ashok Nagar, India
fixnix.co

Flashpoint (140)
Threat Intelligence / Dark Web Intel
New York, NY, USA
flashpoint-intel.com

Flexible IR (1)
Operations / Incident Response
Singapore, Singapore
flexibleir.com

Flowmon Networks (122)
Network Monitoring
San Diego, CA, USA
flowmon.com

FlowTraq (3)
Network / Netflow Analysis
Manchester, NH, USA
flowtraq.com

Fluency Corp. (5)
Security Analytics / Network Traffic
College Park, MD, USA
fluencysecurity.com

Flying Cloud (8)
Data Security / Data Flow Analytics
Santa Cruz, CA, USA
flyingcloudtech.com

ForAllSecure (32)
Application Security / Appsec Fuzzing
Pittsburgh, PA, USA
forallsecure.com

ForcePoint (2,495)
GRC / DLP
Austin, TX, USA
forcepoint.com

ForceShield (14)
IoT Security / Bot Protection
Taipei, Taiwan
forceshield.com

Foregenix (81)
GRC / Vulnerability Scanning
Boston, MA, USA
foregenix.com

Forensic Innovations (1)
GRC / Data Discovery & Forensics
St. Johns, FL, USA
fid3.com

ForeScout Technologies (1,133)
Network Access Control
San Jose, CA, USA
forescout.com

Foreseeti (19)
GRC / Vulnerability Scanning
Stockholm, Sweden
foreseeti.com

ForgeRock (547)
IAM
San Francisco, CA, USA
forgerock.com

Fornetix (23)
Data Security / Key Management
Frederick, MD, USA
fornetix.com

Fortanix (37)
Application Security / Runtime Encryption
Mountain View, CA, USA
fortanix.com

Forter (179)
Fraud Prevention
Tel Aviv-Yafo, Israel
Forter.com

Forticode (24)
IAM / Password Grids
Melbourne, Australia
forticode.com

Fortify 24x7 (3)
MSSP / Managed Security Services
Los Angeles, CA, USA
fortify24x7.com

Fortinet (5,735)
Network / UTM
Sunnyvale, CA, USA
fortinet.com

Fortiphyd Logic (7)
IoT Security / ICS
Norcross, GA, USA
fortiphyd.com

FortMesa (3)
GRC / Risk Management
Austerlitz, NY, USA
fortmesa.com

FortyCloud (2)
Network / Cloud VPN
Overland Park, KS, USA
40cloud.com

ForumSystems (28)
Network / XML Firewall
Needham, MA, USA
forumsys.com

Fossa (41)
Application Security /
Open Source Vulnerability
Management
San Francisco, CA, USA
fossa.com

Fox-IT (303)
MSSP / MDR
Delft, Netherlands
fox-it.com

Foxpass (5)
IAM / Cloud LDAP, Google App Authentication
Management
San Francisco, CA, USA
foxpass.com

FoxT (595)
IAM / Authentication
Eden Prairie, MN, USA
foxt.com

Fractal Industries (121)
Operations / Incident
Response
Reston, VA, USA
fractalindustries.com

FraudLabs (5)
Fraud Prevention / Fraud
Detection
Bayan Baru, Malaysia
fraudlabspro.com

Fraudmarc (6)
Fraud Prevention / Email
Fraud Prevention
Atlanta, GA, USA
fraudmarc.com

FRS Labs (18)
Fraud Prevention / Fraud
Detection
Bangalore, India
frslabs.com

FST Biometrics (47)
IAM / Facial Recognition
Biometrics
Holon, Israel
fstbm.com

Fudo Security (42)
IAM / Privileged Access
Management
Newark, CA, USA
fudosecurity.com

Full Armor Systems (6)
Network / Content URL
Filtering
Conroe, TX, USA
fullarmorsys.com

FullArmor (24)
Network / Policy Management
Boston, MA, USA
fullarmor.com

FuseMail (56)
Email Security
Burnaby, Canada
fusemail.com

Futurae (12)
IAM / Authentication
Zürich, Switzerland
futurae.com

FutureX (58)
Data Security / Encryption
HSM
Bulverde, TX, USA
futurex.com

Fuzzbuzz (4)
Application Security /
Appsec Fuzzing
Mountain View, CA, USA
fuzzbuzz.io

Fyde (28)
IAM / Access Control
Palo Alto, CA, USA
fyde.com

G Data Software (285)
Endpoint / Anti-virus
Bochum, Germany
gdatasoftware.com

GajShield (37)
Network / Firewall
Mumbai, India
gajshield.com

Galaxkey (24)
Data Security / Secure File
and Message Transfer
London, UK
galaxkey.com

Galvanize (444)
GRC / Risk Management
Vancouver, Canada
wegalvanize.com

Gama Operations (7)
Network / Secure PBX
Petah Tikva, Israel
gamaoperations.com

GamaSec (4)
GRC / Web Scanning
Herzelia Pituach, Israel
gamasec.com

Garrison (159)
Network / Browser Isolation
London, UK
garrison.com

Gatefy (12)
Email Security
Miami, FL, USA
gatefy.com

GateWatcher (39)
Network / Threat Detection
Paris, France
gatewatcher.com

GB & Smith (57)
GRC / SAP Audit
Lille, France
gbandsmith.com

Gemalto (11,210)
IAM
Meudon Cedex, France
gemalto.com

GENAPT Technology Labs (11)
GRC Platform
Hyderabad, India
genapt.com

Genians (51)
IoT Security / Device Fingerprinting
Anyang-si, South Korea
genians.com

GeoCodex (6)
IAM / Access Control
Hollywood, CA, USA
geocodex.com

GeoLang (7)
GRC / DLP
Cardiff, UK
geolang.com

GeoTrust Inc. (32)
Data Security / Encryption
Mountain View, CA, USA
geotrust.com

GetData Forensics (9)
GRC / Forensics
Kogarah, Australia
forensicexplorer.com

GFI Software (417)
Email Security / Anti-spam
Austin, TX, USA
gfi.com

GhangorCloud (10)
GRC / DLP
San Jose, CA, USA
ghangorcloud.com

Note: Numbers in parentheses indicate employee count

GhostMail (1)
Email Security / Secure
Email
Zug, Switzerland
ghostmail.com

Gigamon (866)
Network / Span Port
Mirroring
Santa Clara, CA, USA
gigamon.com

GigaNetworks (20)
MSSP / Managed Security
Services
Miami, FL, USA
giganetworks.com

GigaTrust (37)
Data Security / Document
Security
Herndon, VA, USA
gigatrust.com

Gita Technologies (42)
Network / SIGINT Offensive
Tel Aviv, Israel
gitatechnologies.com

GitGuardian (24)
Threat Intelligence /
Github Credential Monitoring
Paris, France
gitguardian.com

Gladius.io (8)
Network / DDoS Defense
Washington, DC, USA
gladius.io

Glasswall Solutions (63)
Operations / Document
Scrubbing
West End, UK
glasswallsolutions.com

GlassWire
Endpoint Firewall
Austin, TX, USA
glasswire.com

Gleg
GRC / Vulnerability Management
Moscow, Russia
gleg.net

Glimmerglass (17)
Fraud Prevention / Cyber
Terrorism & Fraud Prevention
Hayward, CA, USA
glimmerglass.com

Glitchi (1)
Data Security / Secure
Photo Sharing
Palo Alto, CA, USA
glitchi.me

Global ID
IAM / Biometrics
Lausanne, Switzerland
global-id.ch

Global Velocity (10)
Data Security / Cloud DLP
St. Louis, MO, USA
globalvelocity.com

GlobalSCAPE, Inc. (128)
Network / Secure File
Transfer
San Antonio, TX, USA
globalscape.com

GlobalSign (377)
IAM / Authentication &
Identity Service Provider
Portsmouth, NH, USA
globalsign.com

Gluu (18)
IAM / Access Control
Austin, TX, USA
gluu.org

Go-Trust (11)
IAM / Authentication
Taichung City, Taiwan
go-trust.com

GoAnywhere (1)
Data Security / Automated
& Secure File Transfer
Ashland, NE, USA
goanywhere.com

**GOCOM Systems and
Solutions Corporation** (23)
Network / Firewall
Mandaluyong City, Philippines
gocomsystems.net

Gold Lock (1)
Data Security / Mobile
Encryption
Ramat Gan, Israel
secure.gold-lock.com

GovReady
GRC / Self-Serve Scanning
Washington, DC, USA
govready.com

GrammaTech (95)
Application Security /
Code Scanning
Ithaca, NY, USA
grammatech.com

Granite (22)
GRC / Risk Management
Tampere, Finland
granitegrc.com

Graphite Software (14)
Endpoint / Mobile Containers
Ottawa, Canada
graphitesoftware.com

Graphus (12)
Email Security / Anti-phishing
Reston, VA, USA
graphus.ai

Great Bay Software (26)
IAM / Network Access
Control
Bloomington, MN, USA
greatbaysoftware.com

GreatHorn (35)
Email Security / Anti-phishing
Waltham, MA, USA
greathorn.com

Green Armor (1)
IAM
Hackensack, NJ, USA
greenarmor.com

Green Hills Software (1,183)
Endpoint / Secure OS
Santa Barbara, CA, USA
ghs.com

GreeNet (16)
Network / DPI for Carriers
Beijing, China
greenet.net.cn

GreenTeam Internet (1)
Network / Cloud URL
Filtering
Tel Aviv-Yafo, Israel
greentm.co.uk

Greenview Data, Inc. (11)
MSSP / Managed Services
Ann Arbor, MI, USA
greenviewdata.com

Grey Wizard (17)
Network Web Protection
Poznań, Poland
greywizard.com

GreyCortex (34)
Network / Traffic Analysis
Brno, Czech Republic
greycortex.com

GreyNoise (7)
Threat Intelligence / Dark
Web Collection
Washington, DC, USA
greynoise.io

Ground Labs (43)
GRC / Data Discovery
Singapore, Singapore
groundlabs.com

GroupSense (23)
Threat Intelligence / Dark
Web Collection
Arlington, VA, USA
groupsense.io

GTB Technologies (50)
GRC / Data Leak Preven-
tion (DLP)
Newport Beach, CA, USA
gtbtechnologies.com

Guard Knox (26)
IoT Security / Automotive
Tel Aviv, Israel
guardknox.com

Guardian Analytics (98)
GRC / Forensics
Mountain View, CA, USA
guardiananalytics.com

Guardian Digital Inc. (2)
Endpoint / Secure Linux
Midland Park, NJ, USA
guardiandigital.com

GuardiCore (141)
Application Security / App
Monitoring
Tel Aviv, Israel
guardicore.com

Guardsquare (47)
Application Security /
Mobile App Protection
Leuven, Belgium
guardsquare.com

Guidepoint Security (304)
MSSP / Managed Services
Herndon, VA, USA
guidepointsecurity.com

Guidewire (2,219)
GRC / Security Ratings
Foster City, CA, USA
guidewire.com

GuruCul (129)
Security Analytics
El Segundo, CA, USA
gurucul.com

Gyomo (3)
Training / Anti-phishing
Herndon, VA, USA
gyomo.com

H3C (2,806)
Network / Secure Gateway
Beijing, China
h3c.com

Hack the Box (115)
Training / Cyber Range
Kent, UK
hackthebox.eu

HackerOne (813)
Operations / Zero Day
Research and Bounties
San Francisco, CA, USA
hackerone.com

HALOCK Security Labs
(35)
Operations / Incident
Response
Schaumburg, IL, USA
halock.com

Halon (22)
Email Security / Anti-spam
Gothenburg, Sweden
halon.io

Haltdos (12)
Network / DDoS Defense
Noida, India
haltdos.com

Hauri (3)
Endpoint / Anti-virus
Seoul, South Korea
hauri.net

Hawk Network Defense (5)
Security Analytics
Dallas, TX, USA
hawkdefense.com

Haystax (62)
Security Analytics / Threat
Analytics
McLean, VA, USA
haystax.com

HDIV Security (21)
Application Security /
Code Analysis
Donostia-San Sebastián,
Spain
hdivsecurity.com

HDN (17)
Network / Security
Switches
Guro-gu, South Korea
handream.net

Helm Solutions (22)
GRC / Compliance Man-
agement
New York, NY, USA
helm.global

Help Systems (596)
Endpoint / IBM iSecurity
Products
Eden Prairie, MN, USA
helpsystems.com

HENSOLDT Cyber
IoT Security / IoT
Taufkirchen, Germany
hensoldt-cyber.com

Herjavec Group (329)
MSSP / Managed Services
Toronto, Canada
herjavecgroup.com

**Hermetric Software
Services**
Network / Web Security
Kiryat Tiv'on, Israel
hermetric.com

Hexamail (2)
Email Security / Anti-spam
and Anti-virus
Pensham, UK
hexamail.com

Note: Numbers in parentheses indicate employee count

Hexis Cyber Solutions (11)
Endpoint / EDR
Hanover, MD, USA
hexiscyber.com

HID Global (2,110)
IAM / Authentication
Austin, TX, USA
hidglobal.com

Hideez (20)
IAM / Hardware Credential Storage
Redwood City, CA, USA
hideez.com

HighCastle Cybersecurity (3)
MSSP / Managed Services
New York, NY, USA
highcastlecybersecurity.com

Hillstone Networks (267)
Network / Data Analytics Firewall Protection
Santa Clara, CA, USA
hillstonenet.com

Hitachi ID Systems, Inc. (140)
IAM
Calgary, Canada
Hitachi-id.com

Hmatix (4)
IoT Security / IoT Network Security
San Jose, CA, USA
hmatix.com

HOB Networking (1)
Network / VPN
Cadolzburg, Germany
hob.de

HoloNet Security (11)
Operations / Incident Investigation
Sunnyvale, CA, USA
holonetsecurity.com

Hopzero (14)
Network / Hop Minimization
Austin, TX, USA
hopzero.com

Horangi (71)
Network / AWS Vulnerability Scanning
Singapore, Singapore
horangi.com

Hornetsecurity (73)
Email Security
Hannover, Germany
hornetsecurity.com

Huawei (4,000)
Network / Firewalls
Shenzhen, China
www1.huawei.com/en/products/data-communication/network-security/index.htm

Hueya (6)
Training / Phishing Simulation
Bend, OR, USA
hueya.io

Human Presence (10)
Network Bot Detection
Greenville, SC, USA
humanpresence.io

Humio (37)
Security Analytics / Log Analysis
London, UK
humio.com

Humming Heads (2)
Endpoint / Whitelisting
Tokyo, Japan
hummingheads.co.jp/english/product/dep/index.html

Hunters.AI (22)
Security Analytics / Breach Detection and Response
Tel Aviv, Israel
hunters.ai

Huntress Labs (10)
Operations / SaaS Malware Discovery
Baltimore, MD, USA
huntresslabs.com

Huntsman (21)
Security Analytics / SIEM
Chatswood, Australia
huntsmansecurity.com

Hushmail (366)
Data Security / Private Email
Vancouver, Canada
hushmail.com

Hyas (18)
Threat Intelligence / Attribution Intelligence
Victoria, Canada
hyas.com

Hyperion Gray (9)
Network / Open Source Web Security
Concord, NC, USA
hyperiongray.com

Hypersecu Information Systems, Inc. (9)
IAM / OTP Tokens
Richmond, Canada
hypersecu.com

Hypersonica (6)
Network / Web Safety
London, UK
hypersonica.com

Hypori (12)
Endpoint / Mobile Device Management
Austin, TX, USA
hypori.com

HYPR (62)
IAM / Biometrics
New York, NY, USA
hypr.com

Hysolate (40)
Endpoint / Workspace Isolation via VMs
Tel Aviv-Yafo, Israel
hysolate.com

HyTrust (147)
Operations / Cloud Security Automation
Mountain View, CA, USA
hytrust.com

i-Sprint (94)
IAM
Singapore, Singapore
i-sprint.com

I-Tracing (126)
MSSP / Managed Security Services
Puteaux, France
i-tracing.com

I-Trap Internet Security Services (1)
Network / Intrusion Detection System
Doylestown, OH, USA
i-trap.net

IBM (2,000)
MSSP / Managed Services
Armonk, NY, USA
ibm.com

iboss (249)
Network / Secure Web Gateway
Boston, MA, USA
iboss.com

Icon Labs (acquired by Sectigo)
IoT Security / PKI for IoT
IA, USA
iconlabs.com

ICS2 (1)
IoT Security / ICS
Jerusalem, Israel
ics2.com

ID Control (3)
IAM
The Hague, Netherlands
idcontrol.com

ID Experts (73)
GRC / Incident Response
Portland, OR, USA
idexperscorp.com

ID R&D Inc. (16)
IAM / Biometrics
New York, NY, USA
idrnd.net

ID.me (139)
IAM / Credential Management
McLean, VA, USA
id.me

idappcom (8)
Network / Packet Capture
and Analysis
Ludlow, UK
idappcom.com

Idaptive (118)
IAM / Access Management
Santa Clara, CA, USA
idaptive.com

Idax Software (6)
IAM / IAM
Petersfield, UK
idaxsoftware.com

IDECSI (22)
Email Security / Email
Monitoring and Auditing
Paris, France
idecsi.com/en

IDEE Blockchain Software
(18)
IAM / Identity Platform
Munich, Germany
getidee.com

IDEMIA (10,787)
IAM / Identity Augmentation
Reston, VA, USA
idemia.com

IDENprotect (9)
IAM / Authentication
London, UK
idenprotect.com

IDenticard (101)
IAM / Access Control
Manheim, PA, USA
identicard.com

Identify Security Software
(2)
IAM / Biometrics
Boca Raton, FL, USA
identifyss.com

Identify3D (26)
Data Security / Design
Data Encryption
San Francisco, CA, USA
identify3d.com

Identity Automation (111)
IAM / Identity Management
Houston, TX, USA
identityautomation.com

IdentityLogix (3)
IAM / Access Data Analytics
Crown Point, IN, USA
identitylogix.com

Identiv (208)
IAM / Credentials
Fremont, CA, USA
identiv.com

**IdenTrust (part of HID
Global)** (68)
Data Security / Certificate
Authority
Fremont, CA, USA
identrust.com

Idera (365)
GRC / SQL Compliance
Houston, TX, USA
idera.com

IDnomic (121)
IAM / IAM
Issy-les-Moulineaux,
France
idnomic.com

IDology (79)
IAM / Authentication
Atlanta, GA, USA
idology.com

IDRRA (5)
GRC / Third Party Risk
Management
New York, NY, USA
idrra.com

iDSync (5)
IAM / AD Integration
Perrysburg, OH, USA
idsync.com

idwall (103)
Fraud Prevention / Fraud
Detection
São Paulo, Brazil
idwall.co

Igloo Security (46)
MSSP / Managed Security
Services
Seoul, South Korea
igloosec.co.kr

IGLOO Software (163)
GRC / Security Management
Kitchener, Canada
igloosoftware.com

**Ikarus Security Software
GmbH** (25)
Endpoint / Android AV
Vienna, Austria
ikarussecurity.com

Ilantus (193)
IAM / Identity Management
Schaumburg, IL, USA
ilantus.com

Illumio (337)
Endpoint Monitoring
Sunnyvale, CA, USA
illumio.com

illusive Networks (112)
Deception
New York, NY, USA
illusivenetworks.com

ImageWare Systems, Inc.
(95)
IAM / Biometrics
San Diego, CA, USA
iwsinc.com

Immersive Labs (94)
Training / Cyber Range
Bristol, UK
immersivelabs.com

Immunant (4)
Application Security /
Code Hardening
Irvine, CA, USA
immunant.com

Immunity (43)
GRC / Vulnerability Management
Miami, FL, USA
immunityinc.com

Immuniweb
Application Security / Web
Scanning
Geneva, Switzerland
immuniweb.com

Impact (423)
Fraud Prevention / Ad
Tech Security
Santa Barbara, CA, USA
impact.com

Imperva (1,185)
Network / Web Application
Firewall
Redwood Shores, CA, USA
imperva.com

Note: Numbers in parentheses indicate employee count

Imprivata, Inc. (538)
IAM
Lexington, MA, USA
imprivata.com

Impulse (35)
IAM / Network Access
Control
Tampa, FL, USA
impulse.com

Imvision Technologies (17)
Network Behavior Analysis
Ramat Gan, Israel
imvisiontech.com

InBay Technologies (20)
IAM / Mobile Authenti-
cator
Kanata, Canada
inbaytech.com

InCyber (5)
Operations / Employee
Monitoring
Cherry Hill Township, DE,
USA
incyber1.com

Indegy (60)
IoT Security / Visibility
for ICS
New York, NY, USA
indegy.com

Indeni (70)
Operations / Security
Automation
San Francisco, CA, USA
indeni.com

Indusface (57)
Network / Cloud WAF
Vodadora, India
indusface.com

Infineon (1,000)
IAM / Smart Card Solu-
tions
Neubiberg, Germany
infineon.com

InfoAssure (12)
Data Security / Security for
Documents
Chestertown, MD, USA
infoassure.net

Infoblox, Inc. (1,255)
Network / DNS Security
Santa Clara, CA, USA
infoblox.com

Infobyte (47)
Network / Intrusion Detection Platform
Miami, FL, USA
infobytesec.com

Infocyte (37)
Endpoint Detection
Austin, TX, USA
infocyte.com

InfoExpress Inc. (41)
IAM / Network Access
Control
Santa Clara, CA, USA
infoexpress.com

Infor (200)
GRC / Continuous Mon-
itoring
New York, NY, USA
infor.com

Informatica (500)
Data Security / Data
Masking
Redwood City, CA, USA
informatica.com

**Information Security
Corporation** (17)
Data Security / PKI
Oak Park, IL, USA
infoseccorp.com

infOsci (9)
Data Security / Certificate
Management
Washington, DC, USA
Ci4.us

Infosec Global (31)
Data Security / Certificate
Discovery
North York, Canada
infosecglobal.com

Infosec Inc. (16)
Endpoint / Mainframe
Event Monitoring
Centreville, VA, USA
infosecinc.com

Infowatch (176)
GRC / DLP
Moscow, Russia
infowatch.com

InGate (23)
Network / Firewall
Sundbyberg, Sweden
ingate.com

Inky (25)
Email Security / An-
ti-phishing
Rockville, MD, USA
inky.com

Innefu Labs Pvt Ltd. (90)
Network / Internet Surveillance for Law Enforcement
New Delhi, India
innefu.com

Innosec (8)
GRC / DLP
Hod HaSharon, Israel
innosec.com

**Innovya Traceless
Biometrics** (3)
IAM / Biometrics
Kiryat Ono, Israel
innovya.com

Inpher (23)
Data Security / Processing
of Private Data
New York, NY, USA
inpher.io

Inpixon (67)
Network / Rogue Wifi AP
Location
Palo Alto, CA, USA
inpixon.com

InQuest (25)
Data Security / DLP
Arlington, VA, USA
inquest.net

INSIDE Secure (200)
Endpoint / Smartphone &
Mobile Device Security
Meyreuil, France
insidesecure.com

Insider Spyder (2)
Operations / Employee
Monitoring
Chantilly, VA, USA
insiderspyder.com

Insignary (12)
Application Security /
Open Source Vulnerability
Management
Seoul, South Korea
insignary.com

Instasafe (27)
Network / Cloud VPN
Gateway
Bangalore, India
instasafe.com

Intego Inc. (18)
Network / Personal Fire-
wall
Seattle, WA, USA
intego.com

Integrated Corporation (1)
IAM
Sheungwan, Hong Kong
integrated.com

Intel 471 (50)
Threat Intelligence / Threat
Actor Intelligence
Amsterdam, Netherlands
intel471.com

Inteligensa (88)
IAM / Smart Card Solutions
Caracas, Venezuela
Inteligensa.com

Intelisecure (181)
MSSP / Managed Services
Greenwood Village, CO, USA
intelisecure.com

Inteller (3)
Threat Intelligence Platform
Israel
inteller.com

Intelliagg (5)
Threat Intelligence
London, UK
intelliagg.com

IntelliGO Networks (30)
Security Analytics / Breach Detection
Toronto, Canada
intelligonetworks.com

Intensity Analytics (10)
IAM / Behavior Metrics
Warrenton, VA, USA
intensityanalytics.com

Intercrypto
Data Security / File Encryption
Seattle, WA, USA
intercrypto.com

Interface Masters Technologies (63)
Network / Intrusion Prevention
San Jose, CA, USA
interfacemasters.com

Interfocus Technologies (4)
Operations / User Behavior Monitoring
Costa Mesa, CA, USA
interfocus.us

Interguard (8)
Operations / Employee Monitoring
Westport, CT, USA
interguardsoftware.com

Interlink Networks (6)
IAM
Ann Arbor, MI, USA
interlinknetworks.com

Interset (86)
Security Analytics
Ottawa, Canada
interset.com

Intertrust Technologies (252)
IoT Security / PKI for IoT
Sunnyvale, CA, USA
intertrust.com

Intezer (30)
Operations / Malware Analysis
New York, NY, USA
intezer.com

Intrinsic (6)
Application Security / Appsec Code Hardening
San Francisco, CA, USA
intrinsic.com

Intrinsic-ID (37)
IAM / Device Authentication
Sunnyvale, CA, USA
intrinsic-id.com

Introspective Networks (7)
Network / VPN
Broomfield, CO, USA
introspectivenetworks.com

Intruder (9)
GRC / Vulnerability Scanner
London, UK
intruder.io

Intrusion Inc. (27)
Network / IDS and IPS
Richardson, TX, USA
intrusion.com

Intsights (150)
Threat Intelligence / Deep & Dark Web
New York, NY, USA
intsights.com

Intufo
IAM / Access Control
Washington, DC, USA
intufo.com

Invincea (27)
Operations / Incident Response
Fairfax, VA, USA
invincea.com

Invinsec (14)
MSSP / Managed Security Services
Cheltenham, UK
invinsec.com

InvizBox (6)
Network / Portable VPN hardware
Dublin, Ireland
invizbox.com

inWebo (28)
IAM / Strong Authentication
Paris, France
inwebo.com

Ioetec (4)
IoT Security / Device Security
Sheffield, UK
ioetec.com

Ionic Security (145)
Data Security / Data Privacy & Protection
Atlanta, GA, USA
ionicsecurity.com

Ionu (2)
Data Security / Secure Data Management
Los Gatos, CA, USA
ionu.com

IoT Defense (2)
IoT Security / Network, Home Firewall for IoT Devices
Falls Church, VA, USA
iotdef.com

IoTSploit
IoT Security / IoT Scanning
Singapore, Singapore
iotsploit.co

Iovation (214)
IAM / Authentication
Portland, OR, USA
iovation.com

IP Infusion (331)
MSSP / Managed Services
Santa Clara, CA, USA
ipinfusion.com

IProov (32)
IAM / Authentication
London, UK
iproov.com

Ipswitch (325)
Network / Secure File Transfer
Burlington, MA, USA
ipswitch.com

IPV Security (17)
MSSP / Monitoring
Ra'anana, Israel
ipvsecurity.com

IPV Tec (1)
Network / Website Monitoring
Ra'anana, Israel
ipvtec.com

Note: Numbers in parentheses indicate employee count

IPVanish (8)
Network / VPN
Dallas, TX, USA
ipvanish.com

Iraje (18)
IAM / Access Control
Mumbai, India
iraje.com

Irdeto (1,169)
IoT Security / Entertainment Systems
Hoofddorp, Netherlands
irdeto.com

Iris Network Systems (23)
Network / Netflow Analysis
Alpharetta, GA, USA
irisns.com

IRM Security (82)
GRC / Risk Management
Cheltenham, UK
irmsecurity.com

IronNet Cybersecurity (245)
Network / Traffic Analysis
Fulton, MD, USA
ironnet.com

IronScales (36)
GRC / Anti-phishing Gamification
Tel Aviv, Israel
ironscales.com

IS Decisions (29)
IAM / Access Control
Bidart, France
isdecisions.com

ISARA (56)
Data Security / Encryption
Waterloo, Canada
isara.com

ISARR (4)
GRC / Asset Management
London, UK
isarr.com

IsItYou (3)
IAM / Mobile Face Recognition
Lod, Israel
isityou.biz

IStorage (36)
Data Security / Hardware Encryption
Perivale, UK
istorage-uk.com

IT Security, Inc. (1)
Network / Application, Cloud & Network Security
Pittsburgh, PA, USA
it-security-inc.com

ITC Secure Networking (136)
MSSP / Managed Security Services
London, UK
itcsecure.com

ITConcepts (99)
IAM / IAM for Small Business
Bonn, Germany
itconcepts.net

iTrust (46)
GRC / Vulnerability Management
Labege, France
itrust.fr

iTrust, Inc. (3)
GRC / Third Party Risk Scores
Atlanta, GA, USA
itrustinc.com

itWatch (1)
Endpoint Security & Data Loss Prevention
Munich, Germany
itwatch.info

Ivanti (1,461)
Endpoint Management
South Jordan, UT, USA
ivanti.com

iWelcome (75)
IAM / Identity Management
Amersfoort, Netherlands
iwelcome.com

Ixia (1,271)
Network Visibility
Calabasas, CA, USA
ixiacom.com

iZOOlogic (10)
Threat Intelligence
London, UK
izoologic.com

Janus Technologies, Inc. (6)
Endpoint / BIOS Protection
Sunnyvale, CA, USA
janustech.com

Janusnet (11)
Data Security / Data Classification
Milsons Point, Australia
janusnet.com

JASK (acquired by Sumo Logic, 2019) (121)
Security Analytics / SIEM
Austin, TX, USA
jask.com

Jazz Networks (74)
Security Analytics / UEBA
Uxbridge, UK
jazznetworks.com

Jemurai (5)
Operations / Security Program Dashboard
Chicago, IL, USA
jemurai.com

Jeronix (1)
IAM / Identity Intelligence
Israel
jeronix.com

Jiran (1)
GRC / DLP
Daejeon, South Korea
jiran.com

JOESecurity (8)
Operations / Malware Analysis
Reinach, Switzerland
joesecurity.org

JpU (15)
IoT Security / IoT
Petah Tikva, Israel
jpu.io

Jscrambler (40)
Application Security / Security for Javascript
San Francisco, CA, USA
jscrambler.com

Jumio (322)
Fraud Prevention / Identity Verification
Palo Alto, CA, USA
jumio.com

Juniper Networks (2,000)
Network / Firewall
Sunnyvale, CA, USA
juniper.net

K2 Cyber Security (2)
Application Security / Appsec, Zero Day Prevention
San Jose, CA, USA
k2io.com

K7Computing (330)
Endpoint / AV
Sholinganallur, India
k7computing.com

Kandji (10)
Endpoint / MDM for Apple Devices
San Diego, CA, USA
kandji.io

Kaprica Security (3)
Endpoint / Mobile Device
Security
College Park, MD, USA
kaprica.com

Karamba Security (46)
IoT Security / Automotive
Defense
Hod HaSharon, Israel
karambasecurity.com

Kasada (22)
Network / Web Defense
Sydney, Australia
kasada.io

Kaseya (575)
IAM / Managed SSO and
MFA
New York, NY, USA
kaseya.com

Kaspersky Lab (3,608)
Endpoint / Anti-virus
Moscow, Russia
kaspersky.com

Kaymera (38)
Endpoint / Mobile Defense
Herzliya, Israel
kaymera.com

Kazuar (21)
Data Security / Secure
Work Environment
Tel Aviv, Israel
kazuar-tech.com

KeeeX (8)
Data Security / Document
Security
Marseille, France
keeex.me

KeePass Password Safe
IAM / IAM
Metzingen, Germany
keepass.info

Keeper Security, Inc. (139)
IAM / Password Manager
Chicago, IL, USA
keepersecurity.com

KeepSafe (21)
Data Security / Mobile
Encryption
San Francisco, CA, USA
getkeepsafe.com

Keezel (11)
Network / Wifi Firewall
Amsterdam, Netherlands
keezel.co

**Kenna Security
(rebranded from Risk I/O)**
(153)
VM and Threat Feeds
San Francisco, CA, USA
kennasecurity.com

Kernel, Inc. (1)
MSSP / Managed Services
Fayetteville, AR, USA
kernelops.com

KernelCare (1)
Endpoint / Linux Kernel
Patching
Palo Alto, CA, USA
kernelcare.com

Kernelios (10)
Training / Simulation and
Training
Rishon LeZion, Israel
kernelios.com

Kernelsec
Data Security / Document
Encryption
Shanghai, China
serpurity.com

KETS Quantum Security
(12)
Data Security / Secure
Communications
Bristol, UK
kets-quantum.com

Keyfactor (94)
Data Security / PKI as a
Service
Independence, OH, USA
keyfactor.com

KeyNexus (11)
Data Security / Cloud Key
Storage
Victoria, Canada
keynexus.net

Keyp (8)
IAM / Identity Platform
Munich, Germany
keyp.io

Keypasco AB (16)
IAM / Multi-factor Au-
thentication
Gothenburg, Sweden
keypasco.com

Keystroke DNA (7)
IAM / Biometrics Key-
stroke Analysis
Tallinn, Estonia
keystrokedna.com

KEYW (1,061)
Operations / Forensics
Hanover, MD, USA
keywcorp.com

Kindite (20)
Data Security / Encryption
Tel Aviv, Israel
kindite.com

KinectIQ (11)
IAM / Identity-Based
Encryption
Woodbury, MN, USA
knectiq.com

Kingston Technology
(1,384)
Data Security / Encrypted
Storage
Fountain Valley, CA, USA
kingston.com

**Klocwork (a Rogue Wave
company)** (299)
Application Security /
Source Code Analysis
Louisville, CO, USA
roguewave.com

KMSChain (3)
Data Security / Cloud Key
Management
Yerevan, Armenia
kmschain.com

KnowBe4 (620)
GRC / Phishing and Secu-
rity Awareness
Clearwater, FL, USA
knowbe4.com

Kobalt (5)
MSSP / Managed Security
Services
Vancouver, Canada
kobalt.io

KOBIL Systems (92)
IAM / Authentication
Worms, Germany
kobil.com

Konduto (89)
Fraud Prevention / Fraud
Detection
São Paulo, Brazil
konduto.com

KoolSpan, Inc. (43)
Data Security / Secure
Communications
Bethesda, MD, USA
koolspan.com

Kount (161)
Fraud Prevention / Identity
Verification
Boise, ID, USA
kount.com

Kovrr (19)
GRC / Risk Monitoring for
Insurance Providers
London, UK
kovrr.com

Kratikal Tech (76)
GRC / Risk Measurement
Noida, India
kratikal.com

Note: Numbers in parentheses indicate employee count

Kriptos (17)
Data Security / Data Classification
Sausalito, CA, USA
kriptos.io

Kroll (200)
Operations / Risk Mitigation & Response
New York, NY, USA
kroll.com

KromTech (625)
Endpoint / Android AV
London, UK
kromtech.com

Kryptaxe (2)
Fraud Prevention / Account Takeover Protection
New York, NY, USA
kryptaxe.com

Kryptus (48)
Data Security / HSM
Campinas São Paulo, Brazil
kryptus.com

Kyber Security (3)
Data Security / Software Protection
Montreal, Canada
kybersecurity.com

KYND (17)
GRC / Risk Management
London, UK
kynd.io

L7 Defense (7)
Network API Security
Be'er Sheva, Israel
l7defense.com

Lacework (65)
Application Security / Cloud Deployment Security
Mountain View, CA, USA
lacework.com

LastLine (143)
Threat Intelligence / Honeynet Malware IOCs
Redwood City, CA, USA
lastline.com

LastPass (23)
IAM / Password Manager
Fairfax, VA, USA
lastpass.com

Lastwall (11)
IAM / Access Management
Mountain View, CA, USA
lastwall.com

Lavabit (182)
Email Security / Encrypted Email
Dallas, TX, USA
lavabit.com

LeapFILE (7)
Data Security / Secure File Transfer
Cupertino, CA, USA
leapfile.com

LeapYear Technologies (28)
Data Security / Analyze Private Information
Berkeley, CA, USA
leapyear.ai

Ledger (176)
Data Security / USB Key Storage for Cryptocurrencies
Paris, France
ledger.com

Lepide (158)
Data Security / Data Discovery
Austin, TX, USA
lepide.com

Levl Technologies (20)
IoT Security / Device Identity
Palo Alto, CA, USA
levltech.com

LGS Innovations (840)
Application Security / Code Security
Herndon, VA, USA
lgsinnovations.com

Libraesva (13)
Email Security
Lecco, Italy
libraesva.com

LifeLock, Symantec (415)
IAM / Personal Identity Theft Protection
Tempe, AZ, USA
lifelock.com

LifeRaft (35)
Threat Intelligence / OSINT Monitoring
Halifax, Canada
liferaftinc.com

Light Point Security (6)
Network / Secure Web Gateway Proxy
Baltimore, MD, USA
lightpointsecurity.com

Link11 (28)
Network / DDoS Defense
Frankfurt, Germany
link11.de

Liopa (8)
IAM / Biometrics, Liveness Detection
Belfast, UK
liopa.ai

LockLizard Ltd. (1)
Data Security / IRM
London, UK
locklizard.com

LockPath, Inc. (89)
GRC / IT Governance, Risk & Compliance
Overland Park, KS, USA
lockpath.com

Locurity (1)
IAM / Cloud Authentication
Baltimore, MD, USA
locurity.com

LOGbinder (1)
GRC / Application Security Intelligence
Wilmington, DE, USA
logbinder.com

LogDNA (79)
Security Analytics
Mountain View, CA, USA
logdna.com

Loggly (18)
Operations / Log Aggregation
Austin, TX, USA
loggly.com

LogicGate, Inc. (60)
GRC
Chicago, IL, USA
logicgate.com

LogicHub (35)
Operations / Automated Incident Response
Mountain View, CA, USA
logichub.com

LogMeIn (300)
IAM / Password Manager
Boston, MA, USA
logmeininc.com

LogPoint (199)
Security Analytics / SIEM
Copenhagen, Denmark
logpoint.com

LogRhythm (627)
GRC / Log Management
Boulder, CO, USA
logrhythm.com

Logsign (52)
Security Analytics / SIEM
Istanbul, Turkey
logsign.com

Logz.io (157)
Security Analytics /
Cloud Log Collection and
Analysis
Boston, MA, USA
logz.io

LOKD (7)
Data Security / Secure
Communications
Larnaca, Cyprus
lokd.com

Loki (6)
Network / UTM
Izmir, Turkey
getloki.com

**Lookingglass Cyber
Solutions** (308)
Threat Intelligence
Reston, VA, USA
lookingglasscyber.com

Lookout (412)
Endpoint / Mobile Security
for Android & iOS Apps
San Francisco, CA, USA
lookout.com

Loom Systems (28)
Operations / Incident
Response
San Francisco, CA, USA
loomsystems.com

LSoft Technologies (5)
Data Security / Erasure
Mississauga, Canada
lsoft.net

Lucent Sky (3)
Application Security /
Source Code Analysis and
Repair
San Francisco, CA, USA
lucentsky.com

Lucideus (251)
GRC / Risk Measurement
Okhla Phase III, India
lucideus.com

LUCY Security (8)
GRC / Anti-phishing
Training
Zug, Switzerland
lucysecurity.com

Lumeta (48)
Network Discovery
Somerset, NJ, USA
lumeta.com

LunarLine (114)
GRC / VM and Log Man-
agement
Arlington, VA, USA
lunarline.com

Lybero.net (10)
Data Security / Multi-ad-
min Key Authorization
Villers-Lès-Nancy, France
lybero.net

**Lynx Software
Technologies** (86)
Endpoint / Containers
San Jose, CA, USA
lynx.com

Macmon (37)
Network Access Control
Berlin, Germany
macmon.eu

Made4Biz (1)
IAM / Mobile Authentica-
tion (Banking)
Savyon, Israel
israeldefense.co.il/en

Magen (1)
Network / Surveillance
Tel Aviv, Israel
ma-gen.com

MagicCube (1)
IAM / Secure Digital
Transactions
Santa Clara, CA, USA
magic3inc.com

Magnet Forensics (240)
Operations / Forensics
Waterloo, Canada
magnetforensics.com

Maidsafe (1)
Data Security / Block-
chain-like Payment System
Ayr, UK
maidsafe.net

MailCleaner (7)
Email Security
Saint-Sulpice, Switzerland
mailcleaner.net

MailInBlack (53)
Email Security / Anti-spam
Marseille, France
mailinblack.com

Mailspect (1)
Email Security
Tarrytown, NY, USA
mailspect.com

Mako Networks Ltd. (40)
MSSP / Managed Services
Elgin, IL, USA
makonetworks.com

MalCrawler (16)
IoT Security / Anti-mal-
ware
Washington, DC, USA
malcrawler.com

Malware Patrol (1)
Threat Intelligence Feed
São Paulo, Brazil
malwarepatrol.net

Malwarebytes (709)
Endpoint / Anti-virus
Santa Clara, CA, USA
malwarebytes.org

Managed Methods (22)
GRC / Cloud Access
Monitor
Boulder, CO, USA
managedmethods.com

**ManageEngine (Zoho
Corp.)** (87)
GRC / Security Manage-
ment
Pleasanton, CA, USA
manageengine.com

Mancala Networks (5)
Network Monitoring
Meylan, France
mancalanetworks.com

Mantis Networks (8)
Network / Visibility
Reston, VA, USA
mantisnet.com

Mantix4 (5)
Security Analytics / Threat
Hunting
Englewood, CO, USA
mantix4.com

MarkMonitor (504)
Threat Intelligence / Brand
Monitoring
San Francisco, CA, USA
markmonitor.com

Masergy (594)
MSSP / Managed Services
Plano, TX, USA
masergy.com

Matrix42 (250)
Endpoint / EDR
Paris, France
matrix42.com

Max Secure Software (95)
Endpoint Protection
Pune, India
maxpcsecure.com

Maxmind (52)
Fraud Prevention / Geolo-
cation
Waltham, MA, USA
maxmind.com

Maxxsure (29)
GRC / Risk Management
Richardson, TX, USA
maxxsure.com

Note: Numbers in parentheses indicate employee count

MazeBolt Technologies
Testing for DDoS
Ramat Gan, Israel
mazebolt.com

MB Connect Line (24)
IoT Security / ICS Firewall
Dinkelsbühl, Germany
mbconnectline.com

MBX (134)
Endpoint / Appliance
& Embedded Systems
Security
Libertyville, IL, USA
mbx.com

McAfee (9,663)
Endpoint / AV
Santa Clara, CA, USA
mcafee.com

MeasuredRisk (27)
GRC / Risk Management
Arlington, VA, USA
measuredrisk.com

Medcrypt (17)
IoT Security / Medical
Device Protection
Encinitas, CA, USA
medcrypt.co

MediGate (47)
IoT Security / Medical
Devices
Tel Aviv, Israel
medigate.io

Menlo Security (150)
Network / Browser Isola-
tion
Palo Alto, CA, USA
menlosecurity.com

MessageControl (15)
Email Security / An-
ti-phishing
Chicago, IL, USA
mailcontrol.net

MessageSolution Inc. (21)
GRC / Email Archiving
Milpitas, CA, USA
messagesolution.com

Messageware (16)
Email Security / OWA
Security
Mississauga, Canada
messageware.com

**Meta Networks
(Proofpoint)** (22)
Network / Zero-Trust
Networking
Tel Aviv-Yafo, Israel
metanetworks.com

MetaFlows (1)
Network Monitoring
San Diego, CA, USA
metaflows.com

Metascan (5)
GRC / Web Scanning
Moscow, Russia
metascan.ru

Methodware (5)
GRC / Risk Framework
London, UK
methodware.com

MetricStream (1,712)
GRC / IT Governance, Risk
& Compliance
Palo Alto, CA, USA
metricstream.com

Mi-Token (109)
IAM / 2FA Tokens
Austin, TX, USA
mi-token.com

Micro Focus (239)
Security Analytics / SIEM
Newbury, UK
microfocus.com

Microsoft (2,000)
IAM / IAM
Redmond, WA, USA
microsoft.com

MicroStrategy (200)
IAM / Mobile Identity
Platform
Tysons Corner, VA, USA
microstrategy.com

MicroWorld Technologies
(191)
GRC / Vulnerability Man-
agement
Novi, MI, USA
nemasisva.com

**Militus Cybersecurity
Solutions** (2)
Network / NBAD
Newport Beach, CA, USA
milituscyber.com

Milton Security Group (41)
Network Access Control
Inline
Fullerton, CA, USA
miltonsecurity.com

Mimecast (1,501)
Email Security / Microsoft
Exchange Email Security
London, UK
mimecast.com

Mimir Networks (3)
Network / DDoS Defense
Sydney, Canada
mimirnetworks.com

**Minded Security UK
Limited** (22)
Endpoint / Malware De-
tection
Rome, Italy
mindedsecurity.com

MindoLife (11)
Network / IDS and Net-
work Management
Haifa, Israel
mindolife.com

Mindpass (5)
IAM / Visual Password
Manager
Boulder, CO, USA
mindpassco.com

Minereye (19)
GRC / Self-Learning Data
Discovery
Hod HaSharon, Israel
minereye.com

Minerva Labs (25)
Endpoint / Malware Pre-
vention
Petah Tikva, Israel
minerva-labs.com

Minim (40)
IoT Security / Home
Protection
Manchester, NH, USA
minim.co

miniOrange (27)
IAM / SSO
Pune, India
miniorange.com

MIRACL (30)
IAM / Multi-factor Au-
thentication
London, UK
miracl.com

Mirobase
GRC / DLP and Employee
Monitoring
Ukraine
mirobase.com

Mission Secure (43)
IoT Security / ICS
Charlottesville, VA, USA
missionsecure.com

MistNet (17)
Operations / Cloud-Based
Threat Hunting
Mountain View, CA, USA
mistnet.ai

MixMode (17)
Operations / Network
Forensics
San Diego, CA, USA
mixmode.ai

MMOX (6)
MSSP / SMB Solutions
The Hague, Netherlands
mmox.co

Mnemonic (227)
MSSP / MDR
Oslo, Norway
mnemonic.no

Mo An Technology
Application Security /
Scanning and Data Flow
Mapping
Hangzhou, China
moresec.cn

Mobbu (3)
IAM / QRcode Authentication
Hove, UK
mobbu.com

MobileIron (973)
Endpoint / Mobile Device
& App Security
Mountain View, CA, USA
mobileiron.com

Mobiwol
Endpoint / Firewall for
Android
Tel Aviv, Israel
mobiwol.com

Mocana Corporation (73)
Application Security /
Mobile App Security
Sunnyvale, CA, USA
mocana.com

Modoosone (1)
IAM / Privileged Access
Management
Seoul, South Korea
modoosone.com

Modulo (214)
GRC / IT Governance, Risk
& Compliance
Rio de Janeiro, Brazil
modulo.com

Moka5 (6)
Endpoint / Virtual Desktops for PCs and Macs
Redwood City, CA, USA
Moka5.com

Monarx (10)
Network / Webshell Detection and Blocking
Cottonwood Heights, UT,
USA
monarx.com

Morphisec (83)
Endpoint Obfuscation
Be'er Sheva, Israel
morphisec.com

MTG AG (230)
IoT Security / ICS Key
Management
Darmstadt, Germany
mtg.de

MXTools
Threat Intelligence
Brossard, Canada
mxtools.com

My1login (24)
IAM / Identity Management
London, UK
my1login.com

MyPermissions
Endpoint / Control Data
Privacy on Mobile Devices
Ramat Gan, Israel
mypermissions.com

Myra Security (18)
Network / Web Defense
Munich, Germany
myracloud.com

MyWorkDrive (12)
Data Security / Secure File
Storage
San Francisco, CA, USA
myworkdrive.com

N-Dimension Solutions
(14)
IoT Security / ICS
Richmond Hill, Canada
n-dimension.com

N-Stalker (12)
GRC / Web Application
Security Scanner
São Paulo, Brazil
nstalker.com

Namogoo (90)
Application Security / Web
Scanning
Ra'anana, Israel
namogoo.com

Nanitor (7)
GRC
Kópavogur, Iceland
nanitor.com

Nanolock (16)
IoT Security / Automotive
Nitzanei Oz, Israel
nanolocksecurity.com

NanoVMs, Inc. (5)
Endpoint / Secure Containers
San Francisco, CA, USA
nanovms.com

Napatech (97)
Operations / Network
Acceleration Cards
Soeborg, Denmark
napatech.com

Nasdaq Bwise (67)
GRC
's-Hertogenbosch, Netherlands
bwise.com

Nation-E (8)
IoT Security / Energy
Security
Herzliya, Israel
nation-e.com

Navaho Technologies (12)
Endpoint / Hardened
Linux
Brockenhurst, UK
navaho.co.uk

Naval Dome (3)
IoT Security / Security for
Ships
Ra'anana, Israel
navaldome.com

NC4 (168)
GRC / Risk Management
El Segundo, CA, USA
nc4.com

nCipher (268)
Data Security / Encryption
Cambridge, UK
ncipher.com

NCP Engineering (47)
Network / VPN
Mountain View, CA, USA
Ncp-e.com

nCrypted Cloud (27)
Data Security / Encryption
Boston, MA, USA
ncryptedcloud.com

Nehemiah Security (48)
GRC / Risk Management
Tysons, VA, USA
nehemiahsecurity.com

Nelysis (17)
IoT Security / Monitor
Physical Systems
Wilmington, DE, USA
nelysis.com

NeoCertified (10)
Email Security / Secure
Email
Centennial, CO, USA
neocertified.com

Note: Numbers in parentheses indicate employee count

neoEYED (8)
IAM / 2FA
Bangalore, India
neoeyed.com

Netecs Evohop (1)
Network / Gateway Security Platform
Norco, CA, USA
evohop.com

NetFlow Auditor (9)
Network Monitoring
Sydney, Australia
netflowauditor.com

NetFlow Logic (5)
Network / Netflow Concentrator
Atherton, CA, USA
netflowlogic.com

NetFort (acquired by Rapid7, April 2019) (13)
Network Traffic Capture and Analysis
Galway, Ireland
netfort.com

NETGEAR (300)
Network / Firewall
San Jose, CA, USA
netgear.com

Nethone (44)
Fraud Prevention / Anti-fraud
Warsaw, Poland
nethone.com

Netintelligence (5)
MSSP / Managed Services
Glasgow, UK
netintelligence.com

Netlib (4)
Data Security / Encryption Database
Stamford, CT, USA
netlib.com

NetLinkz (1)
Network / Zero-Trust Networking
Sydney, Australia
netlinkz.com

NetMonastery (49)
GRC / Cloud-Based SIEM
Mumbai, India
dnif.it

NetMotion Wireless (153)
Network / Wireless Security
Seattle, WA, USA
netmotionwireless.com

NetNinja (1)
Network / Wifi Hot Spot Encryption
San Francisco, CA, USA
getnetninja.com

Netography (10)
Network / DDoS Defense
San Francisco, CA, USA
netography.com

NetPilot (2)
Network / UTM
Bristol, UK
netpilot.com

NETprotocol Limited (8)
MSSP / Firewall Management
Wakefield, UK
netprotocol.net

NetScout (3,018)
Network / Situational Awareness & Incident Response
Westford, MA, USA
netscout.com

Netsfere
Data Security / Secure Messaging
Arlington Heights, IL, USA
netsfere.com

Netshield (16)
Network / Gateway Vulnerability Scanning Appliance
Nashua, NH, USA
netshieldcorp.com

NetSkope (780)
Application Security / Cloud Application Security
Santa Clara, CA, USA
netskope.com

Netsparker (87)
GRC / Web Scanning
London, UK
netsparker.com

NetSPI (128)
GRC / Vulnerability Scanning
Minneapolis, MN, USA
netspi.com

NetSTAR, Inc. (28)
Network / Secure Web Gateway
Bellevue, WA, USA
NetSTAR-inc.com

Netsurion (364)
MSSP / Managed Security Services
Houston, TX, USA
netsurion.com

Netsweeper (57)
Network / Web Filtering
Waterloo, Canada
netsweeper.com

Netswitch Technology Management (22)
MSSP / MDR
South San Francisco, CA, USA
netswitch.net

Nettoken (4)
GRC / Password Manager
London, UK
nettoken.io

Network Box USA (14)
MSSP / Managed Services
Houston, TX, USA
networkboxusa.com

Network Critical (24)
Network / Intrusion Prevention
Caversham, UK
networkcritical.com

Network Intelligence (567)
Operations / Firewall Policy Management
Mumbai, India
niiconsulting.com

NetWrix Corporation (318)
GRC / Auditor
Irvine, CA, USA
netWrix.com

Neural Legion (11)
Application Security / Dynamic Code Analysis
Tel Aviv, Israel
neuralegion.com

Neuralys (16)
Operations / Risk Mitigation
Bethesda, MD, USA
neuralys.io

NeuroMesh (2)
IoT Security / Device Inoculation
Cambridge, MA, USA
neuromesh.co

NeuShield (6)
Data Security / Data Mirroring for Ransomware Recovery
Fremont, CA, USA
neushield.com

Neustar (300)
Network / DDoS Defense
Sterling, VA, USA
neustar.biz

NeuVector, Inc. (28)
Endpoint / Container
Security
San Jose, CA, USA
neuvector.com

Nevis Networks (60)
IAM / Access Control
Pune, India
nevisnetworks.com

NewBanking (10)
IAM / IAM
Copenhagen, Denmark
newbanking.com

NewSky Security (12)
IoT Security / Device
Monitoring
Redmond, WA, USA
newskysecurity.com

Nexcom (1)
Network Security Appli-
ances
New Taipei City, Taiwan
nexcom.com

NextLabs (144)
Data Security / IRM
San Mateo, CA, USA
nextlabs.com

NextNine (23)
IoT Security / OT security
Petah Tikva, Israel
nextnine.com

Nexusguard (180)
Network / DDoS Defense
Tsuen Wan, Hong Kong
nexusguard.com

Niagra Networks (49)
Network Monitoring
San Jose, CA, USA
niagranetworks.com

NICE Actimize (961)
Fraud Prevention / Fraud
Detection
Hoboken, NJ, USA
niceactimize.com

NIKSUN (281)
Network / NBAD
Princeton, NJ, USA
niksun.com

Nimbusec (12)
GRC / Web Scanning
Linz, Austria
nimbusec.com

NIMIS Cybersecurity (2)
Operations / Automated
Pen Testing
Melbourne, Australia
nimis.ai

NitroKey (2)
Data Security / Encryption
Berlin, Germany
nitrokey.com

NNT (47)
Operations / Workflow
Automation
Naples, FL, USA
newnettechnologies.com

Noble (14)
Network / Anomaly De-
tection
London, UK
noblecss.io

NodeSource (21)
Application Security /
Appsec Serverless
San Francisco, CA, USA
nodesource.com

Nok Nok Labs (35)
IAM / Unified Authentica-
tion Infrastructure
San Jose, CA, USA
noknok.com

Nokia (250)
Endpoint / Mobile Security
Espoo, Finland
networks.nokia.com

Nominet (250)
Network / DNS Threat
Detection
Oxford, UK
nominet.com

Nopsec (27)
GRC / Vulnerability Risk
Management
Brooklyn, NY, USA
nopsec.com

NordVPN
Network / VPN Consumer
Panama City, Panama
nordvpn.com

Norma
IoT Security / Wireless
Seoul, South Korea
norma.co.kr

Normshield (26)
GRC / Security Scores
Vienna, VA, USA
normshield.com

Nova Leah (25)
IoT Security / Medical
Device Vulnerability Man-
agement
Dundalk, Ireland
novaleah.com

Novetta Solutions (810)
Network Traffic Monitor-
ing
McLean, VA, USA
novetta.com

NoviFlow (44)
Network / SDN
Montreal, Canada
noviflow.com

NowSecure (68)
Endpoint / Mobile Security
Chicago, IL, USA
nowsecure.com

Nozomi Security (116)
IoT Security / ICS
San Francisco, CA, USA
nozominetworks.com

NP Core (16)
Endpoint / EDR
Seoul, South Korea
npcore.com

nProtect (15)
Endpoint / Mobile
Guro-gu, South Korea
nprotect.com

NRI Secure Technologies
(398)
MSSP / SOC as a Service
Otemachi Chiyoda-ku,
Japan
Nri-secure.com

NS1 (113)
Network / DNS Security
New York, NY, USA
ns1.com

NS8 (80)
Fraud Prevention / An-
ti-fraud
Las Vegas, NV, USA
ns8.com

Nsauditor (1)
GRC / Vulnerability
Scanner
Las Vegas, NV, USA
nsauditor.com

NSFocus (468)
Network / DDoS Defense
Santa Clara, CA, USA
nsfocus.com

nsKnox
Fraud Prevention / Pay-
ment Verification
Tel Aviv, Israel
nsknox.net

NSS Labs (101)
Testing / Product Testing
Austin, TX, USA
nsslabs.com

Note: Numbers in parentheses indicate employee count

NTrepid (222)
Operations / Forensics and Linkage
Herndon, VA, USA
ntrepidcorp.com

Nu Quantum (5)
Data Security / Quantum Cryptography
London, UK
nu-quantum.com

Nucleon Cyber (3)
Threat Intelligence / Aggregation
Tampa, FL, USA
nucleon.sh

Nucleus Cyber (9)
Data Security / Data Discovery and Classification
Boston, MA, USA
nucleuscyber.com

Nucleus Security (6)
GRC / Vulnerability Management
Sarasota, FL, USA
nucleussec.com

NuCypher (18)
Data Security / Credential Encryption
San Francisco, CA, USA
nucypher.com

NuData Security (101)
Fraud Prevention / Online Fraud Detection
Vancouver, Canada
nudatasecurity.com

NuID Inc. (7)
IAM / Trustless Authentication
Seattle, WA, USA
nuid.io

Nuix (468)
Security Analytics / Analytics for Digital Investigations
Sydney, Australia
nuix.com

Nuro (5)
Data Security / Secure Messaging
Tel Aviv, Israel
nuro.im

Nuspire (117)
MSSP / Managed Services
Commerce, MI, USA
nuspire.com

Nuweba (13)
Application Security / Serverless Security
Tel Aviv, Israel
nuweba.com

nwStor (8)
Data Security / Network & Cloud Data Security
Shatin, Hong Kong
nwstor.com

NXM Labs (28)
IoT Security / Device Security
San Francisco, CA, USA
nxmlabs.com

NXT-ID (11)
IoT Security / Mobile Security
Sebastian, FL, USA
nxt-id.com

Nyotron (62)
Endpoint / EDR
Herzliya, Israel
nyotron.com

ObserveIT (acquired by Proofpoint, 2019) (179)
GRC / Employee Behavior Monitoring
Boston, MA, USA
observeit.com

Obsidian Security (55)
Network / Cloud Monitoring
Newport Beach, CA, USA
obsidiansecurity.com

Octatco (3)
IAM / Fingerprint USB Devices
Seongnam, South Korea
octatco.com

ODI (11)
Data Security / Document Scrubbing
Rosh HaAyin, Israel
odi-x.com

Odo Security (18)
Network / Zero-Trust Networking
Tel Aviv, Israel
odo.io

Okera (46)
Data Security / Data Governance
San Francisco, CA, USA
okera.com

Okta, Inc. (1,934)
IAM
San Francisco, CA, USA
okta.com

Omada A/S (239)
IAM
Copenhagen, Denmark
omada.net

Omniquad Ltd. (30)
Endpoint / Anti-spyware
London, UK
omniquad.com

Onapsis Inc. (209)
Data Security / SAP Security
Boston, MA, USA
onapsis.com

OnDMARC (15)
Email Security / DMARC
London, UK
ondmarc.com

One App
Endpoint / Android AV
oneappessentials.com

One Identity (461)
Network / Firewall
Aliso Viejo, CA, USA
oneidentity.com

OneLogin (283)
IAM / Identity Management
San Francisco, CA, USA
onelogin.com

OnePath (547)
MSSP / Managed Services
Kennesaw, GA, USA
1path.com

OneSpan (formerly Vasco) (559)
IAM / Identity Products
Chicago, IL, USA
onespan.com

OneTrust (667)
GRC / Third Party Risk Management
Atlanta, GA, USA
onetrust.com

OneVisage (8)
IAM / Biometrics
Lausanne, Switzerland
onevisage.com

Onion ID (5)
IAM / Privileged Access Management
Hayward, CA, USA
onionid.com

OnlyMyEmail (12)
Network / Anti-spam
Brighton, MI, USA
onlymyemail.com

Onspring (26)
GRC / Audit Management
Overland Park, KS, USA
onspring.com

OPAC (104)
Network / Zero-Trust Networking
Herndon, VA, USA
opaq.com

Open Systems (257)
MSSP / Managed Services
Zürich, Switzerland
open-systems.com

Open Zeppelin (25)
Application Security for
Blockchain
San Francisco, CA, USA
openzeppelin.com

OpenIAM (13)
IAM / Identity Management
Cortlandt Manor, NY, USA
openiam.com

OpenText (500)
IAM / Federated Identity
Waterloo, Canada
opentext.com

OpenVPN (63)
Network / VPN
Pleasanton, CA, USA
openvpn.net

OPSWAT (205)
Endpoint Security
San Francisco, CA, USA
opswat.com

Optimal IdM (12)
IAM / Single Sign-On
(SSO)
Lutz, FL, USA
optimalidm.com

Optiv (200)
MSSP / Managed Services
Denver, CO, USA
optiv.com

Oracle (450)
IAM
Redwood Shores, CA, USA
oracle.com

Orca Security (25)
Operations / Cloud Vulnerability Scanning
Tel Aviv, Israel
orca.security

Ordr (61)
IoT Security / Device
Management
Santa Clara, CA, USA
ordr.net

Origone (5)
Email Security / Anti-phishing
Paris, France
orisecure.com

Osano (12)
GRC / Data Privacy Compliance
Austin, TX, USA
osano.com

Osirium (45)
IAM / Privileged Access
Management
Theale, UK
osirium.com

Ostendio (12)
GRC / Compliance Management
Arlington, VA, USA
ostendio.com

Outpost24 (161)
GRC / Vulnerability Risk
Management
Karlskrona, Sweden
outpost24.com

OutThink (15)
GRC / Employee Behavior
Monitoring
London, UK
outthinkthreats.com

Owl Cyber Defense (62)
Network / Air Gap
Danbury, CT, USA
owlcyberdefense.com

OxCEPT
IoT Security / Device
Authentication
London, UK
oxcept.com

Oxford Biochronometrics
(12)
Fraud Prevention / Click
Fraud Prevention
London, UK
oxford-biochron.com

P-X Systems (2)
Network / IDS
Amsterdam, Netherlands
p-x.systems

PacketViper (23)
Deception
Pittsburgh, PA, USA
packetviper.com

Paladin Cyber (14)
Email Security / Anti-phishing
San Francisco, CA, USA
meetpaladin.com

Paladion (960)
Testing / Cybersecurity
Testing & Monitoring
Reston, VA, USA
paladion.net

Palantir Technologies
(2,339)
Security Analytics / Link
Analysis
Palo Alto, CA, USA
palantir.com

Palo Alto Networks (6,488)
Network / UTM
Santa Clara, CA, USA
paloaltonetworks.com

Panaseer (50)
GRC / Security Management Platform
London, UK
panaseer.com

Panda Security (633)
Endpoint / Anti-virus
Bilbao, Spain
pandasecurity.com/usa

Pango (86)
IAM / Consumer VPN
Redwood City, CA, USA
pango.co

Panopticon Labs (4)
Fraud Prevention / Virtual
Identity Theft Protection
Columbus, OH, USA
panopticonlabs.com

Panorays (33)
GRC / Vulnerability Assessment for Third Parties
New York, NY, USA
panorays.com

Paraben Corporation (18)
GRC / Digital Forensics &
Data Recovery
Aldie, VA, USA
paraben.com

Paramount Defenses Inc.
(1)
IAM / Privileged Access
Management for AD
Newport Beach, CA, USA
paramountdefenses.com

Parasoft (254)
Application Security /
Security Testing
Monrovia, CA, USA
parasoft.com

Passfaces Corporation
IAM / 2FA
Reston, VA, USA
passfaces.com

**PassMark Software Pvt
Ltd.** (7)
IAM
Surry Hills, Australia
passmark.com

PasswordPing (13)
Fraud Prevention / Compromised Credentials
Boulder, CO, USA
passwordping.com

Note: Numbers in parentheses indicate employee count

Paterva (4)
Operations / Maltego
Enhancement
Pretoria, South Africa
paterva.com

Patriot (55)
Endpoint / Mobile Device
Security Management
Frederick, MD, USA
patriot-tech.com

Patronus.io (6)
Application Security / Web
Scanning
Berlin, Germany
patronus.io

PatternEx (20)
Operations / Security
Automation
San Jose, CA, USA
patternex.com

Payfone (95)
Fraud Prevention / An-
ti-fraud
New York, NY, USA
payfone.com

Paymetric (133)
Data Security / Encryption
Atlanta, GA, USA
paymetric.com

PC VARK (39)
Endpoint / Android AV
Jaipur, India
pcvark.com

Pcysys (30)
Operations / Automated
Pen Testing
Petah Tikva, Israel
pcysys.com

PeachTech (3)
Testing / Fuzzing
Seattle, WA, USA
peach.tech

Pearl Software Inc. (14)
Network / Web Filtering
Exton, PA, USA
pearlsoftware.com

Penango (2)
Data Security / Encryption
for Gmail & Google Apps
Los Angeles, CA, USA
penango.com

Penta Security (114)
Network / Web Application
Firewall
Seoul, South Korea
pentasecurity.com

Perception Point (35)
Email Security / An-
ti-phishing
Tel Aviv, Israel
perception-point.io

Perch (39)
MSSP / SOC
Tampa, FL, USA
perchsecurity.com

Perfectcloud (10)
Data Security / Secure
Cloud Storage
Toronto, Canada
perfectcloud.io

Perimeter 81 (38)
Network / Secure Web
Gateway
Tel Aviv, Israel
perimeter81.com

PerimeterX (146)
Network / Website Defense
Tel Aviv-Yafo, Israel
perimeterx.com

Perpetual Encryption
Data Security / OTP En-
cryption
London, UK
perpetualencryption.com

Perseus. (23)
Email Security / An-
ti-phishing
Berlin, Germany
perseus.de

Pervade Software (6)
GRC
Cardiff, UK
pervade-software.com

Perytons (3)
Network / IoT Defense
Ness Ziona, Israel
perytons.com

PFP Cybersecurity (25)
Endpoint Protection (Pow-
er Anomoly)
Vienna, VA, USA
pfpcybersecurity.com

PhishCloud (9)
Email Security / An-
ti-phishing
Renton, WA, USA
phishcloud.com

PhishLabs (142)
GRC / Anti-phishing
Charleston, SC, USA
phishlabs.com

PhishX (4)
GRC / Security Awareness
Training
Cotia, Brazil
phishx.io

Phoenix Technologies
(502)
Endpoint / Secure PC
Campbell, CA, USA
phoenix.com

Phosphorus (12)
IoT Security / Agentless
Patch Management
Atlanta, GA, USA
phosphorus.io

Picus Security (53)
GRC / IT Security Control
Monitoring
Ankara, Turkey
picussecurity.com

Pindrop Security (292)
IAM / Authentication,
Audio
Atlanta, GA, USA
pindropsecurity.com

Ping Identity Corporation
(882)
IAM
Denver, CO, USA
pingidentity.com

Pinn (26)
IAM / Authentication
Redwood City, CA, USA
pinn.ai

Pirean (Echostar) (65)
IAM / Identity Manage-
ment
London, UK
pirean.com

PistolStar Inc. (15)
Fraud Prevention / Au-
thentication
Bedford, NH, USA
pistolstar.com

PivotPoint Security (25)
GRC / Risk Assessment
Hamilton, NJ, USA
pivotpointsecurity.com

PixAlert (14)
GRC / Data Discovery
Dublin, Ireland
pixalert.com

Pixelpin (15)
IAM / Password Manage-
ment
London, UK
pixelpin.io

pixlcloud (1)
Security Analytics / Visualization
San Francisco, CA, USA
pixlcloud.com

PIXM, Inc. (9)
Email Security / An-
ti-phishing
Brooklyn, NY, USA
pixm.net

PKWARE (142)
Data Security / Data
Privacy
Milwaukee, WI, USA
pkware.com

PlainID (37)
IAM / Authorization
Tel Aviv, Israel
plainid.com

Plixer (94)
Network / Netflow Anal-
ysis
Kennebunk, ME, USA
plixer.com

Plurilock (18)
IAM / Behavior-Based
Biometrics
Victoria, Canada
plurilock.com

PNF Software (5)
Application Security /
Reverse Engineering for
Android
Redwood City, CA, USA
pnfsoftware.com

Pointsecure (3)
GRC / OpenVMS Com-
pliance
Houston, TX, USA
pointsecure.com

PointSharp AB (13)
Endpoint / Mobile Security
Stockholm, Sweden
pointsharp.com

Polarity (39)
Operations / Onscreen
Data Augmentation
Farmington, CT, USA
polarity.io

Polylogyx (9)
Endpoint / EDR with
OSQuery
Pleasanton, CA, USA
polylogyx.com

PolySwarm (25)
Endpoint / Malware De-
tection
San Diego, CA, USA
polyswarm.io

Polyverse (25)
Endpoint / OS Random-
izing
Bellevue, WA, USA
polyverse.io

Port80 Software (2)
Endpoint / IIS Security
San Diego, CA, USA
port80software.com

Portnox (32)
Endpoint / MDM
Ra'anana, Israel
portnox.com

Portshift (10)
Application Security /
Identity-Based Workload
Protection
Tel Aviv-Yafo, Israel
portshift.io

PortSwigger (30)
GRC / Vulnerability
Scanner
Knutsford, UK
portswigger.net

Positive Technologies
(483)
Network / Web Application
Firewall
Framingham, MA, USA
ptsecurity.com

Post-Quantum (15)
IAM / Authentication
London, UK
post-quantum.com

Pradeo (19)
Application Security /
Mobile App Security
Paris, France
pradeo.net

Preempt Security (58)
Security Analytics / UEBA
Ramat Gan, Israel
preemptsecurity.com

PreEmptive Solutions (32)
Application Security / App
Hardening
Mayfield Village, OH, USA
preemptive.com

PresiNET Systems Corp.
(8)
Network Monitoring
Victoria, Canada
presinet.com

Prevailion (26)
Threat Intelligence
Fulton, MD, USA
prevailion.com

Prevalent AI (21)
GRC / Risk Management
London, UK
prevalent.ai

Prevalent Networks (95)
GRC / Third Party Risk
Management
Warren, NJ, USA
prevalent.net

Note: Numbers in parentheses indicate employee count

PreVeil (23)
Data Security / File and
Email Encryption
Boston, MA, USA
preveil.com

Prifender (20)
GRC / Data Privacy
Tel Aviv, Israel
prifender.com

PrimeKey Solutions (61)
Data Security / PKI & Digital Signature Solutions
Solna, Sweden
primekey.com

Prismo Systems (16)
Network / Zero-Trust
Networking
San Francisco, CA, USA
prismosystems.com

Privacera (22)
Data Security / Data Governance
Fremont, CA, USA
privacera.com

Privacy Analytics (101)
Data Security / Healthcare
Data Privacy
Ottawa, Canada
privacy-analytics.com

Privacyware (1)
Endpoint / IIS Security
New Albany, OH, USA
privacyware.com

Privakey, Inc. (10)
Fraud Prevention / Transaction Intent
Philadelphia, PA, USA
privakey.com

Privitar (109)
Data Security / Data
Masking
London, UK
privitar.com

Privoro (38)
Endpoint / Hardened Cases for Mobile Phones
Chandler, AZ, USA
privoro.com

Privus (9)
Data Security / Secure
Communications
Zug, Switzerland
privus.global

Privva (10)
GRC / Third Party Risk
Arlington, VA, USA
privva.com

ProactEye (2)
Security Analytics / CASB
and UEBA
Pune, India
proacteye.com

Probely (1)
Application Security / Web
Scanning
Lisbon, Portugal
probely.com

Process Software (21)
Email Security
Framingham, MA, USA
process.com

ProcessUnity (74)
GRC / Third Party Risk
Management
Concord, MA, USA
processunity.com

Proficio (132)
MSSP / MDR
Carlsbad, CA, USA
proficio.com

Profitap (31)
Network / Traffic Capture
Eindhoven, Netherlands
profitap.com

Promia (29)
GRC / Network Asset
Discovery
Skillman, NJ, USA
promia.com

Promisec (40)
Endpoint Security Intelligence
Holon, Israel
promisec.com

Promon (43)
Application Security / In-App Protection for Mobile
Oslo, Norway
promon.co

Proofpoint, Inc. (2,764)
Email Security / Anti-malware, Anti-spam, and
Anti-phishing
Sunnyvale, CA, USA
proofpoint.com

Prophecy International
(32)
Data Security / Secure File
Transfer
Adelaide, Australia
prophecyinternational.com

Prosa Security (1)
Application Security / Development Collaboration
Platform
Oslo, Norway
prosasecurity.com

Protect2020 (2)
Training / SaaS Platform
Camberley, UK
p2020academy.com

Protected Media (28)
Network / Advertising
Security
Petah Tikva, Israel
protected.media

Protectimus (28)
IAM / Two-Factor Authentication
London, UK
protectimus.com

ProtectStar (2)
Data Security / Erasure
Miami, FL, USA
protectstar.com/en

**ProtectWise (acquired by
Verizon, March 2019)** (70)
Network Data Capture
Denver, CO, USA
protectwise.com

Protego (48)
Application Security / App
Hardening
Baltimore, MD, USA
protego.io

Protegrity (309)
Application Security
Stamford, CT, USA
protegrity.com

Protenus (65)
GRC / Medical Record
Access Monitoring
Baltimore, MD, USA
protenus.com

Proteus-Cyber, Ltd. (4)
GRC
London, UK
proteuscyber.com

Protocol 46 (20)
Network / Firewall
Saint Paul, MN, USA
protocol46.com

Proxim (155)
Network / Wireless Security
San Jose, CA, USA
proxim.com

Psafe Technology (102)
Endpoint / Anti-virus
San Francisco, CA, USA
psafe.com

Pulse Secure (532)
IAM / Authentication
San Jose, CA, USA
pulsesecure.net

Pushfor, Inc. (19)
Data Security / Secure
Content Sharing
Wimbledon, UK
pushfor.com

Pwnie Express (17)
Testing / Wireless Scanning
Boston, MA, USA
pwnieexpress.com

Pyramid Computer GmbH
(64)
Network / Firewall
Freiburg, Germany
pyramid.de

Q-Branch Labs (3)
Network / VPN Device
Wilmington, DE, USA
q-branch-labs.com

Q6 Cyber (40)
Threat Intelligence / Dark
Web Mining
Miami, FL, USA
q6cyber.com

QEDit (24)
Data Security / Data
Privacy
Tel Aviv, Israel
qed-it.com
QEYnet (3)
Data Security
Vaughan, Canada
qeynet.com

Qgroup, GmbH (8)
Network / Firewall
Frankfurt am Main, Ger-
many
qgroup.de

Qihoo 360 Total Security
(2,022)
Endpoint / AV
Beijing, China
360totalsecurity.com

Qingteng (15)
Operations / Asset Discovery and Protection
Beijing, China
qingteng.cn/en/index.html

Qomplx (94)
Security Analytics / Monitoring and Response
Reston, VA, USA
qomplx.com/cyber

QoSient (1)
Network Monitoring
New York, NY, USA
qosient.com

Qosmos, Division of ENEA
(79)
Network / DPI Technology
Paris, France
qosmos.com

Qrator (32)
Network / DDoS Defense
Prague, Czech Republic
qrator.net

Qredo (13)
Data Security / App En-
cryption
London, UK
qredo.com

**Quadrant Information
Security** (29)
Security Analytics / SIEM
Jacksonville, FL, USA
quadrantsec.com

Qualys (1,167)
GRC / Vulnerability man-
agement
Foster City, CA, USA
qualys.com

QuantLR (4)
Data Security, Quantum
Key Distribution
Jerusalem, Israel
quantlr.com

Quantum Digital Solutions
(3)
Data Security / Key Man-
agement
Los Angeles, CA, USA
qdsc.us

Quantum Signal, LLC (36)
IAM / Biometrics
Saline, MI, USA
quantumsignal.com

Quantum Xchange (12)
Data Security / Quantum
Key Distribution
Newton, MA, USA
quantumxc.com

Quick Heal (1,263)
Endpoint, Server (Linux),
and UTM
Pune, India
quickheal.com

Quintessence Labs (38)
Data Security / Quantum
Optics & Cryptographic
Security
Deakin, Australia
quintessencelabs.com

QuoScient GmbH (36)
Operations / Security
Operations Platform
Frankfurt am Main, Ger-
many
quoscient.io

Quotium (21)
GRC / Data Storage Mon-
itoring
Paris, France
quotium.com

Quside (19)
Data Security / Quantum
RNG
Barcelona, Spain
quside.com

Qustodio (79)
Endpoint / Mobile Parental
Controls
Redondo Beach, CA, USA
qustodio.com

Quttera (5)
Network / Malware Scan-
ning of Websites
Herzliya Pituach, Israel
quttera.com

R&K Cyber Solutions (11)
MSSP / Managed Security
Services
Manassas, VA, USA
rkcybersolutions.com

R-Vision (44)
Operations / Incident
Response Platform
Moscow, Russia
rvision.pro

Racktop Systems (42)
Data Security / Secure
Storage
Fulton, MD, USA
racktopsystems.com

Radiant Logic (104)
IAM / LDAP, SSO
Novato, CA, USA
radiantlogic.com

RadiFlow (42)
IoT Security / ICS
Tel Aviv, Israel
radiflow.com

Radware (1,196)
Network / Load Balanc-
ing, DDoS Defense, IPS,
Firewall
Tel Aviv, Israel
radware.com

Rambus (881)
Data Security / Semicon-
ductor Security R&D
Sunnyvale, CA, USA
rambus.com

Note: Numbers in parentheses indicate employee count

RangeForce (26)
Operations / Training
White Plains, NY, USA
rangeforce.com

RANK Software, Inc. (20)
Security Analytics / Threat
Hunting
Toronto, Canada
ranksoftwareinc.com

Raonsecure (10)
IAM / Biometrics
Santa Clara, CA, USA
raonsecure.com

Rapid 7 (1,447)
GRC / Vulnerability Man-
agement
Boston, MA, USA
rapid7.com

RavenWhite Security, Inc.
(2)
IAM / Cookies
Menlo Park, CA, USA
ravenwhite.com

RaviRaj Technologies (4)
IAM / Biometrics
Pune, India
ravirajtech.com

Rawstream (3)
Network / DNS-Based
Security
London, UK
rawstream.com

Raz-Lee Security (20)
Endpoint / IBM iSeries
Security
Herzliya, Israel
razlee.com

RazorSecure
IoT Security / Automotive
Basingstoke, UK
web.razorsecure.com

RCDevs (13)
IAM / IAM
Belvaux, Luxembourg
rcdevs.com

RealVNC (67)
Network / Remote Access
Cambridge, UK
realvnc.com/en

ReaQta (20)
Endpoint / EDR
Amsterdam, Netherlands
reaqta.com

Reblaze Technologies Ltd.
(34)
Network / Web Proxy
Defense
Tel Aviv, Israel
reblaze.com

**Recorded Future
(acquired by FireEye,
2019)** (392)
Threat Intelligence
Somerville, MA, USA
recordedfuture.com

Red Balloon Security (26)
Endpoint / Embedded
Device Security
New York, NY, USA
redballoonsecurity.com

Red Button (3)
Network / DDoS Defense
Tel Aviv, Israel
red-button.net

Red Canary (96)
Endpoint Detection
Denver, CO, USA
redcanary.com

Red Database Security (2)
Data Security / Database
Security
Heusenstamm, Germany
red-database-security.de

Red Lambda (21)
Endpoint Security
Lake Mary, FL, USA
redlambda.com

Red Piranha (41)
Network / UTM
Melbourne, Australia
redpiranha.net

Red Sift (38)
Endpoint / Open Platform
London, UK
redsift.com

Redborder
Network / IDS Based on
SNORT
Sevilla, Spain
redborder.com

RedJack (31)
Network Monitoring
Silver Spring, MD, USA
redjack.com

RedMarlin, Inc. (8)
Email Security / Phishing
Detection
Mountain View, CA, USA
redmarlin.ai

RedScan (60)
MSSP / MDR
London, UK
redscan.com

RedSeal (188)
GRC / Security Posture
San Jose, CA, USA
redseal.net

RedShield Security (36)
Network / Web Application
Defense
Wellington, New Zealand
redshield.co

RedShift Networks (24)
Network / VoIP Security
San Ramon, CA, USA
redshiftnetworks.com

Redstout (5)
Network / UTM
Lisbon, Portugal
redstout.com

Refirm Labs (12)
IoT Security / Firmware
Analysis and Monitoring
Fulton, MD, USA
refirmlabs.com

Regulus (16)
IoT Security / Automotive
Haifa, Israel
regulus.com

RelateData (3)
Network Monitoring
London, UK
relatedata.com

Reliaquest (380)
Security Analytics / Threat
Hunting
Tampa, FL, USA
reliaquest.com

Remediant (32)
IAM / Privileged Access
Management
San Francisco, CA, USA
remediant.com

remote.it (6)
Network / Zero-Trust
Networking
Palo Alto, CA, USA
remote.it

RepKnight (22)
Threat Intelligence / Dark
Web Breach Alert
Belfast, UK
repknight.com

Reposify (15)
Operations / Asset Dis-
covery
Bnei Brak, Israel
reposify.com

Reprivata (3)
Network / Microsegmen-
tation
Palo Alto, CA, USA
reprivata.com

ReSec Technologies (14)
Data Security / Document
Scrubbing
Caesarea, Israel
resec.co

Reservoir Labs (28)
Security Analytics / Re-
al-Time Threat Visibility
New York, NY, USA
reservoir.com

Resolver (224)
GRC / Risk Management
Toronto, Canada
resolver.com

Respond Software (53)
Security Analytics / Au-
tomated Incident Identifi-
cation
Mountain View, CA, USA
respond-software.com

Responsight (8)
Network / UEBA
Melbourne, Australia
responsight.com

Rether Networks Inc. (1)
Endpoint / Host Intrusion
Prevention
Centereach, NY, USA
rether.com

Return Path (518)
Fraud Prevention / Email
Fraud Prevention
New York, NY, USA
returnpath.com

RevenueStream (4)
Fraud Prevention /
Revenue Stream Fraud
Prevention
Israel
revenue-stream.com

Reversing Labs (152)
Operations / Malware
Analysis
Cambridge, MA, USA
reversinglabs.com

Rhebo (23)
IoT Security / ICS
Leipzig, Germany
rhebo.com

**Ridgeback Network
Defense** (14)
Deception
Baltimore, MD, USA
ridgebacknet.com

RioRey (17)
Network / DDoS Defense
Bethesda, MD, USA
riorey.com

Rippleshot (15)
Fraud Prevention / Fraud
Detection
Chicago, IL, USA
rippleshot.com

RIPS Technologies GmbH
(28)
Application Security / Static Code Analysis for PHP
and Java
Bochum, Germany
ripstech.com

Riscure (109)
Testing / Security Product
Test Labs
Delft, Netherlands
riscure.com

Note: Numbers in parentheses indicate employee count

Risk Based Security (27)
GRC / Cyber Risk Analytics
Richmond, VA, USA
riskbasedsecurity.com

Risk Ledger (10)
GRC / Third Party Risk Assessment
London, UK
riskledger.com

Risk.Ident (62)
Fraud Prevention / Fraud Detection
Hamburg, Germany
riskident.com

Riskified (335)
Fraud Prevention / e-Commerce Transaction Monitoring
Tel Aviv, Israel
riskified.com

RiskIQ (166)
GRC / External Threat Platform
San Francisco, CA, USA
riskiq.com

RiskLens (67)
GRC / Risk Calculations
Spokane, WA, USA
risklens.com

RiskRecon (75)
GRC / Third Party Risk Management
Salt Lake City, UT, USA
riskrecon.com

RiskSense, Inc. (103)
GRC / Vulnerability Management
Albuquerque, NM, USA
risksense.com

RiskWatch International (18)
GRC / Risk Management
Sarasota, FL, USA
riskwatch.com

Rivetz (19)
Data Security / Secure Communications
Richmond, MD, USA
rivetz.com

Rocket Software, Inc. (1,211)
Network / Secure Terminal Emulation
Waltham, MA, USA
rocketsoftware.com

Rofori Corporation (5)
GRC / Risk Management
Zionsville, IN, USA
rofori.com

Rohde & Schwarz Cybersecurity (51)
Application Security / App Containers
Meudon, France
Rohd-schwarz.com

Romad (43)
Endpoint / AV
Kiev, Ukraine
romad-systems.com

Rook Security (29)
MSSP / Managed Services
Carmel, IN, USA
rooksecurity.com

root9B (29)
Security Analytics / Threat Hunting Platform
Colorado Springs, CO, USA
root9b.com

Route 1 (39)
IAM
Toronto, Canada
route1.com

RSA Security, Division of EMC/Dell (3,161)
IAM
Bedford, MA, USA
rsa.com

Rsam (172)
IAM / IT Governance, Risk & Compliance
Secaucus, NJ, USA
rsam.com

RSD (705)
IAM / Information Governance Solutions
Geneva, Switzerland
rsd.com

Rubica (27)
Network / VPN
San Francisco, CA, USA
rubica.com

Rubicon Labs (12)
Data Security / Key Management
San Francisco, CA, USA
rubiconlabs.io

Rublon (2)
IAM / 2FA
Zielona Gora, Poland
rublon.com

RunSafe Security (15)
IoT Security / Firmware Hardening
McLean, VA, USA
runsafesecurity.com

Safe-T (56)
Data Security / Secure Data Exchange
Herzliya Pituach, Israel
safe-t.com

SafeBreach (56)
Operations / Automated Pen Testing
Tel Aviv, Israel
safebreach.com

SafeDNS (34)
Network / DNS Filtering
Alexandria, VA, USA
safedns.com/en

SafeGuard Cyber (37)
GRC / Employee Social Media Management
Charlottesville, VA, USA
safeguardcyber.com

Safehouse Technologies (7)
Network Cloud Proxy
Scottsdale, AZ, USA
safehousetechnologies.com

SafeLogic (8)
Data Security / Cryptographic Libraries
Palo Alto, CA, USA
safelogic.com

SafelyLocked (2)
Data Security / Encryption
Atlanta, GA, USA
safelylocked.com

SafeNet AT (64)
Data Security / Encryption
Abingdon, MD, USA
safenetat.com

SafenSoft (7)
Endpoint Protection
Los Angeles, CA, USA
safensoft.com

SafeRide Technologies (22)
IoT Security / Automotive
Tel Aviv-Yafo, Israel
saferide.io

SaferPass (18)
IAM / Password Manager
Bratislava, Slovakia
saferpass.net

SaferVPN (26)
Network / Consumer VPN
New York, NY, USA
safervpn.com

SafeUM (4)
Data Security / Private Messenger
Reykjavík, Iceland
safeum.com

Safewhere (2)
IAM / Identity Management
Virum, Denmark
safewhere.com

Sage Data Security (32)
Network / Firewall
Portland, ME, USA
sagedatasecurity.com

Saife (1)
Data Security / Secure Data Transfer
Chandler, AZ, USA
saifeinc.com

SailPoint (1,093)
IAM / Identity Governance
Austin, TX, USA
sailpoint.com

Saint Corporation (18)
GRC / Vulnerability Management
Bethesda, MD, USA
saintcorporation.com

Salt Security (19)
Network / API Attack Detection
Palo Alto, CA, USA
salt.security

SaltDNA (16)
Data Security / Secure Communications
Belfast, UK
saltdna.com

SaltStack (94)
Operations / Orchestration
Lehi, UT, USA
saltstack.com

SaltyCloud (6)
Operations / Workflow Automation
Austin, TX, USA
saltycloud.com

Salviol Global Analytics (17)
Fraud Prevention / Fraud Detection
Reading, UK
salviol.com

SAM (51)
Network / Home Gateway Defense
Tel Aviv, Israel
securingsam.com

Sangfor (1444)
Network / UTM
Shenzhen, China
sangfor.com

Sapian Cyber (28)
Security Analytics / Breach Detection
Joondalup, Australia
sapiencyber.com.au

SAS Institute (100)
Fraud Prevention / Anti-fraud
Cary, NC, USA
sas.com

Sasa Software (17)
Data Security / File Scrubbing
Sasa, Israel
sasa-software.com

Saviynt (295)
IAM / Cloud Access Governance
El Segundo, CA, USA
saviynt.com

ScadaFence (33)
IoT Security / ICS
Tel Aviv, Israel
scadafence.com

Scalarr (34)
Fraud Prevention / Mobile Ad Fraud
Wilmington, DE, USA
scalarr.io

Scantist (11)
GRC / Vulnerability Management
Singapore, Singapore
scantist.com

SCIT Labs, Inc. (10)
Endpoint / Dynamic Image Replacement for Servers
Clifton, VA, USA
scitlabs.com

Scytale (27)
IAM / Identity Management for Cloud
San Francisco, CA, USA
scytale.io

SCYTHE (22)
Testing / Attack Simulation and Automated Pen Testing
Arlington, VA, USA
scythe.io

SDG Corporation (616)
GRC
Norwalk, CT, USA
sdgc.com

SDS (19)
Endpoint / z/OS Security
Minneapolis, MN, USA
sdsusa.com

Seagate Technology (100)
Data Security / Encryption
Cupertino, CA, USA
seagate.com

Searchguard (5)
Data Security / Security for Elasticsearch
Berlin, Germany
search-guard.com

SearchInform (97)
Operations / Employee Monitoring
Moscow, Russia
searchinform.com

Searchlight Security (2)
Threat Intelligence / Dark Web Intel
Portsmouth, UK
slcyber.io

SEC Consult (109)
Application Security / Code Testing
Vienna, Austria
sec-consult.com

Secberus (9)
GRC / Compliance for Cloud Environments
Miami, FL, USA
secberus.com

SecBI (25)
Security Analytics
Tel Aviv, Israel
secbi.com

Seccom Global (25)
MSSP / Managed Services
Sydney, Australia
seccomglobal.com

Seceon (56)
Security Analytics / SIEM
Westford, MA, USA
seceon.com

Seclab (19)
Data Security / Secure File Transfer
Montpellier, France
seclab-security.com

Seclore (199)
Data Security / IRM
Mumbai, India
seclore.com

Seclytics (10)
Security Analytics / Threat Intelligence
San Diego, CA, USA
seclytics.com

Secnap (14)
MSSP / Managed Services
Fort Lauderdale, FL, USA
secnap.com

Note: Numbers in parentheses indicate employee count

SecNeo (22)
Application Security /
Mobile App Protection
San Jose, CA, USA
secneo.com

SECNOLOGY (25)
Security Analytics / Big
Data Mining & Security
El Granada, CA, USA
secnology.com

Secoda Risk Management
(5)
GRC
London, UK
secoda.com

Secomba (12)
Data Security / Encryption
for Dropbox
Augsburg, Germany
boxcryptor.com/en

Secon Cyber (135)
MSSP / MDR
Surrey, UK
seconcyber.com

Seconize (6)
GRC / Risk Management
Singapore, Singapore
seconize.co

SecPod Technologies (52)
Endpoint / EDR
Tulsa, OK, USA
secpod.com

SecPoint (17)
GRC / Vulnerability
Scanning
Copenhagen, Denmark
secpoint.com

Secret Double Octopus
(32)
Data Security / Two-Chan-
nel Encryption
Tel Aviv, Israel
doubleoctopus.com

SecSign (4)
IAM / 2FA for Mobile
Devices
Henderson, NV, USA
secsign.com

Sectigo (156)
Data Security / PKI CA
Roseland, NJ, USA
sectigo.com

Secucloud (70)
Network / Cloud Proxy
Security
Hamburg, Germany
secucloud.com

Secudit, Ltd. (6)
GRC / Vulnerability
Scanning
Veszprém, Hungary
secudit.com

Secudrives (1)
Data Security / Data En-
cryption & Destruction
Seoul, South Korea
secudrives.com

SecuGen (20)
IAM / Biometric Finger
Scanners
Santa Clara, CA, USA
secugen.com

Secui (1)
Network / Firewall
Seoul, South Korea
secui.com

SecuLetter (3)
Operations / Malware
Analysis
Seongnam-si, South Korea
seculetter.com

SecuPi (22)
Application Security /
Cloud App Monitoring
London, UK
secupi.com

**Secure Access
Technologies** (13)
IAM / Mobile Single Sign-
On
Menlo Park, CA, USA
secureaccesstechnologies.
com

Secure Channels (24)
Data Security / Encryption
Irvine, CA, USA
securechannels.com

Secure Crossing R&D
IoT Security / ICS
Dearborn, MI, USA
securecrossing.com

Secure Decisions (4)
Security Analytics / Securi-
ty Visualization for Cyber
Defense
Northport, NY, USA
securedecisions.com

Secure Mentem (5)
GRC / Security Awareness
Training
Annapolis, MD, USA
securementem.com

Secure Push (10)
Fraud Prevention / Identity
Assurance
Migdal Tefen, Israel
securepush.com

Secure24 (627)
GRC / Secure Hosting
Southfield, MI, USA
secure-24.com

Secure64 (36)
Network / DNS Security
Fort Collins, CO, USA
secure64.com

SecureAge Technology
(25)
Data Security / Encryption
West Chester, PA, USA
secureage.com

SecureAuth (278)
IAM / Acces Control
Irvine, CA, USA
secureauth.com

SecureCode Warrior (106)
Application Security /
Code Security
Sydney, Australia
securecodewarrior.com

Secured Communication
(20)
Data Security / Secure
Communications
San Francisco, CA, USA
securedcommunications.
com

Secured Universe (2)
Endpoint / Mobile Device
Security
San Diego, CA, USA
secureduniverse.com

SecureData, Inc. (65)
Data Security / Encrypted
Hard Drives
Los Angeles, CA, USA
securedata.com

SecuredTouch (34)
IAM / Touchscreen Bio-
metrics
Ramat Gan, Israel
securedtouch.com

SecureIC (44)
Endpoint / Tools for Secure
Chip Design
France
secureic.com

SecureKey (107)
IAM / Identity Manage-
ment
Toronto, Canada
securekey.com

SecureLink (146)
IAM / Third Party Access
Controls
Austin, TX, USA
securelink.com

SecureLogix Corporation (72)
Network / VoIP Security
San Antonio, TX, USA
securelogix.com

SecurelyShare (26)
Data Security / Vault
Indira Nagar, India
securelyshare.com

Secureme2 (5)
MSSP / MDR
Rijen, Netherlands
secureme2.eu/en

SecurEnvoy (34)
IAM / Tokenless 2FA
Basingstoke, UK
securenvoy.com

SecureRF Corporation (19)
IAM / Device Authentication
Shelton, CT, USA
securerf.com

SecureSight Technologies (6)
Training / Collaborative Learning
Ulhasnagar, India
securesighttech.in

SecureSky (16)
MSSP / Cloud MDR
Omaha, NE, USA
securesky.com

SecureStack (4)
GRC / Configuration Management
Docklands, Australia
securestack.com

SecureSwitch (1)
Network / Air Gap Switches
Pittsburgh, PA, USA
secureswitch.com

SecureTeam (1)
Data Security / DRM
Rishon LeZion, Israel
secureteam.net

SecureWorks (2,692)
MSSP / Managed Services
Atlanta, GA, USA
secureworks.com

Securicy (16)
GRC / Policy Management
Sydney, Canada
securicy.com

SecuriGo (1)
Application Security / Cloud App Information Exposure
Haifa, Israel
securigo.com

Securithings (16)
IoT Security / Device Management
Ramat Gan, Israel
securithings.com

SECURITI.ai (130)
Data Security / Discovery for PII
San Jose, CA, USA
securiti.ai

Security Compass (205)
GRC / Policy Compliance
Toronto, Canada
securitycompass.com

Security Compliance Corporation (1)
IAM / Access Control
Orinda, CA, USA
securitycompliancecorp.com

Security First (33)
Data Security for Documents
Rancho Santa Margarita, CA, USA
securityfirstcorp.com

Security Innovation (143)
Application Security
Wilmington, MA, USA
securityinnovation.com

Security Mentor (11)
GRC / Security Awareness Training
Pacific Grove, CA, USA
securitymentor.com

Security On-Demand (72)
MSSP / Managed Firewalls
San Diego, CA, USA
securityondemand.com

Security Weaver (88)
Data Security / IRM
Lehi, UT, USA
securityweaver.com

SecurityCTRL
Network / Intrusion Detection
Edinburgh, UK
securityctrl.com

SecurityDAM (27)
Network / DDoS Defense
Ramat HaHayal, Israel
securitydam.com

SecurityFirst (31)
Data Security / IRM
Rancho Santa Margarita, CA, USA
securityfirst.com

SecurityMetrics (291)
GRC / Vulnerability Scanning and Compliance
Orem, UT, USA
securitymetrics.com

SecurityScorecard (175)
GRC / Risk Measurement
New York, NY, USA
securityscorecard.com

SecurityZONES (6)
Threat Intelligence / Spamhaus
London, UK
securityzones.net

SecurLinx (11)
IAM / Biometrics
Morgantown, WV, USA
securlinx.com

Securonix (368)
Security Analytics / UEBA
Addison, TX, USA
securonix.com

SecurStar (6)
Data Security / Full Disk Encryption
Munich, Germany
securestar.com

Secusmart (52)
Data Security / Secure Mobile Phone
Düsseldorf, Germany
secusmart.com

Secutech Solutions (8)
Data Security / USB Token Security
North Ryde, Australia
esecutech.com

Secuware (1)
Data Security / Database Security
London, UK
secuware.uk

Sedicii (17)
IAM / Mobile Authentication
Carriganore, Ireland
sedicii.com

Seed Protocol (3)
Data Security / Encryption
Athens, OH, USA
seed-protocol.com

SegaSec (26)
Email Security / Anti-phishing
Toronto, Canada
segasec.com

Note: Numbers in parentheses indicate employee count

SEGURO (1)
Network / Secure PBX
Petah Tikva, Israel
seguro-com.com

Sekur Me (3)
IAM / Mobile Authentication
Santa Ana, CA, USA
sekur.me

Semmle (61)
Application Security /
Code Analysis
San Francisco, CA, USA
semmle.com

Semperis (23)
IAM / AD State Manager
New York, NY, USA
semperis.com

Sendio (27)
Email Security / Anti-spam
Newport Beach, CA, USA
sendio.com

SendSafely (7)
Data Security / Secure File
and Message Transfer
New York, NY, USA
sendsafely.com

SendThisFile (4)
Data Security / Secure File
Transfer
Wichita, KS, USA
sendthisfile.com

**Senetas Corporation
Limited** (44)
Data Security / Network
Encryptors
South Melbourne, Australia
senetas.com

Senrio (15)
IoT Security / ICS
Portland, OR, USA
senr.io

SenseCy (9)
Threat Intelligence / Deep
Web OSINT
Poleg Netanya, Israel
sensecy.com

Senseity (3)
GRC / Monitoring
Kfar Saba, Israel
senseity.com

Senseon (38)
Security Analytics / Breach
Detection and Response
London, UK
senseon.io

Sensible Vision (6)
IAM / Biometrics
Cape Coral, FL, USA
sensiblevision.com

SensorHound (6)
IoT Security / ICS
West Lafayette, IN, USA
sensorhound.com

Sentar (303)
Application Security /
Code Scanning
Huntsville, AL, USA
sentar.com

Sentegrity (8)
Endpoint / Mobile
Chicago, IL, USA
sentegrity.com

SentiLink (15)
Fraud Prevention / Anti-fraud
San Francisco, CA, USA
sentilink.com

Sentinel IPS (9)
MSSP / Reputation Firewall
Dallas, TX, USA
sentinelips.com

SentinelOne (329)
Endpoint Protection
Platform
Mountain View, CA, USA
sentinelone.com

Sentor (68)
MSSP / Managed SIEM
Stockholm, Sweden
sentor.se

Sentrix (9)
Network / Web App Security and DDoS Sefense
Waltham, MA, USA
sentrix.com

Sentropi (2)
Fraud Prevention
Ahmedabad, India
sentropi.com

SentryBay (16)
Endpoint / Anti-malware
London, UK
sentrybay.com

SentryCard (5)
IAM / 2FA Cards and OTP
Chicago, IL, USA
sentrycard.com

Sentrycom (2)
Data Security / Encryption
Haifa, Israel
sentry-com.net

Sentryo (28)
IoT Security / ICS
Lyon, France
sentryo.net

Seon (15)
Fraud Prevention / Fraud
Detection
Budapest, Hungary
seon.io

Sepio Systems (11)
IoT Security / IoT Network
Security
Gaithersburg, MD, USA
sepio.systems

Sepior (17)
Data Security / Encryption
and Key Management
Aarhus, Denmark
sepior.com

Seppmail (9)
Email Security / Email
Encryption
Neuenhof, Switzerland
seppmail.com

Septier Communication
(79)
Network / SIGINT Offensive
Petah Tikva, Israel
septier.com

Seqrite (21)
Endpoint / Protection and
Encryption
Pune, India
seqrite.com

Sequitur Labs (12)
Endpoint / Embedded
Security
Fall City, WA, USA
sequiturlabs.com

Sequretek (231)
Endpoint / AV
Mumbai, India
sequretek.com

Sera-Brynn (20)
GRC / Cyber Risk Management
Suffolk, VA, USA
sera-brynn.com

Sergeant Laboratories
(20)
GRC / Risk Management
Onalaska, WI, USA
sgtlabs.com

SertintyONE (6)
Data Security / IRM
Nashville, TN, USA
sertintyone.com

ServiceNow (500)
Operations / Orchestration
Santa Clara, CA, USA
servicenow.com

Seworks (221)
Operations / Automated
Pen Testing
San Francisco, CA, USA
se.works

Shaka Technologies (5)
Network / DLP
Witham, UK
shakatechnologies.com

Shape Security (333)
Network / Web Application
Firewall
Mountain View, CA, USA
shapesecurity.com

ShareVault (27)
Data Security / Vault
Los Gatos, CA, USA
sharevault.com

Sharktech (13)
Network / DDoS Defense
Las Vegas, NV, USA
sharktech.net

**Shenzhen Excelsecu Data
Technology** (42)
IAM / OTP
Shenzhen, China
excelsecu.com

**Sherpas Cyber Security
Group** (3)
Data Security / Secure
Storage
Gaithersburg, MD, USA
sherpascyber.com

Shevirah (3)
Operations / Mobile
Testing
Herndon, VA, USA
shevirah.com

SHIELD Crypto Systems
(3)
Data Security / Encryption
Toronto, Canada
shieldcryptosystems.com

**Shield Square (acquired
by Radware, 2019)** (61)
Network / Anti-bot, An-
ti-scraping
Bangalore, India
shieldsquare.com

ShieldIOT (10)
IoT Security / For Service
Providers
Herzliya, Israel
shieldiot.io

ShieldX (57)
Network / Cloud Mi-
crosegmentation
San Jose, CA, USA
shieldx.com

ShiftLeft (45)
Application Security /
Appsec Code Hardening
Santa Clara, CA, USA
shiftleft.io

ShoCard (18)
IAM / Identity Manage-
ment
Cupertino, CA, USA
shocard.com

SIEMonster (9)
Security Analytics
New York, NY, USA
siemonster.com

Siemplify (79)
Security Analytics / Threat
Detection and Response
New York, NY, USA
siemplify.co

Sift Security (3)
Security Analytics / Cloud
Monitoring
Palo Alto, CA, USA
siftsecurity.com

SIGA Cyber Alert System
(20)
IoT Security / ICS
Ashkelon, Israel
sigasec.com

Signal Science (142)
Network / WAF
Culver City, CA, USA
signalsciences.com

Signifyd (281)
Fraud Prevention / e-Com-
merce Fraud Prevention
San Jose, CA, USA
signifyd.com

SignPass (4)
IAM / Handwriting Bio-
metrics
Tel Aviv, Israel
sign-pass.com

Silent Circle (37)
Data Security / Encrypted
Communication
Fairfax, VA, USA
silentcircle.com

Silicon Forensics (9)
Operations / Forensic
Hardware
Pomona, CA, USA
siliconforensics.com

Silobreaker (36)
Threat Intelligence Man-
agement
London, UK
silobreaker.com

Silverfort (42)
IAM / Clienteles Multi-factor
Tel Aviv, Israel
silverfort.io

SilverLakeMasterSAM (25)
IAM / Privileged Access
Management
Singapore, Singapore
mastersam.com

**Silverskin Information
Security** (20)
GRC / Skills Measurement
and Compliance
Helsinki, Finland
silverskin.com

Simeio Solutions (423)
IAM / IAM
Atlanta, GA, USA
simeiosolutions.com

SimSpace (57)
Training / Cyber Range
Boston, MA, USA
simspace.com

Singular Security (6)
GRC / IT Security & Com-
pliance Risk Management
Tustin, CA, USA
singularsecurity.com

SiteLock (200)
Network / Website Security
Scottsdale, AZ, USA
sitelock.com

Sixgill (28)
Threat Intelligence / Dark
Web Intel
Netanya, Israel
cybersixgill.com

Skout Cybersecurity (76)
Security Analytics /
Streaming Data Analysis
New York, NY, USA
getskout.com

Skurio (26)
Threat Intelligence / Brand
Monitoring
Belfast, UK
skurio.com

Skybox Security (352)
Operations / Security
Management
San Jose, CA, USA
skyboxsecurity.com

Note: Numbers in parentheses indicate employee count

SkyFormation (8)
Network / CASB
Giv'at Shmuel, Israel
skyformation.com

Skymatic (4)
Data Security
Sankt Augustin, Germany
skymatic.de

SlashNext (97)
Email Security / Anti-phishing
Pleasanton, CA, USA
slashnext.com

Smokescreen Technologies Pvt. Ltd. (32)
Deception / Complete Deception Platform
Mumbai, India
smokescreen.io

Smoothwall (116)
Network / UTM
Leeds, UK
smoothwall.com

Smufs (3)
IAM / Finger Scanners for Mobile
Ramat Negev, Israel
smufsbio.com

SMX (301)
Email Security
Auckland, New Zealand
smxemail.com

Snaptrust (1)
Application Security
Potsdam, Germany
snaptrust.com

SNDBOX (3)
Application Security / Malware Analysis
Giv'atayim, Israel
sndbox.com

Snyk (205)
Application Security / Appsec Open Source Vulns
London, UK
snyk.io

SOC Prime (64)
Threat Intelligence Platform
Kiev, Ukraine
socprime.com

Socure (76)
IAM / Online Identity Verification
New York, NY, USA
socure.com

SocView (7)
Operations / Alert Management
London, UK
socview.com

Softex (13)
IAM / Authentication
Austin, TX, USA
softexinc.com

SOFTwarfare (8)
Application Security / Integration Security
Prairie Village, KS, USA
softwarfare.com

Softwin SRL (195)
Endpoint / Anti-virus
Bucharest, Romania
softwin.ro

SoHo Token Labs (1)
Application Security /
Static Code Analysis
New York, NY, USA
sohotokenlabs.com

Solarflare (210)
Network Security Monitoring
Irvine, CA, USA
solarflare.com

Solarwinds (400)
Security Analytics / SIEM
Austin, TX, USA
solarwinds.com

SolSoft (24)
Operations / Policy Management
Bristol, UK
solsoft.co.uk

Solutionary (NTT) (128)
MSSP / Managed Services
Omaha, NE, USA
solutionary.com

Solutions-II (97)
MSSP / Monitoring
Littleton, CO, USA
solutions-ii.com

Somansa (36)
GRC / DLP
San Jose, CA, USA
somansatech.com

Sonatype (321)
Application Security /
Open Source Scanning
Fulton, MD, USA
sonatype.com

Sonavation (48)
IAM / Ultrasound Biometrics
Palm Beach Gardens, FL,
USA
sonavation.com

SonicWall (1,907)
Network / UTM
Milpitas, CA, USA
sonicwall.com

Sonikpass (4)
IAM / Identity Verification,
Mobile
Los Angeles, CA, USA
sonikpass.com

Sonrai Security (39)
IAM / Identity Data
Security
New Brunswick, Canada
sonraisecurity.com

Sophos (3,408)
Endpoint / Anti-virus
Abingdon, UK
sophos.com

Source Defense (32)
Network / Client-Side
Protection against Third
Party Attacks
Be'er Sheva, Israel
sourcedefense.com

South River Technologies
(11)
Data Security / Secure File
Transfer
Annapolis, MD, USA
southrivertech.com

SparkCognition (247)
Endpoint / AV
Austin, TX, USA
sparkcognition.com

Sparrow
Application Security /
Code Scanning
Mapo-gu, South Korea
sparrowfasoo.com

**Specialized Security
Services Inc.** (43)
MSSP / Managed Services
Plano, TX, USA
s3security.com

Specops Software Inc. (49)
IAM / Password Management
Stockholm, Sweden
specopssoft.com

SpeQtral (11)
Data Security / Quantum
Key Distribution
Singapore, Singapore
speqtral.space

**SPHERE Technology
Solutions** (33)
IAM / Privileged Access
Management
Hoboken, NJ, USA
sphereco.com

Spherical Defence (11)
Application Security / API
Security
London, UK
sphericaldefence.com

Spideroak (37)
Data Security / Zero
Knowledge Storage
Mission, KS, USA
spideroak.com

Spirent Communications
(200)
Testing / Security Instrumentation
Crawley, UK
spirent.com

**Spirion (was Identity
Finder)** (107)
Data Security / Data Discovery
St. Petersburg, FL, USA
spirion.com

Splunk (1,000)
Security Analytics / SIEM
San Francisco, CA, USA
splunk.com

SpyCloud (44)
Threat Intelligence / Dark
Web Collection
Austin, TX, USA
spycloud.com

**Spydex, Inc. (division of
Edison Commerce Corp.)**
(1)
Endpoint / Anti-spyware
Wilmington, DE, USA
spydex.com

SPYRUS (27)
Data Security / Encryption
San Jose, CA, USA
spyrus.com

SQR Systems (10)
Data Security / Secure
Communications
London, UK
sqrsystems.com

Sqreen (47)
Application Security /
Agent-Based Monitoring
of Apps
Saint-Cloud, France
sqreen.com

Squadra Technologies (3)
GRC / DLP
Las Vegas, NV, USA
squadratechnologies.com

SS8 (125)
Security Analytics
Milpitas, CA, USA
ss8.com

**SSH Communications
Security** (145)
Data Security / Secure File
Transfer
Helsinki, Finland
ssh.com

SSL.com (20)
Data Security / Certificate
Authority
Houston, TX, USA
ssl.com

Innovate with Intention.
Securely.

Every business wants to accelerate innovation. But innovation can create risk.
Spirent empowers you to "innovate with intention"—take responsible risks backed by actionable intelligence and solid security. Now you can build a culture of continuous innovation without the constant fear of threats and attacks. You can build security into innovations rather than bolt them on. You can see security as the catalyst for innovation rather than the obstacle. And you can leverage great ideas from everywhere—with confidence.

Ospirent™
Promise. Assured.

StackPath (305)
Network / WAF and DDoS
at the Edge
Dallas, TX, USA
stackpath.com

Stackrox (62)
Endpoint / Trusted Computing
Mountain View, CA, USA
stackrox.com

StackStorm (1)
Operations / Orchestration
San Jose, CA, USA
stackstorm.com

Star Lab (38)
Application Security / Research and Development
Washington, DC, USA
starlab.io

STEALIEN (9)
Application Security /
Appsec
Seoul, South Korea
stealien.com

Stealth Software (7)
Data Security / Encryption
Scottsdale, AZ, USA
stealth-soft.com

**STEALTHbits
Technologies, Inc.** (202)
Security Analytics / Threat
Prevention
Hawthorne, NJ, USA
stealthbits.com

SteelCloud (34)
GRC / Configuration Management
Ashburn, VA, USA
steelcloud.com

Steganos (1)
Data Security / Encryption
Munich, Germany
steganos.com/en

Stellar Cyber (31)
Security Analytics / Threat
Detection & Network
Forensics
Santa Clara, CA, USA
stellarcyber.ai

**StepNexus (Division of
Multos International)** (54)
IAM / Authentication
Singapore, Singapore
multosinternational.com/
secure-services/stepnexus.
html

STOPzilla by iS3 (1)
Endpoint / AV
Dover, DE, USA
stopzilla.com

**StormShield (was NetASQ
and Arcoon)** (276)
Network / UTM
Issy-les-Moulineaux,
France
stormshield.com

Storro (5)
Data Security / Encrypted
Storage
Hengelo, Netherlands
storro.com

Stratus Digital Systems (8)
Endpoint / Server Rotation
Eugene, OR, USA
stratusdigitalsystems.com

Stridepoint (5)
Network / Secure Network
Fabric
Tampa, FL, USA
stridepoint.com

StrikeForce Technologies
(20)
IAM
Edison, NJ, USA
strikeforcetech.com

Strobes (3)
GRC / Vulnerability Management
Frisco, TX, USA
strobes.co

StrongKey (18)
Data Security / Key Management
Durham, NC, USA
strongkey.com

Sttarx (3)
Data Security / Network
Encryption
Washington, DC, USA
sttarx.com

Styra (25)
Endpoint / Kubernetes
Access Controls
Redwood City, CA, USA
styra.com

Suavei (10)
IoT Security / Vulnerability
Management
Las Vegas, NV, USA
suavei.com

SubpicoCat (2)
Network / IPS
Sydney, Australia
subpicocat.com

Subuno (2)
Fraud Prevention for SMB
Seattle, WA, USA
subuno.com

Sucuri (63)
Network / Website Defense
Menifee, CA, USA
sucuri.net

Sumo Logic (629)
Security Analytics / SIEM
Redwood City, CA, USA
sumologic.com

Note: Numbers in parentheses indicate employee count

SUPERAntiSpyware (2)
Endpoint / Anti-spyware
Eugene, OR, USA
superantispyware.com

Surance.io (5)
IoT Security / Home Device Protection
Ramat HaSharon, Israel
surance.io

SureCloud (72)
GRC / Cloud Platform
Plano, TX, USA
surecloud.com

SureID (120)
IAM
Portland, OR, USA
sureid.com

SurePass ID (3)
IAM / Secure Single Sign-On
Winter Garden, FL, USA
surepassid.com

Surety (40)
Data Security / Data Protection
Naples, FL, USA
surety.com

Surevine (27)
Data Security / Secure Collaboration
Guildford, UK
surevine.com

SurfWatch Labs (14)
GRC / Cyber Risk Intelligence Analytics
Sterling, VA, USA
surfwatchlabs.com

Swascan (27)
GRC / Web Scanning
Cassina de' Pecchi, Italy
swascan.com

Sweepatic (7)
Threat Intelligence / Brand Monitoring
Leuven, Belgium
sweepatic.com

Swimlane (75)
Operations / Incident Response
Louisville, CO, USA
swimlane.com

SwissSign Group
Data Security / Certificate Authority
Glattbrugg, Switzerland
swisssign.com

SwivelSecure (50)
IAM / Authentication
Wetherby, UK
swivelsecure.com

Sword Active Risk (78)
GRC / Risk Management
Maidenhead, UK
sword-activerisk.com

Syccure (4)
IAM / Access Control
Albany, NY, USA
syccure.com

Syferlock (6)
IAM / Software-Based Authentication
Shelton, CT, USA
syferlock.com

Syhunt (2)
Application Security / Code Scanning
Rio de Janeiro, Brazil
syhunt.com

Symantec Corporation (acquired by Broadcom, 2019) (25,745)
Endpoint / Anti-virus
Mountain View, CA, USA
symantec.com

Symphony (315)
Data Security / Secure Messaging and Collaboration
Palo Alto, CA, USA
Symphony.com

Synack (155)
Testing
Redwood City, CA, USA
synack.com

Syncdog (8)
Endpoint / Mobile Security
Reston, VA, USA
syncdog.com

Syncplicity by Axway (57)
Data Security / Secure File Storage
Santa Clara, CA, USA
syncplicity.com

Syncsort (474)
IAM / iSeries Access Control
Pearl River, NY, USA
syncsort.com

Syncurity Networks (20)
Operations / Incident Response Workflow
Bethesda, MD, USA
syncurity.net

Syneidis (15)
Data Security / File Encryption
Barcelona, Spain
syneidis.com

SynerComm (55)
Network & Security Infrastructure
Brookdfield, WI, USA
synercomm.com

Synopsys (100)
Application Security / Software Testing & Security
Mountain View, CA, USA
synopsys.com

Sysdig (227)
Endpoint / Kubernetes Security
Davis, CA, USA
sysdig.com

Tala Security (31)
Application Security / Web App Analysis
Fremont, CA, USA
talasecurity.io

TamosSoft (1)
Network Monitoring
Christchurch, New Zealand
tamos.com

Tanium (952)
Endpoint Visibility and Control
Emeryville, CA, USA
tanium.com

TargetProof (3)
Fraud Prevention / Identity Verification & Fraud Prevention
Atlanta, GA, USA
targetproof.com

Tascet (8)
GRC / Risk Management
Madison, WI, USA
tascet.com

Tata Communications (1200)
MSSP / Managed Services
Mumbai, India
tatacommunications.com

Tavve Software (15)
Network / Packet Routing
Morrisville, NC, USA
tavve.com

Team Cymru (46)
Threat Intelligence IoCs Malware
Lake Mary, FL, USA
team-cymru.org

TechR2 (29)
Data Security / Erasure
Reynoldsburg, OH, USA
techr2.com

TecSec (23)
Data Security / Key Management
McLean, VA, USA
tecsec.com

Tehama (39)
Network / Secure Virtual
Desktops
Ottawa, Canada
tehama.io

TEHTRIS (37)
Endpoint / AV
San Francisco, CA, USA
tehtris.com

TELEGRID Technologies (5)
Data Security / Network
Encryption Monitoring
Florham Park, NJ, USA
telegrid.com

Telemate Software (22)
Security Analytics / SIEM
Norcross, GA, USA
telemate.net

Telemessage (64)
GRC / Text Messaging
Security
Petah Tikva, Israel
telemessage.com

TeleSign Corporation (307)
IAM / Mobile Identity
Verification
Marina del Rey, CA, USA
telesign.com

Telesoft Technologies (86)
Network / Netflow Monitoring Tools
Annapolis Junction, MD,
USA
Telesoft-technologies.com

Telos (556)
GRC / Risk Management
Ashburn, VA, USA
telos.com

Tempered Networks (65)
Network / Zero-Trust
Networking
Seattle, WA, USA
temperednetworks.com

**Tempest Security
Intelligence** (249)
GRC / Data Classification
and Discovery
Recife, Brazil
tempest.com.br

Templarbit (13)
Application Security /
Appsec Code Hardening
San Francisco, CA, USA
templarbit.com

Tenable Network Security
(1,328)
GRC / Vulnerability Management
Columbia, MD, USA
tenable.com

Tencent (650)
Endpoint / Android AV
Shenzhen, China
tencent.com

Tenzir (4)
Network Forensics
Hamburg, Germany
tenzir.com

TeraDact (7)
Data Security / Secure
Information Sharing
Missoula, MT, USA
teradact.com

Terafence (11)
IoT Security / ICS Gateway
Haifa, Israel
terafence.com

Teramind (64)
Operations / Employee
Monitoring
Aventura, FL, USA
teramind.co

Terbium Labs (42)
GRC / Risk Monitoring
Baltimore, MD, USA
terbiumlabs.com

Terranova Security (55)
Training / Security Training
Laval, Canada
terranovasecurity.com

Teskalabs (9)
Network / Secure Mobile
Gateway
London, UK
teskalabs.com

Tesorion (146)
MSSP / Managed Services
Leusden, Netherlands
tesorion.nl

Tesseract (29)
Data Security / Encryption
Mexico City, Mexico
tesseract.mx

Tessian (124)
Email Security / Anti-phishing
New York, NY, USA
tessian.com

Tetrane (11)
Application Security /
Reverse Engineering
Macon, France
tetrane.com

Thales (910)
IAM / Authentication
Plantation, FL, USA
thalesesecurity.com

The Barrier Group (2)
Threat Intelligence Platform
Minneapolis, MN, USA
thebarriergroup.com

The Cyberfort Group (17)
MSSP / Managed SOC
Thatcham, UK
cyberfortgroup.com

The DigiTrust Group (23)
MSSP / Managed Endpoint
and WAF
Los Angeles, CA, USA
digitrustgroup.com

The Email Laundry (11)
Network / Managed
Services
Naas, Ireland
theemaillaundry.com

The Media Trust (79)
Fraud Prevention / Ad
Tech Security
McLean, VA, USA
themediatrust.com

ThetaRay (87)
Security Analytics
Hod HaSharon, Israel
thetaray.com

Thinkst Canary (9)
Deception / Target Agents
Deployed in Operations
Edinvale, South Africa
canary.tools

ThirdPartyTrust (22)
GRC / Third Party Risk
Chicago, IL, USA
thirdpartytrust.com

ThisIsMe (13)
IAM / Onboarding
Cape Town, South Africa
thisisme.com

Note: Numbers in parentheses indicate employee count

Threat Stack (136)
Network / Cloud Security
Monitoring
Boston, MA, USA
threatstack.com

ThreatConnect (117)
Threat Intelligence
Arlington, VA, USA
threatconnect.com

ThreatGuard, Inc. (4)
GRC / Auditing and Mon-
itoring
San Antonio, TX, USA
threatguard.com

ThreatLandscape (24)
Threat Intelligence
San Jose, CA, USA
threatlandscape.com

ThreatLocker
Endpoint / Whitelisting
Maitland, FL, USA
threatlocker.com

ThreatMetrix (260)
Fraud Prevention
San Jose, CA, USA
threatmetrix.com
ThreatModeler Software
(39)
Application Security / Vul-
nerability Management
Jersey City, NJ, USA
threatmodeler.com

ThreatQuotient (104)
Threat Intelligence Plat-
form
Reston, VA, USA
threatquotient.com

ThreatSTOP, Inc (30)
Network / Cloud Reputa-
tion Service
Carlsbad, CA, USA
threatstop.com

ThreatTrack Security (72)
Endpoint Security
Clearwater, FL, USA
threattracksecurity.com

ThreatWarrior (5)
Network Monitoring and
Defense
Austin, TX, USA
threatwarrior.com

ThreatX (20)
Network / Web Application
Firewall
Louisville, CO, USA
threatx.com

Thred Tech (45)
Threat Intelligence Plat-
form
London, Canada
thredtech.com

Threshing Floor (3)
Security Analytics / SIEM
Enrichment
Washington, DC, USA
threshingfloor.io

Thycotic Software (355)
IAM / Password & Access
Management
Washington, DC, USA
thycotic.com

TIBCO Software Inc. (500)
Data Security / Big Data
Security
Palo Alto, CA, USA
tibco.com

Tigera (80)
Endpoint / Kubernetes
Security
San Francisco, CA, USA
tigera.io

Tinfoil Security (15)
Application Security / App
Scanning
Mountain View, CA, USA
tinfoilsecurity.com

Titan IC (22)
Network / IDS
Belfast, UK
Titan-ic.com

TitanHQ (52)
Network / DNS Filtering
Galway, Ireland
titanhq.com

Titania Ltd. (48)
GRC / Configuration
Auditing
Worcester, UK
titania.com

TITUS (250)
GRC / DLP
Ottawa, Canada
titus.com

TNT Software (5)
Operations / Security
Management
Vancouver, WA, USA
tntsoftware.com

Todyl (5)
Network / Remote Access
Protection
New York, NY, USA
todyl.com

TokenEx (32)
Data Security / Tokeniza-
tion
Edmond, OK, USA
tokenex.com

TokenOne (11)
IAM
Sydney, Australia
tokenone.com

In 2020, T.E.N. is proudly celebrating 10 years of Connecting, Collaborating, & Celebrating. Join the celebration by visiting **ten-inc.com**

ToothPic (22)
Operations / Forensics Cameras
Turin, Italy
toothpic.eu

Tophat Security (2)
MSSP / Managed SIEM
Wilmington, DE, USA
tophatsecurity.com

Topia Technology (19)
Data Security / Encryption with Shredding
Tacoma, WA, USA
topiatechnology.com

Torsion Information Security (7)
Data Security / File Access Monitoring
London, UK
torsionis.com

Tortuga Logic (25)
Data Security / Hardware Root of Trust Verification
San Diego, CA, USA
tortugalogic.com

Total Defense (32)
Endpoint / PC, Mobile & Internet Security
Hauppauge, NY, USA
totaldefense.com

Total Digital Security (4)
Network / Consumer VPN
West Palm Beach, FL, USA
totaldigitalsecurity.com

ToucanX
Endpoint Segmentation and Sandboxing
Southfield, MI, USA
toucanx.com

TowerSec (a HARMAN company) (35)
IoT Security / Automotive Security
Hod HaSharon, Israel
tower-sec.com

Townsend Security (21)
Data Security / Encryption and Tokenization
Olympia, WA, USA
townsendsecurity.com

TraceSecurity (100)
GRC
Baton Rouge, LA, USA
tracesecurity.com

TransientX (1)
Network / Zero-Trust Networking
San Francisco, CA, USA
transientx.com

Transmit Security (105)
Fraud Prevention / Anti-fraud
Boston, MA, USA
transmitsecurity.com

Trapezoid (11)
IoT Security / Firmware Monitoring
Miami, FL, USA
trapezoid.com

Trapmine (9)
Endpoint Security
Tallinn, Estonia
trapmine.com

TrapX Security (37)
Deception
San Jose, CA, USA
trapx.com

Traversal Networks
Network / IDS
Brazil
traversalnetworks.com

Treebox Solutions (22)
Data Security / Secure Communications
Singapore, Singapore
treeboxsolutions.com

Trend Micro (6,565)
Endpoint / Anti-virus
Irving, TX, USA
trendmicro.com

Tresorit (115)
Data Security / Secure File Transfer
Budapest, Hungary
tresorit.com

Tresys (52)
Data Security / Data Scrubbing of Removable Media
Columbia, MD, USA
tresys.com

TriagingX (8)
Operations / Malware Sandbox
San Jose, CA, USA
triagingx.com

Tricerion (5)
IAM / Grid Password
Reading, UK
tricerion.com

Trillium Secure (20)
IoT Security / Automotive
Sunnyvale, CA, USA
trilliumsecure.com

Trinity Future-In (11)
Data Security / DRM for Web
Bangalore, India
trifuturein.com

TripWire (Belkin) (465)
GRC / File Integrity Management
Portland, OR, USA
tripwire.com

Trivalent (12)
Data Security / File En-
cryption
Annapolis, MD, USA
trivalent.co

Trovares (8)
Security Analytics / Graph
Analytics
Seattle, WA, USA
trovares.com

True Digital Security (62)
MSSP / Managed SIEM
Tulsa, OK, USA
truedigitalsecurity.com

TrueFort (32)
Application Security /
Appsec Code Hardening
Weehawken, NJ, USA
truefort.com

TrueVault (10)
Data Security / Secure Data
Storage
San Francisco, CA, USA
truevault.com

TruGrid (5)
IAM / Access Control
Schaumburg, IL, USA
trugrid.com

Trulioo (113)
IAM / Identity Verification
Vancouver, Canada
trulioo.com

TrulyProtect (7)
Application Security / App
Security
Rehovot, Israel
trulyprotect.com

Trushield, Inc. (40)
MSSP / Managed Security
Services
Sterling, VA, USA
trushieldinc.com

Trusona (35)
IAM / SSO
Scottsdale, AZ, USA
trusona.com

TruSTAR (65)
Threat Intelligence Plat-
form
San Francisco, CA, USA
trustar.co

TrustArc (304)
GRC / Privacy Assessments
San Francisco, CA, USA
trustarc.com

Trusted Integration (4)
GRC
Alexandria, VA, USA
trustedintegration.com

Trusted Knight (13)
Endpoint
Annapolis, MD, USA
trustedknight.com

Trusted Objects
IoT Security / IoT
Aix-en-Provence, France
trusted-objects.com

Trustelem (5)
IAM / IAM
Paris, France
trustelem.com

TrustGo
Endpoint / Android AV
Santa Clara, CA, USA
trustgo.com

Trustifi (28)
Email Security / Encryp-
tion and Anti-phishing
Las Vegas, NV, USA
trustifi.com

TrustLayers (1)
Data Security / IRM
Cambridge, MA, USA
trustlayers.com

Trustless.ai (11)
Endpoint / Secure Device
Geneva, Switzerland
trustless.ai

Trustlook (19)
Endpoint / Malware
Analysis
San Jose, CA, USA
trustlook.com

Trustonic (93)
Endpoint / Mobile App
Protection
Austin, TX, USA
trustonic.com

TrustPort (14)
Endpoint / Android AV
Brno, Czech Republic
trustport.com/en

**TrustWave (a Singtel
Company)** (1,417)
MSSP / Managed Security
Services
Chicago, IL, USA
trustwave.com

Truvincio (3)
GRC / Security Awareness
Training
Vienna, VA, USA
truvincio.com

Tu Identidad (8)
IAM / 2FA (mobile)
Mexico City, Mexico
tuidentidad.com

Tufin (442)
Operations / Firewall Policy Management
Boston, MA, USA
tufin.com

TunnelBear (47)
Network / VPN
Toronto, Canada
tunnelbear.com

**Twistlock (acquired by
Palo Alto Networks)** (121)
Operations / Container
Security
Portland, OR, USA
twistlock.com

Tychon (25)
GRC / Risk Management
Dashboards
Fredericksburg, VA, USA
tychon.io

Typing DNA (27)
IAM / Biometrics
New York, NY, USA
typingdna.com

Ubble.ai (31)
Fraud Prevention / Identity
Verification
Paris, France
ubble.ai

Ubiq Security (27)
Data Security / Encryption
San Diego, CA, USA
ubiqsecurity.com

Ubirch
IoT Security / Encryption
and Blockchain for ICS
Berlin, Germany
ubirch.de

Ubisecure Solutions, Inc.
(37)
IAM
Espoo, Finland
ubisecure.com

ULedger (5)
Data Security / Blockchain
Applied to Data
Boise, ID, USA
uledger.co

UM-Labs (10)
Endpoint / Hardened OS
for Realtime Comms
London, UK
Um-labs.com

Unbound Tech (45)
Data Security / Key Management
New York, NY, USA
unboundtech.com

Unfraud (1)
Fraud Prevention / Anti-fraud
Ariano Irpino, Italy
unfraud.com

UnifyID (34)
IAM / Behavioral Identity
Redwood City, CA, USA
unify.id

Uniken (125)
IAM / Authentication
Chatham Twp., NJ, USA
uniken.com

Uniloc (6)
IAM
Plano, TX, USA
uniloc.com

Unisys Stealth (500)
Network Cloaking
Blue Bell, PA, USA
unisys.com

United Security Providers (57)
Network / Web Application Firewall
Bern, Switzerland
united-security-providers.com

Unitrends (239)
Data Security / Encryption
Burlington, MA, USA
unitrends.com

Universign (69)
IAM / IAM
Paris, France
universign.com

Unloq (—)
IAM / Authentication and Authorization
London, UK
unloqsystems.com

Untangle (68)
Network / UTM
San Jose, CA, USA
untangle.com

UpGuard (43)
GRC / Configuration Monitoring
Mountain View, CA, USA
upguard.com

Uplevel Security (13)
Operations / Incident Response
New York, NY, USA
uplevelsecurity.com

Upstream (34)
IoT Security / Automotive
Herzliya, Israel
upstream.auto

Uptycs, Inc. (45)
Security Analytics / OS-Query
Waltham, MA, USA
uptycs.com

US Interactive (1)
MSSP / Managed Services
Santa Clara, CA, USA
usinteractive.com

Utimaco (424)
Data Security / Encryption HSMs
Aachen, Germany
utimaco.com/en/home

V-Key (84)
Application Security / Mobile Device & App Security
Singapore, Singapore
v-key.com

V5 Systems (78)
IoT Security / ICS
Fremont, CA, USA
v5systems.us

Vade Secure (112)
Email Security / Anti-phishing
San Francisco, CA, USA
vadesecure.com

VADO Security (3)
Network / Air Gap
Giv'atayim, Israel
vadosecurity.com

Validian (1)
Data Security / Encryption
Nepean, Canada
validian.com

Valimail (108)
Email Security / Anti-phishing
San Francisco, CA, USA
valimail.com

Valtx Cyber Securities (5)
Endpoint Hardening
Surprise, AZ, USA
valtx.com

Vancosys (5)
IAM / IAM
Vancouver, Canada
vancosys.com

Vandyke Software (20)
Data Security / Secure File Transfer
Albuquerque, NM, USA
vandyke.com

Vanguard Integrity Professionals (77)
GRC / Event Monitoring
Las Vegas, NV, USA
go2vanguard.com

Vanquish Labs, Inc. (29)
Endpoint / Anti-spam
Marlborough, MA, USA
vanquish.com

Vario Secure Networks (15)
MSSP / Managed Security Services
Tokyo, Japan
variosecure.net/en

Variti (7)
Network / DDoS Defense
Lucerne, Switzerland
variti.com

vArmour (103)
Endpoint / Server Security
Mountain View, CA, USA
varmour.com

Varonis (1,396)
Data Security / File Collaboration & Data Protection
New York, NY, USA
varonis.com

Vaultize (31)
Data Security / IRM Content Sharing
San Francisco, CA, USA
vaultize.com

Vaulto (3)
Endpoint / Mobile Security
Tel Aviv-Yafo, Israel
vaulto.co

Vdoo (68)
IoT Security / Embedded Systems Security
Tel Aviv, Israel
vdoo.com

Vectra Networks (246)
Security Analytics / Cyber-Attack Detection & Management
San Jose, CA, USA
vectra.ai

Velona Systems (7)
GRC / PBX Security Scanner
Cork, Ireland
velonasystems.com

Venafi (303)
Data Security / Key Management
Salt Lake City, UT, USA
venafi.com

Venustech (260)
Network / UTM
China
venusense.com

Vera (116)
Data Security / IRM
Palo Alto, CA, USA
vera.com

Veracity Industrial Networks (13)
IoT Security / ICS
Aliso Viejo, CA, USA
veracity.io

Veracode (721)
Application Security /
Code Analysis
Burlington, MA, USA
veracode.com

Veriato (formerly SpectorSoft) (51)
GRC / UEBA
Palm Beach Gardens, FL,
USA
veriato.com

VeriClouds (6)
Fraud Prevention / Credential Stuffing Defense
Seattle, WA, USA
vericlouds.com

Veridium (63)
IAM / Authentication
Boston, MA, USA
veridiumid.com

Verifyoo (2)
IAM / Biometrics
Tel Aviv, Israel
verifyoo.com

Verimatrix (281)
Data Security / DRM for
Video
San Diego, CA, USA
verimatrix.com

Verimuchme (1)
IAM / Identity Storage
London, UK
verimuchme.com

Verint (3,132)
Operations / Data Mining
Melville, NY, USA
verint.com

Veriscan Security (10)
GRC / Security Measurement
Karlstad, Sweden
veriscan.se

Verisign (1,323)
MSSP / Managed Services
Reston, VA, USA
verisign.com

**Verizon Business Security
Solutions** (1,000)
MSSP / Managed Services
Basking Ridge, NJ, USA
verizonenterprise.com/
solutions/security

**Verodin (acquired by
FireEye, 2019)** (93)
Testing / Security Instrumentation
McLean, VA, USA
verodin.com

Versa (304)
Network / SDN
San Jose, CA, USA
versa-networks.com

Versasec (23)
IAM
Stockholm, Sweden
versasec.com

Very Good Security (96)
Data Security / Vault
San Francisco, CA, USA
verygoodsecurity.com

VIA3 Corperation (18)
Data Security / Secure
Messaging
Scottsdale, AZ, USA
via3.com

Viascope (6)
IAM / Network Access
Control
Seoul, South Korea
viascope.com

Vicarius (14)
Application Security /
Static and Dynamic Code
Scanning
Jerusalem, Israel
vicarius.io

Vigilante ATI (9)
Threat Intelligence / Dark
Web Research
Phoenix, AZ, USA
vigilante.io

VigiTrust (16)
GRC / Risk Management
Dublin, Ireland
vigitrust.com

Vijilan Security (27)
MSSP / Security for MSPs
Ft. Lauderdale, FL, USA
vijilan.com

VikiSense (5)
IAM / Biometrics MFA
Kiryat Gat, Israel
vikisense.com

Vinsula (2)
Endpoint Protection
Seattle, WA, USA
vinsula.com

Vipre (115)
Endpoint / AV for Desktops
Clearwater, FL, USA
vipre.com

Vir2us (11)
Endpoint / Virtual Environments
Petaluma, CA, USA
vir2us.com

Virgil Security (40)
Data Security / End-to-End
Application Encryption
Manassas, VA, USA
virgilsecurity.com

Virsec (69)
Endpoint / Runtime Protection
San Jose, CA, USA
virsec.com

Virta Labs (4)
IoT Security / Healthcare
Seattle, WA, USA
virtalabs.com

Virtru (118)
Data Security / Google
Apps & Email Privacy
Washington, DC, USA
virtru.com

Virtual Forge (76)
Application Security / SAP
Security
Heidelberg, Germany
virtualforge.com

VirtualArmour (50)
MSSP / Managed Services
Centennial, CO, USA
irtualarmour.com

Visual Click Software (16)
GRC / Auditing for AD
Austin, TX, USA
visualclick.com

Vitrium (20)
Data Security / DRM
Vancouver, Canada
vitrium.com

Vkansee (1)
IAM / Fingerprint Sensors
for Mobile Security
Beijing, China
vkansee.com

VKey (2)
Endpoint / Sandbox for
Apps
Ottawa, Canada
v-key.com

VMRay (50)
Operations / Malware
Analysis
Boston, MA, USA
vmray.com

VMWare (1200)
Endpoint / EDR
Palo Alto, CA, USA
vmware.com]

Vo1t (9)
Data Security / Secure
Storage for Cryptocurren-
cies
London, UK
vo1t.io

**Voice Security Systems
Inc.** (2)
IAM / Biometrics
Dana Point, CA, USA
voice-security.com

Votiro (33)
Network / File Scrubbing
Tel Aviv, Israel
votiro.com

VU Security (454)
IAM / Identity, Authentication, VPN
Buenos Aires, Argentina
vusecurity.com

Vulcan Cyber (33)
GRC / Vulnerability Reme-
diation
Tel Aviv, Israel
vulcan.io

VuNet Systems (30)
Security Analytics / Log
Analysis
Bangalore, India
vunetsystems.com

Vysk (12)
Endpoint / Mobile Device
Security
San Antonio, TX, USA
vysk.com

Wallarm (71)
Network / Cloud WAF
San Francisco, CA, USA
wallarm.com

Wallix (154)
IAM / Privileged Access
Management
Paris, France
wallix.com/en

Wandera (177)
Network / Secure Mobile
Gateway
San Francisco, CA, USA
wandera.com

Wapack Labs (17)
Threat Intelligence / Hacker Account Takeover
New Boston, NH, USA
cms.wapacklabs.com

Waratek (41)
Application Security
Dublin, Ireland
waratek.com

WaryMe (9)
GRC
Cesson-Sévigné, France
waryme.com

Watchdata (202)
IAM / PKI
Singapore, Singapore
watchdata.com

**WatchGuard
Technologies, Inc.** (720)
Network / UTM
Seattle, WA, USA
watchguard.com

Watchtower AI (12)
Data Security / Data Dis-
covery
San Francisco, CA, USA
watchtower.ai

Waterfall (72)
IoT Security / ICS Air Gap
Firewall
Rosh HaAyin, Israel
waterfall-security.com

Wavecrest Computing (15)
Network / Secure Web
Gateway
Melbourne, FL, USA
wavecrest.net

we45 (33)
Application Security
Sunnyvale, CA, USA
we45.com

WebARX (4)
Network / Web Application
Firewall
London, UK
webarxsecurity.com

Webgap (3)
Network / Remote Browser
Isolation
Walnut, CA, USA
webgap.io

**Webroot Software
(acquired by Carbonite,
2019; then acquired by
OpenText)** (796)
Endpoint / Anti-malware
Broomfield, CO, USA
webroot.com

webScurity Inc. (1)
Network / Web Application
Firewall
Minneapolis, MN, USA
webscurity.com

WebTitan (TitanHQ) (53)
Network / Content and
Email Filtering
Salthill, Ireland
webtitan.com

Wedge Networks (40)
Network / Cloud Proxy
Security
Calgary, Canada
wedgenetworks.com

Westgate Cyber Security
(4)
Network / Zero-Trust
Networking
Cwmbran, UK
westgatecyber.com

Wetstone (15)
Operations / Forensics
Cortland, NY, USA
wetstonetech.com

Whistic (35)
Operations / Vendor Man-
agement
Pleasant Grove, UT, USA
whistic.com

White Canyon Inc. (24)
Data Security / Erasure
American Fork, UT, USA
whitecanyon.com

White Cloud Security (15)
Endpoint / Whitelisting
Austin, TX, USA
whitecloudsecurity.com

White Cyber Knight (7)
GRC / Risk Management
Tel Aviv, Israel
wck-grc.com

Note: Numbers in parentheses indicate employee count

White Hawk Software (5)
Application Security /
Tamperproofing
Palo Alto, CA, USA
whitehawksoftware.com

White Ops (115)
Fraud Prevention / Ad
Tech Security
New York, NY, USA
whiteops.com

**WhiteHat Security
(acquired by NTT, 2019)**
(370)
GRC / Web Application
Security
San Jose, CA, USA
whitehatsec.com

WhiteSource (154)
Application Security /
Open Source Security and
License Management
Giv'atayim, Israel
whitesourcesoftware.com

Wickr (43)
Data Security / Secure
Communications
San Francisco, CA, USA
wickr.com

Widevine Technologies (6)
Data Security / DRM
Kirkland, WA, USA
widevine.com

WifiWall (2)
Network / Wifi Firewall
Kfar Haim, Israel
wifiwall.com

WiKID Systems (4)
IAM / 2FA OTP with AD
Atlanta, GA, USA
wikidsystems.com

WindTalker Security (8)
Data Security / File En-
cryption and Sharing
Cumming, GA, USA
windtalkersecurity.com

WinGate (Qbik) (1)
Network / Gateway Securi-
ty, VPN
Auckland, New Zealand
wingate.com

WinMagic Inc. (108)
Data Security / Encryption
Mississauga, Canada
winmagic.com

Winston Privacy (12)
Network / Private Brows-
ing
Chicago, IL, USA
winstonprivacy.com

Wintego (10)
Network / Wifi Offensive
Yokne'am Illit, Israel
wintego.com

Wirewheel (51)
Data Security / Customer
Data Protection
Arlington, VA, USA
wirewheel.io

WireX (20)
Operations / Network
Forensics
Sunnyvale, CA, USA
wirexsystems.com

Wisekey (124)
IoT Security / Root of
Trust Chips
Geneva, Switzerland
wisekey.com

WiseSec (10)
Operations / Microgeolo-
cation
Yokne'am Illit, Israel
wisesec.com

Wispero (2)
IoT Security / Anomaly
Detection
San Jose, CA, USA
wispero.com

WitFoo (10)
Operations / Security
Operations Platform
Dunwoody, GA, USA
witfoo.com

WithNetworks
Endpoint / EDR
Yongsan-gu, South Korea
withnetworks.com

WiTopia (9)
Network / VPN
Reston, VA, USA
witopia.com

Woleet (15)
Data Security / Blockchain
for Signatures
Rennes, France
woleet.io

wolfSSL (26)
Network / Open Source
Internet Security
Edmonds, WA, USA
wolfssl.com

Wontok (29)
Fraud Prevention / An-
ti-fraud Technology
Pyrmont, Australia
wontok.com

WootCloud (17)
Endpoint / Device Control
San Jose, CA, USA
wootcloud.com

Workshare (213)
Data Security / File En-
cryption and Sharing
London, UK
workshare.com

Workspot (80)
Operations / Secure Re-
mote Access
Campbell, CA, USA
workspot.com

WWN Software LLC (10)
Data Security / Encrypted
Data Sharing
Washington, DC, USA
wwnsoftware.com

WWPass (21)
IAM / Authentication &
Access Solutions
Nashua, NH, USA
wwpass.com

Wymsical (6)
IAM / Identity Manager
Greenwich, CT, USA
wymsical.com

X-Ways (8)
Operations / Forensics
Delhi, India
x-ways.net

Xabyss
Network / Traffic Capture
and Analysis
Seoul, South Korea
xabyss.com

Xage Security (40)
IoT Security / ICS
Palo Alto, CA, USA
xage.com

Xahive (5)
Data Security / Secure
Messaging
Ottawa, Canada
xahive.com

Xbridge Systems (8)
GRC / DLP for z/OS
San Jose, CA, USA
xbridgesystems.com

Xenarmor (1)
Data Security / SSL Certificate Management
Bangalore, India
xenarmor.com

XM Cyber (60)
Operations / Breach and
Attack Simulation
Herzliya, Israel
xmcyber.com

XOOUi (1)
Data Security / Encryption
State College, PA, USA
xooui.com

Xpandion (19)
GRC / Risk Management
Tel Aviv, Israel
xpandion.com

XTN Cognitive Security
(19)
IAM / Identity Verification
Boston, MA, USA
Xtn-lab.com

Xton Technologies (4)
IAM / Privileged Access
Management
Trevose, PA, USA
xtontech.com

YAXA (2)
Network / UEBA
Concord, MA, USA
yaxa.io

YazamTech (3)
Data Security / File Scrubbing
Ra'anana, Israel
yazamtech.com

YesWeHack (49)
Operations / Bug Bounty
Paris, France
yeswehack.com

Yogosha (28)
Operations / Bug Bounty
Platform
Paris, France
yogosha.com

Yottaa (83)
Network / DDoS Defense
Waltham, MA, USA
yottaa.com

Yubico (188)
IAM / Authentication
Tokens
Stockholm, Sweden
yubico.com

Zapper Software (1)
Data Security / DRM
Rosedale, Canada
zappersoftware.com/home.
html

ZecOps (19)
Operations / Automated
Defense
San Francisco, CA, USA
zecops.com

Zecurion (43)
Data Security / Database
Security
Moscow, Russia
zecurion.com

Zemana (33)
Endpoint / Android AV
Ankara, Turkey
zemana.com

Zen Internet (464)
MSSP / Managed Services
Rochdale, UK
zen.co.uk

Note: Numbers in parentheses indicate employee count

ZenMate (13)
Network / VPN
Berlin, Germany
zenmate.com

Zentera Systems (27)
Network / Zero-Trust
Networking
San Jose, CA, USA
zentera.net

Zercurity (2)
GRC / OSQuery
London, UK
zercurity.com

Zerho (2)
Security Analytics / Machine Learning
Crestview, VA, USA
zerho.info

ZeroFOX (187)
Threat Intelligence / Social
Media Monitoring
Baltimore, MD, USA
zerofox.com

Zeronorth (40)
GRC / Vulnerability Management
Boston, MA, USA
zeronorth.io

Zertificon Solutions (49)
Email Security / Secure
Email
Berlin, Germany
zertificon.com/en

Zettaset (31)
Data Security / Encryption,
Databases
Mountain View, CA, USA
zettaset.com

Ziften (33)
Endpoint Visibility
Austin, TX, USA
ziften.com

Zighra (8)
IAM / Biometrics, Kinetic
Ottawa, Canada
zighra.com

Zignsec (16)
IAM / Identity Verification
Solna, Sweden
zignsec.com

Zimperium (164)
Endpoint / Mobile Device
Security
Dallas, TX, USA
zimperium.com

**Zingbox (acquired by Palo
Alto Networks)** (83)
IoT Security / IoT
Mountain View, CA, USA
zingbox.com

Ziroh Labs (17)
Data Security
Bangalore, India
ziroh.com

Zivver (83)
Email Security / Encrypted
Email
Amsterdam, Netherlands
zivver.com

Zix Corp. (391)
Data Security / Secure
Messaging
Dallas, TX, USA
zixcorp.com

Zoloz (33)
IAM / Biometrics
Haidian District, China
zoloz.com

Zorus (11)
Network / Cloud Proxy
Monroe, CT, USA
zorustech.com

Zscaler (1,504)
Network / Cloud Security
Layer
San Jose, CA, USA
zscaler.com

Zumigo (21)
IAM / Identity Verification
San Jose, CA, USA
zumigo.com

Zvelo (41)
Network / URL Categorization
Greenwood VillageCO,
CO, USA
zvelo.com

ZyLAB (91)
GRC / e-discovery
Amsterdam, Netherlands
zylab.com

Zymbit (2)
IoT Security / Device Security Modules
Santa Barbara, CA, USA
zymbit.com

Zyston (41)
MSSP / Managed Security
Services
Dallas, TX, USA
zyston.com

Zyudly Labs (23)
Operations / Cloud Security for AWS
Palo Alto, CA, USA
zyudlylabs.com

**ZyXEL Communications
Corp.** (33)
Network / Firewall
Anaheim, CA, USA
zyxel.com/us/en/homepage.shtml

Listings By Country

Number of Vendors in Top 20 Countries

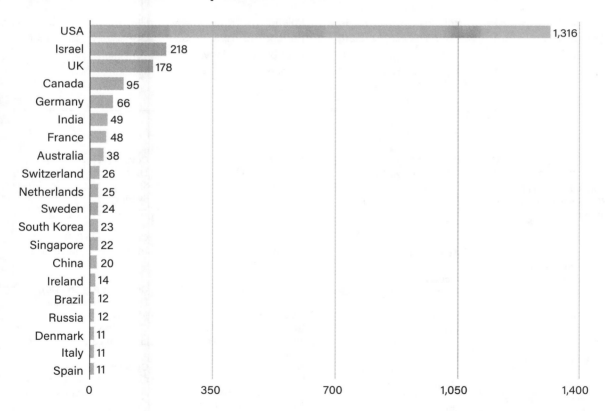

Country	Number of Vendors
USA	1,316
Israel	218
UK	178
Canada	95
Germany	66
India	49
France	48
Australia	38
Switzerland	26
Netherlands	25
Sweden	24
South Korea	23
Singapore	22
China	20
Ireland	14
Brazil	12
Russia	12
Denmark	11
Italy	11
Spain	11

Number of Vendors per Country

Argentina 2	Egypt 1	Kuwait 2	Russia 12
Armenia 2	Estonia 3	Luxembourg 1	Singapore 22
Australia 38	Finland 9	Malaysia 2	Slovakia 2
Austria 8	France 48	Malta 1	South Africa 4
Bahrain 1	Germany 66	Mexico 2	South Korea 27
Belgium 2	Greece 1	Morocco 1	Spain 11
Brazil 12	Hong Kong 3	Netherlands 25	Sweden 24
British Virgin Islands ... 1	Hungary 3	New Zealand 6	Switzerland 26
Bulgaria 1	Iceland 2	Norway 4	Taiwan 6
Canada 95	India 49	Panama 1	Turkey 5
Chile 1	Indonesia 1	Philippines 1	UK 178
China 20	Ireland 14	Poland 4	Ukraine 3
Cyprus 1	Israel 218	Portugal 3	USA 1,316
Czech Republic 7	Italy 11	Republic of Moldova ... 1	Venezuela 1
Denmark 11	Japan 6	Romania 6	Vietnam 1

ARGENTINA

Defense Balance (13)
GRC / Security Awareness
Training
Cordoba
smartfense.com

VU Security (454)
IAM / Identity, Authentication, VPN
Buenos Aires
vusecurity.com

ARMENIA

BeSafe (8)
Data Security / Cloud Key
Management
Yerevan
besafe.io

KMSChain (3)
Data Security / Cloud Key
Management
Yerevan
kmschain.com

AUSTRALIA

Aiculus (5)
Application Security / API
Security
Melbourne
aiculus.co

Anixis (1)
IAM / Password Management
Glenmore Park
anixis.com

Archimigo (7)
GRC / Compliance Management
Melbourne
archimigo.io

Cloud Conformity (51)
GRC / AWS Compliance
Monitoring
Sydney
cloudconformity.com

Cloudpurge (1)
Network / Virtualized
Remote Browsing
Sydney
cloudpurge.info

Cog (127)
IoT Security / Microvirtualization Framework
Sydney
cog.systems

ContentKeeper (37)
Network / Content URL
Filtering
Braddon
contentkeeper.com

Covata (22)
Data Security / Secure File
Sharing
Sydney
covata.com

CryptoPhoto (34)
IAM / 2FA Using Images
cryptophoto.com

Cryptsoft Pty Ltd. (10)
Data Security / PKI and
Identity
Greenslopes
cryptsoft.com

Cydarm (4)
Operations / Incident Response Case Management
Docklands
cydarm.com

Dekko Secure (7)
Data Security / Encryption
Sydney
dekkosecure.com

Note: Numbers in parentheses indicate employee count

Ditno (6)
Network / Cloud Firewall Management and WAF
Sydney
ditno.com

E-Certify (2)
IAM
Wayville
ecertify.com

EFTsure (14)
Fraud Prevention / EFT Protection
North Sydney
home.eftsure.com.au

Forticode (24)
IAM / Password Grids
Melbourne
forticode.com

GetData Forensics (9)
GRC / Forensics
Kogarah
forensicexplorer.com

Huntsman (21)
Security Analytics / SIEM
Chatswood
huntsmansecurity.com

Janusnet (11)
Data Security / Data Classification
Milsons Point
janusnet.com

Kasada (22)
Network / Web Defense
Sydney
kasada.io

NetFlow Auditor (9)
Network Monitoring
Sydney
netflowauditor.com

NetLinkz (1)
Network / Zero-Trust Networking
Sydney
netlinkz.com

NIMIS Cybersecurity (2)
Operations / Automated Pen Testing
Melbourne
nimis.ai

Nuix (468)
Security Analytics / Analytics for Digital Investigations
Sydney
nuix.com

PassMark Software Pvt Ltd. (7)
IAM
Surry Hills
passmark.com

Prophecy International (32)
Data Security / Secure File Transfer
Adelaide
prophecyinternational.com

Quintessence Labs (38)
Data Security / Quantum Optics & Cryptographic Security
Deakin
quintessencelabs.com

Red Piranha (41)
Network / UTM
Melbourne
redpiranha.net

Responsight (8)
Network / UEBA
Melbourne
responsight.com

Sapian Cyber (28)
Security Analytics / Breach Detection
Joondalup
sapiencyber.com.au

Seccom Global (25)
MSSP / Managed Services
Sydney
seccomglobal.com

SecureCode Warrior (106)
Application Security / Code Security
Sydney
securecodewarrior.com

SecureStack (4)
GRC / Configuration Management
Docklands
securestack.com

Secutech Solutions (8)
Data Security / USB Token Security
North Ryde
esecutech.com

Senetas Corporation Limited (44)
Data Security / Network Encryptors
South Melbourne
senetas.com

SubpicoCat (2)
Network / IPS
Sydney
subpicocat.com

TokenOne (11)
IAM
Sydney
tokenone.com

Wontok (29)
Fraud Prevention / Anti-fraud Technology
Pyrmont
wontok.com

AUSTRIA

Appray (2)
Application Security / Mobile App Scanning
Vienna
app-ray.co

Cubro (64)
Network / Packet Capture
Vienna
cubro.com

CYAN Network Security (2)
Network / Secure Web Gateway
Vienna
cyannetworks.com

CYBERTRAP (20)
Deception
Wiener Neustadt
cybertrap.com

Ikarus Security Software GmbH (25)
Endpoint / Android AV
Vienna
ikarussecurity.com

Nimbusec (12)
GRC / Web Scanning
Linz
nimbusec.com

SEC Consult (109)
Application Security / Code Testing
Vienna
sec-consult.com

BAHRAIN

CTM360 (34)
Security Analytics / Breach Detection
Seef
ctm360.com

BELGIUM

Guardsquare (47)
Application Security / Mobile App Protection
Leuven
guardsquare.com

Sweepatic (7)
Threat Intelligence / Brand Monitoring
Leuven
sweepatic.com

BRAZIL

Aker (72)
Network / Web Filtering
Brasilia
aker.com.br

Certisign Certificador
(754)
IAM / IAM
São Paulo
certisign.com.br

idwall (103)
Fraud Prevention / Fraud
Detection
São Paulo
idwall.co

Konduto (89)
Fraud Prevention / Fraud
Detection
São Paulo
konduto.com

Kryptus (48)
Data Security / HSM
Campinas São Paulo
kryptus.com

Malware Patrol (1)
Threat Intelligence Feed
São Paulo
malwarepatrol.net

Modulo (214)
GRC / IT Governance, Risk
& Compliance
Rio de Janeiro
modulo.com

N-Stalker (12)
GRC / Web Application
Security Scanner
São Paulo
nstalker.com

PhishX (4)
GRC / Security Awareness
Training
Cotia
phishx.io

Syhunt (2)
Application Security /
Code Scanning
Rio de Janeiro
syhunt.com

**Tempest Security
Intelligence** (249)
GRC / Data Classification
and Discovery
Recife
tempest.com.br

Traversal Networks
Network / IDS
traversalnetworks.com

BRITISH VIRGIN ISLANDS

ExpressVPN (12)
Network / VPN
Tortola
expressvpn.com

BULGARIA

1H (8)
Network / Security for
Webhosting
Sofia
1h.com

CANADA

1Password (67)
IAM / Password Manage-
ment
Toronto
1password.com

2Keys (77)
MSSP / Managed Identity
Platform
Ottawa
2keys.ca

Absolute Software (578)
Endpoint / Mobile Device
Security
Vancouver
absolute.com/en

Adaware (51)
Endpoint / Anti-virus
Montreal
adaware.com

Aprivacy (5)
Data Security / Secure
Communications
Kitchener
aprivacy.com

Arc4dia (5)
Security Analytics / Breach
Detection and Response
Montreal
arc4dia.com

Beauceron (24)
GRC / Risk Measurement
Fredericton
beauceronsecurity.com

Bibu Labs (3)
Deception / Decoys
Toronto
bibulabs.com

BicDroid (7)
Data Security / Encryption
Waterloo
bicdroid.com

BioConnect (64)
IAM / Biometrics
Toronto
bioconnect.com

Bluink (16)
IAM / Mobile Authenti-
cator
Ottawa
bluink.ca

**CBL Data Recovery
Technologies Inc.** (36)
Data Security / Data Re-
covery and Data Destruc-
tion
Markham
cbldata.com

Certicom (167)
Data Security / Encryption,
PKI
Mississauga
certicom.com

**Cicada Security
Technology** (2)
Endpoint / Device Theft
Prevention
Montreal
cicadasecurity.com

Cloudmask (10)
Email Security
Ottawa
cloudmask.com

CMD (33)
Endpoint / Linux Security
Vancouver
cmd.com

Cord3 Innovation Inc. (15)
Data Security / Zero
Knowledge File Encryption
Ottawa
cord3inc.com

Corsa (32)
Network / Zero-Trust
Networking
Ottawa
corsa.com

Crypto4A Inc. (14)
Data Security / Entropy as
a Service
Ottawa
crypto4a.com

**Cryptomill Cybersecurity
Solutions** (16)
Data Security
Toronto
cryptomill.com

Note: Numbers in parentheses indicate employee count

Cybeats (12)
Operations / Incident
Response
Aurora
cybeats.com

Cybernetiq (13)
GRC / Risk Measurement
Ottawa
cybernetiq.ca

Cyphercor – LoginTC (6)
IAM / Two-Factor Authentication
Kanata
logintc.com

D3 Security (101)
Operations / Incident
Management
Vancouver
d3security.com

DataPassports (3)
Data Security / IRM
Toronto
datapassports.com

Datex Inc. (29)
Data Security / Network
Data Masking
Mississauga
datex.ca

Defence Intelligence (23)
Operations / Malware
Protection
Kanata
defintel.com

Delve Labs (21)
GRC / Vulnerability Management
Montreal
delve-labs.com

Difenda Labs (37)
MSSP / MDR
Oakville
difenda.com

DOSarrest (26)
Network / DDoS Defense
Richmond
dosarrest.com

Echosec (22)
Threat Intelligence / Intel
Gathering Tool
Victoria
echosec.net

eSentire (424)
MSSP / MDR
Cambridge
esentire.com

**Ethoca (acquired by
Mastercard)** (221)
Fraud Prevention / Transaction Data
Toronto
ethoca.com

Faronics Technologies Inc.
(133)
Endpoint Security
Vancouver
faronics.com

Field Effect Software (28)
MSSP / MDR
Ottawa
fieldeffect.com

Fingerprint-IT (1)
IAM / Biometrics
Vancouver
fingerprint-it.com

FixMeStick (17)
Endpoint / AV
Montreal
fixmestick.com

FuseMail (56)
Email Security
Burnaby
fusemail.com

Galvanize (444)
GRC / Risk Management
Vancouver
wegalvanize.com

Graphite Software (14)
Endpoint / Mobile Containers
Ottawa
graphitesoftware.com

Herjavec Group (329)
MSSP / Managed Services
Toronto
herjavecgroup.com

Hitachi ID Systems, Inc.
(140)
IAM
Calgary
Hitachi-id.com

Hushmail (366)
Data Security / Private
Email
Vancouver
hushmail.com

Hyas (18)
Threat Intelligence / Attribution Intelligence
Victoria
hyas.com

**Hypersecu Information
Systems, Inc.** (9)
IAM / OTP Tokens
Richmond
hypersecu.com

IGLOO Software (163)
GRC / Security Management
Kitchener
igloosoftware.com

InBay Technologies (20)
IAM / Mobile Authenticator
Kanata
inbaytech.com

Infosec Global (31)
Data Security / Certificate
Discovery
North York
infosecglobal.com

IntelliGO Networks (30)
Security Analytics / Breach
Detection
Toronto
intelligonetworks.com

Interset (86)
Security Analytics
Ottawa
interset.com

ISARA (56)
Data Security / Encryption
Waterloo
isara.com

KeyNexus (11)
Data Security / Cloud Key
Storage
Victoria
keynexus.net

Kobalt (5)
MSSP / Managed Security
Services
Vancouver
kobalt.io

Kyber Security (3)
Data Security / Software
Protection
Montreal
kybersecurity.com

LifeRaft (35)
Threat Intelligence /
OSINT Monitoring
Halifax
liferaftinc.com

LSoft Technologies (5)
Data Security / Erasure
Mississauga
lsoft.net

Magnet Forensics (240)
Operations / Forensics
Waterloo
magnetforensics.com

Messageware (16)
Email Security / OWA
Security
Mississauga
messageware.com

Mimir Networks (3)
Network / DDoS Defense
Sydney
mimirnetworks.com

MXTools
Threat Intelligence
Brossard
mxtools.com

N-Dimension Solutions
(14)
IoT Security / ICS
Richmond Hill
n-dimension.com

Netsweeper (57)
Network / Web Filtering
Waterloo
netsweeper.com

NoviFlow (44)
Network / SDN
Montreal
noviflow.com

NuData Security (101)
Fraud Prevention / Online
Fraud Detection
Vancouver
nudatasecurity.com

OpenText (500)
IAM / Federated Identity
Waterloo
opentext.com

Perfectcloud (10)
Data Security / Secure
Cloud Storage
Toronto
perfectcloud.io

Plurilock (18)
IAM / Behavior-Based
Biometrics
Victoria
plurilock.com

PresiNET Systems Corp.
(8)
Network Monitoring
Victoria
presinet.com

Privacy Analytics (101)
Data Security / Healthcare
Data Privacy
Ottawa
privacy-analytics.com

QEYnet (3)
Data Security
Vaughan
qeynet.com

RANK Software, Inc. (20)
Security Analytics / Threat
Hunting
Toronto
ranksoftwareinc.com

Resolver (224)
GRC / Risk Management
Toronto
resolver.com

Route 1 (39)
IAM
Toronto
route1.com

SecureKey (107)
IAM / Identity Manage-
ment
Toronto
securekey.com

Securicy (16)
GRC / Policy Management
Sydney
securicy.com

Security Compass (205)
GRC / Policy Compliance
Toronto
securitycompass.com

SegaSec (26)
Email Security / An-
ti-phishing
Toronto
segasec.com

SHIELD Crypto Systems
(3)
Data Security / Encryption
Toronto
shieldcryptosystems.com

Sonrai Security (39)
IAM / Identity Data
Security
New Brunswick
sonraisecurity.com

Tehama (39)
Network / Secure Virtual
Desktops
Ottawa
tehama.io

Terranova Security (55)
Training / Security Training
Laval
terranovasecurity.com

Thred Tech (45)
Threat Intelligence Plat-
form
London
thredtech.com

TITUS (250)
GRC / DLP
Ottawa
titus.com

Trulioo (113)
IAM / Identity Verification
Vancouver
trulioo.com

TunnelBear (47)
Network / VPN
Toronto
tunnelbear.com

Validian (1)
Data Security / Encryption
Nepean
validian.com

Vancosys (5)
IAM / IAM
Vancouver
vancosys.com

Vitrium (20)
Data Security / DRM
Vancouver
vitrium.com

VKey (2)
Endpoint / Sandbox for
Apps
Ottawa
v-key.com

Wedge Networks (40)
Network / Cloud Proxy
Security
Calgary
wedgenetworks.com

WinMagic Inc. (108)
Data Security / Encryption
Mississauga
winmagic.com

Xahive (5)
Data Security / Secure
Messaging
Ottawa
xahive.com

Zapper Software (1)
Data Security / DRM
Rosedale
zappersoftware.com/home.
html

Zighra (8)
IAM / Biometrics, Kinetic
Ottawa
zighra.com

CHILE

Camel Secure (7)
GRC
Santiago
camelsecure.com

CHINA

Anchiva (10)
Network / UTM
Beijing
en.anchiva.com

Note: Numbers in parentheses indicate employee count

Antiy Labs (1)
Endpoint / Malware
Analysis
Beijing
antiy.net

Cheetah Mobile (1,948)
Endpoint / Android AV
Beijing
cmcm.com

Cloudscreen (1)
Data Security / Discovery,
Classification
Yuhang District
cloudscreen.com

DBApp Security (22)
Application Security / Web
Application & Database
Security
Hangzhou
dbappsecurity.com

Excelsecu (43)
Data Security / PKI and
Data Encryption
Shenzhen
excelsecu.com/en/index.
html

Feitian Technologies (8)
IAM
Beijing
ftsafe.com

GreeNet (16)
Network / DPI for Carriers
Beijing
greenet.net.cn

H3C (2,806)
Network / Secure Gateway
Beijing
h3c.com

Huawei (4,000)
Network / Firewalls
Shenzhen
www1.huawei.com/en/
products/data-communi-
cation/network-security/
index.htm

Kernelsec
Data Security / Document
Encryption
Shanghai
serpurity.com

Mo An Technology
Application Security /
Scanning and Data Flow
Mapping
Hangzhou
moresec.cn

Qihoo 360 Total Security
(2,022)
Endpoint / AV
Beijing
360totalsecurity.com

Qingteng (15)
Operations / Asset Discovery and Protection
Beijing
qingteng.cn/en/index.html

Sangfor (1444)
Network / UTM
Shenzhen
sangfor.com

**Shenzhen Excelsecu Data
Technology** (42)
IAM / OTP
Shenzhen
excelsecu.com

Tencent (650)
Endpoint / Android AV
Shenzhen
tencent.com

Venustech (260)
Network / UTM
venusense.com

Vkansee (1)
IAM / Fingerprint Sensors
for Mobile Security
Beijing
vkansee.com

Zoloz (33)
IAM / Biometrics
Haidian District
zoloz.com

CYPRUS

LOKD (7)
Data Security / Secure
Communications
Larnaca
lokd.com

CZECH REPUBLIC

Avast Software (1,390)
Endpoint / Anti-virus
Prague
avast.com

Caligare (1)
Network Monitoring
Netflow
Prague
caligare.com

**Compelson Labs
(Mobiledit)** (17)
GRC / Forensics
Prague
mobiledit.com/home

Cryptelo (6)
Data Security / Secure Data
Transfer
Prague
cryptelo.com

GreyCortex (34)
Network / Traffic Analysis
Brno
greycortex.com

Qrator (32)
Network / DDoS Defense
Prague
qrator.net

TrustPort (14)
Endpoint / Android AV
Brno
trustport.com/en

DENMARK

Arama Tech (4)
GRC / Compliance Con-
trols
Glostrop
aramatech.com

CardLab
IAM / IAM
Herlev
cardlab.com

Cryptomathic (67)
Data Security / Key Man-
agement, PKI
Aarhus
cryptomathic.com

FastpassCorp (106)
IAM / Password Manage-
ment
Kongens Lyngby
fastpasscorp.com

LogPoint (199)
Security Analytics / SIEM
Copenhagen
logpoint.com

Napatech (97)
Operations / Network
Acceleration Cards
Soeborg
napatech.com

NewBanking (10)
IAM / IAM
Copenhagen
newbanking.com

Omada A/S (239)
IAM
Copenhagen
omada.net

Safewhere (2)
IAM / Identity Manage-
ment
Virum
safewhere.com

SecPoint (17)
GRC / Vulnerability
Scanning
Copenhagen
secpoint.com

Sepior (17)
Data Security / Encryption
and Key Management
Aarhus
sepior.com

EGYPT

BlueKaizen (5)
Training
bluekaizen.org

ESTONIA

Cybexer (12)
Opertions / Cyber Range
Tallinn
cybexer.com

Keystroke DNA (7)
IAM / Biometrics Key-
stroke Analysis
Tallinn
keystrokedna.com

Trapmine (9)
Endpoint Security
Tallinn
trapmine.com

FINLAND

Arctic Security (20)
Threat Intelligence
Oulu
arcticsecurity.com

Bittium (1,907)
Data Security / Secure
Communications
Oulu
bittium.com

Envault (3)
Data Security
Espoo
envaultcorp.com

F-Secure (4,545)
Endpoint / AV
Helsinki
f-secure.com

Granite (22)
GRC / Risk Management
Tampere
granitegrc.com

Nokia (250)
Endpoint / Mobile Security
Espoo
networks.nokia.com

**Silverskin Information
Security** (20)
GRC / Skills Measurement
and Compliance
Helsinki
silverskin.com

**SSH Communications
Security** (145)
Data Security / Secure File
Transfer
Helsinki
ssh.com

Ubisecure Solutions, Inc.
(37)
IAM
Espoo
ubisecure.com

FRANCE

6WIND (76)
Network / IPSec VPN
Router
Montigny-le-Bretonneux
6wind.com

Akheros (4)
Network / NBAD
Paris
akheros.fr

Alsid (31)
Network / AD Defense
Paris
alsid.com

Atos Group (450)
IAM / IAM
Bezons
atos.net/en

Capgemini (250)
MSSP / Identity as a
Service
Paris
capgemini.com

Citalid (6)
GRC
Versailles
citalid.com

Cosmian (8)
Data Security
Paris
cosmian.com

Cryptosense (8)
GRC / VM for Cryptogra-
py
Paris
cryptosense.com

CybelAngel (87)
GRC / OSINT Data Leak
Detection
Paris
cybelangel.com

Cyberwatch (15)
GRC
Paris
cyberwatch.fr

Cyrating (2)
GRC / Risk Scores
Paris
cyrating.com

GateWatcher (39)
Network / Threat Detec-
tion
Paris
gatewatcher.com

GB & Smith (57)
GRC / SAP Audit
Lille
gbandsmith.com

Gemalto (11,210)
IAM
Meudon Cedex
gemalto.com

GitGuardian (24)
Threat Intelligence /
Github Credential Moni-
toring
Paris
gitguardian.com

I-Tracing (126)
MSSP / Managed Security
Services
Puteaux
i-tracing.com

IDECSI (22)
Email Security / Email
Monitoring and Auditing
Paris
idecsi.com/en

IDnomic (121)
IAM / IAM
Issy-les-Moulineaux
idnomic.com

INSIDE Secure (200)
Endpoint / Smartphone &
Mobile Device Security
Meyreuil
insidesecure.com

inWebo (28)
IAM / Strong Authenti-
cation
Paris
inwebo.com

IS Decisions (29)
IAM / Access Control
Bidart
isdecisions.com

Note: Numbers in parentheses indicate employee count

iTrust (46)
GRC / Vulnerability Management
Labege
itrust.fr

KeeeX (8)
Data Security / Document Security
Marseille
keeex.me

Ledger (176)
Data Security / USB Key Storage for Cryptocurrencies
Paris
ledger.com

Lybero.net (10)
Data Security / Multi-admin Key Authorization
Villers-Lès-Nancy
lybero.net

MailInBlack (53)
Email Security / Anti-spam
Marseille
mailinblack.com

Mancala Networks (5)
Network Monitoring
Meylan
mancalanetworks.com

Matrix42 (250)
Endpoint / EDR
Paris
matrix42.com

Origone (5)
Email Security / Anti-phishing
Paris
orisecure.com

Pradeo (19)
Application Security / Mobile App Security
Paris
pradeo.net

Qosmos, Division of ENEA (79)
Network / DPI Technology
Paris
qosmos.com

Quotium (21)
GRC / Data Storage Monitoring
Paris
quotium.com

Rohde & Schwarz Cybersecurity (51)
Application Security / App Containers
Meudon
Rohd-schwarz.com

Seclab (19)
Data Security / Secure File Transfer
Montpellier
seclab-security.com

SecureIC (44)
Endpoint / Tools for Secure Chip Design
secureic.com

Sentryo (28)
IoT Security / ICS
Lyon
sentryo.net

Sqreen (47)
Application Security / Agent-Based Monitoring of Apps
Saint-Cloud
sqreen.com

StormShield (was NetASQ and Arcoon) (276)
Network / UTM
Issy-les-Moulineaux
stormshield.com

Tetrane (11)
Application Security / Reverse Engineering
Macon
tetrane.com

Trusted Objects
IoT Security / IoT
Aix-en-Provence
trusted-objects.com

Trustelem (5)
IAM / IAM
Paris
trustelem.com

Ubble.ai (31)
Fraud Prevention / Identity Verification
Paris
ubble.ai

Universign (69)
IAM / IAM
Paris
universign.com

Wallix (154)
IAM / Privileged Access Management
Paris
wallix.com/en

WaryMe (9)
GRC
Cesson-Sévigné
waryme.com

Woleet (15)
Data Security / Blockchain for Signatures
Rennes
woleet.io

YesWeHack (49)
Operations / Bug Bounty
Paris
yeswehack.com

Yogosha (28)
Operations / Bug Bounty Platform
Paris
yogosha.com

GERMANY

achelos GmbH (33)
Testing / TLS Testing
Paderborn
achelos.de

Adjust (290)
Fraud Prevention / Bot Detection
Berlin
adjust.com

ADVA Optical Networking (2,241)
Network / Secure Switching
Munich
advaoptical.com

Allgeier IT (63)
MSSP / Managed Email Security
Bremen
Allgeier-it.de

Alyne (34)
GRC / Risk Measurement
Munich
alyne.com

Auconet (12)
IAM / Network Access Control
Berlin
Auconet.com

AUTHADA (14)
Fraud Prevention / Using Mobile Identity
Darmstadt
authada.de

Avira (454)
Endpoint / Anti-virus
Tettnang
avira.com

Baramundi Software (98)
GRC / Endpoint Management
Augsburg
baramundi.com

Beta Systems Software AG (222)
IAM
Berlin
betasystems.com

Boxcryptor (12)
Data Security / Cloud Encryption
Augsburg
boxcryptor.com

Brainloop (124)
Data Security / Secure Collaboration
Munich
brainloop.com/us

Build38 (13)
Application Security / Mobile App Protection
Munich
build38.com

Bundesdruckerei (387)
IAM / Authentication PKI
Berlin
bundesdruckerei.de/en

Charismathics (4)
IoT Security / IoT
Munich
charismathics.com

Code Intelligence (15)
Application Security / Appsec
Bonn
code-intelligence.com

Crashtest Security (8)
Application Security / Appsec
Munich
crashtest-security.com

cryptovision (27)
IAM / Smart Card Solutions
Gelsenkirchen
cryptovision.com

Cryptshare (50)
Email Security / Encrypted File and Email on Azure
Freiburg
cryptshare.com

DRACOON (42)
Data Security / File Sharing
Regensburg
dracoon.com

DriveLock (47)
Endpoint Device Control, DLP
Munich
drivelock.com

Drooms (116)
Data Security / Data Rooms
Frankfurt am Main
drooms.com

EgoSecure (21)
Data Security / Data-at-Rest Encryption
Ettlingen
egosecure.com

eperi (26)
Data Security / Encryption
Pfungstadt
eperi.de/en

ESNC (4)
GRC / SAP Security
Grünwald
esnc.de

G Data Software (285)
Endpoint / Anti-virus
Bochum
gdatasoftware.com

HENSOLDT Cyber
IoT Security / IoT
Taufkirchen
hensoldt-cyber.com

HOB Networking (1)
Network / VPN
Cadolzburg
hob.de

Hornetsecurity (73)
Email Security / Managed Email Security
Hannover
hornetsecurity.com

IDEE Blockchain Software (18)
IAM / Identity Platform
Munich
getidee.com

Infineon (1,000)
IAM / Smart Card Solutions
Neubiberg
infineon.com

ITConcepts (99)
IAM / IAM for Small Business
Bonn
itconcepts.net

itWatch (1)
Endpoint Security & Data Loss Prevention
Munich
itwatch.info

KeePass Password Safe
IAM / IAM
Metzingen
keepass.info

Keyp (8)
IAM / Identity Platform
Munich
keyp.io

KOBIL Systems (92)
IAM / Authentication
Worms
kobil.com

Link11 (28)
Network / DDoS Defense
Frankfurt
link11.de

Macmon (37)
Network Access Control
Berlin
macmon.eu

MB Connect Line (24)
IoT Security / ICS Firewall
Dinkelsbühl
mbconnectline.com

MTG AG (230)
IoT Security / ICS Key Management
Darmstadt
mtg.de

Myra Security (18)
Network / Web Defense
Munich
myracloud.com

NitroKey (2)
Data Security / Encryption
Berlin
nitrokey.com

Patronus.io (6)
Application Security / Web Scanning
Berlin
patronus.io

Perseus. (23)
Email Security / Anti-phishing
Berlin
perseus.de

Pyramid Computer GmbH (64)
Network / Firewall
Freiburg
pyramid.de

Qgroup, GmbH (8)
Network / Firewall
Frankfurt am Main
qgroup.de

QuoScient GmbH (36)
Operations / Security Operations Platform
Frankfurt am Main
quoscient.io

Note: Numbers in parentheses indicate employee count

Red Database Security (2)
Data Security / Database
Security
Heusenstamm
red-database-security.de

Rhebo (23)
IoT Security / ICS
Leipzig
rhebo.com

RIPS Technologies GmbH
(28)
Application Security / Static Code Analysis for PHP
and Java
Bochum
ripstech.com

Risk.Ident (62)
Fraud Prevention / Fraud
Detection
Hamburg
riskident.com

Searchguard (5)
Data Security / Security for
Elasticsearch
Berlin
search-guard.com

Secomba (12)
Data Security / Encryption
for Dropbox
Augsburg
boxcryptor.com/en

Secucloud (70)
Network / Cloud Proxy
Security
Hamburg
secucloud.com

SecurStar (6)
Data Security / Full Disk
Encryption
Munich
securestar.com

Secusmart (52)
Data Security / Secure
Mobile Phone
Düsseldorf
secusmart.com

Skymatic (4)
Data Security
Sankt Augustin
skymatic.de

Snaptrust (1)
Application Security
Potsdam
snaptrust.com

Steganos (1)
Data Security / Encryption
Munich
steganos.com/en

Tenzir (4)
Network Forensics
Hamburg
tenzir.com

Ubirch
IoT Security / Encryption
and Blockchain for ICS
Berlin
ubirch.de

Utimaco (424)
Data Security / Encryption
HSMs
Aachen
utimaco.com/en/home

Virtual Forge (76)
Application Security / SAP
Security
Heidelberg
virtualforge.com

ZenMate (13)
Network / VPN
Berlin
zenmate.com

Zertificon Solutions (49)
Email Security / Secure
Email
Berlin
zertificon.com/en

GREECE

**Crypteia Networks
(PCCW)** (15)
Threat Intelligence Platform and Analytics
Neo Psychiko
crypteianetworks.com

HONG KONG

Integrated Corporation (1)
IAM
Sheungwan
integrated.com

Nexusguard (180)
Network / DDoS Defense
Tsuen Wan
nexusguard.com

nwStor (8)
Data Security / Network &
Cloud Data Security
Shatin
nwstor.com

HUNGARY

Secudit, Ltd. (6)
GRC / Vulnerability
Scanning
Veszprém
secudit.com

Seon (15)
Fraud Prevention / Fraud
Detection
Budapest
seon.io

Tresorit (115)
Data Security / Secure File
Transfer
Budapest
tresorit.com

ICELAND

Nanitor (7)
GRC
Kópavogur
nanitor.com

SafeUM (4)
Data Security / Private
Messenger
Reykjavík
safeum.com

INDIA

Arcon (342)
GRC / Rights Management
Mumbai
arconnet.com

Attify (12)
Application Security /
Mobile App Security
Bangalore
attify.com

Authshield Labs Pvt. Ltd.
(1)
IAM / Two-Factor Authentication
Delhi
auth-shield.com

BioEnable (84)
IAM / Access Control,
Biometrics
Pune
bioenabletech.com

Block Armour (6)
Network / Zero-Trust
Networking
Mumbai
blockarmour.com

CloudSEK (42)
GRC / Risk Management
Bangalore
cloudsek.com

CopyNotify (1)
Data Security / Device
Control for SMB
Pune
copynotify.com

**CyberEye Research Labs
& Security Solutions** (22)
GRC / Security Awareness
Training
Hyderabad
cybereyelabs.io

DataResolve (82)
Security Analytics / UEBA
Noida
dataresolve.com

DNIF (6)
Security Analytics / SIEM
Mumbai
dnif.it

Ensurity (42)
IAM / 2FA
Hyderabad
ensurity.com

EScan (187)
Endpoint / AV
Mumbai
escanav.com

**eSphere Security
Solutions Pvt** (2)
Endpoint / Mobile Defense
Ahmedabad
espheresecurity.com

Fixnix (45)
GRC / SaaS for SMB
Ashok Nagar
fixnix.co

FRS Labs (18)
Fraud Prevention / Fraud
Detection
Bangalore
frslabs.com

GajShield (37)
Network / Firewall
Mumbai
gajshield.com

GENAPT Technology Labs
(11)
GRC Platform
Hyderabad
genapt.com

Haltdos (12)
Network / DDoS Defense
Noida
haltdos.com

Indusface (57)
Network / Cloud WAF
Vodadora
indusface.com

Innefu Labs Pvt Ltd. (90)
Network / Internet Surveillance for Law Enforcement
New Delhi
innefu.com

Instasafe (27)
Network / Cloud VPN
Gateway
Bangalore
instasafe.com

Iraje (18)
IAM / Access Control
Mumbai
iraje.com

K7Computing (330)
Endpoint / AV
Sholinganallur
k7computing.com

Kratikal Tech (76)
GRC / Risk Measurement
Noida
kratikal.com

Lucideus (251)
GRC / Risk Measurement
Okhla Phase III
lucideus.com

Max Secure Software (95)
Endpoint Protection
Pune
maxpcsecure.com

miniOrange (27)
IAM / SSO
Pune
miniorange.com

neoEYED (8)
IAM / 2FA
Bangalore
neoeyed.com

NetMonastery (49)
GRC / Cloud-Based SIEM
Mumbai
dnif.it

Network Intelligence (567)
Operations / Firewall Policy Management
Mumbai
niiconsulting.com

Nevis Networks (60)
IAM / Access Control
Pune
nevisnetworks.com

PC VARK (39)
Endpoint / Android AV
Jaipur
pcvark.com

ProactEye (2)
Security Analytics / CASB
and UEBA
Pune
proacteye.com

Quick Heal (1,263)
Endpoint, Server (Linux),
and UTM
Pune
quickheal.com

RaviRaj Technologies (4)
IAM / Biometrics
Pune
ravirajtech.com

Seclore (199)
Data Security / IRM
Mumbai
seclore.com

SecurelyShare (26)
Data Security / Vault
Indira Nagar
securelyshare.com

SecureSight Technologies
(6)
Training / Collaborative
Learning
Ulhasnagar
securesighttech.in

Sentropi (2)
Fraud Prevention
Ahmedabad
sentropi.com

Seqrite (21)
Endpoint / Protection and
Encryption
Pune
seqrite.com

Sequretek (231)
Endpoint / AV
Mumbai
sequretek.com

**Shield Square (acquired
by Radware, 2019)** (61)
Network / Anti-bot, An-
ti-scraping
Bangalore
shieldsquare.com

**Smokescreen
Technologies Pvt. Ltd.** (32)
Deception / Complete
Deception Platform
Mumbai
smokescreen.io

Tata Communications
(1200)
MSSP / Managed Services
Mumbai
tatacommunications.com

Trinity Future-In (11)
Data Security / DRM for
Web
Bangalore
trifuturein.com

Note: Numbers in parentheses indicate employee count

VuNet Systems (30)
Security Analytics / Log
Analysis
Bangalore
vunetsystems.com

X-Ways (8)
Operations / Forensics
Delhi
x-ways.net

Xenarmor (1)
Data Security / SSL Certificate Management
Bangalore
xenarmor.com

Ziroh Labs (17)
Data Security
Bangalore
ziroh.com

IRELAND

Acsia (372)
Security Analytics / UEBA
Dublin
acsia.io

Adaptive Mobile (133)
Endpoint / Mobile Device
Security
Dublin
adaptivemobile.com

edgescan (45)
GRC / Vulnerability Man-
agement
Dublin
edgescan.com

Famoc (42)
Endpoint / MDM
Midleton
fancyfon.com

InvizBox (6)
Network / Portable VPN
hardware
Dublin
invizbox.com

**NetFort (acquired by
Rapid7, April 2019)** (13)
Network Traffic Capture
and Analysis
Galway
netfort.com

Nova Leah (25)
IoT Security / Medical
Device Vulnerability Man-
agement
Dundalk
novaleah.com

PixAlert (14)
GRC / Data Discovery
Dublin
pixalert.com

Sedicii (17)
IAM / Mobile Authenti-
cation
Carriganore
sedicii.com

The Email Laundry (11)
Network / Managed
Services
Naas
theemaillaundry.com

TitanHQ (52)
Network / DNS Filtering
Galway
titanhq.com

Velona Systems (7)
GRC / PBX Security
Scanner
Cork
velonasystems.com

VigiTrust (16)
GRC / Risk Management
Dublin
vigitrust.com

Waratek (41)
Application Security
Dublin
waratek.com

WebTitan (TitanHQ) (53)
Network / Content and
Email Filtering
Salthill
webtitan.com

ISRAEL

ACID Technologies (2)
Threat Intelligence
Tel Aviv-Yafo
acid-tech.co

Actifile (4)
GRC / DLP
Herzliya
actifile.com

Agat Software (29)
Network / Security for
Unified Comms
Jerusalem
agatsoftware.com

alcide (29)
Endpoint / Container
Security
Tel Aviv
alcide.io

Algosec (395)
Operations / Firewall Policy Management
Petah Tikva
algosec.com

Allot (926)
Network / Content URL
Filtering
Hod HaSharon
allot.com

APERIO Systems
IoT Security / ICS
Haifa
aperio-systems.com

AppDome (62)
Application Security
Tel Aviv
appdome.com

Applicure (7)
Network / Web Application
Firewall
Ramat Gan
applicure.com

AppSec Labs (18)
Application Security / Mo-
bile Application Security
Testing
Kfar Saba
appsec-labs.com

**Aqua Security Software,
Inc.** (136)
Endpoint / Container
Security
Ramat Gan
aquasec.com

ArcusTeam
IoT Security / Vulnerability
Management
Tel Aviv-Yafo
arcusteam.com

Argus Cyber Security (139)
IoT Security / Automotive
Cybersecurity
Tel Aviv
argus-sec.com

Arilou Technologies (20)
IoT Security / Automotive
Security
Ramat Gan
ariloutech.com

Assac Networks (1)
Endpoint / Mobile Device
Protection
Ramat HaSharon
assacnetworks.com

Ayyeka (42)
IoT Security / Secure
Remote Monitoring
Jerusalem
ayyeka.com

Barillet (24)
GRC / Manager of Managers
Be'er Sheva
barillet.co.il

Be Strategic Solutions (7)
Training / Crisis Simulation
Tel Aviv
best.be-strategic.solutions

Beame.io
IAM / Mobile Authenticator
Tel Aviv
beame.io

BigID, Inc. (105)
Data Security / Data Discovery
Tel Aviv-Yafo
bigid.com

BioCatch (111)
Fraud Prevention / Authentication Through Behavior
Tel Aviv-Yafo
biocatch.com

BIS Guard (1)
Application Security / Code Wrappers to Prevent Tampering
Ofra
bisguard.com

BitDam (24)
Endpoint / Anti-malware
Tel Aviv
bitdam.com

BrandShield (18)
Fraud Prevention / Brand Abuse Discovery
Ramat HaSharon
brandshield.com

Bufferzone (21)
Endpoint Sandbox
Giv'atayim
bufferzonesecurity.com

Bugsec Group (87)
MSSP / Managed Security Services
Rishon LeZion
bugsec.com

C2A Security (17)
IoT Security / Automotive
Jerusalem
c2a-sec.com

CalCom (28)
Endpoint / Server Hardening via MSFT System Center
Lod
calcomsoftware.com

Cato Networks (118)
Network / Cloud Security Layer
Tel Aviv
catonetworks.com

Cellebrite (789)
Endpoint / Mobile Forensics
Petah Tikva
cellebrite.com

Cellrox (15)
Endpoint / Mobile Virtualization
Tel Aviv
cellrox.com

Cervello (9)
IoT Security / Railway
Tel Aviv
cervellosec.com

CGS Tower Networks (12)
Network Taps
Rosh HaAyin
cgstowernetworks.com

ChameleonX (8)
Application Security / Runtime Protection
Tel Aviv
chameleonx.com

Check Point Software (5,604)
Network / UTM
Tel Aviv
checkpoint.com

Checkmarx (1)
Application Security / Software Development Security
Ramat Gan
checkmarx.com

CipherSiP (7)
IoT Security / Automotive
Haifa
ciphersip.com

Commugen (21)
GRC / Risk Management
Tel Aviv
commugen.com

ComSignTrust (3)
Data Security / Digital Signatures for Data
Tel Aviv
comsigntrust.com

ControlGuard (8)
Endpoint / Device Control
Herzlia Pituach
atrog.com

Coronet (85)
Network / Endpoint Radio Protection
Tel Aviv-Yafo
coro.net

Critifence (6)
IoT Security / ICS
Herzliya
critifence.com

Cronus (17)
Testing / Attacker Simulation
Haifa
cronus-cyber.com

Crusoe Security (6)
Network / Web Browsing Isolation
Neve Yarak
crusoesecurity.com

Cy-oT (12)
IoT Security / Wireless Monitoring
Tel Aviv
Cy-ot.com

Cyabra (11)
Threat Intelligence / Fake News Defense
Tel Aviv
cyabra.com

Cybellum (9)
Endpoint / In-Memory Prevention
Tel Aviv-Yafo
cybellum.com

Cyber 2.0 (16)
Endpoint / EDR
Tel Aviv
cyber20.com

Cyber Driveware
Network Malware Defense
Herzliya
cyberdriveware.com

Cyber Observer Ltd. (22)
GRC / Security Management
Caesarea
cyber-observer.com

CyberArk Software (1,228)
IAM / Privileged Access Management
Petah Tikva
cyberark.com

Cyberbit (334)
Training / Cyber Range
Ra'anana
cyberbit.com

Note: Numbers in parentheses indicate employee count

Cybeready (16)
GRC / Anti-phishing
Training
Tel Aviv
cybeready.co.il

Cybergym (47)
Training / Cyber Range
Hadera
cybergym.com

Cyberhat (47)
MSSP / Managed SOC
Tel Aviv
cyberhat.co.il

Cyberint (87)
Threat Intelligence
Petah Tikva
cyberint.com

CyberObserver (22)
Operations / Manager of
Managers
Caesarea
cyber-observer.com

CyberSeal (3)
Network / SIGINT Offensive
Yehud
cyber-seal.net

Cybonet (was PineApp)
(41)
Email Security / AV and
Sandboxing
Matam
cybonet.com/en

Cycurity (45)
Security Analytics
Tel Aviv
cycurity.com

Cydome
IoT Security / ICS Maritime
Tel Aviv
cydome.io

CYFORT Security (2)
Threat Intelligence
Herzliya
cyfort.com

Cylus (23)
IoT Security / Railway
Tel Aviv
cylus.com

Cymmetria (23)
Deception (Honeypots)
Tel Aviv
cymmetria.com

Cymotive (75)
IoT Security / Automotive
Tel Aviv
cymotive.com

Cympire (12)
Training / Cyber Range
Tel Aviv
cympire.com

Cymulate (57)
Operations / Breach and
Attack Simulation
Rishon LeZion
cymulate.com

Cynerio (19)
IoT Security / Medical
Device Security
Ramat Gan
cynerio.co

Cynet (97)
Operations / APT Discovery via Agentless Scan
Rishon LeZion
cynet.com

Cytegic (17)
GRC / Risk Profiling
Tel Aviv
cytegic.com

D-ID (25)
IAM / Anti-facial Recognition
Tel Aviv
deidentification.co

Dax Asparna Ltd. (11)
Data Security / Encrypted
File Sync and Social Conversations
Afula
asparna.com

Dcoya (7)
GRC / Anti-phishing
Training
Tel Aviv
dcoya.com

Deceptive Bytes (3)
Deception
Holon
deceptivebytes.com

Deep Instinct (91)
Endpoint Machine Learning
Tel Aviv
deepinstinct.com

Digital Confidence Ltd. (1)
GRC / DLP
Tel Aviv
digitalconfidence.com

DocAuthority (34)
GRC / DLP
Ra'anana
docauthority.com

Dojo by BullGuard (1)
Network / Home Wifi
Security
Ra'anana
dojo.bullguard.com

**Dome9 (acquired by
Check Point in 2018)** (82)
Network / Cloud Firewall
Policy Management
Tel Aviv
dome9.com

Empow (34)
Security Analytics / SIEM
Ramat Gan
empow.co

Engage Technologies
IoT Security / Code Automation
Kibbutz
engageiot.com

Enigmatos (5)
IoT Security / Automotive
Yavne
enigmatos.com

Fenror7 (6)
Operations / Lateral Movement Detection
Herzliya
fenror7.com

FireDome (19)
IoT Security / IoT for
Device Manufacturers
Tel Aviv
firedome.io

FirstPoint Mobile Guard
(12)
Endpoint / Mobile Device
Protection
Netanya
firstpoint-mg.com

Forter (179)
Fraud Prevention
Tel Aviv-Yafo
Forter.com

FST Biometrics (47)
IAM / Facial Recognition
Biometrics
Holon
fstbm.com

Gama Operations (7)
Network / Secure PBX
Petah Tikva
gamaoperations.com

GamaSec (4)
GRC / Web Scanning
Herzelia Pituach
gamasec.com

Gita Technologies (42)
Network / SIGINT Offensive
Tel Aviv
gitatechnologies.com

Gold Lock (1)
Data Security / Mobile
Encryption
Ramat Gan
secure.gold-lock.com

GreenTeam Internet (1)
Network / Cloud URL
Filtering
Tel Aviv-Yafo
greentm.co.uk

Guard Knox (26)
IoT Security / Automotive
Tel Aviv
guardknox.com

GuardiCore (141)
Application Security / App
Monitoring
Tel Aviv
guardicore.com

**Hermetric Software
Services**
Network / Web Security
Kiryat Tiv'on
hermetric.com

Hunters.AI (22)
Security Analytics / Breach
Detection and Response
Tel Aviv
hunters.ai

Hysolate (40)
Endpoint / Workspace
Isolation via VMs
Tel Aviv-Yafo
hysolate.com

ICS2 (1)
IoT Security / ICS
Jerusalem
ics2.com

Imvision Technologies (17)
Network Behavior Analysis
Ramat Gan
imvisiontech.com

Innosec (8)
GRC / DLP
Hod HaSharon
innosec.com

**Innovya Traceless
Biometrics** (3)
IAM / Biometrics
Kiryat Ono
innovya.com

Inteller (3)
Threat Intelligence Platform
inteller.com

IPV Security (17)
MSSP / Monitoring
Ra'anana
ipvsecurity.com

IPV Tec (1)
Network / Website Monitoring
Ra'anana
ipvtec.com

IronScales (36)
GRC / Anti-phishing Gamification
Tel Aviv
ironscales.com

IsItYou (3)
IAM / Mobile Face Recognition
Lod
isityou.biz

Jeronix (1)
IAM / Identity Intelligence
jeronix.com

JpU (15)
IoT Security / IoT
Petah Tikva
jpu.io

Karamba Security (46)
IoT Security / Automotive
Defense
Hod HaSharon
karambasecurity.com

Kaymera (38)
Endpoint / Mobile Defense
Herzliya
kaymera.com

Kazuar (21)
Data Security / Secure
Work Environment
Tel Aviv
kazuar-tech.com

Kernelios (10)
Training / Simulation and
Training
Rishon LeZion
kernelios.com

Kindite (20)
Data Security / Encryption
Tel Aviv
kindite.com

L7 Defense (7)
Network API Security
Be'er Sheva
l7defense.com

Made4Biz (1)
IAM / Mobile Authentication (Banking)
Savyon
israeldefense.co.il/en

Magen (1)
Network / Surveillance
Tel Aviv
ma-gen.com

MazeBolt Technologies
Testing for DDoS
Ramat Gan
mazebolt.com

MediGate (47)
IoT Security / Medical
Devices
Tel Aviv
medigate.io

**Meta Networks
(Proofpoint)** (22)
Network / Zero-Trust
Networking
Tel Aviv-Yafo
metanetworks.com

MindoLife (11)
Network / IDS and Network Management
Haifa
mindolife.com

Minereye (19)
GRC / Self-Learning Data
Discovery
Hod HaSharon
minereye.com

Minerva Labs (25)
Endpoint / Malware Prevention
Petah Tikva
minerva-labs.com

Mobiwol
Endpoint / Firewall for
Android
Tel Aviv
mobiwol.com

Morphisec (83)
Endpoint Obfuscation
Be'er Sheva
morphisec.com

MyPermissions
Endpoint / Control Data
Privacy on Mobile Devices
Ramat Gan
mypermissions.com

Namogoo (90)
Application Security / Web
Scanning
Ra'anana
namogoo.com

Note: Numbers in parentheses indicate employee count

Nanolock (16)
IoT Security / Automotive
Nitzanei Oz
nanolocksecurity.com

Nation-E (8)
IoT Security / Energy
Security
Herzliya
nation-e.com

Naval Dome (3)
IoT Security / Security for
Ships
Ra'anana
navaldome.com

Neural Legion (11)
Application Security / Dynamic Code Analysis
Tel Aviv
neuralegion.com

NextNine (23)
IoT Security / OT security
Petah Tikva
nextnine.com

nsKnox
Fraud Prevention / Payment Verification
Tel Aviv
nsknox.net

Nuro (5)
Data Security / Secure
Messaging
Tel Aviv
nuro.im

Nuweba (13)
Application Security /
Serverless Security
Tel Aviv
nuweba.com

Nyotron (62)
Endpoint / EDR
Herzliya
nyotron.com

ODI (11)
Data Security / Document
Scrubbing
Rosh HaAyin
odi-x.com

Odo Security (18)
Network / Zero-Trust
Networking
Tel Aviv
odo.io

Orca Security (25)
Operations / Cloud Vulnerability Scanning
Tel Aviv
orca.security

Pcysys (30)
Operations / Automated
Pen Testing
Petah Tikva
pcysys.com

Perception Point (35)
Email Security / Anti-phishing
Tel Aviv
perception-point.io

Perimeter 81 (38)
Network / Secure Web
Gateway
Tel Aviv
perimeter81.com

PerimeterX (146)
Network / Website Defense
Tel Aviv-Yafo
perimeterx.com

Perytons (3)
Network / IoT Defense
Ness Ziona
perytons.com

PlainID (37)
IAM / Authorization
Tel Aviv
plainid.com

Portnox (32)
Endpoint / MDM
Ra'anana
portnox.com

Portshift (10)
Application Security /
Identity-Based Workload
Protection
Tel Aviv-Yafo
portshift.io

Preempt Security (58)
Security Analytics / UEBA
Ramat Gan
preemptsecurity.com

Prifender (20)
GRC / Data Privacy
Tel Aviv
prifender.com

Promisec (40)
Endpoint Security Intelligence
Holon
promisec.com

Protected Media (28)
Network / Advertising
Security
Petah Tikva
protected.media

QEDit (24)
Data Security / Data
Privacy
Tel Aviv
qed-it.com

QuantLR (4)
Data Security, Quantum
Key Distribution
Jerusalem
quantlr.com

Quttera (5)
Network / Malware Scanning of Websites
Herzliya Pituach
quttera.com

RadiFlow (42)
IoT Security / ICS
Tel Aviv
radiflow.com

Radware (1,196)
Network / Load Balancing, DDoS Defense, IPS,
Firewall
Tel Aviv
radware.com

Raz-Lee Security (20)
Endpoint / IBM iSeries
Security
Herzliya
razlee.com

Reblaze Technologies Ltd.
(34)
Network / Web Proxy
Defense
Tel Aviv
reblaze.com

Red Button (3)
Network / DDoS Defense
Tel Aviv
red-button.net

Regulus (16)
IoT Security / Automotive
Haifa
regulus.com

Reposify (15)
Operations / Asset Discovery
Bnei Brak
reposify.com

ReSec Technologies (14)
Data Security / Document
Scrubbing
Caesarea
resec.co

RevenueStream (4)
Fraud Prevention /
Revenue Stream Fraud
Prevention
revenue-stream.com

Riskified (335)
Fraud Prevention /
e-Commerce Transaction
Monitoring
Tel Aviv
riskified.com

Safe-T (56)
Data Security / Secure Data
Exchange
Herzliya Pituach
safe-t.com

SafeBreach (56)
Operations / Automated
Pen Testing
Tel Aviv
safebreach.com

SafeRide Technologies
(22)
IoT Security / Automotive
Tel Aviv-Yafo
saferide.io

SAM (51)
Network / Home Gateway
Defense
Tel Aviv
securingsam.com

Sasa Software (17)
Data Security / File Scrubbing
Sasa
sasa-software.com

ScadaFence (33)
IoT Security / ICS
Tel Aviv
scadafence.com

SecBI (25)
Security Analytics
Tel Aviv
secbi.com

Secret Double Octopus
(32)
Data Security / Two-Chan-
nel Encryption
Tel Aviv
doubleoctopus.com

Secure Push (10)
Fraud Prevention / Identity
Assurance
Migdal Tefen
securepush.com

SecuredTouch (34)
IAM / Touchscreen Bio-
metrics
Ramat Gan
securedtouch.com

SecureTeam (1)
Data Security / DRM
Rishon LeZion
secureteam.net

SecuriGo (1)
Application Security /
Cloud App Information
Exposure
Haifa
securigo.com

Securithings (16)
IoT Security / Device
Management
Ramat Gan
securithings.com

SecurityDAM (27)
Network / DDoS Defense
Ramat HaHayal
securitydam.com

SEGURO (1)
Network / Secure PBX
Petah Tikva
seguro-com.com

SenseCy (9)
Threat Intelligence / Deep
Web OSINT
Poleg Netanya
sensecy.com

Senseity (3)
GRC / Monitoring
Kfar Saba
senseity.com

Sentrycom (2)
Data Security / Encryption
Haifa
sentry-com.net

Septier Communication
(79)
Network / SIGINT Offen-
sive
Petah Tikva
septier.com

ShieldIOT (10)
IoT Security / For Service
Providers
Herzliya
shieldiot.io

SIGA Cyber Alert System
(20)
IoT Security / ICS
Ashkelon
sigasec.com

SignPass (4)
IAM / Handwriting Bio-
metrics
Tel Aviv
sign-pass.com

Silverfort (42)
IAM / Clienteles Multi-factor
Tel Aviv
silverfort.io

Sixgill (28)
Threat Intelligence / Dark
Web Intel
Netanya
cybersixgill.com

SkyFormation (8)
Network / CASB
Giv'at Shmuel
skyformation.com

Smufs (3)
IAM / Finger Scanners for
Mobile
Ramat Negev
smufsbio.com

SNDBOX (3)
Application Security /
Malware Analysis
Giv'atayim
sndbox.com

Source Defense (32)
Network / Client-Side
Protection against Third
Party Attacks
Be'er Sheva
sourcedefense.com

Surance.io (5)
IoT Security / Home De-
vice Protection
Ramat HaSharon
surance.io

Telemessage (64)
GRC / Text Messaging
Security
Petah Tikva
telemessage.com

Terafence (11)
IoT Security / ICS Gateway
Haifa
terafence.com

ThetaRay (87)
Security Analytics
Hod HaSharon
thetaray.com

**TowerSec (a HARMAN
company)** (35)
IoT Security / Automotive
Security
Hod HaSharon
tower-sec.com

TrulyProtect (7)
Application Security / App
Security
Rehovot
trulyprotect.com

Upstream (34)
IoT Security / Automotive
Herzliya
upstream.auto

Note: Numbers in parentheses indicate employee count

VADO Security (3)
Network / Air Gap
Giv'atayim
vadosecurity.com

Vaulto (3)
Endpoint / Mobile Security
Tel Aviv-Yafo
vaulto.co

Vdoo (68)
IoT Security / Embedded
Systems Security
Tel Aviv
vdoo.com

Verifyoo (2)
IAM / Biometrics
Tel Aviv
verifyoo.com

Vicarius (14)
Application Security /
Static and Dynamic Code
Scanning
Jerusalem
vicarius.io

VikiSense (5)
IAM / Biometrics MFA
Kiryat Gat
vikisense.com

Votiro (33)
Network / File Scrubbing
Tel Aviv
votiro.com

Vulcan Cyber (33)
GRC / Vulnerability Reme-
diation
Tel Aviv
vulcan.io

Waterfall (72)
IoT Security / ICS Air Gap
Firewall
Rosh HaAyin
waterfall-security.com

White Cyber Knight (7)
GRC / Risk Management
Tel Aviv
wck-grc.com

WhiteSource (154)
Application Security /
Open Source Security and
License Management
Giv'atayim
whitesourcesoftware.com

WifiWall (2)
Network / Wifi Firewall
Kfar Haim
wifiwall.com

Wintego (10)
Network / Wifi Offensive
Yokne'am Illit
wintego.com

WiseSec (10)
Operations / Microgeolo-
cation
Yokne'am Illit
wisesec.com

XM Cyber (60)
Operations / Breach and
Attack Simulation
Herzliya
xmcyber.com

Xpandion (19)
GRC / Risk Management
Tel Aviv
xpandion.com

YazamTech (3)
Data Security / File Scrubbing
Ra'anana
yazamtech.com

ITALY

Boole Server (22)
Data Security / Secure File
Synch and Share
Milan
booleserver.com

Cleafy (21)
Fraud Prevention / An-
ti-fraud
Milan
cleafy.com

DFLabs (56)
Operations / Automat-
ed Incident & Breach
Response
Milan
dflabs.com

Endian (26)
Network / UTM
Bolzano
endian.com

ERMES Cyber Security (11)
Data Security / DLP and
Web Browsing Protection
Turin
ermessecurity.com

Exein (9)
IoT Security / IoT
Rome
exein.io

Libraesva (13)
Email Security
Lecco
libraesva.com

**Minded Security UK
Limited** (22)
Endpoint / Malware De-
tection
Rome
mindedsecurity.com

Swascan (27)
GRC / Web Scanning
Cassina de' Pecchi
swascan.com

ToothPic (22)
Operations / Forensics
Cameras
Turin
toothpic.eu

Unfraud (1)
Fraud Prevention / An-
ti-fraud
Ariano Irpino
unfraud.com

JAPAN

Authlete (9)
IAM / OAuth Gateways
Tokyo
authlete.com

Blue Planet-works (13)
Application Security /
Isolation
Tokyo
blueplanet-works.com

Cyber-SIGN (1)
IAM / Biometrics Hand-
writing
Setagaya
witswell.com

Humming Heads (2)
Endpoint / Whitelisting
Tokyo
hummingheads.co.jp/en-
glish/product/dep/index.
html

NRI Secure Technologies
(398)
MSSP / SOC as a Service
Otemachi Chiyoda-ku
Nri-secure.com

Vario Secure Networks
(15)
MSSP / Managed Security
Services
Tokyo
variosecure.net/en

KUWAIT

Alsharq International Co.
(6)
Data Security / Certificate
Authority
alsharq.com.kw

Cyberkov (5)
GRC / Risk Assessment
Kuwait City
cyberkov.com

LUXEMBOURG

RCDevs (13)
IAM / IAM
Belvaux
rcdevs.com

MALAYSIA

Ensign Infosecurity (255)
MSSP / Managed Services
Kuala Lumpur
ensigninfosecurity.com

FraudLabs (5)
Fraud Prevention / Fraud
Detection
Bayan Baru
fraudlabspro.com

MALTA

Acunetix (53)
GRC / Vunerability Scanner (Web)
Mriehel
acunetix.com

MEXICO

Tesseract (29)
Data Security / Encryption
Mexico City
tesseract.mx

Tu Identidad (8)
IAM / 2FA (mobile)
Mexico City
tuidentidad.com

MOROCCO

Buglab (10)
Operations / Pen Testing
Network
Casablanca
buglab.io

NETHERLANDS

CipherMail (1)
Email Security / Secure
Email
Amsterdam
ciphermail.com

Compumatica (16)
Data Security / Secure
Remote Access
Uden
compumatica.com

CyberSprint (28)
GRC / Vulnerability
Scanner
The Hague
cybersprint.com

Deeptrace (7)
Data Security / Deep Fake
Detection
Amsterdam
deeptracelabs.com

Dynasec BV (20)
GRC / Compliance Management
Eindhoven
dynasec.org

EclecticIQ (110)
Threat Intelligence Platform
Amsterdam
eclecticiq.com

Elastic (200)
Security Analytics / SIEM
Amsterdam
elastic.co

ERPScan (21)
GRC / Business Application Security SAP
Amsterdam
erpscan.io

Fox-IT (303)
MSSP / MDR
Delft
fox-it.com

ID Control (3)
IAM
The Hague
idcontrol.com

Intel 471 (50)
Threat Intelligence / Threat
Actor Intelligence
Amsterdam
intel471.com

Irdeto (1,169)
IoT Security / Entertainment Systems
Hoofddorp
irdeto.com

iWelcome (75)
IAM / Identity Management
Amersfoort
iwelcome.com

Keezel (11)
Network / Wifi Firewall
Amsterdam
keezel.co

MMOX (6)
MSSP / SMB Solutions
The Hague
mmox.co

Nasdaq Bwise (67)
GRC
's-Hertogenbosch
bwise.com

P-X Systems (2)
Network / IDS
Amsterdam
p-x.systems

Profitap (31)
Network / Traffic Capture
Eindhoven
profitap.com

ReaQta (20)
Endpoint / EDR
Amsterdam
reaqta.com

Riscure (109)
Testing / Security Product
Test Labs
Delft
riscure.com

Secureme2 (5)
MSSP / MDR
Rijen
secureme2.eu/en

Storro (5)
Data Security / Encrypted
Storage
Hengelo
storro.com

Tesorion (146)
MSSP / Managed Services
Leusden
tesorion.nl

Zivver (83)
Email Security / Encrypted
Email
Amsterdam
zivver.com

ZyLAB (91)
GRC / e-discovery
Amsterdam
zylab.com

NEW ZEALAND

Darkscope (2)
Threat Intelligence
Wellington
darkscope.com

Note: Numbers in parentheses indicate employee count

Endace (136)
Network / IDS
Ellerslie
endace.com

RedShield Security (36)
Network / Web Application
Defense
Wellington
redshield.co

SMX (301)
Email Security
Auckland
smxemail.com

TamosSoft (1)
Network Monitoring
Christchurch
tamos.com

WinGate (Qbik) (1)
Network / Gateway Security, VPN
Auckland
wingate.com

NORWAY

Crypho AS (5)
Data Security / Private
Messaging
Tønsberg
crypho.com

Mnemonic (227)
MSSP / MDR
Oslo
mnemonic.no

Promon (43)
Application Security / In-App Protection for Mobile
Oslo
promon.co

Prosa Security (1)
Application Security / Development Collaboration
Platform
Oslo
prosasecurity.com

PANAMA

NordVPN
Network / VPN Consumer
Panama City
nordvpn.com

PHILIPPINES

**GOCOM Systems and
Solutions Corporation** (23)
Network / Firewall
Mandaluyong City
gocomsystems.net

POLAND

Cyberus Labs (12)
IAM / 2FA (mobile)
Kraków
cyberuslabs.com

Grey Wizard (17)
Network Web Protection
Poznań
greywizard.com

Nethone (44)
Fraud Prevention / Anti-fraud
Warsaw
nethone.com

Rublon (2)
IAM / 2FA
Zielona Gora
rublon.com

PORTUGAL

**AnubisNetworks
(BitSight)** (35)
Email Security / Email
Protection
Lisbon
anubisnetworks.com

Probely (1)
Application Security / Web
Scanning
Lisbon
probely.com

Redstout (5)
Network / UTM
Lisbon
redstout.com

REPUBLIC OF
MOLDOVA

Dekart (1)
Data Security / Encryption
Chisinau
dekart.com

ROMANIA

BitDefender (1,600)
Endpoint / Anti-virus
Bucharest
bitdefender.com

CoSoSys (63)
Network / DLP
Cluj-Napoca
endpointprotector.com

CTF365 (8)
Training / Capture the Flag
Exercise
Cluj-Napoca
ctf365.com

CyberGhost (67)
Network / VPN
Bucharest
cyberghostvpn.com

east-tec (8)
Data Security / Erasure
Oradea
east-tec.com

Softwin SRL (195)
Endpoint / Anti-virus
Bucharest
softwin.ro

RUSSIA

BI.ZONE (81)
Threat Intelligence Aggregator
Moscow
bi.zone

Cezurity (9)
Endpoint / EDR
St. Petersburg
cezurity.com

CyberSafe Software (3)
Data Security / Full Disk
Encryption
Krasnodar
cybersafesoft.com

Dr. Web (1)
Endpoint / Android AV
Moscow
drweb.com

Elcomsoft (16)
Operations / Forensics
Moscow
elcomsoft.com

Gleg
GRC / Vulnerability Management
Moscow
gleg.net

Infowatch (176)
GRC / DLP
Moscow
infowatch.com

Kaspersky Lab (3,608)
Endpoint / Anti-virus
Moscow
kaspersky.com

Metascan (5)
GRC / Web Scanning
Moscow
metascan.ru

R-Vision (44)
Operations / Incident
Response Platform
Moscow
rvision.pro

SearchInform (97)
Operations / Employee
Monitoring
Moscow
searchinform.com

Zecurion (43)
Data Security / Database
Security
Moscow
zecurion.com

SINGAPORE

Anqlave (10)
IAM / 2FA
Singapore
anqlave.com

AppKnox (19)
Application Security / Mo-
bile Application Security
Testing
Singapore
appknox.com

Apvera (12)
GRC / User Activity Mon-
itoring
Singapore
apvera.com

Avnos (27)
Endpoint / Application
Whitelisting
Singapore
avnos.io

Banff Cyber (1)
MSSP / Website Deface-
ment Monitoring
Singapore
banffcyber.com

Cura Software Solutions
(90)
GRC / Risk Management
Singapore
curasoftware.com

Custodio Technologies (13)
Security Analytics / Breach
Detection and Response
Ubi
custodio.com.sg

Dathena Science (51)
Data Security / Discovery
and Classification
Singapore
dathena.io

Deep Identity Pte Ltd. (85)
IAM / IAM
Singapore
deepidentity.com

Flexible IR (1)
Operations / Incident
Response
Singapore
flexibleir.com

Ground Labs (43)
GRC / Data Discovery
Singapore
groundlabs.com

Horangi (71)
Network / AWS Vulnera-
bility Scanning
Singapore
horangi.com

i-Sprint (94)
IAM
Singapore
i-sprint.com

IoTSploit
IoT Security / IoT Scan-
ning
Singapore
iotsploit.co

Scantist (11)
GRC / Vulnerability Man-
agement
Singapore
scantist.com

Seconize (6)
GRC / Risk Management
Singapore
seconize.co

SilverLakeMasterSAM (25)
IAM / Privileged Access
Management
Singapore
mastersam.com

SpeQtral (11)
Data Security / Quantum
Key Distribution
Singapore
speqtral.space

**StepNexus (Division of
Multos International)** (54)
IAM / Authentication
Singapore
multosinternational.com/
secure-services/stepnexus.
html

Treebox Solutions (22)
Data Security / Secure
Communications
Singapore
treeboxsolutions.com

V-Key (84)
Application Security / Mobile Device & App Security
Singapore
v-key.com

Watchdata (202)
IAM / PKI
Singapore
watchdata.com

SLOVAKIA

Ardaco (27)
Data Security / Secure
Communications
Bratislava
ardaco.com

SaferPass (18)
IAM / Password Manager
Bratislava
saferpass.net

SOUTH AFRICA

Entersekt (144)
IAM / Authentication &
Fraud Protection for Banks
Stellenbosch
entersekt.com

Paterva (4)
Operations / Maltego
Enhancement
Pretoria
paterva.com

Thinkst Canary (9)
Deception / Target Agents
Deployed in Operations
Edinvale
canary.tools

ThisIsMe (13)
IAM / Onboarding
Cape Town
thisisme.com

SOUTH KOREA

Ahnlab (429)
Endpoint / Anti-virus
Gyeonggi-do
ahnlab.com

Ahope (21)
Application Security /
Mobile
Seoul
ahope.net/main

Note: Numbers in parentheses indicate employee count

Aircuve (1)
IAM / Authentication
Seoul
aircuve.com/wp/en

Amgine Securus (2)
Network and Endpoint
Monitoring
amgine.co.kr

ESTsoft (402)
Endpoint / Android AV
Seoul
estsoft.com

Everspin (15)
Endpoint / Dynamic Image
Replacement
Seoul
everspin.global

Fasoo.com, Inc. (105)
GRC / Digital Rights Man-
agement
Seoul
fasoo.com

Genians (51)
IoT Security / Device Fingerprinting
Anyang-si
genians.com

Hauri (3)
Endpoint / Anti-virus
Seoul
hauri.net

HDN (17)
Network / Security
Switches
Guro-gu
handream.net

Igloo Security (46)
MSSP / Managed Security
Services
Seoul
igloosec.co.kr

Insignary (12)
Application Security /
Open Source Vulnerability
Management
Seoul
insignary.com

Jiran (1)
GRC / DLP
Daejeon
jiran.com

Modoosone (1)
IAM / Privileged Access
Management
Seoul
modoosone.com

Norma
IoT Security / Wireless
Seoul
norma.co.kr

NP Core (16)
Endpoint / EDR
Seoul
npcore.com

nProtect (15)
Endpoint / Mobile
Guro-gu
nprotect.com

Octatco (3)
IAM / Fingerprint USB
Devices
Seongnam
octatco.com

Penta Security (114)
Network / Web Application
Firewall
Seoul
pentasecurity.com

Secudrives (1)
Data Security / Data En-
cryption & Destruction
Seoul
secudrives.com

Secui (1)
Network / Firewall
Seoul
secui.com

SecuLetter (3)
Operations / Malware
Analysis
Seongnam-si
seculetter.com

Sparrow
Application Security /
Code Scanning
Mapo-gu
sparrowfasoo.com

STEALIEN (9)
Application Security /
Appsec
Seoul
stealien.com

Viascope (6)
IAM / Network Access
Control
Seoul
viascope.com

WithNetworks
Endpoint / EDR
Yongsan-gu
withnetworks.com

Xabyss
Network / Traffic Capture
and Analysis
Seoul
xabyss.com

SPAIN

BIID (22)
IAM / Mobile Identity
Platform
Sant Cugat del Vallès
biid.com

Blueliv (67)
Threat Intelligence
Barcelona
blueliv.com

Buguroo (45)
Fraud Prevention / Behav-
ior Monitoring
Alcobendas
buguroo.com

Continuum Security (30)
Application Security /
Open Source Scanning
Huesca
continuumsecurity.net

CounterCraft (26)
Deception
Donostia-San Sebastian
countercraft.eu

Enigmedia (17)
Data Security / Secure
Communications
San Sebastian
enigmedia.es

HDIV Security (21)
Application Security /
Code Analysis
Donostia-San Sebastián
hdivsecurity.com

Panda Security (633)
Endpoint / Anti-virus
Bilbao
pandasecurity.com/usa

Quside (19)
Data Security / Quantum
RNG
Barcelona
quside.com

Redborder
Network / IDS Based on
SNORT
Sevilla
redborder.com

Syneidis (15)
Data Security / File En-
cryption
Barcelona
syneidis.com

SWEDEN

Advenica (50)
Network / Air Gap
Malmö
advenica.com

Axiomatics (45)
IAM / Database Access
Control
Stockholm
axiomatics.com

Baffin Bay Networking (34)
Network / Threat Detection & Network Forensics
Stockholm
baffinbaynetworks.com

Clavister (142)
Network / UTM
Örnsköldsvik
clavister.com

Columbitech (12)
Network / Mobile VPN
Stockholm
columbitech.com

CovR
IAM / Mobile Authenticator
Malmö
covrsecurity.com

Debricked (17)
GRC / Vulnerability Management
Malmö
debricked.com

Defentry (10)
Opertions / Web Scanning
Stockholm
defentry.com

Detectify (82)
Application Security / Web Scanning
Stockholm
detectify.com

Fingerprint Cards AB (286)
IAM / Biometrics
Gothenburg
fingerprints.com

Foreseeti (19)
GRC / Vulnerability Scanning
Stockholm
foreseeti.com

Halon (22)
Email Security / Anti-spam
Gothenburg
halon.io

InGate (23)
Network / Firewall
Sundbyberg
ingate.com

Keypasco AB (16)
IAM / Multi-factor Authentication
Gothenburg
keypasco.com

Outpost24 (161)
GRC / Vulnerability Risk Management
Karlskrona
outpost24.com

PointSharp AB (13)
Endpoint / Mobile Security
Stockholm
pointsharp.com

PrimeKey Solutions (61)
Data Security / PKI & Digital Signature Solutions
Solna
primekey.com

Sentor (68)
MSSP / Managed SIEM
Stockholm
sentor.se

Specops Software Inc. (49)
IAM / Password Management
Stockholm
specopssoft.com

Veriscan Security (10)
GRC / Security Measurement
Karlstad
veriscan.se

Versasec (23)
IAM
Stockholm
versasec.com

Yubico (188)
IAM / Authentication Tokens
Stockholm
yubico.com

Zignsec (16)
IAM / Identity Verification
Solna
zignsec.com

SWITZERLAND

AdNovum (1)
IAM
Zürich
adnovum.ch

Agora SecureWare (4)
Data Security / Secure Collaboration
Bioggio
agora-secureware.com

BinaryEdge (5)
Opertions / Internet Scanning
Zürich
binaryedge.io

BioID (10)
IAM / Biometrics
Sachseln
bioid.com

BioWatch
IAM / Biometrics
Martigny
biowatchid.com

Compass Security AG
Data Security / Secure File Transfer
Rapperswil-Jona
csnc.ch

Crypto International AG (1)
Data Security / Hardware for Crypto
Steinhausen
crypto.ch

cyel (5)
Network / IP Address Morphing
Bern
cyel.ch

Exeon Analytics (10)
Security Analytics / Network Monitoring
Zürich
exeon.ch

Futurae (12)
IAM / Authentication
Zürich
futurae.com

GhostMail (1)
Email Security / Secure Email
Zug
ghostmail.com

Global ID
IAM / Biometrics
Lausanne
global-id.ch

Immuniweb
Application Security / Web Scanning
Geneva
immuniweb.com

JOESecurity (8)
Operations / Malware Analysis
Reinach
joesecurity.org

Note: Numbers in parentheses indicate employee count

LUCY Security (8)
GRC / Anti-phishing
Training
Zug
lucysecurity.com

MailCleaner (7)
Email Security
Saint-Sulpice
mailcleaner.net

OneVisage (8)
IAM / Biometrics
Lausanne
onevisage.com

Open Systems (257)
MSSP / Managed Services
Zürich
open-systems.com

Privus (9)
Data Security / Secure
Communications
Zug
privus.global

RSD (705)
IAM / Information Gover-
nance Solutions
Geneva
rsd.com

Seppmail (9)
Email Security / Email
Encryption
Neuenhof
seppmail.com

SwissSign Group
Data Security / Certificate
Authority
Glattbrugg
swisssign.com

Trustless.ai (11)
Endpoint / Secure Device
Geneva
trustless.ai

United Security Providers
(57)
Network / Web Application
Firewall
Bern
united-security-providers.
com

Variti (7)
Network / DDoS Defense
Lucerne
variti.com

Wisekey (124)
IoT Security / Root of
Trust Chips
Geneva
wisekey.com

TAIWAN

D-Link Systems, Inc.
(1,000)
Network / UTM
Taipei City
us.dlink.com

DragonSoft (31)
Application Security WAF
and Scanning
New Taipei City
dragonsoft.com.tw

Egis Technology (1)
IAM / Biometrics under
Display Fingerprint Sensor
Taipei
egistec.com

ForceShield (14)
IoT Security / Bot Protection
Taipei
forceshield.com

Go-Trust (11)
IAM / Authentication
Taichung City
go-trust.com

Nexcom (1)
Network Security Appli-
ances
New Taipei City
nexcom.com

TURKEY

Extunda (8)
IoT Security / IoT Device
Management
Istanbul
extunda.com

Logsign (52)
Security Analytics / SIEM
Istanbul
logsign.com

Loki (6)
Network / UTM
Izmir
getloki.com

Picus Security (53)
GRC / IT Security Control
Monitoring
Ankara
picussecurity.com

Zemana (33)
Endpoint / Android AV
Ankara
zemana.com

UNITED KINGDOM

0 Patch (10)
Endpoint / Micropatching
London
0patch.com

1E (424)
Endpoint Detection and
Response (EDR)
London
1e.com

3ami Network Security (1)
GRC / Activity Auditing
Wigan
3ami.com

Abatis UK Ltd. (3)
Endpoint Protection
Egham
abatis-hdf.com

Acuity Risk Management
(8)
GRC / Risk Management
London
acuityrm.com

AimBrain (16)
IAM / Biometrics
London
aimbrain.com

AppsPicket (2)
IAM / Authentication
Hammersmith
appspicket.com

AquilAI
Email Security / An-
ti-phishing
Cheltenham
aquil.ai

ArQit (13)
Network / Post-quantum
Defense
London
arqit.io

Assuria (20)
Security Analytics / SIEM
Reading
assuria.com

Atar Labs (32)
Operations / Security
Orchestration
London
atarlabs.io

AuthLogics (6)
IAM / Authentication
Bracknell
authlogics.com

Aves Network Security (6)
Endpoint / Temporary
Patching
London
avesnetsec.com

Avoco Secure (6)
IAM / Cloud Authentication
London
secure2trust.com

B-Secur (37)
IAM / Biometrics (ECG)
Belfast
b-secur.com

BAE Systems (150)
MSSP / Managed Services
Guildford
baesystems.com

Barac (11)
Network / NBAD
London
barac.io

Becrypt (62)
Data Security / Encryption
London
becrypt.com/uk

BitNinja (18)
Endpoint / Server Protection
London
bitninja.io

Blancco (251)
Data Security / Erasure
Bishops Stortford
blancco.com/en

Bluecat Networks (10)
Network / DNS Security
Bracknell
bluecatnetworks.com

Bob's Business (27)
GRC / Security Awareness
Training
Barnsley
bobsbusiness.co.uk

Boldon James (76)
GRC / DLP (Data Classification)
Farnborough
boldonjames.com

British Telecom (300)
MSSP / Managed Services
London
bt.com

BSI Group (50)
Training / Standards Certification
London
bsigroup.com

Bulletproof (23)
MSSP / Managed SIEM
Stevenage
bulletproof.co.uk

BullGuard Ltd. (129)
Endpoint / Anti-virus
London
bullguard.com

Callsign (129)
IAM / Authentication
London
callsign.com

Cambridge Intelligence (35)
Security Analytics / Data
Visualization
Cambridge
cambridge-intelligence.com

Cellcrypt (4)
Data Security / Secure
Communications
London
cellcrypt.com

CensorNet (78)
Network / Content URL
Filtering
Basingstoke
censornet.com

Citicus (4)
GRC
London
citicus.com

Clearswift (193)
Email Security
Theale
clearswift.com

Codified Security (5)
Application Security /
Code Scanning
London
codifiedsecurity.com

Communication Security Group (16)
Data Security / Secure
Communications
London
csghq.com

Corax (31)
GRC / Security Ratings
London
coraxcyber.com

Cortex Insight (4)
Security Analytics / Vulnerability Measurement
London
cortexinsight.com

Crypta Labs (13)
Data Security / Encryption
(RNG)
London
cryptalabs.com

Crypto Quantique (24)
IoT Security / Embedded
Security
Egham
cryptoquantique.com

Cyan Forensics (9)
Operations / Endpoint
Forensics
Edinburgh
cyanforensics.com

CyberCPR (1)
Operations / Secure Incident Response Management
Cheltenham
cybercpr.com

CyberOwl (26)
GRC / Risk Measurement
Birmingham
cyberowl.io

CyberSafe Ltd. (7)
IAM / Access Control for
SAP
Longford
cybersafe.com

Cyberseer (11)
MSSP / Threat Intel
London
cyberseer.net

Cybersmart (18)
GRC / Compliance Automation
London
cybersmart.co.uk

CybSafe (39)
GRC / Security Awareness
Training
London
cybsafe.com

Cyjax (10)
Threat Intelligence
London
cyjax.com

CyNation (14)
GRC / Third Party Risk
Assessment
London
cynation.com

Darkbeam (5)
Threat Intelligence
London
darkbeam.com

Data Encryption Systems (4)
Data Security / Software
DRM
Taunton
des.co.uk

Note: Numbers in parentheses indicate employee count

Deep-Secure (48)
Network / Air Gap (Data Diodes)
Malvern
deep-secure.com

Deepnet Security (14)
IAM / Identity Management
London
deepnetsecurity.com

DeepView (7)
Data Security / DL Detection Through Social Media Monitoring
London
deepview.com

Device Authority (23)
IAM / Device Authentication
Reading
deviceauthority.com

Digital Detective (3)
GRC / Forensics
Folkestone
digital-detective.net

DISUK Limited (2)
Data Security / Encryption
Northampton
disuk.com

Egress (198)
Email Security
London
egress.com

Elemendar (4)
Threat Intelligence Analysis
Stourbridge
elemendar.com

Encedo (2)
Data Security / Encrypted Networks
London
encedo.com

Encode (98)
Security Analytics
London
encodegroup.com

Exonar (52)
Data Security / Data Discovery
Newbury
exonar.com

Galaxkey (24)
Data Security / Secure File and Message Transfer
London
galaxkey.com

Garrison (159)
Network / Browser Isolation
London
garrison.com

GeoLang (7)
GRC / DLP
Cardiff
geolang.com

Glasswall Solutions (63)
Operations / Document Scrubbing
West End
glasswallsolutions.com

Hack the Box (115)
Training / Cyber Range
Kent
hackthebox.eu

Hexamail (2)
Email Security / Anti-spam and Anti-virus
Pensham
hexamail.com

Humio (37)
Security Analytics / Log Analysis
London
humio.com

Hypersonica (6)
Network / Web Safety
London
hypersonica.com

idappcom (8)
Network / Packet Capture and Analysis
Ludlow
idappcom.com

Idax Software (6)
IAM / IAM
Petersfield
idaxsoftware.com

IDENprotect (9)
IAM / Authentication
London
idenprotect.com

Immersive Labs (94)
Training / Cyber Range
Bristol
immersivelabs.com

Intelliagg (5)
Threat Intelligence
London
intelliagg.com

Intruder (9)
GRC / Vulnerability Scanner
London
intruder.io

Invinsec (14)
MSSP / Managed Security Services
Cheltenham
invinsec.com

Ioetec (4)
IoT Security / Device Security
Sheffield
ioetec.com

IProov (32)
IAM / Authentication
London
iproov.com

IRM Security (82)
GRC / Risk Management
Cheltenham
irmsecurity.com

ISARR (4)
GRC / Asset Management
London
isarr.com

IStorage (36)
Data Security / Hardware Encryption
Perivale
istorage-uk.com

ITC Secure Networking (136)
MSSP / Managed Security Services
London
itcsecure.com

iZOOlogic (10)
Threat Intelligence
London
izoologic.com

Jazz Networks (74)
Security Analytics / UEBA
Uxbridge
jazznetworks.com

KETS Quantum Security (12)
Data Security / Secure Communications
Bristol
kets-quantum.com

Kovrr (19)
GRC / Risk Monitoring for Insurance Providers
London
kovrr.com

KromTech (625)
Endpoint / Android AV
London
kromtech.com

KYND (17)
GRC / Risk Management
London
kynd.io

Liopa (8)
IAM / Biometrics, Liveness
Detection
Belfast
liopa.ai

LockLizard Ltd. (1)
Data Security / IRM
London
locklizard.com

Maidsafe (1)
Data Security / Block-
chain-like Payment System
Ayr
maidsafe.net

Methodware (5)
GRC / Risk Framework
London
methodware.com

Micro Focus (239)
Security Analytics / SIEM
Newbury
microfocus.com

Mimecast (1,501)
Email Security / Microsoft
Exchange Email Security
London
mimecast.com

MIRACL (30)
IAM / Multi-factor Au-
thentication
London
miracl.com

Mobbu (3)
IAM / QRcode Authenti-
cation
Hove
mobbu.com

My1login (24)
IAM / Identity Manage-
ment
London
my1login.com

Navaho Technologies (12)
Endpoint / Hardened
Linux
Brockenhurst
navaho.co.uk

nCipher (268)
Data Security / Encryption
Cambridge
ncipher.com

Netintelligence (5)
MSSP / Managed Services
Glasgow
netintelligence.com

NetPilot (2)
Network / UTM
Bristol
netpilot.com

NETprotocol Limited (8)
MSSP / Firewall Manage-
ment
Wakefield
netprotocol.net

Netsparker (87)
GRC / Web Scanning
London
netsparker.com

Nettoken (4)
GRC / Password Manager
London
nettoken.io

Network Critical (24)
Network / Intrusion Pre-
vention
Caversham
networkcritical.com

Noble (14)
Network / Anomaly De-
tection
London
noblecss.io

Nominet (250)
Network / DNS Threat
Detection
Oxford
nominet.com

Nu Quantum (5)
Data Security / Quantum
Cryptography
London
nu-quantum.com

Omniquad Ltd. (30)
Endpoint / Anti-spyware
London
omniquad.com

OnDMARC (15)
Email Security / DMARC
London
ondmarc.com

Osirium (45)
IAM / Privileged Access
Management
Theale
osirium.com

OutThink (15)
GRC / Employee Behavior
Monitoring
London
outthinkthreats.com

OxCEPT
IoT Security / Device
Authentication
London
oxcept.com

Oxford Biochronometrics
(12)
Fraud Prevention / Click
Fraud Prevention
London
oxford-biochron.com

Panaseer (50)
GRC / Security Manage-
ment Platform
London
panaseer.com

Perpetual Encryption
Data Security / OTP En-
cryption
London
perpetualencryption.com

Pervade Software (6)
GRC
Cardiff
pervade-software.com

Pirean (Echostar) (65)
IAM / Identity Manage-
ment
London
pirean.com

Pixelpin (15)
IAM / Password Manage-
ment
London
pixelpin.io

PortSwigger (30)
GRC / Vulnerability
Scanner
Knutsford
portswigger.net

Post-Quantum (15)
IAM / Authentication
London
post-quantum.com

Prevalent AI (21)
GRC / Risk Management
London
prevalent.ai

Privitar (109)
Data Security / Data
Masking
London
privitar.com

Protect2020 (2)
Training / SaaS Platform
Camberley
p2020academy.com

Note: Numbers in parentheses indicate employee count

Protectimus (28)
IAM / Two-Factor Authentication
London
protectimus.com

Proteus-Cyber, Ltd. (4)
GRC
London
proteuscyber.com

Pushfor, Inc. (19)
Data Security / Secure
Content Sharing
Wimbledon
pushfor.com

Qredo (13)
Data Security / App Encryption
London
qredo.com

Rawstream (3)
Network / DNS-Based
Security
London
rawstream.com

RazorSecure
IoT Security / Automotive
Basingstoke
web.razorsecure.com

RealVNC (67)
Network / Remote Access
Cambridge
realvnc.com/en

Red Sift (38)
Endpoint / Open Platform
London
redsift.com

RedScan (60)
MSSP / MDR
London
redscan.com

RelateData (3)
Network Monitoring
London
relatedata.com

RepKnight (22)
Threat Intelligence / Dark
Web Breach Alert
Belfast
repknight.com

Risk Ledger (10)
GRC / Third Party Risk
Assessment
London
riskledger.com

SaltDNA (16)
Data Security / Secure
Communications
Belfast
saltdna.com

Salviol Global Analytics
(17)
Fraud Prevention / Fraud
Detection
Reading
salviol.com

Searchlight Security (2)
Threat Intelligence / Dark
Web Intel
Portsmouth
slcyber.io

Secoda Risk Management
(5)
GRC
London
secoda.com

Secon Cyber (135)
MSSP / MDR
Surrey
seconcyber.com

SecuPi (22)
Application Security /
Cloud App Monitoring
London
secupi.com

SecurEnvoy (34)
IAM / Tokenless 2FA
Basingstoke
securenvoy.com

SecurityCTRL
Network / Intrusion Detection
Edinburgh
securityctrl.com

SecurityZONES (6)
Threat Intelligence /
Spamhaus
London
securityzones.net

Secuware (1)
Data Security / Database
Security
London
secuware.uk

Senseon (38)
Security Analytics / Breach
Detection and Response
London
senseon.io

SentryBay (16)
Endpoint / Anti-malware
London
sentrybay.com

Shaka Technologies (5)
Network / DLP
Witham
shakatechnologies.com

Silobreaker (36)
Threat Intelligence Management
London
silobreaker.com

Skurio (26)
Threat Intelligence / Brand
Monitoring
Belfast
skurio.com

Smoothwall (116)
Network / UTM
Leeds
smoothwall.com

Snyk (205)
Application Security /
Appsec Open Source Vulns
London
snyk.io

SocView (7)
Operations / Alert Management
London
socview.com

SolSoft (24)
Operations / Policy Management
Bristol
solsoft.co.uk

Sophos (3,408)
Endpoint / Anti-virus
Abingdon
sophos.com

Spherical Defence (11)
Application Security / API
Security
London
sphericaldefence.com

Spirent Communications
(200)
Testing / Security Instrumentation
Crawley
spirent.com

SQR Systems (10)
Data Security / Secure
Communications
London
sqrsystems.com

Surevine (27)
Data Security / Secure
Collaboration
Guildford
surevine.com

SwivelSecure (50)
IAM / Authentication
Wetherby
swivelsecure.com

Sword Active Risk (78)
GRC / Risk Management
Maidenhead
sword-activerisk.com

Teskalabs (9)
Network / Secure Mobile
Gateway
London
teskalabs.com

The Cyberfort Group (17)
MSSP / Managed SOC
Thatcham
cyberfortgroup.com

Titan IC (22)
Network / IDS
Belfast
Titan-ic.com

Titania Ltd. (48)
GRC / Configuration
Auditing
Worcester
titania.com

**Torsion Information
Security** (7)
Data Security / File Access
Monitoring
London
torsionis.com

Tricerion (5)
IAM / Grid Password
Reading
tricerion.com

UM-Labs (10)
Endpoint / Hardened OS
for Realtime Comms
London
Um-labs.com

Unloq
IAM / Authentication and
Authorization
London
unloqsystems.com

Verimuchme (1)
IAM / Identity Storage
London
verimuchme.com

Vo1t (9)
Data Security / Secure
Storage for Cryptocurren-
cies
London
vo1t.io

WebARX (4)
Network / Web Application
Firewall
London
webarxsecurity.com

Westgate Cyber Security
(4)
Network / Zero-Trust
Networking
Cwmbran
westgatecyber.com

Workshare (213)
Data Security / File En-
cryption and Sharing
London
workshare.com

Zen Internet (464)
MSSP / Managed Services
Rochdale
zen.co.uk

Zercurity (2)
GRC / OSQuery
London
zercurity.com

UKRAINE

Mirobase
GRC / DLP and Employee
Monitoring
mirobase.com

Romad (43)
Endpoint / AV
Kiev
romad-systems.com

SOC Prime (64)
Threat Intelligence Plat-
form
Kiev
socprime.com

VENEZUELA

Inteligensa (88)
IAM / Smart Card Solu-
tions
Caracas
Inteligensa.com

VIETNAM

CyRadar
Endpoint / EDR
Hanoi
cyradar.com

Note: Numbers in parentheses indicate employee count

US Listings By State

Number of Vendors in Top 20 States

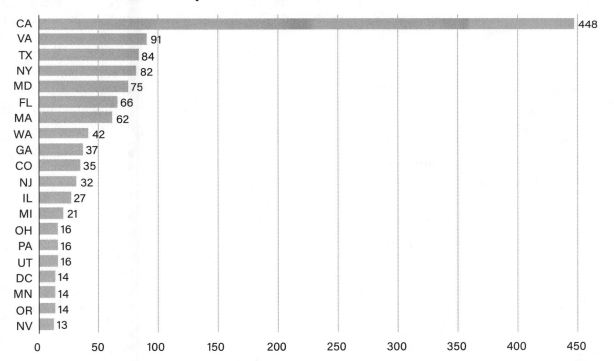

Number of Vendors per State

AL	3	ID	4	MT	1	PA	16
AR	11	IL	27	NC	8	SC	2
AZ	7	IN	5	NE	3	SD	1
CA	448	KS	8	NH	8	TN	3
CO	35	LA	4	NJ	32	TX	84
CT	11	MA	62	NM	2	UT	16
DC	14	MD	75	NV	13	VA	91
DE	10	ME	3	NY	82	WA	42
FL	66	MI	21	OH	16	WI	5
GA	37	MN	14	OK	3	WV	1
IA	2	MO	3	OR	14	WY	1

ALABAMA

Adtran Inc. (200)
Network / Firewalls
Huntsville
adtran.com

Cyber Operations, LLC (1)
Operations / ACL Management
Pelham
cyberoperations.com

Sentar (303)
Application Security /
Code Scanning
Huntsville
sentar.com

ARIZONA

Avertium (108)
MSSP / Managed Services
Phoenix
avertium.com

Axway (2,035)
GRC / Secure File Transfer
Phoenix
axway.com

BOSaNOVA (19)
Network / Secure Terminal
Emulation
Phoenix
bosanova.net

CYR3CON (55)
GRC / Vulnerability
Ranking
Tempe
cyr3con.ai

Early Warning (904)
Fraud Prevention / Identity
Assurance
Scottsdale
earlywarning.com

Emailage (174)
Email Security
Chandler
emailage.com

LifeLock, Symantec (415)
IAM / Personal Identity
Theft Protection
Tempe
lifelock.com

Privoro (38)
Endpoint / Hardened Cases for Mobile Phones
Chandler
privoro.com

Safehouse Technologies (7)
Network Cloud Proxy
Scottsdale
safehousetechnologies.com

Saife (1)
Data Security / Secure Data
Transfer
Chandler
saifeinc.com

SiteLock (200)
Network / Website Security
Scottsdale
sitelock.com

Stealth Software (7)
Data Security / Encryption
Scottsdale
stealth-soft.com

Trusona (35)
IAM / SSO
Scottsdale
trusona.com

Valtx Cyber Securities (5)
Endpoint Hardening
Surprise
valtx.com

VIA3 Corperation (18)
Data Security / Secure
Messaging
Scottsdale
via3.com

Vigilante ATI (9)
Threat Intelligence / Dark
Web Research
Phoenix
vigilante.io

ARKANSAS

Kernel, Inc. (1)
MSSP / Managed Services
Fayetteville
kernelops.com

Note: Numbers in parentheses indicate employee count

CALIFORNIA

42Crunch (19)
Application Security / API Security
Irvine
42crunch.com

4iQ (100)
Threat Intelligence / Stolen Identities
Los Altos
4iQ.com

802Secure (48)
IoT Security / IoT Network Monitoring
Emeryville
802secure.com

8e14 Networks (5)
Network / Microsegmentation
San Francisco
8e14.net

A10 Networks (821)
Network / DDoS Defense Appliance
San Jose
a10networks.com

Abnormal Security (21)
Email Security / Anti-phishing
San Francisco
abnormalsecurity.com

Abusix (19)
Threat Intelligence
San Jose
abusix.com

Acalvio Technologies (64)
Deception
Santa Clara
acalvio.com

Accellion (180)
Data Security / IRM
Palo Alto
accellion.com

Aegify (19)
GRC / Risk Management
San Jose
aegify.com

Aerohive Networks (557)
IAM / Network Access Control
Milpitas
aerohive.com

Agari (184)
Email Security
Foster City
agari.com

AlertEnterprise (147)
IAM / Physical Identity & Access Management
Fremont
alertenterprise.com

alertsec (5)
GRC / Encryption Monitoring for Third Parties
Palo Alto
alertsec.com

Allgress (42)
GRC / Compliance
Livermore
allgress.com

AlphaGuardian Networks (1)
IoT Security / ICS Monitoring
San Ramon
alphaguardian.net

Altitude Networks (10)
Data Security / File Monitoring
San Francisco
altitudenetworks.com

Ambitrace (3)
Data Security / Data Tracking and Logging
San Francisco
ambitrace.com

Anchorage (48)
Data Security / Secure Storage
San Francisco
anchorage.com

Anjuna (10)
Data Security / Runtime Encryption
Palo Alto
anjuna.io

Anomali (301)
Threat Intelligence Platform
Redwood City
anomali.com

Apollo Information Systems (20)
MSSP / Managed Security Services
Los Gatos
apollo-is.com

Aporeto (44)
Endpoint / Container Security
San Jose
aporeto.com

Apozy (4)
Endpoint / Content URL Filtering
San Francisco
apozy.com

AppOmni (19)
Data Security / Cloud DLP
San Francisco
appomni.com

AppVision (10)
Application Security / Appsec Code Hardening and Monitoring
San Francisco
appvision.net

Apricorn (23)
Data Security / Encrypted Storage
Poway
apricorn.com

Aptible (40)
GRC / Compliance Management
San Francisco
aptible.com

Araali Networks (4)
Application Security / Appsec for Containers
Fremont
araalinetworks.com

Arctic Wolf Networks (236)
Security Analytics / SIEM
Sunnyvale
arcticwolf.com

Area 1 Security (78)
Email Security / Anti-phishing
Redwood City
area1security.com

ArecaBay (6)
Application Security / API Security
Los Altos
arecabay.com

Arkose Labs (59)
Fraud Prevention / Graduated Friction
San Francisco
arkoselabs.com

Armis (150)
IoT Security / Device Discovery and Protection
Palo Alto
armis.com

Armor Scientific (7)
IAM / Authentication
Newport Beach
armorsci.com

Armorblox (42)
Data Security / DLP
Cupertino
armorblox.com

Array Networks (OSS Corp.) (193)
Network / SSL VPN
Milpitas
arraynetworks.com

Aruba Networks, an HP Company (150)
Network / UEBA
Santa Clara
arubanetworks.com

Arxan Technology (153)
Application Security
San Francisco
arxan.com

AT&T Cybersecurity (297)
Security Analytics / SIEM
San Mateo
alienvault.com

AttackFlow (5)
Application Security /
Appsec Code Scanning
San Francisco
attackflow.com

AttackIQ, Inc. (61)
Testing / Security Instrumentation
San Diego
attackiq.com

Attivo Networks (165)
Deception
Fremont
attivonetworks.com

Authenex Inc. (13)
IAM / Authentication
Mountain View
authenex.com

Authentic8, Inc. (75)
Network / Cloud Browser Isolation
Redwood City
authentic8.com

Authernative (2)
IAM / Authentication
Redwood City
authernative.com

Authy (3)
IAM / 2FA for Consumers
San Francisco
authy.com

Autonomic Software (13)
Endpoint / Patch Management
Danville
autonomic-software.com

Avatier (35)
IAM / Identity Management Platform
Pleasanton
avatier.com

Avaya (150)
Network / SSL VPN
Santa Clara
avaya.com

Averon (30)
IAM / Mobile Authentication
San Francisco
averon.com

Avi Networks (330)
Network / Web Application Firewall
Santa Clara
avinetworks.com

Aviatrix (90)
Network / Firewall Enablement in the Cloud
Palo Alto
aviatrix.com

Avocado Systems, Inc. (10)
Application Security / App Hardening
San Jose
avocadosys.com

Awake Security (51)
Network Monitoring
Sunnyvale
awakesecurity.com

Axiad IDS (26)
IAM / Authentication
Santa Clara
axiadids.com

Axiado (9)
Endpoint / Secure Hardware
San Jose
axiado.com

Ayehu (55)
Operations / Orchestration
San Jose
ayehu.com

Baffle (30)
Data Security / Database Encryption
Santa Clara
baffle.io

Balbix (52)
GRC / Asset Management
San Jose
balbix.com

Banyan Security (19)
Network / Zero-Trust Networking
San Francisco
banyansecurity.io

Barracuda Networks (1,427)
Network / Anti-spam
Campbell
barracuda.com

Beachhead Solutions, Inc. (15)
Endpoint / MDM
San Jose
beachheadsolutions.com

Behaviosec (41)
Fraud Prevention / Behavior Monitoring
San Francisco
behaviosec.com

Belkasoft (19)
Operations / Mobile Device Forensics
Palo Alto
belkasoft.com

Beyond Security (54)
GRC / Vulnerability Management
San Jose
beyondsecurity.com

Big Switch Networks (218)
Network / DDoS Defense
Santa Clara
bigswitch.com

BitGlass (123)
Security Analytics / Breach Discovery
Campbell
bitglass.com

Bivio Networks (36)
Network / Gateway Security Platform
Pleasanton
bivio.net

BlastWave (16)
Network / Microsegmentation
Mountain View
blastwaveinc.com

Bloombase (20)
Data Security / Network-Attached Encryption
Redwood City
bloombase.com

Blue Hexagon (32)
Security Analytics / Breach Detection
Sunnyvale
bluehexagon.ai

BlueCedar (39)
Endpoint / Mobile Device
Protection
San Francisco
bluecedar.com

BlueTalon (32)
Data Security / Database
Policy Management
Redwood City
bluetalon.com

BroadBridge Networks (3)
Security Analytics / Network Monitoring
Fremont
broadbridgenetworks.com

Broadcom (2,000)
Network / Security Hardware
San Jose
broadcom.com

Bromium (acquired by HP) (131)
Endpoint Sandbox
Cupertino
bromium.com

Bugcrowd (581)
Operations / Bug Reporting Platform
San Francisco
bugcrowd.com

Caplinked (20)
Data Security / Secure Workflow File Sharing
Manhattan Beach
caplinked.com

Castle (51)
Fraud Prevention / User-Trained Account Access
San Francisco
castle.io

Cavirin (69)
GRC / Cloud Compliance
Santa Clara
cavirin.com

CD Networks (322)
Network / DDoS Defense
Diamond Bar
cdnetworks.com

Celestix (25)
IAM
Fremont
celestix.com

Centrify (381)
IAM
Santa Clara
centrify.com

Cequence Security (47)
Security Analytics / NBAD
Sunnyvale
cequence.ai

CESPPA (13)
Operations / Bug Bounty
Manhattan Beach
cesppa.com

Chronicle (part of Google) (133)
Security Analytics / SIEM
Mountain View
chronicle.security

CipherCloud (309)
Data Security / Cloud Visibility & Data Protection
San Jose
ciphercloud.com

ciphertrace (28)
Fraud Prevention / Anti-money Laudering
Menlo Park
ciphertrace.com

Cisco (5,000)
Network / Firewall
San Jose
cisco.com

ClearedIn (16)
Email Security / Anti-phishing
Los Altos
clearedin.com

Cloud Raxak (9)
GRC / Compliance
Los Gatos
cloudraxak.com

Cloudera (247)
Operations / Cloud Security
Palo Alto
cloudera.com

Cloudflare (951)
Network / CDN and DDoS Defense
San Francisco
cloudflare.com

Cloudknox (19)
IAM / Cloud Identity Management
Sunnyvale
cloudknox.io

Cloudmark Inc. (94)
Network / DNS Security
San Francisco
cloudmark.com/en

CloudPassage (60)
Endpoint / Cloud Host Security
San Francisco
cloudpassage.com

Coalition (36)
GRC / Cyber Insurance
San Francisco
thecoalition.com

Cobalt (192)
Application Security / App Testing for Security
San Francisco
cobalt.io

Codenomicon (15)
Application Security / Code Analysis
Mountain View
codenomicon.com

Cognito (6)
Fraud Prevention / Intelligence-Based Authentication
Palo Alto
cognitohq.com

ColorTokens (230)
Network / Zero-Trust Networking
Santa Clara
colortokens.com

Confident Technologies (3)
Fraud Prevention / Anti-fraud CAPTCHAS
Solana Beach
confidenttechnologies.com

Confluera (19)
Security Analytics / Autonomous Detection and Response
Palo Alto
confluera.com

Contrast Security (169)
Application Security
Los Altos
contrastsecurity.com

Corelight (80)
Network / Traffic Analysis
San Francisco
corelight.com

cPacket (60)
Network / Packet Capture
San Jose
cpacket.com

CrowdStrike (1,513)
Endpoint / EDR
Sunnyvale
crowdstrike.com

Crown Sterling (17)
Data Security / Encryption
Newport Beach
crownsterling.io

CryptoMove, Inc. (23)
Data Security / Key Storage
Oakland
cryptomove.com

Cujo AI (150)
Network / Home Security
for Carriers
El Segundo
getcujo.com

Culinda (2)
IoT Security / Medical
Devices
Irvine
culinda.io

Cupp Computing (9)
Endpoint Security
Palo Alto
cuppcomputing.com

**Cyber Advanced
Technology**
Network / IPS
Berkeley
www2.unhackablecloud.
com

CyberCube (61)
GRC / Risk Management
San Francisco
cybcube.com

Cyberinc (43)
Network / Browser Isola-
tion
San Ramon
cyberinc.com

CyberOne (5)
GRC / Policy Management
San Francisco
cb1security.com

Cycognito (43)
GRC / Vulnerability Man-
agement
Palo Alto
cycognito.com

**Cylance (part of
BlackBerry)** (888)
Endpoint / EDR
Irvine
cylance.com

Cypherpath (36)
Application Security /
Containers for Apps
Mountain View
cypherpath.com

Darktrace (889)
Security Analytics / Breach
Detection
San Francisco
darktrace.com

Data Theorem (23)
Application Security /
Mobile App Scanner
Palo Alto
datatheorem.com

DataGuise (125)
Data Security / Database
Security
Fremont
dataguise.com

Datavisor (105)
Security Analytics
Mountain View
datavisor.com

Datiphy (15)
GRC / User Behavior
Monitoring
San Jose
datiphy.com

DB Cybertech (34)
GRC / Data Discovery
San Diego
dbcybertech.com

Deepfence (8)
Network / IPS
Milpitas
deepfence.io

DeepSource (7)
Application Security /
Static Code Analysis for
Python and Go
San Francisco
deepsource.io

DefiniSec (1)
Email Security / Email
Encryption and Backup
El Cerrito
definisec.com

Dellfer (8)
IoT Security / Automotive
Novato
dellfer.com

**Demisto (Palo Alto
Networks)** (158)
Operations / Incident
Response
Cupertino
demisto.com

Detexian (7)
Operations / Monitor
Cloud Configurations
San Diego
detexian.com

DeviceLock (25)
GRC / Endpoint Data Leak
Prevention
San Ramon
devicelock.com

Digital Shadows (180)
Threat Intelligence /
OSINT Dark Web
San Francisco
digitalshadows.com

Direct Risk Management
(2)
IAM / Authentication
Aliso Viejo
directrm.com

Disconnect (16)
Network / Consumer VPN
San Francisco
disconnect.me

Distil Networks (109)
Network / Bot Detection
San Francisco
distilnetworks.com

Druva (643)
Endpoint Data Protection
& Governance
Sunnyvale
druva.com

DTEX Systems (87)
GRC / Insider Threat
Detection
San Jose
dtexsystems.com

eAgency (10)
Endpoint / Mobile Security
Newport Beach
eagency.com

Edgewave (62)
Email Security
La Jolla
edgewave.com

Egnyte (470)
Data Security / Secure File
Sharing
Mountain View
egnyte.com

Elevate Security (21)
GRC / Security Awareness
Training
Berkeley
elevatesecurity.com

Engage Black (7)
Data Security / Code
Signing
Aptos
engageblack.com

Note: Numbers in parentheses indicate employee count

Ensilo (acquired by Fortinet, 2019) (86)
Security Analytics / Breach Detection
San Francisco
ensilo.com

Entreda (22)
Endpoint Monitoring and Control
Santa Clara
entreda.com

ESET (156)
Endpoint / Anti-virus
San Diego
eset.com

Exabeam (358)
Security Analytics / User Behavior Analytics
San Mateo
exabeam.com

Exosphere, Inc. (1)
Endpoint Protection
Campbell
exospheresecurity.com

Expanse (155)
GRC / Vulnerability Scanner
San Francisco
expanse.co

Extenua (4)
Data Security / Secure File Transfer
San Jose
extenua.com

Extreme Networks (280)
IAM / Network Access Control
San Jose
extremenetworks.com

Ezmcom (21)
Endpoint / Security Hardware
Santa Clara
ezmcom.com

Farsight Security (54)
Threat Intelligence Enrichment from DNS
San Mateo
farsightsecurity.com

Fastly (567)
Network / DDoS Defense
San Francisco
fastly.com

Feedzai (368)
Fraud Prevention / Anti-fraud
San Mateo
feedzai.com

FileOpen Systems (8)
Data Security / DRM
Santa Cruz
fileopen.com

FinalCode (5)
Data Security / IRM
San Jose
finalcode.com

FireEye (3,086)
Network / Malware Sandbox
Milpitas
fireeye.com

Flowmon Networks (122)
Network Monitoring
San Diego
flowmon.com

Flying Cloud (8)
Data Security / Data Flow Analytics
Santa Cruz
flyingcloudtech.com

ForeScout Technologies (1,133)
Network Access Control
San Jose
forescout.com

ForgeRock (547)
IAM
San Francisco
forgerock.com

Fortanix (37)
Application Security / Runtim Encryption
Mountain View
fortanix.com

Fortify 24x7 (3)
MSSP / Managed Security Services
Los Angeles
fortify24x7.com

Fortinet (5,735)
Network / UTM
Sunnyvale
fortinet.com

Fossa (41)
Application Security / Open Source Vulnerability Management
San Francisco
fossa.com

Foxpass (5)
IAM / Cloud LDAP, Google App Authentication Management
San Francisco
foxpass.com

Fudo Security (42)
IAM / Privileged Access Management
Newark
fudosecurity.com

Fuzzbuzz (4)
Application Security / Appsec Fuzzing
Mountain View
fuzzbuzz.io

Fyde (28)
IAM / Access Control
Palo Alto
fyde.com

GeoCodex (6)
IAM / Access Control
Hollywood
geocodex.com

GeoTrust Inc. (32)
Data Security / Encryption
Mountain View
geotrust.com

GhangorCloud (10)
GRC / DLP
San Jose
ghangorcloud.com

Gigamon (866)
Network / Span Port Mirroring
Santa Clara
gigamon.com

Glimmerglass (17)
Fraud Prevention / Cyber Terrorism & Fraud Prevention
Hayward
glimmerglass.com

Glitchi (1)
Data Security / Secure Photo Sharing
Palo Alto
glitchi.me

Green Hills Software (1,183)
Endpoint / Secure OS
Santa Barbara
ghs.com

GTB Technologies (50)
GRC / Data Leak Prevention (DLP)
Newport Beach
gtbtechnologies.com

Guardian Analytics (98)
GRC / Forensics
Mountain View
guardiananalytics.com

Guidewire (2,219)
GRC / Security Ratings
Foster City
guidewire.com

GuruCul (129)
Security Analytics
El Segundo
gurucul.com

HackerOne (813)
Operations / Zero Day
Research and Bounties
San Francisco
hackerone.com

Hideez (20)
IAM / Hardware Credential Storage
Redwood City
hideez.com

Hillstone Networks (267)
Network / Data Analytics
Firewall Protection
Santa Clara
hillstonenet.com

Hmatix (4)
IoT Security / IoT Network
Security
San Jose
hmatix.com

HoloNet Security (11)
Operations / Incident
Investigation
Sunnyvale
holonetsecurity.com

HyTrust (147)
Operations / Cloud Security Automation
Mountain View
hytrust.com

Idaptive (118)
IAM / Access Management
Santa Clara
idaptive.com

Identify3D (26)
Data Security / Design
Data Encryption
San Francisco
identify3d.com

Identiv (208)
IAM / Credentials
Fremont
identiv.com

IdenTrust (part of HID Global) (68)
Data Security / Certificate
Authority
Fremont
identrust.com

Illumio (337)
Endpoint Monitoring
Sunnyvale
illumio.com

ImageWare Systems, Inc. (95)
IAM / Biometrics
San Diego
iwsinc.com

Immunant (4)
Application Security /
Code Hardening
Irvine
immunant.com

Impact (423)
Fraud Prevention / Ad
Tech Security
Santa Barbara
impact.com

Imperva (1,185)
Network / Web Application
Firewall
Redwood Shores
imperva.com

Indeni (70)
Operations / Security
Automation
San Francisco
indeni.com

Infoblox, Inc. (1,255)
Network / DNS Security
Santa Clara
infoblox.com

InfoExpress Inc. (41)
IAM / Network Access
Control
Santa Clara
infoexpress.com

Informatica (500)
Data Security / Data
Masking
Redwood City
informatica.com

Inpixon (67)
Network / Rogue Wifi AP
Location
Palo Alto
inpixon.com

**Interface Masters
Technologies** (63)
Network / Intrusion Prevention
San Jose
interfacemasters.com

Interfocus Technologies
(4)
Operations / User Behavior
Monitoring
Costa Mesa
interfocus.us

Intertrust Technologies
(252)
IoT Security / PKI for IoT
Sunnyvale
intertrust.com

Intrinsic (6)
Application Security /
Appsec Code Hardening
San Francisco
intrinsic.com

Intrinsic-ID (37)
IAM / Device Authentication
Sunnyvale
intrinsic-id.com

Ionu (2)
Data Security / Secure Data
Management
Los Gatos
ionu.com

IP Infusion (331)
MSSP / Managed Services
Santa Clara
ipinfusion.com

Ixia (1,271)
Network Visibility
Calabasas
ixiacom.com

Janus Technologies, Inc.
(6)
Endpoint / BIOS Protection
Sunnyvale
janustech.com

Jscrambler (40)
Application Security /
Security for Javascript
San Francisco
jscrambler.com

Jumio (322)
Fraud Prevention / Identity
Verification
Palo Alto
jumio.com

Juniper Networks (2,000)
Network / Firewall
Sunnyvale
juniper.net

K2 Cyber Security (2)
Application Security /
Appsec, Zero Day Prevention
San Jose
k2io.com

Kandji (10)
Endpoint / MDM for Apple
Devices
San Diego
kandji.io

Note: Numbers in parentheses indicate employee count

KeepSafe (21)
Data Security / Mobile
Encryption
San Francisco
getkeepsafe.com

**Kenna Security
(rebranded from Risk I/O)**
(153)
GRC / VM and Threat
Feeds
San Francisco
kennasecurity.com

KernelCare (1)
Endpoint / Linux Kernel
Patching
Palo Alto
kernelcare.com

Kingston Technology
(1,384)
Data Security / Encrypted
Storage
Fountain Valley
kingston.com

Kriptos (17)
Data Security / Data Classification
Sausalito
kriptos.io

Lacework (65)
Application Security /
Cloud Deployment Secu-
rity
Mountain View
lacework.com

LastLine (143)
Threat Intelligence / Honeynet Malware IOCs
Redwood City
lastline.com

Lastwall (11)
IAM / Access Management
Mountain View
lastwall.com

LeapFILE (7)
Data Security / Secure File
Transfer
Cupertino
leapfile.com

LeapYear Technologies
(28)
Data Security / Analyze
Private Information
Berkeley
leapyear.ai

Levl Technologies (20)
IoT Security / Device
Identity
Palo Alto
levltech.com

LogDNA (79)
Security Analytics
Mountain View
logdna.com

LogicHub (35)
Operations / Automated
Incident Response
Mountain View
logichub.com

Lookout (412)
Endpoint / Mobile Security
for Android & iOS Apps
San Francisco
lookout.com

Loom Systems (28)
Operations / Incident
Response
San Francisco
loomsystems.com

Lucent Sky (3)
Application Security /
Source Code Analysis and
Repair
San Francisco
lucentsky.com

**Lynx Software
Technologies** (86)
Endpoint / Containers
San Jose
lynx.com

MagicCube (1)
IAM / Secure Digital
Transactions
Santa Clara
magic3inc.com

Malwarebytes (709)
Endpoint / Anti-virus
Santa Clara
malwarebytes.org

**ManageEngine (Zoho
Corp.)** (87)
GRC / Security Manage-
ment
Pleasanton
manageengine.com

MarkMonitor (504)
Threat Intelligence / Brand
Monitoring
San Francisco
markmonitor.com

McAfee (9,663)
Endpoint / AV
Santa Clara
mcafee.com

Medcrypt (17)
IoT Security / Medical
Device Protection
Encinitas
medcrypt.co

Menlo Security (150)
Network / Browser Isola-
tion
Palo Alto
menlosecurity.com

MessageSolution Inc. (21)
GRC / Email Archiving
Milpitas
messagesolution.com

MetaFlows (1)
Network Monitoring
San Diego
metaflows.com

MetricStream (1,712)
GRC / IT Governance, Risk
& Compliance
Palo Alto
metricstream.com

**Militus Cybersecurity
Solutions** (2)
Network / NBAD
Newport Beach
milituscyber.com

Milton Security Group (41)
Network Access Control
Inline
Fullerton
miltonsecurity.com

MistNet (17)
Operations / Cloud-Based
Threat Hunting
Mountain View
mistnet.ai

MixMode (17)
Operations / Network
Forensics
San Diego
mixmode.ai

MobileIron (973)
Endpoint / Mobile Device
& App Security
Mountain View
mobileiron.com

Mocana Corporation (73)
Application Security /
Mobile App Security
Sunnyvale
mocana.com

Moka5 (6)
Endpoint / Virtual Desk-
tops for PCs and Macs
Redwood City
Moka5.com

MyWorkDrive (12)
Data Security / Secure File
Storage
San Francisco
myworkdrive.com

NanoVMs, Inc. (5)
Endpoint / Secure Containers
San Francisco
nanovms.com

NC4 (168)
GRC / Risk Management
El Segundo
nc4.com

NCP Engineering (47)
Network / VPN
Mountain View
Ncp-e.com

Netecs Evohop (1)
Network / Gateway Security Platform
Norco
evohop.com

NetFlow Logic (5)
Network / Netflow Concentrator
Atherton
netflowlogic.com

NETGEAR (300)
Network / Firewall
San Jose
netgear.com

NetNinja (1)
Network / Wifi Hot Spot Encryption
San Francisco
getnetninja.com

Netography (10)
Network / DDoS Defense
San Francisco
netography.com

NetSkope (780)
Application Security / Cloud Application Security
Santa Clara
netskope.com

Netswitch Technology Management (22)
MSSP / MDR
South San Francisco
netswitch.net

NetWrix Corporation (318)
GRC / Auditor
Irvine
netWrix.com

NeuShield (6)
Data Security / Data Mirroring for Ransomware Recovery
Fremont
neushield.com

NeuVector, Inc. (28)
Endpoint / Container Security
San Jose
neuvector.com

NextLabs (144)
Data Security / IRM
San Mateo
nextlabs.com

Niagra Networks (49)
Network Monitoring
San Jose
niagranetworks.com

NodeSource (21)
Application Security / Appsec Serverless
San Francisco
nodesource.com

Nok Nok Labs (35)
IAM / Unified Authentication Infrastructure
San Jose
noknok.com

Nozomi Security (116)
IoT Security / ICS
San Francisco
nozominetworks.com

NSFocus (468)
Network / DDoS Defense
Santa Clara
nsfocus.com

NuCypher (18)
Data Security / Credential Encryption
San Francisco
nucypher.com

NXM Labs (28)
IoT Security / Device Security
San Francisco
nxmlabs.com

Obsidian Security (55)
Network / Cloud Monitoring
Newport Beach
obsidiansecurity.com

Okera (46)
Data Security / Data Governance
San Francisco
okera.com

Okta, Inc. (1,934)
IAM
San Francisco
okta.com

One Identity (461)
Network / Firewall
Aliso Viejo
oneidentity.com

OneLogin (283)
IAM / Identity Management
San Francisco
onelogin.com

Onion ID (5)
IAM / Privileged Access Management
Hayward
onionid.com

Open Zeppelin (25)
Application Security for Blockchain
San Francisco
openzeppelin.com

OpenVPN (63)
Network / VPN
Pleasanton
openvpn.net

OPSWAT (205)
Endpoint Security
San Francisco
opswat.com

Oracle (450)
IAM
Redwood Shores
oracle.com

Ordr (61)
IoT Security / Device Management
Santa Clara
ordr.net

Paladin Cyber (14)
Email Security / Anti-phishing
San Francisco
meetpaladin.com

Palantir Technologies (2,339)
Security Analytics / Link Analysis
Palo Alto
palantir.com

Palo Alto Networks (6,488)
Network / UTM
Santa Clara
paloaltonetworks.com

Pango (86)
IAM / Consumer VPN
Redwood City
pango.co

Note: Numbers in parentheses indicate employee count

Paramount Defenses Inc.
(1)
IAM / Privileged Access
Management for AD
Newport Beach
paramountdefenses.com

Parasoft (254)
Application Security /
Security Testing
Monrovia
parasoft.com

PatternEx (20)
Operations / Security
Automation
San Jose
patternex.com

Penango (2)
Data Security / Encryption
for Gmail & Google Apps
Los Angeles
penango.com

Phoenix Technologies
(502)
Endpoint / Secure PC
Campbell
phoenix.com

Pinn (26)
IAM / Authentication
Redwood City
pinn.ai

pixlcloud (1)
Security Analytics / Visualization
San Francisco
pixlcloud.com

PNF Software (5)
Application Security /
Reverse Engineering for
Android
Redwood City
pnfsoftware.com

Polylogyx (9)
Endpoint / EDR with
OSQuery
Pleasanton
polylogyx.com

PolySwarm (25)
Endpoint / Malware De-
tection
San Diego
polyswarm.io

Port80 Software (2)
Endpoint / IIS Security
San Diego
port80software.com

Prismo Systems (16)
Network / Zero-Trust
Networking
San Francisco
prismosystems.com

Privacera (22)
Data Security / Data Gov-
ernance
Fremont
privacera.com

Proficio (132)
MSSP / MDR
Carlsbad
proficio.com

Proofpoint, Inc. (2,764)
Email Security / Anti-mal-
ware, Anti-spam, and
Anti-phishing
Sunnyvale
proofpoint.com

Proxim (155)
Network / Wireless Secu-
rity
San Jose
proxim.com

Psafe Technology (102)
Endpoint / Anti-virus
San Francisco
psafe.com

Pulse Secure (532)
IAM / Authentication
San Jose
pulsesecure.net

Qualys (1,167)
GRC / Vulnerability man-
agement
Foster City
qualys.com

Quantum Digital Solutions
(3)
Data Security / Key Man-
agement
Los Angeles
qdsc.us

Qustodio (79)
Endpoint / Mobile Parental
Controls
Redondo Beach
qustodio.com

Radiant Logic (104)
IAM / LDAP, SSO
Novato
radiantlogic.com

Rambus (881)
Data Security / Semicon-
ductor Security R&D
Sunnyvale
rambus.com

Raonsecure (10)
IAM / Biometrics
Santa Clara
raonsecure.com

RavenWhite Security, Inc.
(2)
IAM / Cookies
Menlo Park
ravenwhite.com

RedMarlin, Inc. (8)
Email Security / Phishing
Detection
Mountain View
redmarlin.ai

RedSeal (188)
GRC / Security Posture
San Jose
redseal.net

RedShift Networks (24)
Network / VoIP Security
San Ramon
redshiftnetworks.com

Remediant (32)
IAM / Privileged Access
Management
San Francisco
remediant.com

remote.it (6)
Network / Zero-Trust
Networking
Palo Alto
remote.it

Reprivata (3)
Network / Microsegmen-
tation
Palo Alto
reprivata.com

Respond Software (53)
Security Analytics / Au-
tomated Incident Identifi-
cation
Mountain View
respond-software.com

RiskIQ (166)
GRC / External Threat
Platform
San Francisco
riskiq.com

Rubica (27)
Network / VPN
San Francisco
rubica.com

Rubicon Labs (12)
Data Security / Key Man-
agement
San Francisco
rubiconlabs.io

SafeLogic (8)
Data Security / Cryp-
tographic Libraries
Palo Alto
safelogic.com

SafenSoft (7)
Endpoint Protection
Los Angeles
safensoft.com

Salt Security (19)
Network / API Attack
Detection
Palo Alto
salt.security

Saviynt (295)
IAM / Cloud Access Governance
El Segundo
saviynt.com

Scytale (27)
IAM / Identity Management for Cloud
San Francisco
scytale.io

Seagate Technology (100)
Data Security / Encryption
Cupertino
seagate.com

Seclytics (10)
Security Analytics / Threat
Intelligence
San Diego
seclytics.com

SecNeo (22)
Application Security /
Mobile App Protection
San Jose
secneo.com

SECNOLOGY (25)
Security Analytics / Big
Data Mining & Security
El Granada
secnology.com

SecuGen (20)
IAM / Biometric Finger
Scanners
Santa Clara
secugen.com

**Secure Access
Technologies** (13)
IAM / Mobile Single Sign-
On
Menlo Park
secureaccesstechnologies.
com

Secure Channels (24)
Data Security / Encryption
Irvine
securechannels.com

SecureAuth (278)
IAM / Acces Control
Irvine
secureauth.com

Secured Communication
(20)
Data Security / Secure
Communications
San Francisco
securedcommunications.
com

Secured Universe (2)
Endpoint / Mobile Device
Security
San Diego
secureduniverse.com

SecureData, Inc. (65)
Data Security / Encrypted
Hard Drives
Los Angeles
securedata.com

SECURITI.ai (130)
Data Security / Discovery
for PII
San Jose
securiti.ai

**Security Compliance
Corporation** (1)
IAM / Access Control
Orinda
securitycompliancecorp.
com

Security First (33)
Data Security for Documents
Rancho Santa Margarita
securityfirstcorp.com

Security Mentor (11)
GRC / Security Awareness
Training
Pacific Grove
securitymentor.com

Security On-Demand (72)
MSSP / Managed Firewalls
San Diego
securityondemand.com

SecurityFirst (31)
Data Security / IRM
Rancho Santa Margarita
securityfirst.com

Sekur Me (3)
IAM / Mobile Authentication
Santa Ana
sekur.me

Semmle (61)
Application Security /
Code Analysis
San Francisco
semmle.com

Sendio (27)
Email Security / Anti-spam
Newport Beach
sendio.com

SentiLink (15)
Fraud Prevention / Anti-fraud
San Francisco
sentilink.com

SentinelOne (329)
Endpoint Protection
Platform
Mountain View
sentinelone.com

ServiceNow (500)
Operations / Orchestration
Santa Clara
servicenow.com

Seworks (221)
Operations / Automated
Pen Testing
San Francisco
se.works

Shape Security (333)
Network / Web Application
Firewall
Mountain View
shapesecurity.com

ShareVault (27)
Data Security / Vault
Los Gatos
sharevault.com

ShieldX (57)
Network / Cloud Microsegmentation
San Jose
shieldx.com

ShiftLeft (45)
Application Security /
Appsec Code Hardening
Santa Clara
shiftleft.io

ShoCard (18)
IAM / Identity Management
Cupertino
shocard.com

Sift Security (3)
Security Analytics / Cloud
Monitoring
Palo Alto
siftsecurity.com

Signal Science (142)
Network / WAF
Culver City
signalsciences.com

Note: Numbers in parentheses indicate employee count

Signifyd (281)
Fraud Prevention / e-Commerce Fraud Prevention
San Jose
signifyd.com

Silicon Forensics (9)
Operations / Forensic Hardware
Pomona
siliconforensics.com

Singular Security (6)
GRC / IT Security & Compliance Risk Management
Tustin
singularsecurity.com

Skybox Security (352)
Operations / Security Management
San Jose
skyboxsecurity.com

SlashNext (97)
Email Security / Anti-phishing
Pleasanton
slashnext.com

Solarflare (210)
Network Security Monitoring
Irvine
solarflare.com

Somansa (36)
GRC / DLP
San Jose
somansatech.com

SonicWall (1,907)
Network / UTM
Milpitas
sonicwall.com

Sonikpass (4)
IAM / Identity Verification, Mobile
Los Angeles
sonikpass.com

Splunk (1,000)
Security Analytics / SIEM
San Francisco
splunk.com

SPYRUS (27)
Data Security / Encryption
San Jose
spyrus.com

SS8 (125)
Security Analytics
Milpitas
ss8.com

Stackrox (62)
Endpoint / Trusted Computing
Mountain View
stackrox.com

StackStorm (1)
Operations / Orchestration
San Jose
stackstorm.com

Stellar Cyber (31)
Security Analytics / Threat Detection & Network Forensics
Santa Clara
stellarcyber.ai

Styra (25)
Endpoint / Kubernetes Access Controls
Redwood City
styra.com

Sucuri (63)
Network / Website Defense
Menifee
sucuri.net

Sumo Logic (629)
Security Analytics / SIEM
Redwood City
sumologic.com

Symantec Corporation (acquired by Broadcom, 2019) (25,745)
Endpoint / Anti-virus
Mountain View
symantec.com

Symphony (315)
Data Security / Secure Messaging and Collaboration
Palo Alto
Symphony.com

Synack (155)
Testing
Redwood City
synack.com

Syncplicity by Axway (57)
Data Security / Secure File Storage
Santa Clara
syncplicity.com

Synopsys (100)
Application Security / Software Testing & Security
Mountain View
synopsys.com

Sysdig (227)
Endpoint / Kubernetes Security
Davis
sysdig.com

Tala Security (31)
Application Security / Web App Analysis
Fremont
talasecurity.io

Tanium (952)
Endpoint Visibility and Control
Emeryville
tanium.com

TEHTRIS (37)
Endpoint / AV
San Francisco
tehtris.com

TeleSign Corporation (307)
IAM / Mobile Identity Verification
Marina del Rey
telesign.com

Templarbit (13)
Application Security / Appsec Code Hardening
San Francisco
templarbit.com

The DigiTrust Group (23)
MSSP / Managed Endpoint and WAF
Los Angeles
digitrustgroup.com

ThreatLandscape (24)
Threat Intelligence
San Jose
threatlandscape.com

ThreatMetrix (260)
Fraud Prevention
San Jose
threatmetrix.com

ThreatSTOP, Inc (30)
Network / Cloud Reputation Service
Carlsbad
threatstop.com

TIBCO Software Inc. (500)
Data Security / Big Data Security
Palo Alto
tibco.com

Tigera (80)
Endpoint / Kubernetes Security
San Francisco
tigera.io

Tinfoil Security (15)
Application Security / App Scanning
Mountain View
tinfoilsecurity.com

Tortuga Logic (25)
Data Security / Hardware
Root of Trust Verification
San Diego
tortugalogic.com

TransientX (1)
Network / Zero-Trust
Networking
San Francisco
transientx.com

TrapX Security (37)
Deception
San Jose
trapx.com

TriagingX (8)
Operations / Malware
Sandbox
San Jose
triagingx.com

Trillium Secure (20)
IoT Security / Automotive
Sunnyvale
trilliumsecure.com

TrueVault (10)
Data Security / Secure Data
Storage
San Francisco
truevault.com

TruSTAR (65)
Threat Intelligence Plat-
form
San Francisco
trustar.co

TrustArc (304)
GRC / Privacy Assessments
San Francisco
trustarc.com

TrustGo
Endpoint / Android AV
Santa Clara
trustgo.com

Trustlook (19)
Endpoint / Malware
Analysis
San Jose
trustlook.com

Ubiq Security (27)
Data Security / Encryption
San Diego
ubiqsecurity.com

UnifyID (34)
IAM / Behavioral Identity
Redwood City
unify.id

Untangle (68)
Network / UTM
San Jose
untangle.com

UpGuard (43)
GRC / Configuration
Monitoring
Mountain View
upguard.com

US Interactive (1)
MSSP / Managed Services
Santa Clara
usinteractive.com

V5 Systems (78)
IoT Security / ICS
Fremont
v5systems.us

Vade Secure (112)
Email Security / An-
ti-phishing
San Francisco
vadesecure.com

Valimail (108)
Email Security / An-
ti-phishing
San Francisco
valimail.com

vArmour (103)
Endpoint / Server Security
Mountain View
varmour.com

Vaultize (31)
Data Security / IRM Con-
tent Sharing
San Francisco
vaultize.com

Vectra Networks (246)
Security Analytics /
Cyber-Attack Detection &
Management
San Jose
vectra.ai

Vera (116)
Data Security / IRM
Palo Alto
vera.com

**Veracity Industrial
Networks** (13)
IoT Security / ICS
Aliso Viejo
veracity.io

Verimatrix (281)
Data Security / DRM for
Video
San Diego
verimatrix.com

Versa (304)
Network / SDN
San Jose
versa-networks.com

Very Good Security (96)
Data Security / Vault
San Francisco
verygoodsecurity.com

Vir2us (11)
Endpoint / Virtual Envi-
ronments
Petaluma
vir2us.com

Virsec (69)
Endpoint / Runtime Pro-
tection
San Jose
virsec.com

VMWare (1200)
Endpoint / EDR
Palo Alto
vmware.com

**Voice Security Systems
Inc.** (2)
IAM / Biometrics
Dana Point
voice-security.com

Wallarm (71)
Network / Cloud WAF
San Francisco
wallarm.com

Wandera (177)
Network / Secure Mobile
Gateway
San Francisco
wandera.com

Watchtower AI (12)
Data Security / Data Dis-
covery
San Francisco
watchtower.ai

we45 (33)
Application Security
Sunnyvale
we45.com

Webgap (3)
Network / Remote Browser
Isolation
Walnut
webgap.io

White Hawk Software (5)
Application Security /
Tamperproofing
Palo Alto
whitehawksoftware.com

**WhiteHat Security
(acquired by NTT, 2019)**
(370)
GRC / Web Application
Security
San Jose
whitehatsec.com

Note: Numbers in parentheses indicate employee count

Wickr (43)
Data Security / Secure
Communications
San Francisco
wickr.com

WireX (20)
Operations / Network
Forensics
Sunnyvale
wirexsystems.com

Wispero (2)
IoT Security / Anomaly
Detection
San Jose
wispero.com

WootCloud (17)
Endpoint / Device Control
San Jose
wootcloud.com

Workspot (80)
Operations / Secure Re-
mote Access
Campbell
workspot.com

Xage Security (40)
IoT Security / ICS
Palo Alto
xage.com

Xbridge Systems (8)
GRC / DLP for z/OS
San Jose
xbridgesystems.com

ZecOps (19)
Operations / Automated
Defense
San Francisco
zecops.com

Zentera Systems (27)
Network / Zero-Trust
Networking
San Jose
zentera.net

Zettaset (31)
Data Security / Encryption,
Databases
Mountain View
zettaset.com

**Zingbox (acquired by Palo
Alto Networks)** (83)
IoT Security / IoT
Mountain View
zingbox.com

Zscaler (1,504)
Network / Cloud Security
Layer
San Jose
zscaler.com

Zumigo (21)
IAM / Identity Verification
San Jose
zumigo.com

Zymbit (2)
IoT Security / Device Security Modules
Santa Barbara
zymbit.com

Zyudly Labs (23)
Operations / Cloud Security for AWS
Palo Alto
zyudlylabs.com

**ZyXEL Communications
Corp.** (33)
Network / Firewall
Anaheim
zyxel.com/us/en/homep-
age.shtml

COLORADO

Absio (8)
Data Security / Soft-
ware-Defined Distributed
Key Cryptography (SDKC)
Denver
absio.com

Alpha Recon (14)
Threat Intelligence Plat-
form
Colorado Springs
alpharecon.com

Articsoft Technologies (1)
Data Security / Encryption
PGP
Centennial
articsoft.com

AuthRocket
IAM / Authorization and
User Management
Denver
authrocket.com

Automox (57)
GRC / Patch Management
Boulder
automox.com

Botdoc (10)
Data Security / Secure File
Transfer
Monument
botdoc.io

Circadence (175)
Training / Cyber Range
Boulder
circadence.com

Convercent (173)
GRC / Compliance Man-
agement
Denver
convercent.com

CyberGRX (98)
GRC / Third Party Risk
Denver
cybergrx.com

DarkOwl (25)
Threat Intelligence / Dark
Web Collection
Denver
darkowl.com

deepwatch (133)
MSSP / MDR
Denver
deepwatch.com

DH2i (8)
Network / Zero-Trust
Networking
Fort Collins
dh2i.com

Eclypses (4)
Data Security / Encrypted
Storage
Colorado Springs
certainsafe.com

Intelisecure (181)
MSSP / Managed Services
Greenwood Village
intelisecure.com

Introspective Networks (7)
Network / VPN
Broomfield
introspectivenetworks.com

**Klocwork (a Rogue Wave
company)** (299)
Application Security /
Source Code Analysis
Louisville
roguewave.com

LogRhythm (627)
GRC / Log Management
Boulder
logrhythm.com

Managed Methods (22)
GRC / Cloud Access
Monitor
Boulder
managedmethods.com

Mantix4 (5)
Security Analytics / Threat
Hunting
Englewood
mantix4.com

Mindpass (5)
IAM / Visual Password
Manager
Boulder
mindpassco.com

NeoCertified (10)
Email Security / Secure
Email
Centennial
neocertified.com

Optiv (200)
MSSP / Managed Services
Denver
optiv.com

PasswordPing (13)
Fraud Prevention / Compromised Credentials
Boulder
passwordping.com

Ping Identity Corporation
(882)
IAM
Denver
pingidentity.com

**ProtectWise (acquired by
Verizon, March 2019)** (70)
Network Data Capture
Denver
protectwise.com

Red Canary (96)
Endpoint Detection
Denver
redcanary.com

root9B (29)
Security Analytics / Threat
Hunting Platform
Colorado Springs
root9b.com

Secure64 (36)
Network / DNS Security
Fort Collins
secure64.com

Solutions-II (97)
MSSP / Monitoring
Littleton
solutions-ii.com

Swimlane (75)
Operations / Incident
Response
Louisville
swimlane.com

ThreatX (20)
Network / Web Application
Firewall
Louisville
threatx.com

VirtualArmour (50)
MSSP / Managed Services
Centennial
virtualarmour.com

**Webroot Software
(acquired by Carbonite,
2019; then acquired by
OpenText)** (796)
Endpoint / Anti-malware
Broomfield
webroot.com

Zvelo (41)
Network / URL Categorization
Greenwood VillageCO
zvelo.com

CONNECTICUT

Awareness Technologies
(25)
Operations / Employee
Monitoring
Westport
awarenesstechnologies.com

Interguard (8)
Operations / Employee
Monitoring
Westport
interguardsoftware.com

Netlib (4)
Data Security / Encryption
Database
Stamford
netlib.com

Owl Cyber Defense (62)
Network / Air Gap
Danbury
owlcyberdefense.com

Polarity (39)
Operations / Onscreen
Data Augmentation
Farmington
polarity.io

Protegrity (309)
Application Security
Stamford
protegrity.com

SDG Corporation (616)
GRC
Norwalk
sdgc.com

SecureRF Corporation (19)
IAM / Device Authentication
Shelton
securerf.com

Syferlock (6)
IAM / Software-Based
Authentication
Shelton
syferlock.com

Wymsical (6)
IAM / Identity Manager
Greenwich
wymsical.com

Zorus (11)
Network / Cloud Proxy
Monroe
zorustech.com

DISTRICT OF
COLUMBIA

Enveil (23)
Data Security / Encryption
of Data in Use
Washington
enveil.com

Fast Orientation (5)
Security Analytics / UEBA
Washington
fastorientation.com

Gladius.io (8)
Network / DDoS Defense
Washington
gladius.io

GovReady
GRC / Self-Serve Scanning
Washington
govready.com

GreyNoise (7)
Threat Intelligence / Dark
Web Collection
Washington
greynoise.io

infOsci (9)
Data Security / Certificate
Management
Washington
Ci4.us

Intufo
IAM / Access Control
Washington
intufo.com

MalCrawler (16)
IoT Security / Anti-malware
Washington
malcrawler.com

Star Lab (38)
Application Security / Research and Development
Washington
starlab.io

Sttarx (3)
Data Security / Network
Encryption
Washington
sttarx.com

Threshing Floor (3)
Security Analytics / SIEM
Enrichment
Washington
threshingfloor.io

Thycotic Software (355)
IAM / Password & Access
Management
Washington
thycotic.com

Virtru (118)
Data Security / Google
Apps & Email Privacy
Washington
virtru.com

WWN Software LLC (10)
Data Security / Encrypted
Data Sharing
Washington
wwnsoftware.com

DELAWARE

Aries Security (12)
Training / Cyber Range
Wilmington
ariessecurity.com

Cynash (13)
IoT Security / ICS
Wilmington
cynash.com

InCyber (5)
Operations / Employee
Monitoring
Cherry Hill Township
incyber1.com

LOGbinder (1)
GRC / Application Security
Intelligence
Wilmington
logbinder.com

Nelysis (17)
IoT Security / Monitor
Physical Systems
Wilmington
nelysis.com

Q-Branch Labs (3)
Network / VPN Device
Wilmington
q-branch-labs.com

Scalarr (34)
Fraud Prevention / Mobile
Ad Fraud
Wilmington
scalarr.io

**Spydex, Inc. (division of
Edison Commerce Corp.)**
(1)
Endpoint / Anti-spyware
Wilmington
spydex.com

STOPzilla by iS3 (1)
Endpoint / AV
Dover
stopzilla.com

Tophat Security (2)
MSSP / Managed SIEM
Wilmington
tophatsecurity.com

FLORIDA

5Nine Software (46)
Operations / Hyper-V
Security
West Palm Beach
5nine.com

6Scan (1)
GRC / Vulnerability Man-
agement
Miami Beach
6scan.com

Active Fortress
Endpoint Protection
Tampa
activefortress.com

Aerobyte (10)
Network / Zero-Trust
Networking
Boca Raton
aerobyte.com

AppRiver (221)
Email Security
Gulf Breeze
appriver.com

Arxceo Corporation (3)
Network / Intrusion Pre-
vention
Ponte Vedra Beach
arxceo.com

ASPG (29)
Data Security / Encryption
for Mainframes
Naples
aspg.com

Cienaga Systems (4)
Security Analytics / Cyber
Threat Management
Lakewood Ranch
cienagasystems.net

Cigent (16)
Network Monitoring
Fort Myers
cigent.com

CIPHER Security (187)
MSSP / Managed Security
Services
Miami
cipher.com

Citrix Systems, Inc. (1,000)
Network / Secure Remote
Access
Fort Lauderdale
citrix.com

Cloud24X7 (18)
MSSP Enablement
Fort Lauderdale
cloud24x7.us

ComplyUp (5)
GRC / Compliance
Tampa
complyup.com

Crossmatch (259)
IAM
Palm Beach Gardens
crossmatch.com

Cygna Labs Corp (8)
GRC / Audit of Azure
Environments
Miami Beach
cygnalabs.com

Cypherix Software (1)
Data Security / Encryption
Land O' Lakes
cypherix.com

Cyxtera Technologies
(982)
Network / Zero-Trust
Networking
Coral Gables
cyxtera.com

DigiPortal, Inc. (1)
Network / Anti-spam
Altamonte Springs
digiportal.com

**Digital Authentication
Technologies** (6)
IAM / Location-Based
Authentication
Boca Raton
dathq.com

Digital Hands (79)
MSSP / Managed Security
Services
Tampa
digitalhands.com

Dominode (3)
IAM / Identity Assertion
with Blockchain
Boca Raton
dominode.com

ERMProtect (21)
GRC / Security Awareness
Training
Coral Gables
ermprotect.com

EventTracker (64)
MSSP / Managed Security
Services
Fort Lauderdale
eventtracker.com

FairWarning (168)
Data Security / Cloud Data
Security
Clearwater
fairwarning.com

Faraday (82)
Operations / Manager of
Managers
Miami
faradaysec.com

**Fischer International
Identity** (70)
IAM / IAM
Naples
fischerinternational.com

Forensic Innovations (1)
GRC / Data Discovery &
Forensics
St. Johns
fid3.com

Gatefy (12)
Email Security
Miami
gatefy.com

GigaNetworks (20)
MSSP / Managed Security
Services
Miami
giganetworks.com

Identify Security Software
(2)
IAM / Biometrics
Boca Raton
identifyss.com

Immunity (43)
GRC / Vulnerability Man-
agement
Miami
immunityinc.com

Impulse (35)
IAM / Network Access
Control
Tampa
impulse.com

Infobyte (47)
Network / Intrusion Detection Platform
Miami
infobytesec.com

KnowBe4 (620)
GRC / Phishing and Secu-
rity Awareness
Clearwater
knowbe4.com

NNT (47)
Operations / Workflow
Automation
Naples
newnettechnologies.com

Nucleon Cyber (3)
Threat Intelligence / Ag-
gregation
Tampa
nucleon.sh

Nucleus Security (6)
GRC / Vulnerability Man-
agement
Sarasota
nucleussec.com

NXT-ID (11)
IoT Security / Mobile
Security
Sebastian
nxt-id.com

Optimal IdM (12)
IAM / Single Sign-On
(SSO)
Lutz
optimalidm.com

Perch (39)
MSSP / SOC
Tampa
perchsecurity.com

ProtectStar (2)
Data Security / Erasure
Miami
protectstar.com/en

Q6 Cyber (40)
Threat Intelligence / Dark
Web Mining
Miami
q6cyber.com

**Quadrant Information
Security** (29)
Security Analytics / SIEM
Jacksonville
quadrantsec.com

Red Lambda (21)
Endpoint Security
Lake Mary
redlambda.com

Reliaquest (380)
Security Analytics / Threat
Hunting
Tampa
reliaquest.com

RiskWatch International
(18)
GRC / Risk Management
Sarasota
riskwatch.com

Secberus (9)
GRC / Compliance for
Cloud Environments
Miami
secberus.com

Secnap (14)
MSSP / Managed Services
Fort Lauderdale
secnap.com

Sensible Vision (6)
IAM / Biometrics
Cape Coral
sensiblevision.com

Sonavation (48)
IAM / Ultrasound Bio-
metrics
Palm Beach Gardens
sonavation.com

**Spirion (was Identity
Finder)** (107)
Data Security / Data Dis-
covery
St. Petersburg
spirion.com

Stridepoint (5)
Network / Secure Network
Fabric
Tampa
stridepoint.com

SurePass ID (3)
IAM / Secure Single Sign-
On
Winter Garden
surepassid.com

Surety (40)
Data Security / Data Pro-
tection
Naples
surety.com

Team Cymru (46)
Threat Intelligence IoCs
Malware
Lake Mary
team-cymru.org

Teramind (64)
Operations / Employee
Monitoring
Aventura
teramind.co

Thales (910)
IAM / Authentication
Plantation
thalesesecurity.com

Note: Numbers in parentheses indicate employee count

ThreatLocker
Endpoint / Whitelisting
Maitland
threatlocker.com

ThreatTrack Security (72)
Endpoint Security
Clearwater
threattracksecurity.com

Total Digital Security (4)
Network / Consumer VPN
West Palm Beach
totaldigitalsecurity.com

Trapezoid (11)
IoT Security / Firmware
Monitoring
Miami
trapezoid.com

**Veriato (formerly
SpectorSoft)** (51)
GRC / UEBA
Palm Beach Gardens
veriato.com

Vijilan Security (27)
MSSP / Security for MSPs
Ft. Lauderdale
vijilan.com

Vipre (115)
Endpoint / AV for Desk-
tops
Clearwater
vipre.com

Wavecrest Computing (15)
Network / Secure Web
Gateway
Melbourne
wavecrest.net

GEORGIA

Apptega (11)
GRC / Compliance Plat-
form
Atlanta
apptega.com

**Aunigma Network
Solutions** (5)
Network / Cloud Browser
Proxy
Atlanta
aunigma.com

Basil Security (4)
Operations / Policy En-
forcement
Atlanta
basilsecurity.com

Bastille (1)
Network / Wireless Secu-
rity
Atlanta
bastille.net

BeyondTrust (628)
IAM / Privileged Access
Management
Johns Creek
beyondtrust.com

C1Secure (10)
GRC / Compliance Moni-
toring Platform
Atlanta
c1secure.com

CloudeAssurance (5)
GRC / Risk Management
Atlanta
cloudeassurance.com

ControlScan (137)
MSSP / Managed Security
Services
Alpharetta
controlscan.com

Core Security (181)
GRC / Vulnerability Man-
agement
Roswell
coresecurity.com

Cybraics (38)
Security Analytics
Atlanta
cybraics.com

Cybriant (30)
MSSP / MDR
Alpharetta
cybriant.com

DefenseStorm (57)
GRC / Monitoring for
Compliance for Banks
Atlanta
defensestorm.com

DEVCON (14)
Fraud Prevention / Ad
Tech Security
Atlanta
devcondetect.com

DigitalResolve (5)
Fraud Prevention / Activity
Auditing
Norcross
digitalresolve.com

DigitalStakeout (5)
Threat Intelligence Web
Alpharetta
digitalstakeout.com

**Diligent eSecurity
International** (8)
GRC / Asset Monitoring
Atlanta
desintl.com

Dispersive Networks, Inc.
(69)
Network / VPN
Alpharetta
dispersive.io

Evident ID (51)
IAM / Identity Verification
Atlanta
evidentid.com

Fortiphyd Logic (7)
IoT Security / ICS
Norcross
fortiphyd.com

Fraudmarc (6)
Fraud Prevention / Email
Fraud Prevention
Atlanta
fraudmarc.com

IDology (79)
IAM / Authentication
Atlanta
idology.com

Ionic Security (145)
Data Security / Data Privacy & Protection
Atlanta
ionicsecurity.com

Iris Network Systems (23)
Network / Netflow Anal-
ysis
Alpharetta
irisns.com

iTrust, Inc. (3)
GRC / Third Party Risk
Scores
Atlanta
itrustinc.com

OnePath (547)
MSSP / Managed Services
Kennesaw
1path.com

OneTrust (667)
GRC / Third Party Risk
Management
Atlanta
onetrust.com

Paymetric (133)
Data Security / Encryption
Atlanta
paymetric.com

Phosphorus (12)
IoT Security / Agentless
Patch Management
Atlanta
phosphorus.io

Pindrop Security (292)
IAM / Authentication,
Audio
Atlanta
pindropsecurity.com

SafelyLocked (2)
Data Security / Encryption
Atlanta
safelylocked.com

SecureWorks (2,692)
MSSP / Managed Services
Atlanta
secureworks.com

Simeio Solutions (423)
IAM / IAM
Atlanta
simeiosolutions.com

TargetProof (3)
Fraud Prevention / Identity
Verification & Fraud Pre-
vention
Atlanta
targetproof.com

Telemate Software (22)
Security Analytics / SIEM
Norcross
telemate.net

WiKID Systems (4)
IAM / 2FA OTP with AD
Atlanta
wikidsystems.com

WindTalker Security (8)
Data Security / File En-
cryption and Sharing
Cumming
windtalkersecurity.com

WitFoo (10)
Operations / Security
Operations Platform
Dunwoody
witfoo.com

IDAHO

**AHA Products Group
(part of Comtech EF Data
Corporation)** (1)
Data Security / Encryption
Hardware
Moscow
aha.com

AppDetex (102)
Threat Intelligence / Brand
Monitoring
Boise
appdetex.com

Kount (161)
Fraud Prevention / Identity
Verification
Boise
kount.com

ULedger (5)
Data Security / Blockchain
Applied to Data
Boise
uledger.co

ILLINOIS

AuthLite (1)
IAM / Two-Factor Authen-
tication
Springfield
authlite.com

Cohesive Networks (17)
Network / Cloud Tunnels
over IPSec
Chicago
cohesive.net

Collective Software LLC
(1)
IAM / AD Authentication
Springfield
collectivesoftware.com

Conventus (20)
GRC / Vulnerability Man-
agement
Chicago
conventus.com

CYFIRMA (23)
Threat Intelligence
Oak Park
cyfirma.com

DealRoom (10)
Data Security / Deal Room
Chicago
dealroom.net

Emsisoft (27)
Endpoint / Android AV
Chicago
emsisoft.com

EventSentry (6)
Security Analytics / SIEM
Chicago
eventsentry.com

HALOCK Security Labs
(35)
Operations / Incident
Response
Schaumburg
halock.com

Ilantus (193)
IAM / Identity Manage-
ment
Schaumburg
ilantus.com

**Information Security
Corporation** (17)
Data Security / PKI
Oak Park
infoseccorp.com

Jemurai (5)
Operations / Security
Program Dashboard
Chicago
jemurai.com

Keeper Security, Inc. (139)
IAM / Password Manager
Chicago
keepersecurity.com

LogicGate, Inc. (60)
GRC
Chicago
logicgate.com

Mako Networks Ltd. (40)
MSSP / Managed Services
Elgin
makonetworks.com

MBX (134)
Endpoint / Appliance
& Embedded Systems
Security
Libertyville
mbx.com

MessageControl (15)
Email Security / An-
ti-phishing
Chicago
mailcontrol.net

Netsfere
Data Security / Secure
Messaging
Arlington Heights
netsfere.com

NowSecure (68)
Endpoint / Mobile Security
Chicago
nowsecure.com

OneSpan (formerly Vasco)
(559)
IAM / Identity Products
Chicago
onespan.com

Rippleshot (15)
Fraud Prevention / Fraud
Detection
Chicago
rippleshot.com

Note: Numbers in parentheses indicate employee count

Sentegrity (8)
Endpoint / Mobile
Chicago
sentegrity.com

SentryCard (5)
IAM / 2FA Cards and OTP
Chicago
sentrycard.com

ThirdPartyTrust (22)
GRC / Third Party Risk
Chicago
thirdpartytrust.com

TruGrid (5)
IAM / Access Control
Schaumburg
trugrid.com

**TrustWave (a Singtel
Company)** (1,417)
MSSP / Managed Security
Services
Chicago
trustwave.com

Winston Privacy (12)
Network / Private Brows-
ing
Chicago
winstonprivacy.com

INDIANA

Cimcor (13)
GRC / IT Asset Protection
Merrillville
cimcor.com

IdentityLogix (3)
IAM / Access Data Ana-
lytics
Crown Point
identitylogix.com

Rofori Corporation (5)
GRC / Risk Management
Zionsville
rofori.com

Rook Security (29)
MSSP / Managed Services
Carmel
rooksecurity.com

SensorHound (6)
IoT Security / ICS
West Lafayette
sensorhound.com

IOWA

FastPath (49)
GRC / SaaS Authorizations
Des Moines
gofastpath.com

**Icon Labs (acquired by
Sectigo)**
IoT Security / PKI for IoT
iconlabs.com

KANSAS

DataLocker (39)
Data Security / Encrypted
Removable Memory
Overland Park
datalocker.com

FireMon (224)
Operations / Firewall Policy Management
Overland Park
firemon.com

FortyCloud (2)
Network / Cloud VPN
Overland Park
40cloud.com

LockPath, Inc. (89)
GRC / IT Governance, Risk
& Compliance
Overland Park
lockpath.com

Onspring (26)
GRC / Audit Management
Overland Park
onspring.com

SendThisFile (4)
Data Security / Secure File
Transfer
Wichita
sendthisfile.com

SOFTwarfare (8)
Application Security /
Integration Security
Prairie Village
softwarfare.com

Spideroak (37)
Data Security / Zero
Knowledge Storage
Mission
spideroak.com

LOUISIANA

ArcMail Technology (13)
GRC / Email Archiving
Shreveport
arcmail.com

CenturyLink (2,000)
MSSP / Network Moni-
toring
Monroe
centurylink.com

CyberReef Solutions (2)
IoT Security / ICS
Shreveport
scadaaccess.com

TraceSecurity (100)
GRC
Baton Rouge
tracesecurity.com

MAINE

Defendify (19)
GRC
Portland
defendify.io

Plixer (94)
Network / Netflow Anal-
ysis
Kennebunk
plixer.com

Sage Data Security (32)
Network / Firewall
Portland
sagedatasecurity.com

MARYLAND

A1Logic (3)
Data Security / Memory
Protection
Bethesda
a1logic.com

ADF Solutions (53)
GRC / Forensics
Bethesda
adfsolutions.com

Amtel, Inc. (52)
Endpoint / Mobile Device
Security
Rockville
amtelnet.com

Atomic Mole (2)
GRC / Risk Analytics &
Management
Rockville
atomicmole.com

Attila Security (23)
IoT Security / IoT Firewall
Fulton
attilasec.com

Bandura Cyber (36)
Network / Reputation
Firewall
Columbia
banduracyber.com

Blackpoint (26)
MSSP / MDR
Ellicott City
blackpointcyber.com

Bricata (34)
Network / IPS
Columbia
bricata.com

Brivo (149)
IAM / Physical Identity &
Access Management
Bethesda
brivo.com

Cloudsploit (8)
Network / AWS Config
Testing and Monitoring
Silver Spring
cloudsploit.com

Cryptonite (6)
Network / Segmentation
Rockville
cryptonitenxt.com

Cyber Crucible (6)
Security Analytics / Breach
Detection
Severna Park
cybercrucible.com

Cyber Skyline (5)
Training / Continuous
Training for Cybersecurity
College Park
cyberskyline.com

CyberPoint (2)
GRC
Baltimore
cyberpointllc.com

CyberPoint International
(54)
Endpoint / File Artifact
Detection (mostly PS)
Baltimore
cyberpointllc.com

CyberSecure IPS (11)
Network / IPS
Upper Marlboro
cybersecureips.com

Cybrary (297)
GRC / Training
College Park
cybrary.it

Dragos (164)
IoT Security / ICS
Hanover
dragos.com

Envieta (84)
Data Security / Hardware
Security Modules
Columbia
envieta.com

EZShield (Sontiq) (39)
Fraud Prevention / An-
ti-fraud
Baltimore
ezshield.com

Fidelis Cybersecurity (282)
Security Analytics
Bethesda
fidelissecurity.com

Fluency Corp. (5)
Security Analytics / Net-
work Traffic
College Park
fluencysecurity.com

Fornetix (23)
Data Security / Key Man-
agement
Frederick
fornetix.com

Hexis Cyber Solutions (11)
Endpoint / EDR
Hanover
hexiscyber.com

Huntress Labs (10)
Operations / SaaS Malware
Discovery
Baltimore
huntresslabs.com

InfoAssure (12)
Data Security / Security for
Documents
Chestertown
infoassure.net

Inky (25)
Email Security / An-
ti-phishing
Rockville
inky.com

IronNet Cybersecurity
(245)
Network / Traffic Analysis
Fulton
ironnet.com

Kaprica Security (3)
Endpoint / Mobile Device
Security
College Park
kaprica.com

KEYW (1,061)
Operations / Forensics
Hanover
keywcorp.com

KoolSpan, Inc. (43)
Data Security / Secure
Communications
Bethesda
koolspan.com

Light Point Security (6)
Network / Secure Web
Gateway Proxy
Baltimore
lightpointsecurity.com

Locurity (1)
IAM / Cloud Authentica-
tion
Baltimore
locurity.com

Neuralys (16)
Operations / Risk Mitiga-
tion
Bethesda
neuralys.io

Patriot (55)
Endpoint / Mobile Device
Security Management
Frederick
patriot-tech.com

Prevailion (26)
Threat Intelligence
Fulton
prevailion.com

Protego (48)
Application Security / App
Hardening
Baltimore
protego.io

Protenus (65)
GRC / Medical Record
Access Monitoring
Baltimore
protenus.com

Racktop Systems (42)
Data Security / Secure
Storage
Fulton
racktopsystems.com

RedJack (31)
Network Monitoring
Silver Spring
redjack.com

Refirm Labs (12)
IoT Security / Firmware
Analysis and Monitoring
Fulton
refirmlabs.com

**Ridgeback Network
Defense** (14)
Deception
Baltimore
ridgebacknet.com

RioRey (17)
Network / DDoS Defense
Bethesda
riorey.com

Note: Numbers in parentheses indicate employee count

Rivetz (19)
Data Security / Secure Communications
Richmond
rivetz.com

SafeNet AT (64)
Data Security / Encryption
Abingdon
safenetat.com

Saint Corporation (18)
GRC / Vulnerability Management
Bethesda
saintcorporation.com

Secure Mentem (5)
GRC / Security Awareness Training
Annapolis
securementem.com

Sepio Systems (11)
IoT Security / IoT Network Security
Gaithersburg
sepio.systems

Sherpas Cyber Security Group (3)
Data Security / Secure Storage
Gaithersburg
sherpascyber.com

Sonatype (321)
Application Security / Open Source Scanning
Fulton
sonatype.com

South River Technologies (11)
Data Security / Secure File Transfer
Annapolis
southrivertech.com

Syncurity Networks (20)
Operations / Incident Response Workflow
Bethesda
syncurity.net

Telesoft Technologies (86)
Network / Netflow Monitoring Tools
Annapolis Junction
Telesoft-technologies.com

Tenable Network Security (1,328)
GRC / Vulnerability Management
Columbia
tenable.com

Terbium Labs (42)
GRC / Risk Monitoring
Baltimore
terbiumlabs.com

Tresys (52)
Data Security / Data Scrubbing of Removable Media
Columbia
tresys.com

Trivalent (12)
Data Security / File Encryption
Annapolis
trivalent.co

Trusted Knight (13)
Endpoint
Annapolis
trustedknight.com

ZeroFOX (187)
Threat Intelligence / Social Media Monitoring
Baltimore
zerofox.com

MASSACHUSETTS

Accolade Technology (10)
Network Appliance Security
Franklin
accoladetechnology.com

Akamai Technologies (500)
Network / DDoS Defense
Cambridge
akamai.com

Allegro Software (6)
IoT Security / Embedded Device Security
Boxborough
allegrosoft.com

Apperian (11)
Endpoint / Mobile App Security
Boston
apperian.com

Aquila Technology (16)
Email Security / Anti-phishing
Burlington
aquilatc.com

Arbor Networks (554)
Network / DDoS Defense
Burlington
netscout.com

Augur Systems (1)
Operations / SNMP Traps
Wakefield
augur.com

Basis Technology (131)
Operations / Forensics (Text Analysis)
Cambridge
basistech.com

Belarc Inc. (16)
GRC / IT Asset Management
Maynard
belarc.com

Biscom (169)
Data Security / Secure File Transfer
Chelmsford
biscom.com

BitSight (428)
GRC / Security Ratings
Boston
bitsight.com

Blind Hash (2)
IAM / Password Management
Boston
blindhash.com

BlueRisc (7)
Endpoint / Binary Code Vulnerability Analysis
Amherst
bluerisc.com

Carbon Black (acquired by VMWare) (1,177)
Endpoint / EDR
Waltham
carbonblack.com

CODA Intelligence (6)
GRC / Vulnerability Management
Boston
codaintelligence.com

Corero Network Security (90)
Network / DDoS Defense
Marlborough
corero.com

Countersnipe Systems (11)
Network / IPS
Boston
countersnipe.com

CounterTack (57)
Security Analytics / Real-Time Attack Intelligence
Waltham
countertack.com

CriticalStack (12)
Threat Intelligence Aggregator
Cambridge
criticalstack.com

CSPi (143)
Network / Packet Capture
Lowell
cspi.com

Cybereason (459)
Security Analytics / Breach
Detection
Boston
cybereason.com

Cyberhaven (26)
Network Data Flow Monitoring
Boston
cyberhaven.io

CyberSaint (23)
GRC / Risk Management
Boston
cybersaint.io

CyberX (97)
IoT Security / NBAD for
ICS
Waltham
cyberx-labs.com

Cybric (19)
Operations / Security
Orchestration
Boston
cybric.io

Cygilant (110)
MSSP / MDR
Boston
cygilant.com

CyGlass (27)
Security Analytics / Cloud
SIEM
Littleton
cyglass.com

Delfigo Security (5)
IAM / Mobile Device
Authentication
Boston
delfigosecurity.com

Devo (184)
Security Analytics / Cloud
SIEM
Cambridge
devo.com

Digital Guardian (403)
GRC / DLP
Waltham
digitalguardian.com

Digital Immunity (12)
Endpoint / System Hardening
Burlington
digitalimmunity.com

Dover Microsystems (23)
IoT Security / Firmware
Hardening
Waltham
dovermicrosystems.com

Ecora Software (24)
IAM / Authentication
Boston
ecora.com

Edgewise Networks (34)
Network / Zero-Trust
Networking
Burlington
edgewise.net

Foregenix (81)
GRC / Vulnerability
Scanning
Boston
foregenix.com

ForumSystems (28)
Network / XML Firewall
Needham
forumsys.com

FullArmor (24)
Network / Policy Management
Boston
fullarmor.com

GreatHorn (35)
Email Security / Anti-phishing
Waltham
greathorn.com

iboss (249)
Network / Secure Web
Gateway
Boston
iboss.com

Imprivata, Inc. (538)
IAM
Lexington
imprivata.com

Ipswitch (325)
Network / Secure File
Transfer
Burlington
ipswitch.com

LogMeIn (300)
IAM / Password Manager
Boston
logmeininc.com

Logz.io (157)
Security Analytics /
Cloud Log Collection and
Analysis
Boston
logz.io

Maxmind (52)
Fraud Prevention / Geolocation
Waltham
maxmind.com

nCrypted Cloud (27)
Data Security / Encryption
Boston
ncryptedcloud.com

NetScout (3,018)
Network / Situational
Awareness & Incident
Response
Westford
netscout.com

NeuroMesh (2)
IoT Security / Device
Inoculation
Cambridge
neuromesh.co

Nucleus Cyber (9)
Data Security / Data Discovery and Classification
Boston
nucleuscyber.com

**ObserveIT (acquired by
Proofpoint, 2019)** (179)
GRC / Employee Behavior
Monitoring
Boston
observeit.com

Onapsis Inc. (209)
Data Security / SAP
Security
Boston
onapsis.com

Positive Technologies
(483)
Network / Web Application
Firewall
Framingham
ptsecurity.com

PreVeil (23)
Data Security / File and
Email Encryption
Boston
preveil.com

Process Software (21)
Email Security
Framingham
process.com

ProcessUnity (74)
GRC / Third Party Risk
Management
Concord
processunity.com

Pwnie Express (17)
Testing / Wireless Scanning
Boston
pwnieexpress.com

Note: Numbers in parentheses indicate employee count

Quantum Xchange (12)
Data Security / Quantum
Key Distribution
Newton
quantumxc.com

Rapid 7 (1,447)
GRC / Vulnerability Management
Boston
rapid7.com

Recorded Future (acquired by FireEye, 2019) (392)
Threat Intelligence
Somerville
recordedfuture.com

Reversing Labs (152)
Operations / Malware
Analysis
Cambridge
reversinglabs.com

Rocket Software, Inc. (1,211)
Network / Secure Terminal
Emulation
Waltham
rocketsoftware.com

RSA Security, Division of EMC/Dell (3,161)
IAM
Bedford
rsa.com

Seceon (56)
Security Analytics / SIEM
Westford
seceon.com

Security Innovation (143)
Application Security
Wilmington
securityinnovation.com

Sentrix (9)
Network / Web App Security and DDoS Sefense
Waltham
sentrix.com

SimSpace (57)
Training / Cyber Range
Boston
simspace.com

Threat Stack (136)
Network / Cloud Security
Monitoring
Boston
threatstack.com

Transmit Security (105)
Fraud Prevention / Anti-fraud
Boston
transmitsecurity.com

TrustLayers (1)
Data Security / IRM
Cambridge
trustlayers.com

Tufin (442)
Operations / Firewall Policy Management
Boston
tufin.com

Unitrends (239)
Data Security / Encryption
Burlington
unitrends.com

Uptycs, Inc. (45)
Security Analytics / OS-Query
Waltham
uptycs.com

Vanquish Labs, Inc. (29)
Endpoint / Anti-spam
Marlborough
vanquish.com

Veracode (721)
Application Security /
Code Analysis
Burlington
veracode.com

Veridium (63)
IAM / Authentication
Boston
veridiumid.com

VMRay (50)
Operations / Malware
Analysis
Boston
vmray.com

XTN Cognitive Security (19)
IAM / Identity Verification
Boston
Xtn-lab.com

YAXA (2)
Network / UEBA
Concord
yaxa.io

Yottaa (83)
Network / DDoS Defense
Waltham
yottaa.com

Zeronorth (40)
GRC / Vulnerability Management
Boston
zeronorth.io

MICHIGAN

AaDya Security (24)
MSSP / For SMB
Plymouth
aadyasecurity.com

Authen2cate (3)
IAM / Authentication
Rochester Hills
authen2cate.com

BitLyft (6)
MSSP / Managed SIEM
Lansing
bitlyft.com

Blacksands (13)
Network / Software Defined Perimeter
Ann Arbor
blacksandsinc.com

Blumira (10)
Security Analytics / Threat
Detection and Response
Ann Arbor
blumira.com

Censys (26)
GRC / Asset Management
Ann Arbor
censys.io

Control's Force (10)
Fraud Prevention / Insider
Fraud Detection
Detroit
controlsforce.com

Covisint (OpenText) (247)
IAM / Federated Identity
Management
Southfield
covisent.com

Cybernet (1)
GRC / Security Manager
Ann Arbor
cybersecurity.cybernet.com

DuoSecurity (now part of Cisco) (703)
IAM / Authentication
Ann Arbor
duo.com

Ensure Technologies (26)
IAM
Ypsilanti
ensuretech.com

Greenview Data, Inc. (11)
MSSP / Managed Services
Ann Arbor
greenviewdata.com

Interlink Networks (6)
IAM
Ann Arbor
interlinknetworks.com

MicroWorld Technologies (191)
GRC / Vulnerability Management
Novi
nemasisva.com

Nuspire (117)
MSSP / Managed Services
Commerce
nuspire.com

OnlyMyEmail (12)
Network / Anti-spam
Brighton
onlymyemail.com

Quantum Signal, LLC (36)
IAM / Biometrics
Saline
quantumsignal.com

Secure Crossing R&D
IoT Security / ICS
Dearborn
securecrossing.com

Secure24 (627)
GRC / Secure Hosting
Southfield
secure-24.com

ToucanX
Endpoint Segmentation
and Sandboxing
Southfield
toucanx.com

MINNESOTA

Barrier1 (2)
Network / UTM
Minneapolis
thebarriergroup.com

CloudCover (9)
GRC / Compliance as a
Service
Saint Paul
cloudcover.net

Code 42 Software (505)
Operations / Secure Back-up and Recovery
Minneapolis
code42.com

Datakey (ATEK Access Technologies, LLC) (31)
IAM / Authentication
Eden Prairie
datakey.com

Entrust Datacard (2,148)
Data Security / Key Management, CA
Minneapolis
entrustdatacard.com

FoxT (595)
IAM / Authentication
Eden Prairie
foxt.com

Great Bay Software (26)
IAM / Network Access
Control
Bloomington
greatbaysoftware.com

Help Systems (596)
Endpoint / IBM iSecurity
Products
Eden Prairie
helpsystems.com

KinectIQ (11)
IAM / Identity-Based
Encryption
Woodbury
knectiq.com

NetSPI (128)
GRC / Vulnerability
Scanning
Minneapolis
netspi.com

Protocol 46 (20)
Network / Firewall
Saint Paul
protocol46.com

SDS (19)
Endpoint / z/OS Security
Minneapolis
sdsusa.com

The Barrier Group (2)
Threat Intelligence Platform
Minneapolis
thebarriergroup.com

webScurity Inc. (1)
Network / Web Application
Firewall
Minneapolis
webscurity.com

MISSOURI

**CyberSecurity
Corporation** (1)
IAM / Access Management
Kansas City
goldkey.com

DisruptOps (15)
Operations / Monitor and
Fix Cloud Deployments
Kansas City
disruptops.com

Global Velocity (10)
Data Security / Cloud DLP
St. Louis
globalvelocity.com

MONTANA

TeraDact (7)
Data Security / Secure
Information Sharing
Missoula
teradact.com

NEBRASKA

GoAnywhere (1)
Data Security / Automated
& Secure File Transfer
Ashland
goanywhere.com

SecureSky (16)
MSSP / Cloud MDR
Omaha
securesky.com

Solutionary (NTT) (128)
MSSP / Managed Services
Omaha
solutionary.com

NEVADA

Axiom Cyber Solutions (3)
GRC / Vulnerability
Scanner
Las Vegas
axiomcyber.com

Blackridge (66)
IoT Security / ICS
Reno
Blackridge.us

Cryptyk (17)
Data Security / Secure
Storage
Las Vegas
cryptyk.io

Cybrgen
Data Security / Distributed
Encrypted Storage
Las Vegas
cybrgendev.com

Equiinet (18)
Network / Firewall UTM
for Voice
Las Vegas
equiinet.com

NS8 (80)
Fraud Prevention / Anti-fraud
Las Vegas
ns8.com

Nsauditor (1)
GRC / Vulnerability
Scanner
Las Vegas
nsauditor.com

Note: Numbers in parentheses indicate employee count

SecSign (4)
IAM / 2FA for Mobile
Devices
Henderson
secsign.com

Sharktech (13)
Network / DDoS Defense
Las Vegas
sharktech.net

Squadra Technologies (3)
GRC / DLP
Las Vegas
squadratechnologies.com

Suavei (10)
IoT Security / Vulnerability
Management
Las Vegas
suavei.com

Trustifi (28)
Email Security / Encryp-
tion and Anti-phishing
Las Vegas
trustifi.com

**Vanguard Integrity
Professionals** (77)
GRC / Event Monitoring
Las Vegas
go2vanguard.com

NEW HAMPSHIRE

Bottomline (500)
Fraud Prevention / User
Behavior Analytics
Portsmouth
bottomline.com

FlowTraq (3)
Network / Netflow Anal-
ysis
Manchester
flowtraq.com

GlobalSign (377)
IAM / Authentication &
Identity Service Provider
Portsmouth
globalsign.com

Minim (40)
IoT Security / Home
Protection
Manchester
minim.co

Netshield (16)
Network / Gateway
Vulnerability Scanning
Appliance
Nashua
netshieldcorp.com

PistolStar Inc. (15)
Fraud Prevention / Au-
thentication
Bedford
pistolstar.com

Wapack Labs (17)
Threat Intelligence / Hacker Account Takeover
New Boston
cms.wapacklabs.com

WWPass (21)
IAM / Authentication &
Access Solutions
Nashua
wwpass.com

NEW JERSEY

Acreto Cloud (8)
IoT Security / IoT Mi-
crosegmentation
Jersey City
acreto.io

Authomate (7)
IAM / 2FA (mobile)
Morganville
authomate.com

Avepoint (904)
Data Security / Cloud
Backup
Jersey City
avepoint.com

BIO-key (67)
IAM / Biometrics, Finger-
print
Wall
bio-key.com

BlackStratus (57)
MSSP / Security Platform
for MSPs
Piscataway
blackstratus.com

Clearnetwork (8)
MSSP / SOC as a service
Hazlet
clearnetwork.com

Cognigo (34)
GRC / Data Privacy Com-
pliance for Cloud Storage
Jersey City
cognigo.com

**Communication Devices,
Inc.** (7)
Operations / Secure Re-
mote Management
Boonton
commdevices.com

CommVault (2,532)
Operations / Backup and
Recovery
Tinton Falls
commvault.com

Comodo (1,411)
Data Security / SSL Certificates & PCI Compliance
Clifton
comodo.com

DataMotion (44)
Email Security
Florham Park
datamotion.com

Duality Technologies (18)
Data Security / Encrypted
Data Analysis
Newark
duality.cloud

Ericom (93)
Network / Browser Isola-
tion
Closter
ericomshield.com

FCI Cyber (939)
MSSP / Device Manage-
ment
Bloomfield
fcicyber.com

Green Armor (1)
IAM
Hackensack
greenarmor.com

Guardian Digital Inc. (2)
Endpoint / Secure Linux
Midland Park
guardiandigital.com

Lumeta (48)
Network Discovery
Somerset
lumeta.com

NICE Actimize (961)
Fraud Prevention / Fraud
Detection
Hoboken
niceactimize.com

NIKSUN (281)
Network / NBAD
Princeton
niksun.com

PivotPoint Security (25)
GRC / Risk Assessment
Hamilton
pivotpointsecurity.com

Prevalent Networks (95)
GRC / Third Party Risk
Management
Warren
prevalent.net

Promia (29)
GRC / Network Asset
Discovery
Skillman
promia.com

Rsam (172)
IAM / IT Governance, Risk
& Compliance
Secaucus
rsam.com

Sectigo (156)
Data Security / PKI CA
Roseland
sectigo.com

**SPHERE Technology
Solutions** (33)
IAM / Privileged Access
Management
Hoboken
sphereco.com

**STEALTHbits
Technologies, Inc.** (202)
Security Analytics / Threat
Prevention
Hawthorne
stealthbits.com

StrikeForce Technologies
(20)
IAM
Edison
strikeforcetech.com

TELEGRID Technologies
(5)
Data Security / Network
Encryption Monitoring
Florham Park
telegrid.com

ThreatModeler Software
(39)
Application Security / Vulnerability Management
Jersey City
threatmodeler.com

TrueFort (32)
Application Security /
Appsec Code Hardening
Weehawken
truefort.com

Uniken (125)
IAM / Authentication
Chatham Twp.
uniken.com

**Verizon Business Security
Solutions** (1,000)
MSSP / Managed Services
Basking Ridge
verizonenterprise.com/
solutions/security

NEW MEXICO

RiskSense, Inc. (103)
GRC / Vulnerability Man-
agement
Albuquerque
risksense.com

Vandyke Software (20)
Data Security / Secure File
Transfer
Albuquerque
vandyke.com

NEW YORK

Allure Security (12)
Deception / Document
Decoys, Anti-website
Spoofing
New York
alluresecurity.com

Anchor ID (7)
IAM / Mobile Authenti-
cation
Kingston
anchorid.com

AppMobi (14)
Endpoint / Mobile App
Protection
Poughkeepsie
appmobi.com

**Armjisoft Digital Rights
Management Systems,
Inc.** (1)
Data Security / DRM
New York
armjisoft.com

Avanan (55)
Operations / Security Tool
Deployment
New York
avanan.com

Axio (52)
GRC / Risk Management
New York
axio.com

Axonius (33)
Operations / Orchestration
New York
axonius.com

Barricade IT Security (2)
MSSP / Managed Services
Islip
barricadeitsecurity.com

Bay Dynamics (79)
GRC / Information Risk
Intelligence
New York
baydynamics.com

**Better Mobile App
Security** (19)
Endpoint / Mobile App
Security
New York
better.mobi

Bettercloud (256)
Network / Cloud Activity
Monitoring
New York
bettercloud.com

BlueVoyant (175)
MSSP / MDR
New York
bluevoyant.com

**CA Technologies (part of
Broadcom)** (9,565)
IAM
New York
ca.com

Carve Systems (22)
GRC / Risk Assessment
New York
carvesystems.com

Claroty (145)
IoT Security / ICS
New York
claroty.com

Code Dx (10)
Application Security / Software Assurance Analytics
Northport
codedx.com

Confide (1)
Data Security / Private
Messaging
New York
getconfide.com

Criptext (12)
Email Security / Secure
Email
New York
criptext.com

CyberCentric (2)
GRC / Data Access Mon-
itoring
New York
cybercentric.com

Cyberfense (5)
GRC / Risk Management
New York
cyberfense.com

CyberMDX (36)
IoT Security / Medical
Devices
New York
cybermdx.com

Note: Numbers in parentheses indicate employee count

Cybersafe Solutions (16)
MSSP / MDR
Jericho
cybersafesolutions.com

Cygov (13)
GRC / Compliance and
DLP
New York
cygov.co

Cylera (19)
IoT Security / Medical
Devices
New York
cylera.com

Cyware (89)
Operations / Alert Man-
agement
New York
cyware.com

Dashlane (179)
IAM / Password Manager
New York
dashlane.com

DataDome (38)
Fraud Prevention / Bot
Detection
New York
datadome.co

DigitalShark (3)
Network / Web Defense
New York
digitalshark.org

DomainSkate (2)
Fraud Prevention / Brand
Abuse Discovery
New York
domainskate.com

Flashpoint (140)
Threat Intelligence / Dark
Web Intel
New York
flashpoint-intel.com

FortMesa (3)
GRC / Risk Management
Austerlitz
fortmesa.com

GrammaTech (95)
Application Security /
Code Scanning
Ithaca
grammatech.com

Helm Solutions (22)
GRC / Compliance Man-
agement
New York
helm.global

HighCastle Cybersecurity
(3)
MSSP / Managed Services
New York
highcastlecybersecurity.
com

HYPR (62)
IAM / Biometrics
New York
hypr.com

IBM (2,000)
MSSP / Managed Services
Armonk
ibm.com

ID R&D Inc. (16)
IAM / Biometrics
New York
idrnd.net

IDRRA (5)
GRC / Third Party Risk
Management
New York
idrra.com

illusive Networks (112)
Deception
New York
illusivenetworks.com

Indegy (60)
IoT Security / Visibility
for ICS
New York
indegy.com

Infor (200)
GRC / Continuous Mon-
itoring
New York
infor.com

Inpher (23)
Data Security / Processing
of Private Data
New York
inpher.io

Intezer (30)
Operations / Malware
Analysis
New York
intezer.com

Intsights (150)
Threat Intelligence / Deep
& Dark Web
New York
intsights.com

Kaseya (575)
IAM / Managed SSO and
MFA
New York
kaseya.com

Kroll (200)
Operations / Risk Mitiga-
tion & Response
New York
kroll.com

Kryptaxe (2)
Fraud Prevention / Ac-
count Takeover Protection
New York
kryptaxe.com

Mailspect (1)
Email Security
Tarrytown
mailspect.com

Nopsec (27)
GRC / Vulnerability Risk
Management
Brooklyn
nopsec.com

NS1 (113)
Network / DNS Security
New York
ns1.com

OpenIAM (13)
IAM / Identity Manage-
ment
Cortlandt Manor
openiam.com

Panorays (33)
GRC / Vulnerability As-
sessment for Third Parties
New York
panorays.com

Payfone (95)
Fraud Prevention / An-
ti-fraud
New York
payfone.com

PIXM, Inc. (9)
Email Security / An-
ti-phishing
Brooklyn
pixm.net

QoSient (1)
Network Monitoring
New York
qosient.com

RangeForce (26)
Operations / Training
White Plains
rangeforce.com

Red Balloon Security (26)
Endpoint / Embedded
Device Security
New York
redballoonsecurity.com

Reservoir Labs (28)
Security Analytics / Real-Time Threat Visibility
New York
reservoir.com

Rether Networks Inc. (1)
Endpoint / Host Intrusion Prevention
Centereach
rether.com

Return Path (518)
Fraud Prevention / Email Fraud Prevention
New York
returnpath.com

SaferVPN (26)
Network / Consumer VPN
New York
safervpn.com

Secure Decisions (4)
Security Analytics / Security Visualization for Cyber Defense
Northport
securedecisions.com

SecurityScorecard (175)
GRC / Risk Measurement
New York
securityscorecard.com

Semperis (23)
IAM / AD State Manager
New York
semperis.com

SendSafely (7)
Data Security / Secure File and Message Transfer
New York
sendsafely.com

SIEMonster (9)
Security Analytics
New York
siemonster.com

Siemplify (79)
Security Analytics / Threat Detection and Response
New York
siemplify.co

Skout Cybersecurity (76)
Security Analytics / Streaming Data Analysis
New York
getskout.com

Socure (76)
IAM / Online Identity Verification
New York
socure.com

SoHo Token Labs (1)
Application Security / Static Code Analysis
New York
sohotokenlabs.com

Syccure (4)
IAM / Access Control
Albany
syccure.com

Syncsort (474)
IAM / iSeries Access Control
Pearl River
syncsort.com

Tessian (124)
Email Security / Anti-phishing
New York
tessian.com

Todyl (5)
Network / Remote Access Protection
New York
todyl.com

Total Defense (32)
Endpoint / PC, Mobile & Internet Security
Hauppauge
totaldefense.com

Typing DNA (27)
IAM / Biometrics
New York
typingdna.com

Unbound Tech (45)
Data Security / Key Management
New York
unboundtech.com

Uplevel Security (13)
Operations / Incident Response
New York
uplevelsecurity.com

Varonis (1,396)
Data Security / File Collaboration & Data Protection
New York
varonis.com

Verint (3,132)
Operations / Data Mining
Melville
verint.com

Wetstone (15)
Operations / Forensics
Cortland
wetstonetech.com

White Ops (115)
Fraud Prevention / Ad Tech Security
New York
whiteops.com

NORTH CAROLINA

aPersona (7)
IAM / MFA Platform
Raleigh
apersona.com

Bayshore Networks, Inc. (30)
IoT / ICS
Durham
bayshorenetworks.com

Calyptix Security Corporation (9)
Network / UTM
Charlotte
calyptix.com

Cymatic (15)
Security Analytics / UEBA
Raleigh
cymatic.io

Hyperion Gray (9)
Network / Open Source Web Security
Concord
hyperiongray.com

SAS Institute (100)
Fraud Prevention / Anti-fraud
Cary
sas.com

StrongKey (18)
Data Security / Key Management
Durham
strongkey.com

Tavve Software (15)
Network / Packet Routing
Morrisville
tavve.com

OHIO

AwareHQ (43)
Network / Monitor Social Networks
Columbus
awarehq.com

Axuall (5)
IAM / Identity Verification
Cleveland
axuall.com

Binary Defense (55)
MSSP / SOC as a service
Stow
binarydefense.com

Note: Numbers in parentheses indicate employee count

Cerdant (48)
MSSP / Managed Services
Dublin
cerdant.com

DAtAnchor (13)
Data Security / Document
Security
Columbus
datanchor.net

Emergynt (16)
GRC / Risk Management
Cincinnati
emergynt.com

Emprise (35)
MSSP / Managed Services
Toledo
emptechllc.com

Finite State (22)
IoT Security / Firmware
Monitoring
Columbus
finitestate.io

I-Trap Internet Security Services (1)
Network / Intrusion Detection System
Doylestown
i-trap.net

iDSync (5)
IAM / AD Integration
Perrysburg
idsync.com

Keyfactor (94)
Data Security / PKI as a
Service
Independence
keyfactor.com

Panopticon Labs (4)
Fraud Prevention / Virtual
Identity Theft Protection
Columbus
panopticonlabs.com

PreEmptive Solutions (32)
Application Security / App
Hardening
Mayfield Village
preemptive.com

Privacyware (1)
Endpoint / IIS Security
New Albany
privacyware.com

Seed Protocol (3)
Data Security / Encryption
Athens
seed-protocol.com

TechR2 (29)
Data Security / Erasure
Reynoldsburg
techr2.com

OKLAHOMA

SecPod Technologies (52)
Endpoint / EDR
Tulsa
secpod.com

TokenEx (32)
Data Security / Tokenization
Edmond
tokenex.com

True Digital Security (62)
MSSP / Managed SIEM
Tulsa
truedigitalsecurity.com

OREGON

Acceptto (33)
Fraud Prevention /
Behavior-Based Identity
Verification
Portland
acceptto.com

Anitian (31)
GRC / Compliance Automation
Portland
anitian.com

Apcon (249)
Network / Packet Capture
and Analysis
Wilsonville
apcon.com

Eclypsium (23)
Endpoint / Firmware
Protection
Beaverton
eclypsium.com

Hueya (6)
Training / Phishing Simulation
Bend
hueya.io

ID Experts (73)
GRC / Incident Response
Portland
idexperscorp.com

Iovation (214)
IAM / Authentication
Portland
iovation.com

Senrio (15)
IoT Security / ICS
Portland
senr.io

Stratus Digital Systems (8)
Endpoint / Server Rotation
Eugene
stratusdigitalsystems.com

SUPERAntiSpyware (2)
Endpoint / Anti-spyware
Eugene
superantispyware.com

SureID (120)
IAM
Portland
sureid.com

TripWire (Belkin) (465)
GRC / File Integrity Management
Portland
tripwire.com

Twistlock (acquired by Palo Alto Networks) (121)
Operations / Container
Security
Portland
twistlock.com

PENNSYLVANIA

Certes Networks (49)
Network / VPN
Pittsburgh
certesnetworks.com

Clarabyte (3)
Data Security / Erasure
Pittsburgh
clarabyte.com

Clone Systems (13)
MSSP / Security Monitoring
Philadelphia
clone-systems.com

Dash Solutions (7)
GRC / HIPAA Compliance
Management
Devon
dashsdk.com

EfficientIP (106)
Network / DNS Management
West Chester
efficientip.com

ForAllSecure (32)
Application Security /
Appsec Fuzzing
Pittsburgh
forallsecure.com

IDenticard (101)
IAM / Access Control
Manheim
identicard.com

IT Security, Inc. (1)
Network / Application,
Cloud & Network Security
Pittsburgh
it-security-inc.com

PacketViper (23)
Deception
Pittsburgh
packetviper.com

Pearl Software Inc. (14)
Network / Web Filtering
Exton
pearlsoftware.com

Privakey, Inc. (10)
Fraud Prevention / Trans-
action Intent
Philadelphia
privakey.com

SecureAge Technology
(25)
Data Security / Encryption
West Chester
secureage.com

SecureSwitch (1)
Network / Air Gap Switch-
es
Pittsburgh
secureswitch.com

Unisys Stealth (500)
Network Cloaking
Blue Bell
unisys.com

XOOUi (1)
Data Security / Encryption
State College
xooui.com

Xton Technologies (4)
IAM / Privileged Access
Management
Trevose
xtontech.com

SOUTH CAROLINA

Human Presence (10)
Network Bot Detection
Greenville
humanpresence.io

PhishLabs (142)
GRC / Anti-phishing
Charleston
phishlabs.com

SOUTH DAKOTA

Active Countermeasures
(16)
Security Analytics / Threat
Hunting
Spearfish
activecountermeasures.
com

TENNESSEE

Clearwater (101)
GRC / Risk Management
Nashville
clearwatercompliance.com

Cybera (168)
Network / SDN Applica-
tion & Network Security
Franklin
cybera.net

SertintyONE (6)
Data Security / IRM
Nashville
sertintyone.com

TEXAS

2FA Inc. (11)
IAM / Authentication
Austin
2fa.com

9Star (19)
IAM / Managed Identity
Platform
Austin
9starinc.com

@RISK Technologies (61)
GRC / Risk Measurement
Dallas
atrisktech.com

Accudata Systems, Inc.
(195)
Operations / Security
Management
Houston
accudatasystems.com

**ActivIdentity Corp. (now
HIDGlobal)** (2,307)
IAM / Identity Manage-
ment
Austin
hidglobal.com

Acumera (32)
MSSP / Managed Firewalls
Austin
acumera.net

Alert Logic (659)
GRC / Log Management
Houston
alertlogic.com

AllClear ID (149)
Fraud Prevention / Identity
Protection Service
Austin
allclearid.com

Altr (53)
Data Security for Apps
Austin
altr.com

Armor (243)
MSSP Cloud Security
Richardson
armor.com

Blue Lance Inc. (12)
GRC / Asset Management
Houston
bluelance.com

BMC Software (200)
Security Analytics / SIEM
Houston
bmc.com

Brinqa (37)
GRC / Risk Analytics &
Management
Austin
brinqa.com

BrixBits (3)
Application Security /
Code Hardening
Houston
brixbits.com

ByStorm Software (1)
Data Security / IRM
Magnolia
bystorm.com

ClearDATA (191)
MSSP / HIPAA Cloud
Hosting
Austin
cleardata.com

**Critical Research
Corporation** (1)
Network / Endpoint Dis-
covery
Austin
rumble.run

Critical Start (112)
MSSP / MDR
Plano
criticalstart.com

Cyber adAPT (28)
Security Analytics / Net-
work Traffic Monitoring
Dallas
cyberadapt.com

Cybernance (9)
GRC / Risk Measurement
Austin
cybernance.com

Note: Numbers in parentheses indicate employee count

Data Security Technologies
Data Security / NoSQL Policy Enforcement
Richardson
datasectech.com

Delta Risk (71)
MSSP / MDR
San Antonio
deltarisk.com

Denim Group (94)
GRC / Vulnerability Management
San Antonio
denimgroup.com

DeUmbra (3)
Security Analytics / Visualization
Austin
deumbra.com

Digital Defense (110)
GRC / Vulnerability Management
San Antonio
digitaldefense.com

Elemental Cyber Security (9)
GRC / Vulnerability Management
Dallas
elementalsecurity.com

Encryptics (24)
Data Security / IRM
Addison
encryptics.com

ForcePoint (2,495)
GRC / DLP
Austin
forcepoint.com

Full Armor Systems (6)
Network / Content URL Filtering
Conroe
fullarmorsys.com

FutureX (58)
Data Security / Encryption HSM
Bulverde
futurex.com

GFI Software (417)
Email Security / Anti-spam
Austin
gfi.com

GlassWire
Endpoint Firewall
Austin
glasswire.com

GlobalSCAPE, Inc. (128)
Network / Secure File Transfer
San Antonio
globalscape.com

Gluu (18)
IAM / Access Control
Austin
gluu.org

Hawk Network Defense (5)
Security Analytics
Dallas
hawkdefense.com

HID Global (2,110)
IAM / Authentication
Austin
hidglobal.com

Hopzero (14)
Network / Hop Minimization
Austin
hopzero.com

Hypori (12)
Endpoint / Mobile Device Management
Austin
hypori.com

Identity Automation (111)
IAM / Identity Management
Houston
identityautomation.com

Idera (365)
GRC / SQL Compliance
Houston
idera.com

Infocyte (37)
Endpoint Detection
Austin
infocyte.com

Intrusion Inc. (27)
Network / IDS and IPS
Richardson
intrusion.com

IPVanish (8)
Network / VPN
Dallas
ipvanish.com

JASK (acquired by Sumo Logic, 2019) (121)
Security Analytics / SIEM
Austin
jask.com

Lavabit (182)
Email Security / Encrypted Email
Dallas
lavabit.com

Lepide (158)
Data Security / Data Discovery
Austin
lepide.com

Loggly (18)
Operations / Log Aggregation
Austin
loggly.com

Masergy (594)
MSSP / Managed Services
Plano
masergy.com

Maxxsure (29)
GRC / Risk Management
Richardson
maxxsure.com

Mi-Token (109)
IAM / 2FA Tokens
Austin
mi-token.com

Netsurion (364)
MSSP / Managed Security Services
Houston
netsurion.com

Network Box USA (14)
MSSP / Managed Services
Houston
networkboxusa.com

NSS Labs (101)
Testing / Product Testing
Austin
nsslabs.com

Osano (12)
GRC / Data Privacy Compliance
Austin
osano.com

Pointsecure (3)
GRC / OpenVMS Compliance
Houston
pointsecure.com

SailPoint (1,093)
IAM / Identity Governance
Austin
sailpoint.com

SaltyCloud (6)
Operations / Workflow Automation
Austin
saltycloud.com

SecureLink (146)
IAM / Third Party Access Controls
Austin
securelink.com

SecureLogix Corporation (72)
Network / VoIP Security
San Antonio
securelogix.com

Securonix (368)
Security Analytics / UEBA
Addison
securonix.com

Sentinel IPS (9)
MSSP / Reputation Firewall
Dallas
sentinelips.com

Softex (13)
IAM / Authentication
Austin
softexinc.com

Solarwinds (400)
Security Analytics / SIEM
Austin
solarwinds.com

SparkCognition (247)
Endpoint / AV
Austin
sparkcognition.com

Specialized Security Services Inc. (43)
MSSP / Managed Services
Plano
s3security.com

SpyCloud (44)
Threat Intelligence / Dark Web Collection
Austin
spycloud.com

SSL.com (20)
Data Security / Certificate Authority
Houston
ssl.com

StackPath (305)
Network / WAF and DDoS at the Edge
Dallas
stackpath.com

Strobes (3)
GRC / Vulnerability Management
Frisco
strobes.co

SureCloud (72)
GRC / Cloud Platform
Plano
surecloud.com

ThreatGuard, Inc. (4)
GRC / Auditing and Monitoring
San Antonio
threatguard.com

ThreatWarrior (5)
Network Monitoring and Defense
Austin
threatwarrior.com

Trend Micro (6,565)
Endpoint / Anti-virus
Irving
trendmicro.com

Trustonic (93)
Endpoint / Mobile App Protection
Austin
trustonic.com

Uniloc (6)
IAM
Plano
uniloc.com

Visual Click Software (16)
GRC / Auditing for AD
Austin
visualclick.com

Vysk (12)
Endpoint / Mobile Device Security
San Antonio
vysk.com

White Cloud Security (15)
Endpoint / Whitelisting
Austin
whitecloudsecurity.com

Ziften (33)
Endpoint Visibility
Austin
ziften.com

Zimperium (164)
Endpoint / Mobile Device Security
Dallas
zimperium.com

Zix Corp. (391)
Data Security / Secure Messaging
Dallas
zixcorp.com

Zyston (41)
MSSP / Managed Security Services
Dallas
zyston.com

UTAH

Access Data Corp. (250)
GRC / Forensics
Lindon
accessdata.com

Anonyome Labs (76)
Data Security / Secure Communications
Salt Lake City
anonyome.com

Braintrace (36)
MSSP / MDR
Salt Lake City
braintrace.com

DATASHIELD (38)
MSSP / Managed Security Services
Salt Lake City
datashieldprotect.com

DigiCert (843)
Data Security / Certificate Authority
Lehi
digicert.com

Eastwind (5)
Network Monitoring for Cloud
Salt Lake City
eastwindnetworks.com

Evernym (56)
IAM / Identity Attestation
Herriman
evernym.com

Ivanti (1,461)
Endpoint Management
South Jordan
ivanti.com

Monarx (10)
Network / Webshell Detection and Blocking
Cottonwood Heights
monarx.com

RiskRecon (75)
GRC / Third Party Risk Management
Salt Lake City
riskrecon.com

SaltStack (94)
Operations / Orchestration
Lehi
saltstack.com

Security Weaver (88)
Data Security / IRM
Lehi
securityweaver.com

Note: Numbers in parentheses indicate employee count

SecurityMetrics (291)
GRC / Vulnerability Scanning and Compliance
Orem
securitymetrics.com

Venafi (303)
Data Security / Key Management
Salt Lake City
venafi.com

Whistic (35)
Operations / Vendor Management
Pleasant Grove
whistic.com

White Canyon Inc. (24)
Data Security / Erasure
American Fork
whitecanyon.com

VIRGINIA

418 Intelligence (4)
Threat Intelligence Gamification
Reston
418intelligence.com

Analyst Platform (8)
Threat Intelligence Platform
Reston
analystplatform.com

AppGuard (40)
Endpoint / Application Containment
Chantilly
appguard.us

Atomicorp (15)
Endpoint / Host Intrusion Prevention
Chantilly
atomicorp.com

BiObex (8)
IAM / 2FA
Reston
biobex.com

Blue Ridge Networks (34)
Network / Microsegmentation via Tokens
Chantilly
blueridgenetworks.com

BluVector (Part of Comcast) (44)
Network / IDS
Arlington
bluvector.io

CACI International Inc. (140)
MSSP / Managed Services
Arlington
caci.com

Centripetal (39)
Network / Reputation Firewall
Herndon
centripetalnetworks.com

CertiPath (33)
Data Security / Certificate Authority Monitoring
Reston
certipath.com

Cofense (was PhishMe) (393)
GRC / Anti-phishing Training
Leesburg
cofense.com

CounterFlow AI (14)
Network / Forensics
Crozet
counterflow.ai

Cyber 20/20 (11)
Operations / Behavior-Based Malware Detection
Herndon
cyber2020.com

Cyber Triage
Operations / Incident Response Management
Herndon
cybertriage.com

CyberSponse (67)
Operations / Incident Response & Security Operations
Arlington
cybersponse.com

CyFIR (12)
GRC / Digital Forensics & e-Discovery
Ashburn
cyfir.com

Cyph (2)
Data Security / Encrypted Collaboration
McLean
cyph.com

Cyren (266)
Network / Web, Email & Mobile Security
McLean
cyren.com

Daon (148)
IAM / Identity Assurance
Reston
daon.com

Dark3 (20)
Network / SaaS Network Monitoring
Alexandria
darkcubed.com

Dark Cubed (20)
Security Analytics / Network Monitoring
Charlottesville
darkcubed.com

Datablink (26)
IAM / Authentication
McLean
datablink.com

Divvy Cloud Corp. (48)
Endpoint / Container Security
Arlington
divvycloud.com

Endgame, Inc. (153)
Security Analytics / Security Intelligence and Analytics
Arlington
endgame.com

ESCOM (1)
Network / Anti-spam
Oakton
escom.com

Expel (124)
MSSP / SOC as a Service
Herndon
expel.io

Fractal Industries (121)
Operations / Incident Response
Reston
fractalindustries.com

GigaTrust (37)
Data Security / Document Security
Herndon
gigatrust.com

Graphus (12)
Email Security / Anti-phishing
Reston
graphus.ai

GroupSense (23)
Threat Intelligence / Dark Web Collection
Arlington
groupsense.io

Guidepoint Security (304)
MSSP / Managed Services
Herndon
guidepointsecurity.com

Gyomo (3)
Training / Anti-phishing
Herndon
gyomo.com

Haystax (62)
Security Analytics / Threat
Analytics
McLean
haystax.com

ID.me (139)
IAM / Credential Manage-
ment
McLean
id.me

IDEMIA (10,787)
IAM / Identity Augmen-
tation
Reston
idemia.com

Infosec Inc. (16)
Endpoint / Mainframe
Event Monitoring
Centreville
infosecinc.com

InQuest (25)
Data Security / DLP
Arlington
inquest.net

Insider Spyder (2)
Operations / Employee
Monitoring
Chantilly
insiderspyder.com

Intensity Analytics (10)
IAM / Behavior Metrics
Warrenton
intensityanalytics.com

Invincea (27)
Operations / Incident
Response
Fairfax
invincea.com

IoT Defense (2)
IoT Security / Network,
Home Firewall for IoT
Devices
Falls Church
iotdef.com

LastPass (23)
IAM / Password Manager
Fairfax
lastpass.com

LGS Innovations (840)
Application Security /
Code Security
Herndon
lgsinnovations.com

**Lookingglass Cyber
Solutions** (308)
Threat Intelligence
Reston
lookingglasscyber.com

LunarLine (114)
GRC / VM and Log Man-
agement
Arlington
lunarline.com

Mantis Networks (8)
Network / Visibility
Reston
mantisnet.com

MeasuredRisk (27)
GRC / Risk Management
Arlington
measuredrisk.com

MicroStrategy (200)
IAM / Mobile Identity
Platform
Tysons Corner
microstrategy.com

Mission Secure (43)
IoT Security / ICS
Charlottesville
missionsecure.com

Nehemiah Security (48)
GRC / Risk Management
Tysons
nehemiahsecurity.com

Neustar (300)
Network / DDoS Defense
Sterling
neustar.biz

Normshield (26)
GRC / Security Scores
Vienna
normshield.com

Novetta Solutions (810)
Network Traffic Monitor-
ing
McLean
novetta.com

NTrepid (222)
Operations / Forensics and
Linkage
Herndon
ntrepidcorp.com

OPAC (104)
Network / Zero-Trust
Networking
Herndon
opaq.com

Ostendio (12)
GRC / Compliance Man-
agement
Arlington
ostendio.com

Paladion (960)
Testing / Cybersecurity
Testing & Monitoring
Reston
paladion.net

Paraben Corporation (18)
GRC / Digital Forensics &
Data Recovery
Aldie
paraben.com

Passfaces Corporation
IAM / 2FA
Reston
passfaces.com

PFP Cybersecurity (25)
Endpoint Protection (Pow-
er Anomoly)
Vienna
pfpcybersecurity.com

Privva (10)
GRC / Third Party Risk
Arlington
privva.com

Qomplx (94)
Security Analytics / Monitoring and Response
Reston
qomplx.com/cyber

R&K Cyber Solutions (11)
MSSP / Managed Security
Services
Manassas
rkcybersolutions.com

Risk Based Security (27)
GRC / Cyber Risk Ana-
lytics
Richmond
riskbasedsecurity.com

RunSafe Security (15)
IoT Security / Firmware
Hardening
McLean
runsafesecurity.com

SafeDNS (34)
Network / DNS Filtering
Alexandria
safedns.com/en

SafeGuard Cyber (37)
GRC / Employee Social
Media Management
Charlottesville
safeguardcyber.com

SCIT Labs, Inc. (10)
Endpoint / Dynamic Image
Replacement for Servers
Clifton
scitlabs.com

SCYTHE (22)
Testing / Attack Simula-
tion and Automated Pen
Testing
Arlington
scythe.io

Note: Numbers in parentheses indicate employee count

Sera-Brynn (20)
GRC / Cyber Risk Management
Suffolk
sera-brynn.com

Shevirah (3)
Operations / Mobile Testing
Herndon
shevirah.com

Silent Circle (37)
Data Security / Encrypted Communication
Fairfax
silentcircle.com

SteelCloud (34)
GRC / Configuration Management
Ashburn
steelcloud.com

SurfWatch Labs (14)
GRC / Cyber Risk Intelligence Analytics
Sterling
surfwatchlabs.com

Syncdog (8)
Endpoint / Mobile Security
Reston
syncdog.com

TecSec (23)
Data Security / Key Management
McLean
tecsec.com

Telos (556)
GRC / Risk Management
Ashburn
telos.com

The Media Trust (79)
Fraud Prevention / Ad Tech Security
McLean
themediatrust.com

ThreatConnect (117)
Threat Intelligence
Arlington
threatconnect.com

ThreatQuotient (104)
Threat Intelligence Platform
Reston
threatquotient.com

Trushield, Inc. (40)
MSSP / Managed Security Services
Sterling
trushieldinc.com

Trusted Integration (4)
GRC
Alexandria
trustedintegration.com

Truvincio (3)
GRC / Security Awareness Training
Vienna
truvincio.com

Tychon (25)
GRC / Risk Management Dashboards
Fredericksburg
tychon.io

Verisign (1,323)
MSSP / Managed Services
Reston
verisign.com

Verodin (acquired by FireEye, 2019) (93)
Testing / Security Instrumentation
McLean
verodin.com

Virgil Security (40)
Data Security / End-to-End Application Encryption
Manassas
virgilsecurity.com

Wirewheel (51)
Data Security / Customer Data Protection
Arlington
wirewheel.io

WiTopia (9)
Network / VPN
Reston
witopia.com

Zerho (2)
Security Analytics / Machine Learning
Crestview
zerho.info

WASHINGTON

Adaptiva (47)
Endpoint / Configuration Management
Kirkland
adaptiva.com

AppViewX (244)
Data Security / Encryption and Key Management
Seattle
appviewx.com

Atonomi (4)
IoT Security / Blockchain
Seattle
atonomi.io

Auth0 (480)
IAM / Single Sign-On APIs
Bellevue
auth0.com

C2SEC (6)
GRC / Risk Management
Redmond
c2sec.com

Centri (20)
IoT Security / For Mobile Carriers
Seattle
centritechnology.com

CI Security (68)
MSSP / MDR
Seattle
ci.security

Cloudentity (33)
IAM / Cloud Identity Management
Seattle
cloudentity.com

Cloudneeti (34)
GRC / Compliance Management
Seattle
cloudneeti.com

CodeProof (8)
Application Security / Mobile App Secrity
Bellevue
codeproof.com

ContentGuard (Pendrell Company) (5)
Data Security / IRM File Sharing for Mobile Phones
Kirkland
contentguard.com

DarkLight.ai (20)
Security Analytics
Bellevue
darklight.ai

DataSunrise Database Security (285)
Data Security / Database Security
Seattle
datasunrise.com

DigitSec (7)
Application Security / SFDC Scanner
Seattle
digitsec.com

DomainTools (102)
Threat Intelligence from DNS
Seattle
domaintools.com

ExtraHop Networks (451)
Security Analytics /
Network Detection and
Response
Seattle
extrahop.com

F5 Networks (2,000)
Network / DDoS and
Firewall
Seattle
f5.com

Intego Inc. (18)
Network / Personal Fire-
wall
Seattle
intego.com

Intercrypto
Data Security / File En-
cryption
Seattle
intercrypto.com

Microsoft (2,000)
IAM / IAM
Redmond
microsoft.com

NetMotion Wireless (153)
Network / Wireless Secu-
rity
Seattle
netmotionwireless.com

NetSTAR, Inc. (28)
Network / Secure Web
Gateway
Bellevue
NetSTAR-inc.com

NewSky Security (12)
IoT Security / Device
Monitoring
Redmond
newskysecurity.com

NuID Inc. (7)
IAM / Trustless Authenti-
cation
Seattle
nuid.io

PeachTech (3)
Testing / Fuzzing
Seattle
peach.tech

PhishCloud (9)
Email Security / An-
ti-phishing
Renton
phishcloud.com

Polyverse (25)
Endpoint / OS Random-
izing
Bellevue
polyverse.io

RiskLens (67)
GRC / Risk Calculations
Spokane
risklens.com

Sequitur Labs (12)
Endpoint / Embedded
Security
Fall City
sequiturlabs.com

Subuno (2)
Fraud Prevention for SMB
Seattle
subuno.com

Tempered Networks (65)
Network / Zero-Trust
Networking
Seattle
temperednetworks.com

TNT Software (5)
Operations / Security
Management
Vancouver
tntsoftware.com

Topia Technology (19)
Data Security / Encryption
with Shredding
Tacoma
topiatechnology.com

Townsend Security (21)
Data Security / Encryption
and Tokenization
Olympia
townsendsecurity.com

Trovares (8)
Security Analytics / Graph
Analytics
Seattle
trovares.com

VeriClouds (6)
Fraud Prevention / Cre-
dential Stuffing Defense
Seattle
vericlouds.com

Vinsula (2)
Endpoint Protection
Seattle
vinsula.com

Virta Labs (4)
IoT Security / Healthcare
Seattle
virtalabs.com

**WatchGuard
Technologies, Inc.** (720)
Network / UTM
Seattle
watchguard.com

Widevine Technologies (6)
Data Security / DRM
Kirkland
widevine.com

wolfSSL (26)
Network / Open Source
Internet Security
Edmonds
wolfssl.com

WEST VIRGINIA

SecurLinx (11)
IAM / Biometrics
Morgantown
securlinx.com

WISCONSIN

AristotleInsight (24)
GRC / Discovery and
Analysis of Assets
Onalaska
aristotleinsight.com

PKWARE (142)
Data Security / Data
Privacy
Milwaukee
pkware.com

Sergeant Laboratories
(20)
GRC / Risk Management
Onalaska
sgtlabs.com

SynerComm (55)
Network & Security Infra-
structure
Brookdfield
synercomm.com

Tascet (8)
GRC / Risk Management
Madison
tascet.com

WYOMING

BlackFog (5)
Endpoint / EDR
Cheyenne
blackfog.com

Note: Numbers in parentheses indicate employee count

Listings By Category

The Major Categories

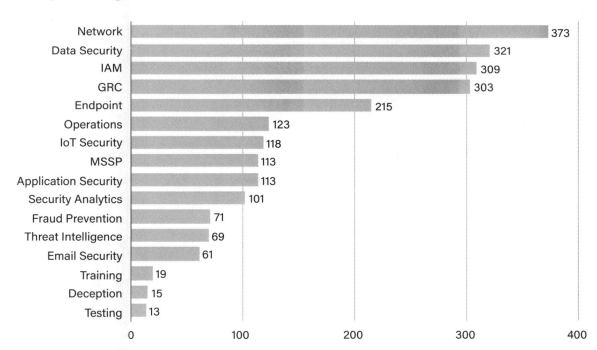

Category	Value
Network	373
Data Security	321
IAM	309
GRC	303
Endpoint	215
Operations	123
IoT Security	118
MSSP	113
Application Security	113
Security Analytics	101
Fraud Prevention	71
Threat Intelligence	69
Email Security	61
Training	19
Deception	15
Testing	13

Number of Vendors per Category

Application Security ... 113	Endpoint 215	IoT Security 118	Security Analytics 101
Data Security 321	Fraud Prevention 71	MSSP 113	Testing 13
Deception 15	GRC 303	Network 373	Threat Intelligence 69
Email Security 61	IAM 309	Operations 123	Training 19

APPLICATION SECURITY

42Crunch (19)
API Security
Irvine, CA, USA
42crunch.com

Ahope (21)
Mobile
Seoul, South Korea
ahope.net/main

Aiculus (5)
API Security
Melbourne, Australia
aiculus.co

AppDome (62)
Application Security
Tel Aviv, Israel
appdome.com

AppKnox (19)
Mobile Application Security Testing
Singapore, Singapore
appknox.com

Appray (2)
Mobile App Scanning
Vienna, Austria
app-ray.co

AppSec Labs (18)
Mobile Application Security Testing
Kfar Saba, Israel
appsec-labs.com

AppVision (10)
Appsec Code Hardening and Monitoring
San Francisco, CA, USA
appvision.net

Araali Networks (4)
Appsec for Containers
Fremont, CA, USA
araalinetworks.com

ArecaBay (6)
API Security
Los Altos, CA, USA
arecabay.com

Arxan Technology (153)
Application Security
San Francisco, CA, USA
arxan.com

AttackFlow (5)
Appsec Code Scanning
San Francisco, CA, USA
attackflow.com

Attify (12)
Mobile App Security
Bangalore, India
attify.com

Avocado Systems, Inc. (10)
App Hardening
San Jose, CA, USA
avocadosys.com

BIS Guard (1)
Code Wrappers to Prevent Tampering
Ofra, Israel
bisguard.com

Blue Planet-works (13)
Isolation
Tokyo, Japan
blueplanet-works.com

BrixBits (3)
Code Hardening
Houston, TX, USA
brixbits.com

Build38 (13)
Mobile App Protection
Munich, Germany
build38.com

ChameleonX (8)
Runtime Protection
Tel Aviv, Israel
chameleonx.com

Checkmarx (1)
Software Development Security
Ramat Gan, Israel
checkmarx.com

Cobalt (192)
App Testing for Security
San Francisco, CA, USA
cobalt.io

Code Dx (10)
Software Assurance Analytics
Northport, NY, USA
codedx.com

Code Intelligence (15)
Appsec
Bonn, Germany
code-intelligence.com

Codenomicon (15)
Code Analysis
Mountain View, CA, USA
codenomicon.com

CodeProof (8)
Mobile App Security
Bellevue, WA, USA
codeproof.com

Codified Security (5)
Code Scanning
London, UK
codifiedsecurity.com

Continuum Security (30)
Open Source Scanning
Huesca, Spain
continuumsecurity.net

Contrast Security (169)
Application Security Software
Los Altos, CA, USA
contrastsecurity.com

Crashtest Security (8)
Appsec
Munich, Germany
crashtest-security.com

Cypherpath (36)
Containers for Apps
Mountain View, CA, USA
cypherpath.com

Data Theorem (23)
Mobile App Scanner
Palo Alto, CA, USA
datatheorem.com

DBApp Security (22)
Web Application & Database Security
Hangzhou, China
dbappsecurity.com

DeepSource (7)
Static Code Analysis for Python and Go
San Francisco, CA, USA
deepsource.io

Detectify (82)
Web Scanning
Stockholm, Sweden
detectify.com

DigitSec (7)
SFDC Scanner
Seattle, WA, USA
digitsec.com

DragonSoft (31)
Application Security WAF and Scanning
New Taipei City, Taiwan
dragonsoft.com.tw

ForAllSecure (32)
Appsec Fuzzing
Pittsburgh, PA, USA
forallsecure.com

Fortanix (37)
Runtime Encryption
Mountain View, CA, USA
fortanix.com

Fossa (41)
Open Source Vulnerability Management
San Francisco, CA, USA
fossa.com

Note: Numbers in parentheses indicate employee count

Fuzzbuzz (4)
Appsec Fuzzing
Mountain View, CA, USA
fuzzbuzz.io

GrammaTech (95)
Code Scanning
Ithaca, NY, USA
grammatech.com

GuardiCore (141)
App Monitoring
Tel Aviv, Israel
guardicore.com

Guardsquare (47)
Mobile App Protection
Leuven, Belgium
guardsquare.com

HDIV Security (21)
Code Analysis
Donostia-San Sebastián,
Spain
hdivsecurity.com

Immunant (4)
Code Hardening
Irvine, CA, USA
immunant.com

Immuniweb
Web Scanning
Geneva, Switzerland
immuniweb.com

Insignary (12)
Open Source Vulnerability
Management
Seoul, South Korea
insignary.com

Intrinsic (6)
Appsec Code Hardening
San Francisco, CA, USA
intrinsic.com

Jscrambler (40)
Security for Javascript
San Francisco, CA, USA
jscrambler.com

K2 Cyber Security (2)
Appsec, Zero Day Prevention
San Jose, CA, USA
k2io.com

Klocwork (a Rogue Wave company) (299)
Source Code Analysis
Louisville, CO, USA
roguewave.com

Lacework (65)
Cloud Deployment Security
Mountain View, CA, USA
lacework.com

LGS Innovations (840)
Code Security
Herndon, VA, USA
lgsinnovations.com

Lucent Sky (3)
Source Code Analysis and
Repair
San Francisco, CA, USA
lucentsky.com

Mo An Technology
Scanning and Data Flow
Mapping
Hangzhou, China
moresec.cn

Mocana Corporation (73)
Mobile App Security
Sunnyvale, CA, USA
mocana.com

Namogoo (90)
Web Scanning
Ra'anana, Israel
namogoo.com

NetSkope (780)
Cloud Application Security
Santa Clara, CA, USA
netskope.com

Neural Legion (11)
Dynamic Code Analysis
Tel Aviv, Israel
neuralegion.com

NodeSource (21)
Appsec Serverless
San Francisco, CA, USA
nodesource.com

Nuweba (13)
Serverless Security
Tel Aviv, Israel
nuweba.com

Open Zeppelin (25)
Application Security for
Blockchain
San Francisco, CA, USA
openzeppelin.com

Parasoft (254)
Security Testing
Monrovia, CA, USA
parasoft.com

Patronus.io (6)
Web Scanning
Berlin, Germany
patronus.io

PNF Software (5)
Reverse Engineering for
Android
Redwood City, CA, USA
pnfsoftware.com

Portshift (10)
Identity-Based Workload
Protection
Tel Aviv-Yafo, Israel
portshift.io

Pradeo (19)
Mobile App Security
Paris, France
pradeo.net

PreEmptive Solutions (32)
App Hardening
Mayfield Village, OH, USA
preemptive.com

Probely (1)
Web Scanning
Lisbon, Portugal
probely.com

Promon (43)
In-App Protection for
Mobile
Oslo, Norway
promon.co

Prosa Security (1)
Development Collaboration Platform
Oslo, Norway
prosasecurity.com

Protego (48)
App Hardening
Baltimore, MD, USA
protego.io

Protegrity (309)
Application Security
Stamford, CT, USA
protegrity.com

RIPS Technologies GmbH (28)
Static Code Analysis for
PHP and Java
Bochum, Germany
ripstech.com

Rohde & Schwarz Cybersecurity (51)
App Containers
Meudon, France
Rohd-schwarz.com

SEC Consult (109)
Code Testing
Vienna, Austria
sec-consult.com

SecNeo (22)
Mobile App Protection
San Jose, CA, USA
secneo.com

SecuPi (22)
Cloud App Monitoring
London, UK
secupi.com

SecureCode Warrior (106)
Code Security
Sydney, Australia
securecodewarrior.com

SecuriGo (1)
Cloud App Information
Exposure
Haifa, Israel
securigo.com

Security Innovation (143)
Application Security
Wilmington, MA, USA
securityinnovation.com

Semmle (61)
Code Analysis
San Francisco, CA, USA
semmle.com

Sentar (303)
Code Scanning
Huntsville, AL, USA
sentar.com

ShiftLeft (45)
Appsec Code Hardening
Santa Clara, CA, USA
shiftleft.io

Snaptrust (1)
Appsec
Potsdam, Germany
snaptrust.com

SNDBOX (3)
Malware Analysis
Giv'atayim, Israel
sndbox.com

Snyk (205)
Appsec Open Source Vulns
London, UK
snyk.io

SOFTwarfare (8)
Integration Security
Prairie Village, KS, USA
softwarfare.com

SoHo Token Labs (1)
Static Code Analysis
New York, NY, USA
sohotokenlabs.com

Sonatype (321)
Open Source Scanning
Fulton, MD, USA
sonatype.com

Sparrow
Code Scanning
Mapo-gu, South Korea
sparrowfasoo.com

Spherical Defence (11)
API Security
London, UK
sphericaldefence.com

Sqreen (47)
Agent-Based Monitoring
of Apps
Saint-Cloud, France
sqreen.com

Star Lab (38)
Research and Development
Washington, DC, USA
starlab.io

STEALIEN (9)
Appsec
Seoul, South Korea
stealien.com

Syhunt (2)
Code Scanning
Rio de Janeiro, Brazil
syhunt.com

Synopsys (100)
Software Testing & Security
Mountain View, CA, USA
synopsys.com

Tala Security (31)
Web App Analysis
Fremont, CA, USA
talasecurity.io

Templarbit (13)
Appsec Code Hardening
San Francisco, CA, USA
templarbit.com

Tetrane (11)
Reverse Engineering
Macon, France
tetrane.com

ThreatModeler Software
(39)
Vulnerability Management
Jersey City, NJ, USA
threatmodeler.com

Tinfoil Security (15)
App Scanning
Mountain View, CA, USA
tinfoilsecurity.com

TrueFort (32)
Appsec Code Hardening
Weehawken, NJ, USA
truefort.com

TrulyProtect (7)
App Security
Rehovot, Israel
trulyprotect.com

V-Key (84)
Mobile Device & App
Security
Singapore, Singapore
v-key.com

Veracode (721)
Code Analysis
Burlington, MA, USA
veracode.com

Vicarius (14)
Static and Dynamic Code
Scanning
Jerusalem, Israel
vicarius.io

Virtual Forge (76)
SAP Security
Heidelberg, Germany
virtualforge.com

Waratek (41)
Application Security
Dublin, Ireland
waratek.com

we45 (33)
Application Security
Sunnyvale, CA, USA
we45.com

White Hawk Software (5)
Tamperproofing
Palo Alto, CA, USA
whitehawksoftware.com

WhiteSource (154)
Open Source Security and
License Management
Giv'atayim, Israel
whitesourcesoftware.com

DATA SECURITY

A1Logic (3)
Memory Protection
Bethesda, MD, USA
a1logic.com

Absio (8)
Software-Defined Distrib-
uted Key Cryptography
(SDKC)
Denver, CO, USA
absio.com

Accellion (180)
IRM
Palo Alto, CA, USA
accellion.com

Agora SecureWare (4)
Secure Collaboration
Bioggio, Switzerland
agora-secureware.com

**AHA Products Group
(part of Comtech EF Data
Corporation)** (1)
Encryption Hardware
Moscow, ID, USA
aha.com

Alsharq International Co.
(6)
Certificate Authority
Kuwait
alsharq.com.kw

Note: Numbers in parenthesis indicate employee count

Altitude Networks (10)
File Monitoring
San Francisco, CA, USA
altitudenetworks.com

Altr (53)
Data Security for Apps
Austin, TX, USA
altr.com

Ambitrace (3)
Data Tracking and Logging
San Francisco, CA, USA
ambitrace.com

Anchorage (48)
Secure Storage
San Francisco, CA, USA
anchorage.com

Anjuna (10)
Runtime Encryption
Palo Alto, CA, USA
anjuna.io

Anonyome Labs (76)
Secure Communications
Salt Lake City, UT, USA
anonyome.com

AppOmni (19)
Cloud DLP
San Francisco, CA, USA
appomni.com

AppViewX (244)
Encryption and Key Management
Seattle, WA, USA
appviewx.com

Apricorn (23)
Encrypted Storage
Poway, CA, USA
apricorn.com

Aprivacy (5)
Secure Communications
Kitchener, Canada
aprivacy.com

Ardaco (27)
Secure Communications
Bratislava, Slovakia
ardaco.com

Armjisoft Digital Rights Management Systems, Inc. (1)
DRM
New York, NY, USA
armjisoft.com

Armorblox (42)
DLP
Cupertino, CA, USA
armorblox.com

Articsoft Technologies (1)
Encryption PGP
Centennial, CO, USA
articsoft.com

ASPG (29)
Encryption for Mainframes
Naples, FL, USA
aspg.com

Avepoint (904)
Cloud Backup
Jersey City, NJ, USA
avepoint.com

Baffle (30)
Database Encryption
Santa Clara, CA, USA
baffle.io

Becrypt (62)
Encryption
London, UK
becrypt.com/uk

BeSafe (8)
Cloud Key Management
Yerevan, Armenia
besafe.io

BicDroid (7)
Encryption
Waterloo, Canada
bicdroid.com

BigID, Inc. (105)
Data Discovery
Tel Aviv-Yafo, Israel
bigid.com

Biscom (169)
Secure File Transfer
Chelmsford, MA, USA
biscom.com

Bittium (1,907)
Secure Communications
Oulu, Finland
bittium.com

Blancco (251)
Erasure
Bishops Stortford, UK
blancco.com/en

Bloombase (20)
Network-Attached Encryption
Redwood City, CA, USA
bloombase.com

BlueTalon (32)
Database Policy Management
Redwood City, CA, USA
bluetalon.com

Boole Server (22)
Secure File Synch and Share
Milan, Italy
booleserver.com

Botdoc (10)
Secure File Transfer
Monument, CO, USA
botdoc.io

Boxcryptor (12)
Cloud Encryption
Augsburg, Germany
boxcryptor.com

Brainloop (124)
Secure Collaboration
Munich, Germany
brainloop.com/us

ByStorm Software (1)
IRM
Magnolia, TX, USA
bystorm.com

Caplinked (20)
Secure Workflow File Sharing
Manhattan Beach, CA, USA
caplinked.com

CBL Data Recovery Technologies Inc. (36)
Data Recovery/Destruction
Markham, Canada
cbldata.com

Cellcrypt (4)
Secure Communications
London, UK
cellcrypt.com

Certicom (167)
Encryption, PKI
Mississauga, Canada
certicom.com

CertiPath (33)
Certificate Authority Monitoring
Reston, VA, USA
certipath.com

CipherCloud (309)
Cloud Visibility & Data Protection
San Jose, CA, USA
ciphercloud.com

Clarabyte (3)
Erasure
Pittsburgh, PA, USA
clarabyte.com

Cloudscreen (1)
Discovery, Classification
Yuhang District, China
cloudscreen.com

Communication Security Group (16)
Secure Communications
London, UK
csghq.com

Comodo (1,411)
SSL Certificates & PCI Compliance
Clifton, NJ, USA
comodo.com

Compass Security AG
Secure File Transfer
Rapperswil-Jona, Switzerland
csnc.ch

Compumatica (16)
Secure Remote Access
Uden, Netherlands
compumatica.com

ComSignTrust (3)
Digital Signatures for Data
Tel Aviv, Israel
comsigntrust.com

Confide (1)
Private Messaging
New York, NY, USA
getconfide.com

ContentGuard (Pendrell Company) (5)
IRM File Sharing for Mobile Phones
Kirkland, WA, USA
contentguard.com

CopyNotify (1)
Device Control for SMB
Pune, India
copynotify.com

Cord3 Innovation Inc. (15)
Zero Knowledge File Encryption
Ottawa, Canada
cord3inc.com

Cosmian (8)
Data Security
Paris, France
cosmian.com

Covata (22)
Secure File Sharing
Sydney, Australia
covata.com

Crown Sterling (17)
Encryption
Newport Beach, CA, USA
crownsterling.io

Crypho AS (5)
Private Messaging
Tønsberg, Norway
crypho.com

Crypta Labs (13)
Encryption (RNG)
London, UK
cryptalabs.com

Cryptelo (6)
Secure Data Transfer
Prague, Czech Republic
cryptelo.com

Crypto International AG (1)
Hardware for Crypto
Steinhausen, Switzerland
crypto.ch

Crypto4A Inc. (14)
Entropy as a Service
Ottawa, Canada
crypto4a.com

Cryptomathic (67)
Key Management, PKI
Aarhus, Denmark
cryptomathic.com

Cryptomill Cybersecurity Solutions (16)
Data Security
Toronto, Canada
cryptomill.com

CryptoMove, Inc. (23)
Key Storage
Oakland, CA, USA
cryptomove.com

Cryptsoft Pty Ltd. (10)
PKI and Identity
Greenslopes, Australia
cryptsoft.com

Cryptyk (17)
Secure Storage
Las Vegas, NV, USA
cryptyk.io

CyberSafe Software (3)
Full Disk Encryption
Krasnodar, Russia
cybersafesoft.com

Cybrgen
Distributed Encrypted Storage
Las Vegas, NV, USA
cybrgendev.com

Cyph (2)
Encrypted Collaboration
McLean, VA, USA
cyph.com

Cypherix Software (1)
Encryption
Land O' Lakes, FL, USA
cypherix.com

Data Encryption Systems (4)
Software DRM
Taunton, UK
des.co.uk

Data Security Technologies
NoSQL Policy Enforcement
Richardson, TX, USA
datasectech.com

DataGuise (125)
Database Security
Fremont, CA, USA
dataguise.com

DataLocker (39)
Encrypted Removable Memory
Overland Park, KS, USA
datalocker.com

DAtAnchor (13)
Document Security
Columbus, OH, USA
datanchor.net

DataPassports (3)
IRM
Toronto, Canada
datapassports.com

DataSunrise Database Security (285)
Database Security
Seattle, WA, USA
datasunrise.com

Datex Inc. (29)
Network Data Masking
Mississauga, Canada
datex.ca

Dathena Science (51)
Discovery/Classification
Singapore, Singapore
dathena.io

Dax Asparna Ltd. (11)
Encrypted File Sync and Social Conversations
Afula, Israel
asparna.com

DealRoom (10)
Deal Room
Chicago, IL, USA
dealroom.net

Deeptrace (7)
Deep Fake Detection
Amsterdam, Netherlands
deeptracelabs.com

DeepView (7)
DL Detection Through Social Media Monitoring
London, UK
deepview.com

Note: Numbers in parenthesis indicate employee count

Dekart (1)
Encryption
Chisinau, Republic of
Moldova
dekart.com

Dekko Secure (7)
Encryption
Sydney, Australia
dekkosecure.com

DigiCert (843)
Certificate Authority
Lehi, UT, USA
digicert.com

DISUK Limited (2)
Encryption
Northampton, UK
disuk.com

DRACOON (42)
File Sharing
Regensburg, Germany
dracoon.com

Drooms (116)
Data Rooms
Frankfurt am Main, Germany
drooms.com

Duality Technologies (18)
Encrypted Data Analysis
Newark, NJ, USA
duality.cloud

east-tec (8)
Erasure
Oradea, Romania
east-tec.com

Eclypses (4)
Encrypted Storage
Colorado Springs, CO,
USA
certainsafe.com

Egnyte (470)
Secure File Sharing
Mountain View, CA, USA
egnyte.com

EgoSecure (21)
Data-at-Rest Encryption
Ettlingen, Germany
egosecure.com

Encedo (2)
Encrypted Networks
London, UK
encedo.com

Encryptics (24)
IRM
Addison, TX, USA
encryptics.com

Engage Black (7)
Code Signing
Aptos, CA, USA
engageblack.com

Enigmedia (17)
Secure Communications
San Sebastian, Spain
enigmedia.es

Entrust Datacard (2,148)
Key Management, CA
Minneapolis, MN, USA
entrustdatacard.com

Envault (3)
Data Security
Espoo, Finland
envaultcorp.com

Enveil (23)
Encryption of Data in Use
Washington, DC, USA
enveil.com

Envieta (84)
Hardware Security Modules
Columbia, MD, USA
envieta.com

eperi (26)
Encryption
Pfungstadt, Germany
eperi.de/en

ERMES Cyber Security (11)
DLP and Web Browsing
Protection
Turin, Italy
ermessecurity.com

Excelsecu (43)
PKI and Data Encryption
Shenzhen, China
excelsecu.com/en/index.
html

Exonar (52)
Data Discovery
Newbury, UK
exonar.com

Extenua (4)
Secure File Transfer
San Jose, CA, USA
extenua.com

FairWarning (168)
Cloud Data Security
Clearwater, FL, USA
fairwarning.com

FileOpen Systems (8)
DRM
Santa Cruz, CA, USA
fileopen.com

FinalCode (5)
IRM
San Jose, CA, USA
finalcode.com

Flying Cloud (8)
Data Flow Analytics
Santa Cruz, CA, USA
flyingcloudtech.com

Fornetix (23)
Key Management
Frederick, MD, USA
fornetix.com

FutureX (58)
Encryption HSM
Bulverde, TX, USA
futurex.com

Galaxkey (24)
Secure File and Message
Transfer
London, UK
galaxkey.com

GeoTrust Inc. (32)
Encryption
Mountain View, CA, USA
geotrust.com

GigaTrust (37)
Document Security
Herndon, VA, USA
gigatrust.com

Glitchi (1)
Secure Photo Sharing
Palo Alto, CA, USA
glitchi.me

Global Velocity (10)
Cloud DLP
St. Louis, MO, USA
globalvelocity.com

GoAnywhere (1)
Automated & Secure File
Transfer
Ashland, NE, USA
goanywhere.com

Gold Lock (1)
Mobile Encryption
Ramat Gan, Israel
secure.gold-lock.com

Hushmail (366)
Private Email
Vancouver, Canada
hushmail.com

Identify3D (26)
Design Data Encryption
San Francisco, CA, USA
identify3d.com

IdenTrust (part of HID Global) (68)
Certificate Authority
Fremont, CA, USA
identrust.com

InfoAssure (12)
Security for Documents
Chestertown, MD, USA
infoassure.net

Informatica (500)
Data Masking
Redwood City, CA, USA
informatica.com

**Information Security
Corporation** (17)
PKI
Oak Park, IL, USA
infoseccorp.com

infOsci (9)
Certificate Management
Washington, DC, USA
Ci4.us

Infosec Global (31)
Certificate Discovery
North York, Canada
infosecglobal.com

Inpher (23)
Processing of Private Data
New York, NY, USA
inpher.io

InQuest (25)
DLP
Arlington, VA, USA
inquest.net

Intercrypto
File Encryption
Seattle, WA, USA
intercrypto.com

Ionic Security (145)
Data Privacy & Protection
Atlanta, GA, USA
ionicsecurity.com

Ionu (2)
Secure Data Management
Los Gatos, CA, USA
ionu.com

ISARA (56)
Encryption
Waterloo, Canada
isara.com

IStorage (36)
Hardware Encryption
Perivale, UK
istorage-uk.com

Janusnet (11)
Data Classification
Milsons Point, Australia
janusnet.com

Kazuar (21)
Secure Work Environment
Tel Aviv, Israel
kazuar-tech.com

KeeeX (8)
Document Security
Marseille, France
keeex.me

KeepSafe (21)
Mobile Encryption
San Francisco, CA, USA
getkeepsafe.com

Kernelsec
Document Encryption
Shanghai, China
serpurity.com

KETS Quantum Security
(12)
Secure Communications
Bristol, UK
kets-quantum.com

Keyfactor (94)
PKI as a Service
Independence, OH, USA
keyfactor.com

KeyNexus (11)
Cloud Key Storage
Victoria, Canada
keynexus.net

Kindite (20)
Encryption
Tel Aviv, Israel
kindite.com

Kingston Technology
(1,384)
Encrypted Storage
Fountain Valley, CA, USA
kingston.com

KMSChain (3)
Cloud Key Management
Yerevan, Armenia
kmschain.com

KoolSpan, Inc. (43)
Secure Communications
Bethesda, MD, USA
koolspan.com

Kriptos (17)
Data Classification
Sausalito, CA, USA
kriptos.io

Kryptus (48)
HSM
Campinas São Paulo, Brazil
kryptus.com

Kyber Security (3)
Software Protection
Montreal, Canada
kybersecurity.com

LeapFILE (7)
Secure File Transfer
Cupertino, CA, USA
leapfile.com

LeapYear Technologies (28)
Analyze Private Informa-
tion
Berkeley, CA, USA
leapyear.ai

Ledger (176)
USB Key Storage for Cryp-
tocurrencies
Paris, France
ledger.com

Lepide (158)
Data Discovery
Austin, TX, USA
lepide.com

LockLizard Ltd. (1)
IRM
London, UK
locklizard.com

LOKD (7)
Secure Communications
Larnaca, Cyprus
lokd.com

LSoft Technologies (5)
Erasure
Mississauga, Canada
lsoft.net

Lybero.net (10)
Multi-admin Key Autho-
rization
Villers-Lès-Nancy, France
lybero.net

Maidsafe (1)
Blockchain-like Payment
System
Ayr, UK
maidsafe.net

MyWorkDrive (12)
Secure File Storage
San Francisco, CA, USA
myworkdrive.com

nCipher (268)
Encryption
Cambridge, UK
ncipher.com

nCrypted Cloud (27)
Encryption
Boston, MA, USA
ncryptedcloud.com

Netlib (4)
Encryption Database
Stamford, CT, USA
netlib.com

Note: Numbers in parenthesis indicate employee count

Netsfere
Secure Messaging
Arlington Heights, IL, USA
netsfere.com

NeuShield (6)
Data Mirroring for Ransomware Recovery
Fremont, CA, USA
neushield.com

NextLabs (144)
IRM
San Mateo, CA, USA
nextlabs.com

NitroKey (2)
Encryption
Berlin, Germany
nitrokey.com

Nu Quantum (5)
Quantum Cryptography
London, UK
nu-quantum.com

Nucleus Cyber (9)
Data Discovery and Classification
Boston, MA, USA
nucleuscyber.com

NuCypher (18)
Credential Encryption
San Francisco, CA, USA
nucypher.com

Nuro (5)
Secure Messaging
Tel Aviv, Israel
nuro.im

nwStor (8)
Network & Cloud Data Security
Shatin, Hong Kong
nwstor.com

ODI (11)
Document Scrubbing
Rosh HaAyin, Israel
odi-x.com

Okera (46)
Data Governance
San Francisco, CA, USA
okera.com

Onapsis Inc. (209)
SAP Security
Boston, MA, USA
onapsis.com

Paymetric (133)
Encryption
Atlanta, GA, USA
paymetric.com

Penango (2)
Encryption for Gmail & Google Apps
Los Angeles, CA, USA
penango.com

Perfectcloud (10)
Secure Cloud Storage
Toronto, Canada
perfectcloud.io

Perpetual Encryption
OTP Encryption
London, UK
perpetualencryption.com

PKWARE (142)
Data Privacy
Milwaukee, WI, USA
pkware.com

PreVeil (23)
File and Email Encryption
Boston, MA, USA
preveil.com

PrimeKey Solutions (61)
PKI & Digital Signature Solutions
Solna, Sweden
primekey.com

Privacera (22)
Data Governance
Fremont, CA, USA
privacera.com

Privacy Analytics (101)
Healthcare Data Privacy
Ottawa, Canada
privacy-analytics.com

Privitar (109)
Data Masking
London, UK
privitar.com

Privus (9)
Secure Communications
Zug, Switzerland
privus.global

Prophecy International (32)
Secure File Transfer
Adelaide, Australia
prophecyinternational.com

ProtectStar (2)
Erasure
Miami, FL, USA
protectstar.com/en

Pushfor, Inc. (19)
Secure Content Sharing
Wimbledon, UK
pushfor.com

QEDit (24)
Data Privacy
Tel Aviv, Israel
qed-it.com

QEYnet (3)
Data Security
Vaughan, Canada
qeynet.com

Qredo (13)
App Encryption
London, UK
qredo.com

QuantLR (4)
Data Security, Quantum Key Distribution
Jerusalem, Israel
quantlr.com

Quantum Digital Solutions (3)
Key Management
Los Angeles, CA, USA
qdsc.us

Quantum Xchange (12)
Quantum Key Distribution
Newton, MA, USA
quantumxc.com

Quintessence Labs (38)
Quantum Optics & Cryptographic Security
Deakin, Australia
quintessencelabs.com

Quside (19)
Quantum RNG
Barcelona, Spain
quside.com

Racktop Systems (42)
Secure Storage
Fulton, MD, USA
racktopsystems.com

Rambus (881)
Semiconductor Security R&D
Sunnyvale, CA, USA
rambus.com

Red Database Security (2)
Database Security
Heusenstamm, Germany
red-database-security.de

ReSec Technologies (14)
Document Scrubbing
Caesarea, Israel
resec.co

Rivetz (19)
Secure Communications
Richmond, MD, USA
rivetz.com

Rubicon Labs (12)
Key Management
San Francisco, CA, USA
rubiconlabs.io

Safe-T (56)
Secure Data Exchange
Herzliya Pituach, Israel
safe-t.com

SafeLogic (8)
Cryptographic Libraries
Palo Alto, CA, USA
safelogic.com

SafelyLocked (2)
Encryption
Atlanta, GA, USA
safelylocked.com

SafeNet AT (64)
Encryption
Abingdon, MD, USA
safenetat.com

SafeUM (4)
Private Messenger
Reykjavík, Iceland
safeum.com

Saife (1)
Secure Data Transfer
Chandler, AZ, USA
saifeinc.com

SaltDNA (16)
Secure Communications
Belfast, UK
saltdna.com

Sasa Software (17)
File Scrubbing
Sasa, Israel
sasa-software.com

Seagate Technology (100)
Encryption
Cupertino, CA, USA
seagate.com

Searchguard (5)
Security for Elasticsearch
Berlin, Germany
search-guard.com

Seclab (19)
Secure File Transfer
Montpellier, France
seclab-security.com

Seclore (199)
IRM
Mumbai, India
seclore.com

Secomba (12)
Encryption for Dropbox
Augsburg, Germany
boxcryptor.com/en

Secret Double Octopus (32)
Two-Channel Encryption
Tel Aviv, Israel
doubleoctopus.com

Sectigo (156)
PKI CA
Roseland, NJ, USA
sectigo.com

Secudrives (1)
Data Encryption & Destruction
Seoul, South Korea
secudrives.com

Secure Channels (24)
Encryption
Irvine, CA, USA
securechannels.com

SecureAge Technology (25)
Encryption
West Chester, PA, USA
secureage.com

Secured Communication (20)
Secure Communications
San Francisco, CA, USA
securedcommunications.com

SecureData, Inc. (65)
Encrypted Hard Drives
Los Angeles, CA, USA
securedata.com

SecurelyShare (26)
Vault
Indira Nagar, India
securelyshare.com

SecureTeam (1)
DRM
Rishon LeZion, Israel
secureteam.net

SECURITI.ai (130)
Discovery for PII
San Jose, CA, USA
securiti.ai

Security First (33)
Data Security for Documents
Rancho Santa Margarita, CA, USA
securityfirstcorp.com

Security Weaver (88)
IRM
Lehi, UT, USA
securityweaver.com

SecurityFirst (31)
IRM
Rancho Santa Margarita, CA, USA
securityfirst.com

SecurStar (6)
Full Disk Encryption
Munich, Germany
securestar.com

Secusmart (52)
Secure Mobile Phone
Düsseldorf, Germany
secusmart.com

Secutech Solutions (8)
USB Token Security
North Ryde, Australia
esecutech.com

Secuware (1)
Database Security
London, UK
secuware.uk

Seed Protocol (3)
Encryption
Athens, OH, USA
seed-protocol.com

SendSafely (7)
Secure File and Message Transfer
New York, NY, USA
sendsafely.com

SendThisFile (4)
Secure File Transfer
Wichita, KS, USA
sendthisfile.com

Senetas Corporation Limited (44)
Network Encryptors
South Melbourne, Australia
senetas.com

Sentrycom (2)
Encryption
Haifa, Israel
sentry-com.net

Sepior (17)
Encryption and Key Management
Aarhus, Denmark
sepior.com

SertintyONE (6)
IRM
Nashville, TN, USA
sertintyone.com

ShareVault (27)
Vault
Los Gatos, CA, USA
sharevault.com

Sherpas Cyber Security Group (3)
Secure Storage
Gaithersburg, MD, USA
sherpascyber.com

SHIELD Crypto Systems (3)
Encryption
Toronto, Canada
shieldcryptosystems.com

Note: Numbers in parenthesis indicate employee count

Silent Circle (37)
Encrypted Communication
Fairfax, VA, USA
silentcircle.com

Skymatic (4)
Data Security
Sankt Augustin, Germany
skymatic.de

South River Technologies
(11)
Secure File Transfer
Annapolis, MD, USA
southrivertech.com

SpeQtral (11)
Quantum Key Distribution
Singapore, Singapore
speqtral.space

Spideroak (37)
Zero Knowledge Storage
Mission, KS, USA
spideroak.com

**Spirion (was Identity
Finder)** (107)
Data Discovery
St. Petersburg, FL, USA
spirion.com

SPYRUS (27)
Encryption
San Jose, CA, USA
spyrus.com

SQR Systems (10)
Secure Communications
London, UK
sqrsystems.com

**SSH Communications
Security** (145)
Secure File Transfer
Helsinki, Finland
ssh.com

SSL.com (20)
Certificate Authority
Houston, TX, USA
ssl.com

Stealth Software (7)
Encryption
Scottsdale, AZ, USA
stealth-soft.com

Steganos (1)
Encryption
Munich, Germany
steganos.com/en

Storro (5)
Encrypted Storage
Hengelo, Netherlands
storro.com

StrongKey (18)
Key Management
Durham, NC, USA
strongkey.com

Sttarx (3)
Network Encryption
Washington, DC, USA
sttarx.com

Surety (40)
Data Protection
Naples, FL, USA
surety.com

Surevine (27)
Secure Collaboration
Guildford, UK
surevine.com

SwissSign Group
Certificate Authority
Glattbrugg, Switzerland
swisssign.com

Symphony (315)
Secure Messaging and
Collaboration
Palo Alto, CA, USA
Symphony.com

Syncplicity by Axway (57)
Secure File Storage
Santa Clara, CA, USA
syncplicity.com

Syneidis (15)
File Encryption
Barcelona, Spain
syneidis.com

TechR2 (29)
Erasure
Reynoldsburg, OH, USA
techr2.com

TecSec (23)
Key Management
McLean, VA, USA
tecsec.com

TELEGRID Technologies
(5)
Network Encryption Mon-
itoring
Florham Park, NJ, USA
telegrid.com

TeraDact (7)
Secure Information
Sharing
Missoula, MT, USA
teradact.com

Tesseract (29)
Encryption
Mexico City, Mexico
tesseract.mx

TIBCO Software Inc. (500)
Big Data Security
Palo Alto, CA, USA
tibco.com

TokenEx (32)
Tokenization
Edmond, OK, USA
tokenex.com

Topia Technology (19)
Encryption with Shredding
Tacoma, WA, USA
topiatechnology.com

**Torsion Information
Security** (7)
File Access Monitoring
London, UK
torsionis.com

Tortuga Logic (25)
Hardware Root of Trust
Verification
San Diego, CA, USA
tortugalogic.com

Townsend Security (21)
Encryption and Tokeni-
zation
Olympia, WA, USA
townsendsecurity.com

Treebox Solutions (22)
Secure Communications
Singapore, Singapore
treeboxsolutions.com

Tresorit (115)
Secure File Transfer
Budapest, Hungary
tresorit.com

Tresys (52)
Data Scrubbing of Remov-
able Media
Columbia, MD, USA
tresys.com

Trinity Future-In (11)
DRM for Web
Bangalore, India
trifuturein.com

Trivalent (12)
File Encryption
Annapolis, MD, USA
trivalent.co

TrueVault (10)
Secure Data Storage
San Francisco, CA, USA
truevault.com

TrustLayers (1)
IRM
Cambridge, MA, USA
trustlayers.com

Ubiq Security (27)
Encryption
San Diego, CA, USA
ubiqsecurity.com

ULedger (5)
Blockchain Applied to Data
Boise, ID, USA
uledger.co

Unbound Tech (45)
Key Management
New York, NY, USA
unboundtech.com

Unitrends (239)
Encryption
Burlington, MA, USA
unitrends.com

Utimaco (424)
Encryption HSMs
Aachen, Germany
utimaco.com/en/home

Validian (1)
Encryption
Nepean, Canada
validian.com

Vandyke Software (20)
Secure File Transfer
Albuquerque, NM, USA
vandyke.com

Varonis (1,396)
File Collaboration & Data
Protection
New York, NY, USA
varonis.com

Vaultize (31)
IRM Content Sharing
San Francisco, CA, USA
vaultize.com

Venafi (303)
Key Management
Salt Lake City, UT, USA
venafi.com

Vera (116)
IRM
Palo Alto, CA, USA
vera.com

Verimatrix (281)
DRM for Video
San Diego, CA, USA
verimatrix.com

Very Good Security (96)
Vault
San Francisco, CA, USA
verygoodsecurity.com

VIA3 Corperation (18)
Secure Messaging
Scottsdale, AZ, USA
via3.com

Virgil Security (40)
End-to-End Application
Encryption
Manassas, VA, USA
virgilsecurity.com

Virtru (118)
Google Apps & Email
Privacy
Washington, DC, USA
virtru.com

Vitrium (20)
DRM
Vancouver, Canada
vitrium.com

Vo1t (9)
Secure Storage for Cryptocurrencies
London, UK
vo1t.io

Watchtower AI (12)
Data Discovery
San Francisco, CA, USA
watchtower.ai

White Canyon Inc. (24)
Erasure
American Fork, UT, USA
whitecanyon.com

Wickr (43)
Secure Communications
San Francisco, CA, USA
wickr.com

Widevine Technologies (6)
DRM
Kirkland, WA, USA
widevine.com

WindTalker Security (8)
File Encryption and
Sharing
Cumming, GA, USA
windtalkersecurity.com

WinMagic Inc. (108)
Encryption
Mississauga, Canada
winmagic.com

Wirewheel (51)
Customer Data Protection
Arlington, VA, USA
wirewheel.io

Woleet (15)
Blockchain for Signatures
Rennes, France
woleet.io

Workshare (213)
File Encryption and
Sharing
London, UK
workshare.com

WWN Software LLC (10)
Encrypted Data Sharing
Washington, DC, USA
wwnsoftware.com

Xahive (5)
Secure Messaging
Ottawa, Canada
xahive.com

Xenarmor (1)
SSL Certificate Manage-
ment
Bangalore, India
xenarmor.com

XOOUi (1)
Encryption
State College, PA, USA
xooui.com

YazamTech (3)
File Scrubbing
Ra'anana, Israel
yazamtech.com

Zapper Software (1)
DRM
Rosedale, Canada
zappersoftware.com/home.
html

Zecurion (43)
Database Security
Moscow, Russia
zecurion.com

Zettaset (31)
Encryption, Databases
Mountain View, CA, USA
zettaset.com

Ziroh Labs (17)
Data Security
Bangalore, India
ziroh.com

Zix Corp. (391)
Secure Messaging
Dallas, TX, USA
zixcorp.com

DECEPTION

Acalvio Technologies (64)
Deception
Santa Clara, CA, USA
acalvio.com

Allure Security (12)
Document Decoys, An-
ti-website Spoofing
New York, NY, USA
alluresecurity.com

Attivo Networks (165)
Deception
Fremont, CA, USA
attivonetworks.com

Bibu Labs (3)
Decoys
Toronto, Canada
bibulabs.com

Note: Numbers in parentheses indicate employee count

CounterCraft (26)
Deception
Donostia-San Sebastian,
Spain
countercraft.eu

CYBERTRAP (20)
Deception
Wiener Neustadt, Austria
cybertrap.com

Cymmetria (23)
Deception (Honeypots)
Tel Aviv, Israel
cymmetria.com

Deceptive Bytes (3)
Deception
Holon, Israel
deceptivebytes.com

illusive Networks (112)
Deception
New York, NY, USA
illusivenetworks.com

PacketViper (23)
Deception
Pittsburgh, PA, USA
packetviper.com

**Ridgeback Network
Defense** (14)
Deception
Baltimore, MD, USA
ridgebacknet.com

**Smokescreen
Technologies Pvt. Ltd.** (32)
Complete Deception
Platform
Mumbai, India
smokescreen.io

Thinkst Canary (9)
Target Agents Deployed in
Operations
Edinvale, South Africa
canary.tools

TrapX Security (37)
Deception
San Jose, CA, USA
trapx.com

EMAIL SECURITY

Abnormal Security (21)
Anti-phishing
San Francisco, CA, USA
abnormalsecurity.com

Agari (184)
Email Security
Foster City, CA, USA
agari.com

**AnubisNetworks
(BitSight)** (35)
Email Protection
Lisbon, Portugal
anubisnetworks.com

AppRiver (221)
Email Security
Gulf Breeze, FL, USA
appriver.com

Aquila Technology (16)
Anti-phishing
Burlington, MA, USA
aquilatc.com

AquilAI
Anti-phishing
Cheltenham, UK
aquil.ai

Area 1 Security (78)
Anti-phishing
Redwood City, CA, USA
area1security.com

CipherMail (1)
Secure Email
Amsterdam, Netherlands
ciphermail.com

ClearedIn (16)
Anti-phishing
Los Altos, CA, USA
clearedin.com

Clearswift (193)
Email Security
Theale, UK
clearswift.com

Cloudmask (10)
Email Security
Ottawa, Canada
cloudmask.com

Criptext (12)
Secure Email
New York, NY, USA
criptext.com

Cryptshare (50)
Encrypted File and Email
on Azure
Freiburg, Germany
cryptshare.com

Cybonet (was PineApp)
(41)
AV and Sandboxing
Matam, Israel
cybonet.com/en

DataMotion (44)
Email Security
Florham Park, NJ, USA
datamotion.com

DefiniSec (1)
Email Encryption and
Backup
El Cerrito, CA, USA
definisec.com

Edgewave (62)
Email Security
La Jolla, CA, USA
edgewave.com

Egress (198)
Email Security
London, UK
egress.com

Emailage (174)
Email Security
Chandler, AZ, USA
emailage.com

FuseMail (56)
Email Security
Burnaby, Canada
fusemail.com

Gatefy (12)
Email Security
Miami, FL, USA
gatefy.com

GFI Software (417)
Anti-spam
Austin, TX, USA
gfi.com

GhostMail (1)
Secure Email
Zug, Switzerland
ghostmail.com

Graphus (12)
Anti-phishing
Reston, VA, USA
graphus.ai

GreatHorn (35)
Anti-phishing
Waltham, MA, USA
greathorn.com

Halon (22)
Anti-spam
Gothenburg, Sweden
halon.io

Hexamail (2)
Anti-spam and Anti-virus
Pensham, UK
hexamail.com

Hornetsecurity (73)
Managed Email Security
Hannover, Germany
hornetsecurity.com

IDECSI (22)
Email Monitoring and
Auditing
Paris, France
idecsi.com/en

Inky (25)
Anti-phishing
Rockville, MD, USA
inky.com

Lavabit (182)
Encrypted Email
Dallas, TX, USA
lavabit.com

Libraesva (13)
Email Security
Lecco, Italy
libraesva.com

MailCleaner (7)
Email Security
Saint-Sulpice, Switzerland
mailcleaner.net

MailInBlack (53)
Anti-spam
Marseille, France
mailinblack.com

Mailspect (1)
Email Security
Tarrytown, NY, USA
mailspect.com

MessageControl (15)
Anti-phishing
Chicago, IL, USA
mailcontrol.net

Messageware (16)
OWA Security
Mississauga, Canada
messageware.com

Mimecast (1,501)
Microsoft Exchange Email
Security
London, UK
mimecast.com

NeoCertified (10)
Secure Email
Centennial, CO, USA
neocertified.com

OnDMARC (15)
DMARC
London, UK
ondmarc.com

Origone (5)
Anti-phishing
Paris, France
orisecure.com

Paladin Cyber (14)
Anti-phishing
San Francisco, CA, USA
meetpaladin.com

Perception Point (35)
Anti-phishing
Tel Aviv, Israel
perception-point.io

Perseus. (23)
Anti-phishing
Berlin, Germany
perseus.de

PhishCloud (9)
Anti-phishing
Renton, WA, USA
phishcloud.com

PIXM, Inc. (9)
Anti-phishing
Brooklyn, NY, USA
pixm.net

Process Software (21)
Email Security
Framingham, MA, USA
process.com

Proofpoint, Inc. (2,764)
Anti-malware, Anti-spam,
and Anti-phishing
Sunnyvale, CA, USA
proofpoint.com

RedMarlin, Inc. (8)
Phishing Detection
Mountain View, CA, USA
redmarlin.ai

SegaSec (26)
Anti-phishing
Toronto, Canada
segasec.com

Sendio (27)
Anti-spam
Newport Beach, CA, USA
sendio.com

Seppmail (9)
Email Encryption
Neuenhof, Switzerland
seppmail.com

SlashNext (97)
Anti-phishing
Pleasanton, CA, USA
slashnext.com

SMX (301)
Email Security
Auckland, New Zealand
smxemail.com

Tessian (124)
Anti-phishing
New York, NY, USA
tessian.com

Trustifi (28)
Encryption and An-
ti-phishing
Las Vegas, NV, USA
trustifi.com

Vade Secure (112)
Anti-phishing
San Francisco, CA, USA
vadesecure.com

Valimail (108)
Anti-phishing
San Francisco, CA, USA
valimail.com

Zertificon Solutions (49)
Secure Email
Berlin, Germany
zertificon.com/en

Zivver (83)
Encrypted Email
Amsterdam, Netherlands
zivver.com

ENDPOINT

0 Patch (10)
Micropatching
London, UK
0patch.com

1E (424)
Endpoint Detection and
Response (EDR)
London, UK
1e.com

Abatis UK Ltd. (3)
Endpoint Protection
Egham, UK
abatis-hdf.com

Absolute Software (578)
Mobile Device Security
Vancouver, Canada
absolute.com/en

Active Fortress
Endpoint Protection
Tampa, FL, USA
activefortress.com

Adaptiva (47)
Configuration Manage-
ment
Kirkland, WA, USA
adaptiva.com

Adaptive Mobile (133)
Mobile Device Security
Dublin, Ireland
adaptivemobile.com

Adaware (51)
Anti-virus
Montreal, Canada
adaware.com

Ahnlab (429)
Anti-virus
Gyeonggi-do, South Korea
ahnlab.com

alcide (29)
Container Security
Tel Aviv, Israel
alcide.io

Note: Numbers in parentheses indicate employee count

Amtel, Inc. (52)
Mobile Device Security
Rockville, MD, USA
amtelnet.com

Antiy Labs (1)
Malware Analysis
Beijing, China
antiy.net

Aporeto (44)
Container Security
San Jose, CA, USA
aporeto.com

Apozy (4)
Content URL Filtering
San Francisco, CA, USA
apozy.com

Apperian (11)
Mobile App Security
Boston, MA, USA
apperian.com

AppGuard (40)
Application Containment
Chantilly, VA, USA
appguard.us

AppMobi (14)
Mobile App Protection
Poughkeepsie, NY, USA
appmobi.com

Aqua Security Software, Inc. (136)
Container Security
Ramat Gan, Israel
aquasec.com

Assac Networks (1)
Mobile Device Protection
Ramat HaSharon, Israel
assacnetworks.com

Atomicorp (15)
Host Intrusion Prevention
Chantilly, VA, USA
atomicorp.com

Autonomic Software (13)
Patch Management
Danville, CA, USA
autonomic-software.com

Avast Software (1,390)
Anti-virus
Prague, Czech Republic
avast.com

Aves Network Security (6)
Temporary Patching
London, UK
avesnetsec.com

Avira (454)
Anti-virus
Tettnang, Germany
avira.com

Avnos (27)
Application Whitelisting
Singapore, Singapore
avnos.io

Axiado (9)
Secure Hardware
San Jose, CA, USA
axiado.com

Beachhead Solutions, Inc. (15)
MDM
San Jose, CA, USA
beachheadsolutions.com

Better Mobile App Security (19)
Mobile App Security
New York, NY, USA
better.mobi

BitDam (24)
Anti-malware
Tel Aviv, Israel
bitdam.com

BitDefender (1,600)
Anti-virus
Bucharest, Romania
bitdefender.com

BitNinja (18)
Server Protection
London, UK
bitninja.io

BlackFog (5)
EDR
Cheyenne, WY, USA
blackfog.com

BlueCedar (39)
Mobile Device Protection
San Francisco, CA, USA
bluecedar.com

BlueRisc (7)
Binary Code Vulnerability
Analysis
Amherst, MA, USA
bluerisc.com

Bromium (acquired by HP) (131)
Endpoint Sandbox
Cupertino, CA, USA
bromium.com

Bufferzone (21)
Endpoint Sandbox
Giv'atayim, Israel
bufferzonesecurity.com

BullGuard Ltd. (129)
Anti-virus
London, UK
bullguard.com

CalCom (28)
Server Hardening via
MSFT System Center
Lod, Israel
calcomsoftware.com

Carbon Black (acquired by VMWare) (1,177)
EDR
Waltham, MA, USA
carbonblack.com

Cellebrite (789)
Mobile Forensics
Petah Tikva, Israel
cellebrite.com

Cellrox (15)
Mobile Virtualization
Tel Aviv, Israel
cellrox.com

Cezurity (9)
EDR
St. Petersburg, Russia
cezurity.com

Cheetah Mobile (1,948)
Android AV
Beijing, China
cmcm.com

Cicada Security Technology (2)
Device Theft Prevention
Montreal, Canada
cicadasecurity.com

CloudPassage (60)
Cloud Host Security
San Francisco, CA, USA
cloudpassage.com

CMD (33)
Linux Security
Vancouver, Canada
cmd.com

ControlGuard (8)
Device Control
Herzlia Pituach, Israel
atrog.com

CrowdStrike (1,513)
EDR
Sunnyvale, CA, USA
crowdstrike.com

Cupp Computing (9)
Endpoint Security
Palo Alto, CA, USA
cuppcomputing.com

Cybellum (9)
In-Memory Prevention
Tel Aviv-Yafo, Israel
cybellum.com

Cyber 2.0 (16)
EDR
Tel Aviv, Israel
cyber20.com

CyberPoint International
(54)
File Artifact Detection
(mostly PS)
Baltimore, MD, USA
cyberpointllc.com

**Cylance (part of
BlackBerry)** (888)
EDR
Irvine, CA, USA
cylance.com

CyRadar
EDR
Hanoi, Vietnam
cyradar.com

Deep Instinct (91)
Endpoint Machine Learning
Tel Aviv, Israel
deepinstinct.com

Digital Immunity (12)
System Hardening
Burlington, MA, USA
digitalimmunity.com

Divvy Cloud Corp. (48)
Container Security
Arlington, VA, USA
divvycloud.com

Dr. Web (1)
Android AV
Moscow, Russia
drweb.com

DriveLock (47)
Endpoint Device Control,
DLP
Munich, Germany
drivelock.com

Druva (643)
Endpoint Data Protection
& Governance
Sunnyvale, CA, USA
druva.com

eAgency (10)
Mobile Security
Newport Beach, CA, USA
eagency.com

Eclypsium (23)
Firmware Protection
Beaverton, OR, USA
eclypsium.com

Emsisoft (27)
Android AV
Chicago, IL, USA
emsisoft.com

Entreda (22)
Endpoint Monitoring and
Control
Santa Clara, CA, USA
entreda.com

EScan (187)
AV
Mumbai, India
escanav.com

ESET (156)
Anti-virus
San Diego, CA, USA
eset.com

**eSphere Security
Solutions Pvt** (2)
Mobile Defense
Ahmedabad, India
espheresecurity.com

ESTsoft (402)
Android AV
Seoul, South Korea
estsoft.com

Everspin (15)
Dynamic Image Replacement
Seoul, South Korea
everspin.global

Exosphere, Inc. (1)
Endpoint Protection
Campbell, CA, USA
exospheresecurity.com

Ezmcom (21)
Security Hardware
Santa Clara, CA, USA
ezmcom.com

F-Secure (4,545)
AV
Helsinki, Finland
f-secure.com

Famoc (42)
MDM
Midleton, Ireland
fancyfon.com

Faronics Technologies Inc.
(133)
Endpoint Security
Vancouver, Canada
faronics.com

FirstPoint Mobile Guard
(12)
Mobile Device Protection
Netanya, Israel
firstpoint-mg.com

FixMeStick (17)
AV
Montreal, Canada
fixmestick.com

G Data Software (285)
Anti-virus
Bochum, Germany
gdatasoftware.com

GlassWire
Endpoint Firewall
Austin, TX, USA
glasswire.com

Graphite Software (14)
Mobile Containers
Ottawa, Canada
graphitesoftware.com

Green Hills Software (1,183)
Secure OS
Santa Barbara, CA, USA
ghs.com

Guardian Digital Inc. (2)
Secure Linux
Midland Park, NJ, USA
guardiandigital.com

Hauri (3)
Anti-virus
Seoul, South Korea
hauri.net

Help Systems (596)
IBM iSecurity Products
Eden Prairie, MN, USA
helpsystems.com

Hexis Cyber Solutions (11)
EDR
Hanover, MD, USA
hexiscyber.com

Humming Heads (2)
Whitelisting
Tokyo, Japan
hummingheads.co.jp/english/product/dep/index.
html

Hypori (12)
Mobile Device Management
Austin, TX, USA
hypori.com

Hysolate (40)
Workspace Isolation via
VMs
Tel Aviv-Yafo, Israel
hysolate.com

**Ikarus Security Software
GmbH** (25)
Android AV
Vienna, Austria
ikarussecurity.com

Illumio (337)
Endpoint Monitoring
Sunnyvale, CA, USA
illumio.com

Note: Numbers in parentheses indicate employee count

Infocyte (37)
Endpoint Detection
Austin, TX, USA
infocyte.com

Infosec Inc. (16)
Mainframe Event Monitoring
Centreville, VA, USA
infosecinc.com

INSIDE Secure (200)
Smartphone & Mobile
Device Security
Meyreuil, France
insidesecure.com

itWatch (1)
Endpoint Security & Data
Loss Prevention
Munich, Germany
itwatch.info

Ivanti (1,461)
Endpoint Management
South Jordan, UT, USA
ivanti.com

Janus Technologies, Inc.
(6)
BIOS Protection
Sunnyvale, CA, USA
janustech.com

K7Computing (330)
AV
Sholinganallur, India
k7computing.com

Kandji (10)
MDM for Apple Devices
San Diego, CA, USA
kandji.io

Kaprica Security (3)
Mobile Device Security
College Park, MD, USA
kaprica.com

Kaspersky Lab (3,608)
Anti-virus
Moscow, Russia
kaspersky.com

Kaymera (38)
Mobile Defense
Herzliya, Israel
kaymera.com

KernelCare (1)
Linux Kernel Patching
Palo Alto, CA, USA
kernelcare.com

KromTech (625)
Android AV
London, UK
kromtech.com

Lookout (412)
Mobile Security for Android & iOS Apps
San Francisco, CA, USA
lookout.com

**Lynx Software
Technologies** (86)
Containers
San Jose, CA, USA
lynx.com

Malwarebytes (709)
Anti-virus
Santa Clara, CA, USA
malwarebytes.org

Matrix42 (250)
EDR
Paris, France
matrix42.com

Max Secure Software (95)
Endpoint Protection
Pune, India
maxpcsecure.com

MBX (134)
Appliance & Embedded
Systems Security
Libertyville, IL, USA
mbx.com

McAfee (9,663)
AV
Santa Clara, CA, USA
mcafee.com

**Minded Security UK
Limited** (22)
Malware Detection
Rome, Italy
mindedsecurity.com

Minerva Labs (25)
Malware Prevention
Petah Tikva, Israel
minerva-labs.com

MobileIron (973)
Mobile Device & App
Security
Mountain View, CA, USA
mobileiron.com

Mobiwol
Firewall for Android
Tel Aviv, Israel
mobiwol.com

Moka5 (6)
Virtual Desktops for PCs
and Macs
Redwood City, CA, USA
Moka5.com

Morphisec (83)
Endpoint Obfuscation
Be'er Sheva, Israel
morphisec.com

MyPermissions
Control Data Privacy on
Mobile Devices
Ramat Gan, Israel
mypermissions.com

NanoVMs, Inc. (5)
Secure Containers
San Francisco, CA, USA
nanovms.com

Navaho Technologies (12)
Hardened Linux
Brockenhurst, UK
navaho.co.uk

NeuVector, Inc. (28)
Container Security
San Jose, CA, USA
neuvector.com

Nokia (250)
Mobile Security
Espoo, Finland
networks.nokia.com

NowSecure (68)
Mobile Security
Chicago, IL, USA
nowsecure.com

NP Core (16)
EDR
Seoul, South Korea
npcore.com

nProtect (15)
Mobile
Guro-gu, South Korea
nprotect.com

Nyotron (62)
EDR
Herzliya, Israel
nyotron.com

Omniquad Ltd. (30)
Anti-spyware
London, UK
omniquad.com

One App
Android AV
oneappessentials.com

OPSWAT (205)
Endpoint Security
San Francisco, CA, USA
opswat.com

Panda Security (633)
Anti-virus
Bilbao, Spain
pandasecurity.com/usa

Patriot (55)
Mobile Device Security
Management
Frederick, MD, USA
patriot-tech.com

PC VARK (39)
Android AV
Jaipur, India
pcvark.com

PFP Cybersecurity (25)
Endpoint Protection (Power Anomoly)
Vienna, VA, USA
pfpcybersecurity.com

Phoenix Technologies (502)
Secure PC
Campbell, CA, USA
phoenix.com

PointSharp AB (13)
Mobile Security
Stockholm, Sweden
pointsharp.com

Polylogyx (9)
EDR with OSQuery
Pleasanton, CA, USA
polylogyx.com

PolySwarm (25)
Malware Detection
San Diego, CA, USA
polyswarm.io

Polyverse (25)
OS Randomizing
Bellevue, WA, USA
polyverse.io

Port80 Software (2)
IIS Security
San Diego, CA, USA
port80software.com

Portnox (32)
MDM
Ra'anana, Israel
portnox.com

Privacyware (1)
IIS Security
New Albany, OH, USA
privacyware.com

Privoro (38)
Hardened Cases for Mobile Phones
Chandler, AZ, USA
privoro.com

Promisec (40)
Endpoint Security Intelligence
Holon, Israel
promisec.com

Psafe Technology (102)
Anti-virus
San Francisco, CA, USA
psafe.com

Qihoo 360 Total Security (2,022)
AV
Beijing, China
360totalsecurity.com

Quick Heal (1,263)
Endpoint, Server (Linux), and UTM
Pune, India
quickheal.com

Qustodio (79)
Mobile Parental Controls
Redondo Beach, CA, USA
qustodio.com

Raz-Lee Security (20)
IBM iSeries Security
Herzliya, Israel
razlee.com

ReaQta (20)
EDR
Amsterdam, Netherlands
reaqta.com

Red Balloon Security (26)
Embedded Device Security
New York, NY, USA
redballoonsecurity.com

Red Canary (96)
Endpoint Detection
Denver, CO, USA
redcanary.com

Red Lambda (21)
Endpoint Security
Lake Mary, FL, USA
redlambda.com

Red Sift (38)
Open Platform
London, UK
redsift.com

Rether Networks Inc. (1)
Host Intrusion Prevention
Centereach, NY, USA
rether.com

Romad (43)
AV
Kiev, Ukraine
romad-systems.com

SafenSoft (7)
Endpoint Protection
Los Angeles, CA, USA
safensoft.com

SCIT Labs, Inc. (10)
Dynamic Image Replacement for Servers
Clifton, VA, USA
scitlabs.com

SDS (19)
z/OS Security
Minneapolis, MN, USA
sdsusa.com

SecPod Technologies (52)
EDR
Tulsa, OK, USA
secpod.com

Secured Universe (2)
Mobile Device Security
San Diego, CA, USA
secureduniverse.com

SecureIC (44)
Tools for Secure Chip Design
France
secureic.com

Sentegrity (8)
Mobile
Chicago, IL, USA
sentegrity.com

SentinelOne (329)
Endpoint Protection Platform
Mountain View, CA, USA
sentinelone.com

SentryBay (16)
Anti-malware
London, UK
sentrybay.com

Seqrite (21)
Protection and Encryption
Pune, India
seqrite.com

Sequitur Labs (12)
Embedded Security
Fall City, WA, USA
sequiturlabs.com

Sequretek (231)
AV
Mumbai, India
sequretek.com

Softwin SRL (195)
Anti-virus
Bucharest, Romania
softwin.ro

Sophos (3,408)
Anti-virus
Abingdon, UK
sophos.com

SparkCognition (247)
AV
Austin, TX, USA
sparkcognition.com

Spydex, Inc. (division of Edison Commerce Corp.) (1)
Anti-spyware
Wilmington, DE, USA
spydex.com

Stackrox (62)
Trusted Computing
Mountain View, CA, USA
stackrox.com

Note: Numbers in parentheses indicate employee count

STOPzilla by iS3 (1)
AV
Dover, DE, USA
stopzilla.com

Stratus Digital Systems (8)
Server Rotation
Eugene, OR, USA
stratusdigitalsystems.com

Styra (25)
Kubernetes Access Controls
Redwood City, CA, USA
styra.com

SUPERAntiSpyware (2)
Anti-spyware
Eugene, OR, USA
superantispyware.com

Symantec Corporation (acquired by Broadcom, 2019) (25,745)
Anti-virus
Mountain View, CA, USA
symantec.com

Syncdog (8)
Mobile Security
Reston, VA, USA
syncdog.com

Sysdig (227)
Kubernetes Security
Davis, CA, USA
sysdig.com

Tanium (952)
Endpoint Visibility and Control
Emeryville, CA, USA
tanium.com

TEHTRIS (37)
AV
San Francisco, CA, USA
tehtris.com

Tencent (650)
Android AV
Shenzhen, China
tencent.com

ThreatLocker
Whitelisting
Maitland, FL, USA
threatlocker.com

ThreatTrack Security (72)
Endpoint Security
Clearwater, FL, USA
threattracksecurity.com

Tigera (80)
Kubernetes Security
San Francisco, CA, USA
tigera.io

Total Defense (32)
PC, Mobile & Internet Security
Hauppauge, NY, USA
totaldefense.com

ToucanX
Endpoint Segmentation and Sandboxing
Southfield, MI, USA
toucanx.com

Trapmine (9)
Endpoint Security
Tallinn, Estonia
trapmine.com

Trend Micro (6,565)
Anti-virus
Irving, TX, USA
trendmicro.com

Trusted Knight (13)
Endpoint
Annapolis, MD, USA
trustedknight.com

TrustGo
Android AV
Santa Clara, CA, USA
trustgo.com

Trustless.ai (11)
Secure Device
Geneva, Switzerland
trustless.ai

Trustlook (19)
Malware Analysis
San Jose, CA, USA
trustlook.com

Trustonic (93)
Mobile App Protection
Austin, TX, USA
trustonic.com

TrustPort (14)
Android AV
Brno, Czech Republic
trustport.com/en

UM-Labs (10)
Hardened OS for Realtime Comms
London, UK
Um-labs.com

Valtx Cyber Securities (5)
Endpoint Hardening
Surprise, AZ, USA
valtx.com

Vanquish Labs, Inc. (29)
Anti-spam
Marlborough, MA, USA
vanquish.com

vArmour (103)
Server Security
Mountain View, CA, USA
varmour.com

Vaulto (3)
Mobile Security
Tel Aviv-Yafo, Israel
vaulto.co

Vinsula (2)
Endpoint Protection
Seattle, WA, USA
vinsula.com

Vipre (115)
AV for Desktops
Clearwater, FL, USA
vipre.com

Vir2us (11)
Virtual Environments
Petaluma, CA, USA
vir2us.com

Virsec (69)
Runtime Protection
San Jose, CA, USA
virsec.com

VKey (2)
Sandbox for Apps
Ottawa, Canada
v-key.com

VMWare (1200)
EDR
Palo Alto, CA, USA
vmware.com

Vysk (12)
Mobile Device Security
San Antonio, TX, USA
vysk.com

Webroot Software (acquired by Carbonite, 2019; then acquired by OpenText) (796)
Anti-malware
Broomfield, CO, USA
webroot.com

White Cloud Security (15)
Whitelisting
Austin, TX, USA
whitecloudsecurity.com

WithNetworks
EDR
Yongsan-gu, South Korea
withnetworks.com

WootCloud (17)
Device Control
San Jose, CA, USA
wootcloud.com

Zemana (33)
Android AV
Ankara, Turkey
zemana.com

Ziften (33)
Endpoint Visibility
Austin, TX, USA
ziften.com

Zimperium (164)
Mobile Device Security
Dallas, TX, USA
zimperium.com

FRAUD PREVENTION

Acceptto (33)
Behavior-Based Identity
Verification
Portland, OR, USA
acceptto.com

Adjust (290)
Bot Detection
Berlin, Germany
adjust.com

AllClear ID (149)
Identity Protection Service
Austin, TX, USA
allclearid.com

Arkose Labs (59)
Graduated Friction
San Francisco, CA, USA
arkoselabs.com

AUTHADA (14)
Fraud Prevention / Using
Mobile Identity
Darmstadt, Germany
authada.de

Behaviosec (41)
Behavior Monitoring
San Francisco, CA, USA
behaviosec.com

BioCatch (111)
Authentication Through
Behavior
Tel Aviv-Yafo, Israel
biocatch.com

Bottomline (500)
User Behavior Analytics
Portsmouth, NH, USA
bottomline.com

BrandShield (18)
Brand Abuse Discovery
Ramat HaSharon, Israel
brandshield.com

Buguroo (45)
Behavior Monitoring
Alcobendas, Spain
buguroo.com

Castle (51)
User-Trained Account
Access
San Francisco, CA, USA
castle.io

ciphertrace (28)
Anti-money Laudering
Menlo Park, CA, USA
ciphertrace.com

Cleafy (21)
Anti-fraud
Milan, Italy
cleafy.com

Cognito (6)
Intelligence-Based Authentication
Palo Alto, CA, USA
cognitohq.com

Confident Technologies
(3)
Anti-fraud CAPTCHAS
Solana Beach, CA, USA
confidenttechnologies.com

Control's Force (10)
Insider Fraud Detection
Detroit, MI, USA
controlsforce.com

DataDome (38)
Bot Detection
New York, NY, USA
datadome.co

DEVCON (14)
Ad Tech Security
Atlanta, GA, USA
devcondetect.com

DigitalResolve (5)
Activity Auditing
Norcross, GA, USA
digitalresolve.com

DomainSkate (2)
Brand Abuse Discovery
New York, NY, USA
domainskate.com

Early Warning (904)
Identity Assurance
Scottsdale, AZ, USA
earlywarning.com

EFTsure (14)
EFT Protection
North Sydney, Australia
home.eftsure.com.au

**Ethoca (acquired by
Mastercard)** (221)
Transaction Data
Toronto, Canada
ethoca.com

EZShield (Sontiq) (39)
Anti-fraud
Baltimore, MD, USA
ezshield.com

Feedzai (368)
Anti-fraud
San Mateo, CA, USA
feedzai.com

Forter (179)
Fraud Prevention
Tel Aviv-Yafo, Israel
Forter.com

FraudLabs (5)
Fraud Detection
Bayan Baru, Malaysia
fraudlabspro.com

Fraudmarc (6)
Email Fraud Prevention
Atlanta, GA, USA
fraudmarc.com

FRS Labs (18)
Fraud Detection
Bangalore, India
frslabs.com

Glimmerglass (17)
Cyber Terrorism & Fraud
Prevention
Hayward, CA, USA
glimmerglass.com

idwall (103)
Fraud Detection
São Paulo, Brazil
idwall.co

Impact (423)
Ad Tech Security
Santa Barbara, CA, USA
impact.com

Jumio (322)
Identity Verification
Palo Alto, CA, USA
jumio.com

Konduto (89)
Fraud Detection
São Paulo, Brazil
konduto.com

Kount (161)
Identity Verification
Boise, ID, USA
kount.com

Kryptaxe (2)
Account Takeover Protec-
tion
New York, NY, USA
kryptaxe.com

Maxmind (52)
Geolocation
Waltham, MA, USA
maxmind.com

Note: Numbers in parentheses indicate employee count

Nethone (44)
Anti-fraud
Warsaw, Poland
nethone.com

NICE Actimize (961)
Fraud Detection
Hoboken, NJ, USA
niceactimize.com

NS8 (80)
Anti-fraud
Las Vegas, NV, USA
ns8.com

nsKnox
Payment Verification
Tel Aviv, Israel
nsknox.net

NuData Security (101)
Online Fraud Detection
Vancouver, Canada
nudatasecurity.com

Oxford Biochronometrics
(12)
Click Fraud Prevention
London, UK
oxford-biochron.com

Panopticon Labs (4)
Virtual Identity Theft
Protection
Columbus, OH, USA
panopticonlabs.com

PasswordPing (13)
Compromised Credentials
Boulder, CO, USA
passwordping.com

Payfone (95)
Anti-fraud
New York, NY, USA
payfone.com

PistolStar Inc. (15)
Authentication
Bedford, NH, USA
pistolstar.com

Privakey, Inc. (10)
Transaction Intent
Philadelphia, PA, USA
privakey.com

Return Path (518)
Email Fraud Prevention
New York, NY, USA
returnpath.com

RevenueStream (4)
Revenue Stream Fraud
Prevention
Israel
revenue-stream.com

Rippleshot (15)
Fraud Detection
Chicago, IL, USA
rippleshot.com

Risk.Ident (62)
Fraud Detection
Hamburg, Germany
riskident.com

Riskified (335)
e-Commerce Transaction
Monitoring
Tel Aviv, Israel
riskified.com

Salviol Global Analytics
(17)
Fraud Detection
Reading, UK
salviol.com

SAS Institute (100)
Anti-fraud
Cary, NC, USA
sas.com

Scalarr (34)
Mobile Ad Fraud
Wilmington, DE, USA
scalarr.io

Secure Push (10)
Identity Assurance
Migdal Tefen, Israel
securepush.com

SentiLink (15)
Anti-fraud
San Francisco, CA, USA
sentilink.com

Sentropi (2)
Fraud Prevention
Ahmedabad, India
sentropi.com

Seon (15)
Fraud Detection
Budapest, Hungary
seon.io

Signifyd (281)
e-Commerce Fraud Pre-
vention
San Jose, CA, USA
signifyd.com

Subuno (2)
Fraud Prevention for SMB
Seattle, WA, USA
subuno.com

TargetProof (3)
Identity Verification &
Fraud Prevention
Atlanta, GA, USA
targetproof.com

The Media Trust (79)
Ad Tech Security
McLean, VA, USA
themediatrust.com

ThreatMetrix (260)
Fraud Prevention
San Jose, CA, USA
threatmetrix.com

Transmit Security (105)
Anti-fraud
Boston, MA, USA
transmitsecurity.com

Ubble.ai (31)
Identity Verification
Paris, France
ubble.ai

Unfraud (1)
Anti-fraud
Ariano Irpino, Italy
unfraud.com

VeriClouds (6)
Credential Stuffing Defense
Seattle, WA, USA
vericlouds.com

White Ops (115)
Ad Tech Security
New York, NY, USA
whiteops.com

Wontok (29)
Anti-fraud Technology
Pyrmont, Australia
wontok.com

GRC

3ami Network Security (1)
Activity Auditing
Wigan, UK
3ami.com

3CM
Cloud Compliance
3cm.io

6Scan (1)
Vulnerability Management
Miami Beach, FL, USA
6scan.com

@RISK Technologies (61)
Risk Measurement
Dallas, TX, USA
atrisktech.com

Access Data Corp. (250)
Forensics
Lindon, UT, USA
accessdata.com

Actifile (4)
DLP
Herzliya, Israel
actifile.com

Acuity Risk Management
(8)
Risk Management
London, UK
acuityrm.com

Acunetix (53)
Vunerability Scanner
(Web)
Mriehel, Malta
acunetix.com

ADF Solutions (53)
Forensics
Bethesda, MD, USA
adfsolutions.com

Aegify (19)
Risk Management
San Jose, CA, USA
aegify.com

Alert Logic (659)
Log Management
Houston, TX, USA
alertlogic.com

alertsec (5)
Encryption Monitoring for
Third Parties
Palo Alto, CA, USA
alertsec.com

Allgress (42)
Compliance
Livermore, CA, USA
allgress.com

Alyne (34)
Risk Measurement
Munich, Germany
alyne.com

Anitian (31)
Compliance Automation
Portland, OR, USA
anitian.com

Apptega (11)
Compliance Platform
Atlanta, GA, USA
apptega.com

Aptible (40)
Compliance Management
San Francisco, CA, USA
aptible.com

Apvera (12)
User Activity Monitoring
Singapore, Singapore
apvera.com

Arama Tech (4)
Compliance Controls
Glostrop, Denmark
aramatech.com

Archimigo (7)
Compliance Management
Melbourne, Australia
archimigo.io

ArcMail Technology (13)
Email Archiving
Shreveport, LA, USA
arcmail.com

Arcon (342)
Rights Management
Mumbai, India
arconnet.com

AristotleInsight (24)
Discovery and Analysis of
Assets
Onalaska, WI, USA
aristotleinsight.com

Atomic Mole (2)
Risk Analytics & Manage-
ment
Rockville, MD, USA
atomicmole.com

Automox (57)
Patch Management
Boulder, CO, USA
automox.com

Axio (52)
Risk Management
New York, NY, USA
axio.com

Axiom Cyber Solutions (3)
Vulnerability Scanner
Las Vegas, NV, USA
axiomcyber.com

Axway (2,035)
Secure File Transfer
Phoenix, AZ, USA
axway.com

Balbix (52)
Asset Management
San Jose, CA, USA
balbix.com

Baramundi Software (98)
Endpoint Management
Augsburg, Germany
baramundi.com

Barillet (24)
Manager of Managers
Be'er Sheva, Israel
barillet.co.il

Bay Dynamics (79)
Information Risk Intelli-
gence
New York, NY, USA
baydynamics.com

Beauceron (24)
Risk Measurement
Fredericton, Canada
beauceronsecurity.com

Belarc Inc. (16)
IT Asset Management
Maynard, MA, USA
belarc.com

Beyond Security (54)
Vulnerability Management
San Jose, CA, USA
beyondsecurity.com

BitSight (428)
Security Ratings
Boston, MA, USA
bitsight.com

Blue Lance Inc. (12)
Asset Management
Houston, TX, USA
bluelance.com

Bob's Business (27)
Security Awareness Train-
ing
Barnsley, UK
bobsbusiness.co.uk

Boldon James (76)
DLP (Data Classification)
Farnborough, UK
boldonjames.com

Brinqa (37)
Risk Analytics & Manage-
ment
Austin, TX, USA
brinqa.com

C1Secure (10)
Compliance Monitoring
Platform
Atlanta, GA, USA
c1secure.com

C2SEC (6)
Risk Management
Redmond, WA, USA
c2sec.com

Camel Secure (7)
GRC
Santiago, Chile
camelsecure.com

Carve Systems (22)
Risk Assessment
New York, NY, USA
carvesystems.com

Cavirin (69)
Cloud Compliance
Santa Clara, CA, USA
cavirin.com

Censys (26)
Asset Management
Ann Arbor, MI, USA
censys.io

Note: Numbers in parentheses indicate employee count

Cimcor (13)
IT Asset Protection
Merrillville, IN, USA
cimcor.com

Citalid (6)
GRC
Versailles, France
citalid.com

Citicus (4)
GRC
London, UK
citicus.com

Clearwater (101)
Risk Management
Nashville, TN, USA
clearwatercompliance.com

Cloud Conformity (51)
AWS Compliance Monitoring
Sydney, Australia
cloudconformity.com

Cloud Raxak (9)
Compliance
Los Gatos, CA, USA
cloudraxak.com

CloudCover (9)
Compliance as a Service
Saint Paul, MN, USA
cloudcover.net

CloudeAssurance (5)
Risk Management
Atlanta, GA, USA
cloudeassurance.com

Cloudneeti (34)
Compliance Management
Seattle, WA, USA
cloudneeti.com

CloudSEK (42)
Risk Management
Bangalore, India
cloudsek.com

Coalition (36)
Cyber Insurance
San Francisco, CA, USA
thecoalition.com

CODA Intelligence (6)
Vulnerability Management
Boston, MA, USA
codaintelligence.com

Cofense (was PhishMe)
(393)
Anti-phishing Training
Leesburg, VA, USA
cofense.com

Cognigo (34)
Data Privacy Compliance
for Cloud Storage
Jersey City, NJ, USA
cognigo.com

Commugen (21)
Risk Management
Tel Aviv, Israel
commugen.com

**Compelson Labs
(Mobiledit)** (17)
Forensics
Prague, Czech Republic
mobiledit.com/home

ComplyUp (5)
Compliance
Tampa, FL, USA
complyup.com

Conventus (20)
Vulnerability Management
Chicago, IL, USA
conventus.com

Convercent (173)
Compliance Management
Denver, CO, USA
convercent.com

Corax (31)
Security Ratings
London, UK
coraxcyber.com

Core Security (181)
Vulnerability Management
Roswell, GA, USA
coresecurity.com

Cryptosense (8)
VM for Cryptograpy
Paris, France
cryptosense.com

Cura Software Solutions
(90)
Risk Management
Singapore, Singapore
curasoftware.com

CybelAngel (87)
OSINT Data Leak Detection
Paris, France
cybelangel.com

Cyber Observer Ltd. (22)
Security Management
Caesarea, Israel
cyber-observer.com

CyberCentric (2)
Data Access Monitoring
New York, NY, USA
cybercentric.com

CyberCube (61)
Risk Management
San Francisco, CA, USA
cybcube.com

Cyberready (16)
Anti-phishing Training
Tel Aviv, Israel
cyberready.co.il

**CyberEye Research Labs
& Security Solutions** (22)
Security Awareness Training
Hyderabad, India
cybereyelabs.io

Cyberfense (5)
Risk Management
New York, NY, USA
cyberfense.com

CyberGRX (98)
Third Party Risk
Denver, CO, USA
cybergrx.com

Cyberkov (5)
Risk Assessment
Kuwait City, Kuwait
cyberkov.com

Cybernance (9)
Risk Measurement
Austin, TX, USA
cybernance.com

Cybernet (1)
Security Manager
Ann Arbor, MI, USA
cybersecurity.cybernet.com

Cybernetiq (13)
Risk Measurement
Ottawa, Canada
cybernetiq.ca

CyberOne (5)
Policy Management
San Francisco, CA, USA
cb1security.com

CyberOwl (26)
Risk Measurement
Birmingham, UK
cyberowl.io

CyberPoint (2)
GRC
Baltimore, MD, USA
cyberpointllc.com

CyberSaint (23)
Risk Management
Boston, MA, USA
cybersaint.io

Cybersmart (18)
Compliance Automation
London, UK
cybersmart.co.uk

CyberSprint (28)
Vulnerability Scanner
The Hague, Netherlands
cybersprint.com

Cyberwatch (15)
GRC
Paris, France
cyberwatch.fr

Cybrary (297)
Training
College Park, MD, USA
cybrary.it

CybSafe (39)
Security Awareness Training
London, UK
cybsafe.com

Cycognito (43)
Vulnerability Management
Palo Alto, CA, USA
cycognito.com

CyFIR (12)
Digital Forensics & e-Discovery
Ashburn, VA, USA
cyfir.com

Cygna Labs Corp (8)
Audit of Azure Environments
Miami Beach, FL, USA
cygnalabs.com

Cygov (13)
Compliance and DLP
New York, NY, USA
cygov.co

CyNation (14)
Third Party Risk Assessment
London, UK
cynation.com

CYR3CON (55)
Vulnerability Ranking
Tempe, AZ, USA
cyr3con.ai

Cyrating (2)
Risk Scores
Paris, France
cyrating.com

Cytegic (17)
Risk Profiling
Tel Aviv, Israel
cytegic.com

Dash Solutions (7)
HIPAA Compliance Management
Devon, PA, USA
dashsdk.com

Datiphy (15)
User Behavior Monitoring
San Jose, CA, USA
datiphy.com

DB Cybertech (34)
Data Discovery
San Diego, CA, USA
dbcybertech.com

Dcoya (7)
Anti-phishing Training
Tel Aviv, Israel
dcoya.com

Debricked (17)
Vulnerability Management
Malmö, Sweden
debricked.com

Defendify (19)
GRC
Portland, ME, USA
defendify.io

Defense Balance (13)
Security Awareness Training
Cordoba, Argentina
smartfense.com

DefenseStorm (57)
Monitoring for Compliance for Banks
Atlanta, GA, USA
defensestorm.com

Delve Labs (21)
Vulnerability Management
Montreal, Canada
delve-labs.com

Denim Group (94)
Vulnerability Management
San Antonio, TX, USA
denimgroup.com

DeviceLock (25)
Endpoint Data Leak Prevention
San Ramon, CA, USA
devicelock.com

Digital Confidence Ltd. (1)
DLP
Tel Aviv, Israel
digitalconfidence.com

Digital Defense (110)
Vulnerability Management
San Antonio, TX, USA
digitaldefense.com

Digital Detective (3)
Forensics
Folkestone, UK
digital-detective.net

Digital Guardian (403)
DLP
Waltham, MA, USA
digitalguardian.com

Diligent eSecurity International (8)
Asset Monitoring
Atlanta, GA, USA
desintl.com

DocAuthority (34)
DLP
Ra'anana, Israel
docauthority.com

DTEX Systems (87)
Insider Threat Detection
San Jose, CA, USA
dtexsystems.com

Dynasec BV (20)
Compliance Management
Eindhoven, Netherlands
dynasec.org

edgescan (45)
Vulnerability Management
Dublin, Ireland
edgescan.com

Elemental Cyber Security (9)
Vulnerability Management
Dallas, TX, USA
elementalsecurity.com

Elevate Security (21)
Security Awareness Training
Berkeley, CA, USA
elevatesecurity.com

Emergynt (16)
Risk Management
Cincinnati, OH, USA
emergynt.com

ERMProtect (21)
Security Awareness Training
Coral Gables, FL, USA
ermprotect.com

ERPScan (21)
Business Application Security SAP
Amsterdam, Netherlands
erpscan.io

ESNC (4)
SAP Security
Grünwald, Germany
esnc.de

Expanse (155)
Vulnerability Scanner
San Francisco, CA, USA
expanse.co

Fasoo.com, Inc. (105)
Digital Rights Management
Seoul, South Korea
fasoo.com

FastPath (49)
SaaS Authorizations
Des Moines, IA, USA
gofastpath.com

Note: Numbers in parentheses indicate employee count

Fixnix (45)
SaaS for SMB
Ashok Nagar, India
fixnix.co

ForcePoint (2,495)
DLP
Austin, TX, USA
forcepoint.com

Foregenix (81)
Vulnerability Scanning
Boston, MA, USA
foregenix.com

Forensic Innovations (1)
Data Discovery & Forensics
St. Johns, FL, USA
fid3.com

Foreseeti (19)
Vulnerability Scanning
Stockholm, Sweden
foreseeti.com

FortMesa (3)
Risk Management
Austerlitz, NY, USA
fortmesa.com

Galvanize (444)
Risk Management
Vancouver, Canada
wegalvanize.com

GamaSec (4)
Web Scanning
Herzelia Pituach, Israel
gamasec.com

GB & Smith (57)
SAP Audit
Lille, France
gbandsmith.com

GENAPT Technology Labs (11)
GRC Platform
Hyderabad, India
genapt.com

GeoLang (7)
DLP
Cardiff, UK
geolang.com

GetData Forensics (9)
Forensics
Kogarah, Australia
forensicexplorer.com

GhangorCloud (10)
DLP
San Jose, CA, USA
ghangorcloud.com

Gleg
Vulnerability Management
Moscow, Russia
gleg.net

GovReady
Self-Serve Scanning
Washington, DC, USA
govready.com

Granite (22)
Risk Management
Tampere, Finland
granitegrc.com

Ground Labs (43)
Data Discovery
Singapore, Singapore
groundlabs.com

GTB Technologies (50)
Data Leak Prevention
(DLP)
Newport Beach, CA, USA
gtbtechnologies.com

Guardian Analytics (98)
Forensics
Mountain View, CA, USA
guardiananalytics.com

Guidewire (2,219)
Security Ratings
Foster City, CA, USA
guidewire.com

Helm Solutions (22)
Compliance Management
New York, NY, USA
helm.global

ID Experts (73)
Incident Response
Portland, OR, USA
idexperscorp.com

Idera (365)
SQL Compliance
Houston, TX, USA
idera.com

IDRRA (5)
Third Party Risk Management
New York, NY, USA
idrra.com

IGLOO Software (163)
Security Management
Kitchener, Canada
igloosoftware.com

Immunity (43)
Vulnerability Management
Miami, FL, USA
immunityinc.com

Infor (200)
Continuous Monitoring
New York, NY, USA
infor.com

Infowatch (176)
DLP
Moscow, Russia
infowatch.com

Innosec (8)
DLP
Hod HaSharon, Israel
innosec.com

Intruder (9)
Vulnerability Scanner
London, UK
intruder.io

IRM Security (82)
Risk Management
Cheltenham, UK
irmsecurity.com

IronScales (36)
Anti-phishing Gamification
Tel Aviv, Israel
ironscales.com

ISARR (4)
Asset Management
London, UK
isarr.com

iTrust (46)
Vulnerability Management
Labege, France
itrust.fr

iTrust, Inc. (3)
Third Party Risk Scores
Atlanta, GA, USA
itrustinc.com

Jiran (1)
DLP
Daejeon, South Korea
jiran.com

**Kenna Security
(rebranded from Risk I/O)**
(153)
VM and Threat Feeds
San Francisco, CA, USA
kennasecurity.com

KnowBe4 (620)
Phishing and Security
Awareness
Clearwater, FL, USA
knowbe4.com

Kovrr (19)
Risk Monitoring for Insurance Providers
London, UK
kovrr.com

Kratikal Tech (76)
Risk Measurement
Noida, India
kratikal.com

KYND (17)
Risk Management
London, UK
kynd.io

LockPath, Inc. (89)
IT Governance, Risk &
Compliance
Overland Park, KS, USA
lockpath.com

LOGbinder (1)
Application Security Intelligence
Wilmington, DE, USA
logbinder.com

LogicGate, Inc. (60)
GRC
Chicago, IL, USA
logicgate.com

LogRhythm (627)
Log Management
Boulder, CO, USA
logrhythm.com

Lucideus (251)
Risk Measurement
Okhla Phase III, India
lucideus.com

LUCY Security (8)
Anti-phishing Training
Zug, Switzerland
lucysecurity.com

LunarLine (114)
VM and Log Management
Arlington, VA, USA
lunarline.com

Managed Methods (22)
Cloud Access Monitor
Boulder, CO, USA
managedmethods.com

**ManageEngine (Zoho
Corp.)** (87)
Security Management
Pleasanton, CA, USA
manageengine.com

Maxxsure (29)
Risk Management
Richardson, TX, USA
maxxsure.com

MeasuredRisk (27)
Risk Management
Arlington, VA, USA
measuredrisk.com

MessageSolution Inc. (21)
Email Archiving
Milpitas, CA, USA
messagesolution.com

Metascan (5)
Web Scanning
Moscow, Russia
metascan.ru

Methodware (5)
Risk Framework
London, UK
methodware.com

MetricStream (1,712)
IT Governance, Risk &
Compliance
Palo Alto, CA, USA
metricstream.com

MicroWorld Technologies
(191)
Vulnerability Management
Novi, MI, USA
nemasisva.com

Minereye (19)
Self-Learning Data Dis-
covery
Hod HaSharon, Israel
minereye.com

Mirobase
DLP and Employee Mon-
itoring
Ukraine
mirobase.com

Modulo (214)
IT Governance, Risk &
Compliance
Rio de Janeiro, Brazil
modulo.com

N-Stalker (12)
Web Application Security
Scanner
São Paulo, Brazil
nstalker.com

Nanitor (7)
GRC
Kópavogur, Iceland
nanitor.com

Nasdaq Bwise (67)
GRC
's-Hertogenbosch, Neth-
erlands
bwise.com

NC4 (168)
Risk Management
El Segundo, CA, USA
nc4.com

Nehemiah Security (48)
Risk Management
Tysons, VA, USA
nehemiahsecurity.com

NetMonastery (49)
Cloud-Based SIEM
Mumbai, India
dnif.it

Netsparker (87)
Web Scanning
London, UK
netsparker.com

NetSPI (128)
Vulnerability Scanning
Minneapolis, MN, USA
netspi.com

Nettoken (4)
Password Manager
London, UK
nettoken.io

NetWrix Corporation (318)
Auditor
Irvine, CA, USA
netWrix.com

Nimbusec (12)
Web Scanning
Linz, Austria
nimbusec.com

Nopsec (27)
Vulnerability Risk Man-
agement
Brooklyn, NY, USA
nopsec.com

Normshield (26)
Security Scores
Vienna, VA, USA
normshield.com

Nsauditor (1)
Vulnerability Scanner
Las Vegas, NV, USA
nsauditor.com

Nucleus Security (6)
Vulnerability Management
Sarasota, FL, USA
nucleussec.com

**ObserveIT (acquired by
Proofpoint, 2019)** (179)
Employee Behavior Mon-
itoring
Boston, MA, USA
observeit.com

OneTrust (667)
Third Party Risk Manage-
ment
Atlanta, GA, USA
onetrust.com

Onspring (26)
Audit Management
Overland Park, KS, USA
onspring.com

Osano (12)
Data Privacy Compliance
Austin, TX, USA
osano.com

Ostendio (12)
Compliance Management
Arlington, VA, USA
ostendio.com

Note: Numbers in parentheses indicate employee count

Outpost24 (161)
Vulnerability Risk Management
Karlskrona, Sweden
outpost24.com

OutThink (15)
Employee Behavior Monitoring
London, UK
outthinkthreats.com

Panaseer (50)
Security Management Platform
London, UK
panaseer.com

Panorays (33)
Vulnerability Assessment for Third Parties
New York, NY, USA
panorays.com

Paraben Corporation (18)
Digital Forensics & Data Recovery
Aldie, VA, USA
paraben.com

Pervade Software (6)
GRC
Cardiff, UK
pervade-software.com

PhishLabs (142)
Anti-phishing
Charleston, SC, USA
phishlabs.com

PhishX (4)
Security Awareness Training
Cotia, Brazil
phishx.io

Picus Security (53)
IT Security Control Monitoring
Ankara, Turkey
picussecurity.com

PivotPoint Security (25)
Risk Assessment
Hamilton, NJ, USA
pivotpointsecurity.com

PixAlert (14)
Data Discovery
Dublin, Ireland
pixalert.com

Pointsecure (3)
OpenVMS Compliance
Houston, TX, USA
pointsecure.com

PortSwigger (30)
Vulnerability Scanner
Knutsford, UK
portswigger.net

Prevalent AI (21)
Risk Management
London, UK
prevalent.ai

Prevalent Networks (95)
Third Party Risk Management
Warren, NJ, USA
prevalent.net

Prifender (20)
Data Privacy
Tel Aviv, Israel
prifender.com

Privva (10)
Third Party Risk
Arlington, VA, USA
privva.com

ProcessUnity (74)
Third Party Risk Management
Concord, MA, USA
processunity.com

Promia (29)
Network Asset Discovery
Skillman, NJ, USA
promia.com

Protenus (65)
Medical Record Access Monitoring
Baltimore, MD, USA
protenus.com

Proteus-Cyber, Ltd. (4)
GRC
London, UK
proteuscyber.com

Qualys (1,167)
Vulnerability management
Foster City, CA, USA
qualys.com

Quotium (21)
Data Storage Monitoring
Paris, France
quotium.com

Rapid 7 (1,447)
Vulnerability Management
Boston, MA, USA
rapid7.com

RedSeal (188)
Security Posture
San Jose, CA, USA
redseal.net

Resolver (224)
Risk Management
Toronto, Canada
resolver.com

Risk Based Security (27)
Cyber Risk Analytics
Richmond, VA, USA
riskbasedsecurity.com

Risk Ledger (10)
Third Party Risk Assessment
London, UK
riskledger.com

RiskIQ (166)
External Threat Platform
San Francisco, CA, USA
riskiq.com

RiskLens (67)
Risk Calculations
Spokane, WA, USA
risklens.com

RiskRecon (75)
Third Party Risk Management
Salt Lake City, UT, USA
riskrecon.com

RiskSense, Inc. (103)
Vulnerability Management
Albuquerque, NM, USA
risksense.com

RiskWatch International (18)
Risk Management
Sarasota, FL, USA
riskwatch.com

Rofori Corporation (5)
Risk Management
Zionsville, IN, USA
rofori.com

SafeGuard Cyber (37)
Employee Social Media Management
Charlottesville, VA, USA
safeguardcyber.com

Saint Corporation (18)
Vulnerability Management
Bethesda, MD, USA
saintcorporation.com

Scantist (11)
Vulnerability Management
Singapore, Singapore
scantist.com

SDG Corporation (616)
GRC
Norwalk, CT, USA
sdgc.com

Secberus (9)
Compliance for Cloud Environments
Miami, FL, USA
secberus.com

Secoda Risk Management
(5)
GRC
London, UK
secoda.com

Seconize (6)
Risk Management
Singapore, Singapore
seconize.co

SecPoint (17)
Vulnerability Scanning
Copenhagen, Denmark
secpoint.com

Secudit, Ltd. (6)
Vulnerability Scanning
Veszprém, Hungary
secudit.com

Secure Mentem (5)
Security Awareness Train-
ing
Annapolis, MD, USA
securementem.com

Secure24 (627)
Secure Hosting
Southfield, MI, USA
secure-24.com

SecureStack (4)
Configuration Manage-
ment
Docklands, Australia
securestack.com

Securicy (16)
Policy Management
Sydney, Canada
securicy.com

Security Compass (205)
Policy Compliance
Toronto, Canada
securitycompass.com

Security Mentor (11)
Security Awareness Train-
ing
Pacific Grove, CA, USA
securitymentor.com

SecurityMetrics (291)
Vulnerability Scanning and
Compliance
Orem, UT, USA
securitymetrics.com

SecurityScorecard (175)
Risk Measurement
New York, NY, USA
securityscorecard.com

Senseity (3)
Monitoring
Kfar Saba, Israel
senseity.com

Sera-Brynn (20)
Cyber Risk Management
Suffolk, VA, USA
sera-brynn.com

Sergeant Laboratories
(20)
Risk Management
Onalaska, WI, USA
sgtlabs.com

**Silverskin Information
Security** (20)
Skills Measurement and
Compliance
Helsinki, Finland
silverskin.com

Singular Security (6)
IT Security & Compliance
Risk Management
Tustin, CA, USA
singularsecurity.com

Somansa (36)
DLP
San Jose, CA, USA
somansatech.com

Squadra Technologies (3)
DLP
Las Vegas, NV, USA
squadratechnologies.com

SteelCloud (34)
Configuration Manage-
ment
Ashburn, VA, USA
steelcloud.com

Strobes (3)
Vulnerability Management
Frisco, TX, USA
strobes.co

SureCloud (72)
Cloud Platform
Plano, TX, USA
surecloud.com

SurfWatch Labs (14)
Cyber Risk Intelligence
Analytics
Sterling, VA, USA
surfwatchlabs.com

Swascan (27)
Web Scanning
Cassina de' Pecchi, Italy
swascan.com

Sword Active Risk (78)
Risk Management
Maidenhead, UK
sword-activerisk.com

Tascet (8)
Risk Management
Madison, WI, USA
tascet.com

Telemessage (64)
Text Messaging Security
Petah Tikva, Israel
telemessage.com

Telos (556)
Risk Management
Ashburn, VA, USA
telos.com

**Tempest Security
Intelligence** (249)
Data Classification and
Discovery
Recife, Brazil
tempest.com.br

Tenable Network Security
(1,328)
Vulnerability Management
Columbia, MD, USA
tenable.com

Terbium Labs (42)
Risk Monitoring
Baltimore, MD, USA
terbiumlabs.com

ThirdPartyTrust (22)
Third Party Risk
Chicago, IL, USA
thirdpartytrust.com

ThreatGuard, Inc. (4)
Auditing and Monitoring
San Antonio, TX, USA
threatguard.com

Titania Ltd. (48)
Configuration Auditing
Worcester, UK
titania.com

TITUS (250)
DLP
Ottawa, Canada
titus.com

TraceSecurity (100)
GRC
Baton Rouge, LA, USA
tracesecurity.com

TripWire (Belkin) (465)
File Integrity Management
Portland, OR, USA
tripwire.com

TrustArc (304)
Privacy Assessments
San Francisco, CA, USA
trustarc.com

Trusted Integration (4)
GRC
Alexandria, VA, USA
trustedintegration.com

Note: Numbers in parentheses indicate employee count

Truvincio (3)
Security Awareness Training
Vienna, VA, USA
truvincio.com

Tychon (25)
Risk Management Dashboards
Fredericksburg, VA, USA
tychon.io

UpGuard (43)
Configuration Monitoring
Mountain View, CA, USA
upguard.com

Vanguard Integrity Professionals (77)
Event Monitoring
Las Vegas, NV, USA
go2vanguard.com

Velona Systems (7)
PBX Security Scanner
Cork, Ireland
velonasystems.com

Veriato (formerly SpectorSoft) (51)
UEBA
Palm Beach Gardens, FL, USA
veriato.com

Veriscan Security (10)
Security Measurement
Karlstad, Sweden
veriscan.se

VigiTrust (16)
Risk Management
Dublin, Ireland
vigitrust.com

Visual Click Software (16)
Auditing for AD
Austin, TX, USA
visualclick.com

Vulcan Cyber (33)
Vulnerability Remediation
Tel Aviv, Israel
vulcan.io

WaryMe (9)
GRC
Cesson-Sévigné, France
waryme.com

White Cyber Knight (7)
Risk Management
Tel Aviv, Israel
wck-grc.com

WhiteHat Security (acquired by NTT, 2019) (370)
Web Application Security
San Jose, CA, USA
whitehatsec.com

Xbridge Systems (8)
DLP for z/OS
San Jose, CA, USA
xbridgesystems.com

Xpandion (19)
Risk Management
Tel Aviv, Israel
xpandion.com

Zercurity (2)
OSQuery
London, UK
zercurity.com

Zeronorth (40)
Vulnerability Management
Boston, MA, USA
zeronorth.io

ZyLAB (91)
e-discovery
Amsterdam, Netherlands
zylab.com

IAM

1Password (67)
Password Management
Toronto, Canada
1password.com

2FA Inc. (11)
Authentication
Austin, TX, USA
2fa.com

9Star (19)
Managed Identity Platform
Austin, TX, USA
9starinc.com

ActivIdentity Corp. (now HIDGlobal) (2,307)
Identity Management
Austin, TX, USA
hidglobal.com

AdNovum (1)
IAM
Zürich, Switzerland
adnovum.ch

Aerohive Networks (557)
Network Access Control
Milpitas, CA, USA
aerohive.com

AimBrain (16)
Biometrics
London, UK
aimbrain.com

Aircuve (1)
Authentication
Seoul, South Korea
aircuve.com/wp/en

AlertEnterprise (147)
Physical Identity & Access Management
Fremont, CA, USA
alertenterprise.com

Anchor ID (7)
Mobile Authentication
Kingston, NY, USA
anchorid.com

Anixis (1)
Password Management
Glenmore Park, Australia
anixis.com

Anqlave (10)
2FA
Singapore, Singapore
anqlave.com

aPersona (7)
MFA Platform
Raleigh, NC, USA
apersona.com

AppsPicket (2)
Authentication
Hammersmith, UK
appspicket.com

Armor Scientific (7)
Authentication
Newport Beach, CA, USA
armorsci.com

Atos Group (450)
IAM
Bezons, France
atos.net/en

Auconet (12)
Network Access Control
Berlin, Germany
Auconet.com

Auth0 (480)
Single Sign-On APIs
Bellevue, WA, USA
auth0.com

Authen2cate (3)
Authentication
Rochester Hills, MI, USA
authen2cate.com

Authenex Inc. (13)
Authentication
Mountain View, CA, USA
authenex.com

Authernative (2)
Authentication
Redwood City, CA, USA
authernative.com

Authlete (9)
OAuth Gateways
Tokyo, Japan
authlete.com

AuthLite (1)
Two-Factor Authentication
Springfield, IL, USA
authlite.com

AuthLogics (6)
Authentication
Bracknell, UK
authlogics.com

Authomate (7)
2FA (mobile)
Morganville, NJ, USA
authomate.com

AuthRocket
Authorization and User
Management
Denver, CO, USA
authrocket.com

Authshield Labs Pvt. Ltd.
(1)
Two-Factor Authentication
Delhi, India
auth-shield.com

Authy (3)
2FA for Consumers
San Francisco, CA, USA
authy.com

Avatier (35)
Identity Management
Platform
Pleasanton, CA, USA
avatier.com

Averon (30)
Mobile Authentication
San Francisco, CA, USA
averon.com

Avoco Secure (6)
Cloud Authentication
London, UK
secure2trust.com

Axiad IDS (26)
Authentication
Santa Clara, CA, USA
axiadids.com

Axiomatics (45)
Database Access Control
Stockholm, Sweden
axiomatics.com

Axuall (5)
Identity Verification
Cleveland, OH, USA
axuall.com

B-Secur (37)
Biometrics (ECG)
Belfast, UK
b-secur.com

Beame.io
Mobile Authenticator
Tel Aviv, Israel
beame.io

**Beta Systems Software
AG** (222)
IAM
Berlin, Germany
betasystems.com

BeyondTrust (628)
Privileged Access Manage-
ment
Johns Creek, GA, USA
beyondtrust.com

BIID (22)
Mobile Identity Platform
Sant Cugat del Vallès,
Spain
biid.com

BIO-key (67)
Biometrics, Fingerprint
Wall, NJ, USA
bio-key.com

BiObex (8)
2FA
Reston, VA, USA
biobex.com

BioConnect (64)
Biometrics
Toronto, Canada
bioconnect.com

BioEnable (84)
Access Control, Biometrics
Pune, India
bioenabletech.com

BioID (10)
Biometrics
Sachseln, Switzerland
bioid.com

BioWatch
Biometrics
Martigny, Switzerland
biowatchid.com

Blind Hash (2)
Password Management
Boston, MA, USA
blindhash.com

Bluink (16)
Mobile Authenticator
Ottawa, Canada
bluink.ca

Brivo (149)
Physical Identity & Access
Management
Bethesda, MD, USA
brivo.com

Bundesdruckerei (387)
Authentication PKI
Berlin, Germany
bundesdruckerei.de/en

CA Technologies (part of
Broadcom) (9,565)
IAM
New York, NY, USA
ca.com

Callsign (129)
Authentication
London, UK
callsign.com

CardLab
IAM
Herlev, Denmark
cardlab.com

Celestix (25)
IAM
Fremont, CA, USA
celestix.com

Centrify (381)
IAM
Santa Clara, CA, USA
centrify.com

Certisign Certificador
(754)
IAM
São Paulo, Brazil
certisign.com.br

Cloudentity (33)
Cloud Identity Manage-
ment
Seattle, WA, USA
cloudentity.com

Cloudknox (19)
Cloud Identity Manage-
ment
Sunnyvale, CA, USA
cloudknox.io

Collective Software LLC
(1)
AD Authentication
Springfield, IL, USA
collectivesoftware.com

Covisint (OpenText) (247)
Federated Identity Man-
agement
Southfield, MI, USA
covisent.com

CovR
Mobile Authenticator
Malmö, Sweden
covrsecurity.com

Crossmatch (259)
IAM
Palm Beach Gardens, FL,
USA
crossmatch.com

CryptoPhoto (34)
2FA Using Images
Australia
cryptophoto.com

Note: Numbers in parentheses indicate employee count

cryptovision (27)
Smart Card Solutions
Gelsenkirchen, Germany
cryptovision.com

Cyber-SIGN (1)
Biometrics Handwriting
Setagaya, Japan
witswell.com

CyberArk Software (1,228)
Privileged Access Management
Petah Tikva, Israel
cyberark.com

CyberSafe Ltd. (7)
Access Control for SAP
Longford, UK
cybersafe.com

CyberSecurity Corporation (1)
Access Management
Kansas City, MO, USA
goldkey.com

Cyberus Labs (12)
2FA (mobile)
Kraków, Poland
cyberuslabs.com

Cyphercor – LoginTC (6)
Two-Factor Authentication
Kanata, Canada
logintc.com

D-ID (25)
Anti-facial Recognition
Tel Aviv, Israel
deidentification.co

Daon (148)
Identity Assurance
Reston, VA, USA
daon.com

Dashlane (179)
Password Manager
New York, NY, USA
dashlane.com

Datablink (26)
Authentication
McLean, VA, USA
datablink.com

Datakey (ATEK Access Technologies, LLC) (31)
Authentication
Eden Prairie, MN, USA
datakey.com

Deep Identity Pte Ltd. (85)
IAM
Singapore, Singapore
deepidentity.com

Deepnet Security (14)
Identity Management
London, UK
deepnetsecurity.com

Delfigo Security (5)
Mobile Device Authentication
Boston, MA, USA
delfigosecurity.com

Device Authority (23)
Device Authentication
Reading, UK
deviceauthority.com

Digital Authentication Technologies (6)
Location-Based Authentication
Boca Raton, FL, USA
dathq.com

Direct Risk Management (2)
Authentication
Aliso Viejo, CA, USA
directrm.com

Dominode (3)
Identity Assertion with Blockchain
Boca Raton, FL, USA
dominode.com

DuoSecurity (now part of Cisco) (703)
Authentication
Ann Arbor, MI, USA
duo.com

E-Certify (2)
IAM
Wayville, Australia
ecertify.com

Ecora Software (24)
Authentication
Boston, MA, USA
ecora.com

Egis Technology (1)
Biometrics under Display Fingerprint Sensor
Taipei, Taiwan
egistec.com

Ensure Technologies (26)
IAM
Ypsilanti, MI, USA
ensuretech.com

Ensurity (42)
2FA
Hyderabad, India
ensurity.com

Entersekt (144)
Authentication & Fraud Protection for Banks
Stellenbosch, South Africa
entersekt.com

Evernym (56)
Identity Attestation
Herriman, UT, USA
evernym.com

FoxT (595)
Authentication
Eden Prairie, MN, USA
foxt.com

FST Biometrics (47)
Facial Recognition Biometrics
Holon, Israel
fstbm.com

Fudo Security (42)
Privileged Access Management
Newark, CA, USA
fudosecurity.com

Futurae (12)
Authentication
Zürich, Switzerland
futurae.com

Fyde (28)
Access Control
Palo Alto, CA, USA
fyde.com

Gemalto (11,210)
IAM
Meudon Cedex, France
gemalto.com

GeoCodex (6)
Access Control
Hollywood, CA, USA
geocodex.com

Global ID
Biometrics
Lausanne, Switzerland
global-id.ch

GlobalSign (377)
Authentication & Identity Service Provider
Portsmouth, NH, USA
globalsign.com

Gluu (18)
Access Control
Austin, TX, USA
gluu.org

Go-Trust (11)
Authentication
Taichung City, Taiwan
go-trust.com

Great Bay Software (26)
Network Access Control
Bloomington, MN, USA
greatbaysoftware.com

Green Armor (1)
IAM
Hackensack, NJ, USA
greenarmor.com

HID Global (2,110)
Authentication
Austin, TX, USA
hidglobal.com

Hideez (20)
Hardware Credential
Storage
Redwood City, CA, USA
hideez.com

Hitachi ID Systems, Inc.
(140)
IAM
Calgary, Canada
Hitachi-id.com

**Hypersecu Information
Systems, Inc.** (9)
OTP Tokens
Richmond, Canada
hypersecu.com

HYPR (62)
Biometrics
New York, NY, USA
hypr.com

i-Sprint (94)
IAM
Singapore, Singapore
i-sprint.com

ID Control (3)
IAM
The Hague, Netherlands
idcontrol.com

ID R&D Inc. (16)
Biometrics
New York, NY, USA
idrnd.net

ID.me (139)
Credential Management
McLean, VA, USA
id.me

Idaptive (118)
Access Management
Santa Clara, CA, USA
idaptive.com

Idax Software (6)
IAM
Petersfield, UK
idaxsoftware.com

IDEE Blockchain Software
(18)
Identity Platform
Munich, Germany
getidee.com

IDEMIA (10,787)
Identity Augmentation
Reston, VA, USA
idemia.com

IDENprotect (9)
Authentication
London, UK
idenprotect.com

IDenticard (101)
Access Control
Manheim, PA, USA
identicard.com

Identify Security Software
(2)
Biometrics
Boca Raton, FL, USA
identifyss.com

Identity Automation (111)
Identity Management
Houston, TX, USA
identityautomation.com

IdentityLogix (3)
Access Data Analytics
Crown Point, IN, USA
identitylogix.com

Identiv (208)
Credentials
Fremont, CA, USA
identiv.com

IDnomic (121)
IAM
Issy-les-Moulineaux,
France
idnomic.com

IDology (79)
Authentication
Atlanta, GA, USA
idology.com

iDSync (5)
AD Integration
Perrysburg, OH, USA
idsync.com

Ilantus (193)
Identity Management
Schaumburg, IL, USA
ilantus.com

ImageWare Systems, Inc.
(95)
Biometrics
San Diego, CA, USA
iwsinc.com

Imprivata, Inc. (538)
IAM
Lexington, MA, USA
imprivata.com

Impulse (35)
Network Access Control
Tampa, FL, USA
impulse.com

InBay Technologies (20)
Mobile Authenticator
Kanata, Canada
inbaytech.com

Infineon (1,000)
Smart Card Solutions
Neubiberg, Germany
infineon.com

InfoExpress Inc. (41)
Network Access Control
Santa Clara, CA, USA
infoexpress.com

**Innovya Traceless
Biometrics** (3)
Biometrics
Kiryat Ono, Israel
innovya.com

Integrated Corporation (1)
IAM
Sheungwan, Hong Kong
integrated.com

Inteligensa (88)
Smart Card Solutions
Caracas, Venezuela
Inteligensa.com

Intensity Analytics (10)
Behavior Metrics
Warrenton, VA, USA
intensityanalytics.com

Interlink Networks (6)
IAM
Ann Arbor, MI, USA
interlinknetworks.com

Intrinsic-ID (37)
Device Authentication
Sunnyvale, CA, USA
intrinsic-id.com

Intufo
Access Control
Washington, DC, USA
intufo.com

inWebo (28)
Strong Authentication
Paris, France
inwebo.com

Iovation (214)
Authentication
Portland, OR, USA
iovation.com

IProov (32)
Authentication
London, UK
iproov.com

Note: Numbers in parentheses indicate employee count

Iraje (18)
Access Control
Mumbai, India
iraje.com

IS Decisions (29)
Access Control
Bidart, France
isdecisions.com

IsItYou (3)
Mobile Face Recognition
Lod, Israel
isityou.biz

ITConcepts (99)
IAM for Small Business
Bonn, Germany
itconcepts.net

iWelcome (75)
Identity Management
Amersfoort, Netherlands
iwelcome.com

Jeronix (1)
Identity Intelligence
Israel
jeronix.com

Kaseya (575)
Managed SSO and MFA
New York, NY, USA
kaseya.com

KeePass Password Safe
IAM
Metzingen, Germany
keepass.info

Keeper Security, Inc. (139)
Password Manager
Chicago, IL, USA
keepersecurity.com

Keyp (8)
Identity Platform
Munich, Germany
keyp.io

Keypasco AB (16)
Multi-factor Authentica-
tion
Gothenburg, Sweden
keypasco.com

Keystroke DNA (7)
Biometrics Keystroke
Analysis
Tallinn, Estonia
keystrokedna.com

KinectIQ (11)
Identity-Based Encryption
Woodbury, MN, USA
knectiq.com

KOBIL Systems (92)
Authentication
Worms, Germany
kobil.com

LastPass (23)
Password Manager
Fairfax, VA, USA
lastpass.com

Lastwall (11)
Access Management
Mountain View, CA, USA
lastwall.com

LifeLock, Symantec (415)
Personal Identity Theft
Protection
Tempe, AZ, USA
lifelock.com

Liopa (8)
Biometrics, Liveness
Detection
Belfast, UK
liopa.ai

Locurity (1)
Cloud Authentication
Baltimore, MD, USA
locurity.com

LogMeIn (300)
Password Manager
Boston, MA, USA
logmeininc.com

Made4Biz (1)
Mobile Authentication
(Banking)
Savyon, Israel
israeldefense.co.il/en

MagicCube (1)
Secure Digital Transactions
Santa Clara, CA, USA
magic3inc.com

Mi-Token (109)
2FA Tokens
Austin, TX, USA
mi-token.com

Microsoft (2,000)
IAM
Redmond, WA, USA
microsoft.com

MicroStrategy (200)
Mobile Identity Platform
Tysons Corner, VA, USA
microstrategy.com

Mindpass (5)
Visual Password Manager
Boulder, CO, USA
mindpassco.com

miniOrange (27)
SSO
Pune, India
miniorange.com

MIRACL (30)
Multi-factor Authentica-
tion
London, UK
miracl.com

Mobbu (3)
QRcode Authentication
Hove, UK
mobbu.com

Modoosone (1)
Privileged Access Manage-
ment
Seoul, South Korea
modoosone.com

My1login (24)
Identity Management
London, UK
my1login.com

neoEYED (8)
2FA
Bangalore, India
neoeyed.com

Nevis Networks (60)
Access Control
Pune, India
nevisnetworks.com

NewBanking (10)
IAM
Copenhagen, Denmark
newbanking.com

Nok Nok Labs (35)
Unified Authentication
Infrastructure
San Jose, CA, USA
noknok.com

NuID Inc. (7)
Trustless Authentication
Seattle, WA, USA
nuid.io

Octatco (3)
Fingerprint USB Devices
Seongnam, South Korea
octatco.com

Okta, Inc. (1,934)
IAM
San Francisco, CA, USA
okta.com

Omada A/S (239)
IAM
Copenhagen, Denmark
omada.net

OneLogin (283)
Identity Management
San Francisco, CA, USA
onelogin.com

OneSpan (formerly Vasco) (559)
Identity Products
Chicago, IL, USA
onespan.com

OneVisage (8)
Biometrics
Lausanne, Switzerland
onevisage.com

Onion ID (5)
Privileged Access Management
Hayward, CA, USA
onionid.com

OpenIAM (13)
Identity Management
Cortlandt Manor, NY, USA
openiam.com

OpenText (500)
Federated Identity
Waterloo, Canada
opentext.com

Optimal IdM (12)
Single Sign-On (SSO)
Lutz, FL, USA
optimalidm.com

Oracle (450)
IAM
Redwood Shores, CA, USA
oracle.com

Osirium (45)
Privileged Access Management
Theale, UK
osirium.com

Pango (86)
Consumer VPN
Redwood City, CA, USA
pango.co

Paramount Defenses Inc. (1)
Privileged Access Management for AD
Newport Beach, CA, USA
paramountdefenses.com

Passfaces Corporation
2FA
Reston, VA, USA
passfaces.com

PassMark Software Pvt Ltd. (7)
IAM
Surry Hills, Australia
passmark.com

Pindrop Security (292)
Authentication, Audio
Atlanta, GA, USA
pindropsecurity.com

Ping Identity Corporation (882)
IAM
Denver, CO, USA
pingidentity.com

Pinn (26)
Authentication
Redwood City, CA, USA
pinn.ai

Pirean (Echostar) (65)
Identity Management
London, UK
pirean.com

Pixelpin (15)
Password Management
London, UK
pixelpin.io

PlainID (37)
Authorization
Tel Aviv, Israel
plainid.com

Plurilock (18)
Behavior-Based Biometrics
Victoria, Canada
plurilock.com

Post-Quantum (15)
Authentication
London, UK
post-quantum.com

Protectimus (28)
Two-Factor Authentication
London, UK
protectimus.com

Pulse Secure (532)
Authentication
San Jose, CA, USA
pulsesecure.net

Quantum Signal, LLC (36)
Biometrics
Saline, MI, USA
quantumsignal.com

Radiant Logic (104)
LDAP, SSO
Novato, CA, USA
radiantlogic.com

Raonsecure (10)
Biometrics
Santa Clara, CA, USA
raonsecure.com

RavenWhite Security, Inc. (2)
Cookies
Menlo Park, CA, USA
ravenwhite.com

RaviRaj Technologies (4)
Biometrics
Pune, India
ravirajtech.com

RCDevs (13)
IAM
Belvaux, Luxembourg
rcdevs.com

Remediant (32)
Privileged Access Management
San Francisco, CA, USA
remediant.com

Route 1 (39)
IAM
Toronto, Canada
route1.com

RSA Security, Division of EMC/Dell (3,161)
IAM
Bedford, MA, USA
rsa.com

Rsam (172)
IT Governance, Risk & Compliance
Secaucus, NJ, USA
rsam.com

RSD (705)
Information Governance Solutions
Geneva, Switzerland
rsd.com

Rublon (2)
2FA
Zielona Gora, Poland
rublon.com

SaferPass (18)
Password Manager
Bratislava, Slovakia
saferpass.net

Safewhere (2)
Identity Management
Virum, Denmark
safewhere.com

SailPoint (1,093)
Identity Governance
Austin, TX, USA
sailpoint.com

Saviynt (295)
Cloud Access Governance
El Segundo, CA, USA
saviynt.com

Scytale (27)
Identity Management for Cloud
San Francisco, CA, USA
scytale.io

SecSign (4)
2FA for Mobile Devices
Henderson, NV, USA
secsign.com

Note: Numbers in parentheses indicate employee count

SecuGen (20)
Biometric Finger Scanners
Santa Clara, CA, USA
secugen.com

**Secure Access
Technologies** (13)
Mobile Single Sign-On
Menlo Park, CA, USA
secureaccesstechnologies.
com

SecureAuth (278)
Acces Control
Irvine, CA, USA
secureauth.com

SecuredTouch (34)
Touchscreen Biometrics
Ramat Gan, Israel
securedtouch.com

SecureKey (107)
Identity Management
Toronto, Canada
securekey.com

SecureLink (146)
Third Party Access Controls
Austin, TX, USA
securelink.com

SecurEnvoy (34)
Tokenless 2FA
Basingstoke, UK
securenvoy.com

SecureRF Corporation (19)
Device Authentication
Shelton, CT, USA
securerf.com

**Security Compliance
Corporation** (1)
Access Control
Orinda, CA, USA
securitycompliancecorp.
com

SecurLinx (11)
Biometrics
Morgantown, WV, USA
securlinx.com

Sedicii (17)
Mobile Authentication
Carriganore, Ireland
sedicii.com

Sekur Me (3)
Mobile Authentication
Santa Ana, CA, USA
sekur.me

Semperis (23)
AD State Manager
New York, NY, USA
semperis.com

Sensible Vision (6)
Biometrics
Cape Coral, FL, USA
sensiblevision.com

SentryCard (5)
2FA Cards and OTP
Chicago, IL, USA
sentrycard.com

**Shenzhen Excelsecu Data
Technology** (42)
OTP
Shenzhen, China
excelsecu.com

ShoCard (18)
Identity Management
Cupertino, CA, USA
shocard.com

SignPass (4)
Handwriting Biometrics
Tel Aviv, Israel
sign-pass.com

Silverfort (42)
Clienteles Multi-factor
Tel Aviv, Israel
silverfort.io

SilverLakeMasterSAM (25)
Privileged Access Management
Singapore, Singapore
mastersam.com

Simeio Solutions (423)
IAM
Atlanta, GA, USA
simeiosolutions.com

Smufs (3)
Finger Scanners for Mobile
Ramat Negev, Israel
smufsbio.com

Socure (76)
Online Identity Verification
New York, NY, USA
socure.com

Softex (13)
Authentication
Austin, TX, USA
softexinc.com

Sonavation (48)
Ultrasound Biometrics
Palm Beach Gardens, FL,
USA
sonavation.com

Sonikpass (4)
Identity Verification,
Mobile
Los Angeles, CA, USA
sonikpass.com

Sonrai Security (39)
Identity Data Security
New Brunswick, Canada
sonraisecurity.com

Specops Software Inc. (49)
Password Management
Stockholm, Sweden
specopssoft.com

**SPHERE Technology
Solutions** (33)
Privileged Access Management
Hoboken, NJ, USA
sphereco.com

**StepNexus (Division of
Multos International)** (54)
Authentication
Singapore, Singapore
multosinternational.com/
secure-services/stepnexus.
html

StrikeForce Technologies
(20)
IAM
Edison, NJ, USA
strikeforcetech.com

SureID (120)
IAM
Portland, OR, USA
sureid.com

SurePass ID (3)
Secure Single Sign-On
Winter Garden, FL, USA
surepassid.com

SwivelSecure (50)
Authentication
Wetherby, UK
swivelsecure.com

Syccure (4)
Access Control
Albany, NY, USA
syccure.com

Syferlock (6)
Software-Based Authentication
Shelton, CT, USA
syferlock.com

Syncsort (474)
iSeries Access Control
Pearl River, NY, USA
syncsort.com

TeleSign Corporation (307)
Mobile Identity Verification
Marina del Rey, CA, USA
telesign.com

Thales (910)
Authentication
Plantation, FL, USA
thalesesecurity.com

ThisIsMe (13)
Onboarding
Cape Town, South Africa
thisisme.com

Thycotic Software (355)
Password & Access Management
Washington, DC, USA
thycotic.com

TokenOne (11)
IAM
Sydney, Australia
tokenone.com

Tricerion (5)
Grid Password
Reading, UK
tricerion.com

TruGrid (5)
Access Control
Schaumburg, IL, USA
trugrid.com

Trulioo (113)
Identity Verification
Vancouver, Canada
trulioo.com

Trusona (35)
SSO
Scottsdale, AZ, USA
trusona.com

Trustelem (5)
IAM
Paris, France
trustelem.com

Tu Identidad (8)
2FA (mobile)
Mexico City, Mexico
tuidentidad.com

Typing DNA (27)
Biometrics
New York, NY, USA
typingdna.com

Ubisecure Solutions, Inc.
(37)
IAM
Espoo, Finland
ubisecure.com

UnifyID (34)
Behavioral Identity
Redwood City, CA, USA
unify.id

Uniken (125)
Authentication
Chatham Twp., NJ, USA
uniken.com

Uniloc (6)
IAM
Plano, TX, USA
uniloc.com

Universign (69)
IAM
Paris, France
universign.com

Unloq
Authentication and Authorization
London, UK
unloqsystems.com

Vancosys (5)
IAM
Vancouver, Canada
vancosys.com

Veridium (63)
Authentication
Boston, MA, USA
veridiumid.com

Verifyoo (2)
Biometrics
Tel Aviv, Israel
verifyoo.com

Verimuchme (1)
Identity Storage
London, UK
verimuchme.com

Versasec (23)
IAM
Stockholm, Sweden
versasec.com

Viascope (6)
Network Access Control
Seoul, South Korea
viascope.com

VikiSense (5)
Biometrics MFA
Kiryat Gat, Israel
vikisense.com

Vkansee (1)
Fingerprint Sensors for
Mobile Security
Beijing, China
vkansee.com

**Voice Security Systems
Inc.** (2)
Biometrics
Dana Point, CA, USA
voice-security.com

VU Security (454)
Identity, Authentication,
VPN
Buenos Aires, Argentina
vusecurity.com

Wallix (154)
Privileged Access Management
Paris, France
wallix.com/en

Watchdata (202)
PKI
Singapore, Singapore
watchdata.com

WiKID Systems (4)
2FA OTP with AD
Atlanta, GA, USA
wikidsystems.com

WWPass (21)
Authentication & Access
Solutions
Nashua, NH, USA
wwpass.com

Wymsical (6)
Identity Manager
Greenwich, CT, USA
wymsical.com

XTN Cognitive Security
(19)
Identity Verification
Boston, MA, USA
Xtn-lab.com

Xton Technologies (4)
Privileged Access Management
Trevose, PA, USA
xtontech.com

Yubico (188)
Authentication Tokens
Stockholm, Sweden
yubico.com

Zighra (8)
Biometrics, Kinetic
Ottawa, Canada
zighra.com

Zignsec (16)
Identity Verification
Solna, Sweden
zignsec.com

Zoloz (33)
Biometrics
Haidian District, China
zoloz.com

Zumigo (21)
Identity Verification
San Jose, CA, USA
zumigo.com

Note: Numbers in parentheses indicate employee count

IOT SECURITY

802Secure (48)
IoT Network Monitoring
Emeryville, CA, USA
802secure.com

Acreto Cloud (8)
IoT Microsegmentation
Jersey City, NJ, USA
acreto.io

Allegro Software (6)
Embedded Device Security
Boxborough, MA, USA
allegrosoft.com

AlphaGuardian Networks (1)
ICS Monitoring
San Ramon, CA, USA
alphaguardian.net

APERIO Systems
ICS
Haifa, Israel
aperio-systems.com

ArcusTeam
Vulnerability Management
Tel Aviv-Yafo, Israel
arcusteam.com

Argus Cyber Security (139)
Automotive Cybersecurity
Tel Aviv, Israel
argus-sec.com

Arilou Technologies (20)
Automotive Security
Ramat Gan, Israel
ariloutech.com

Armis (150)
Device Discovery and
Protection
Palo Alto, CA, USA
armis.com

Atonomi (4)
Blockchain
Seattle, WA, USA
atonomi.io

Attila Security (23)
IoT Firewall
Fulton, MD, USA
attilasec.com

Ayyeka (42)
Secure Remote Monitoring
Jerusalem, Israel
ayyeka.com

Bayshore Networks, Inc.
(30)
ICS
Durham, NC, USA
bayshorenetworks.com

Blackridge (66)
ICS
Reno, NV, USA
Blackridge.us

C2A Security (17)
Automotive
Jerusalem, Israel
c2a-sec.com

Centri (20)
For Mobile Carriers
Seattle, WA, USA
centritechnology.com

Cervello (9)
Railway
Tel Aviv, Israel
cervellosec.com

Charismathics (4)
IoT
Munich, Germany
charismathics.com

CipherSiP (7)
Automotive
Haifa, Israel
ciphersip.com

Claroty (145)
ICS
New York, NY, USA
claroty.com

Cog (127)
Microvirtualization Framework
Sydney, Australia
cog.systems

Critifence (6)
ICS
Herzliya, Israel
critifence.com

Crypto Quantique (24)
Embedded Security
Egham, UK
cryptoquantique.com

Culinda (2)
Medical Devices
Irvine, CA, USA
culinda.io

Cy-oT (12)
Wireless Monitoring
Tel Aviv, Israel
Cy-ot.com

CyberMDX (36)
Medical Devices
New York, NY, USA
cybermdx.com

CyberReef Solutions (2)
ICS
Shreveport, LA, USA
scadaaccess.com

CyberX (97)
NBAD for ICS
Waltham, MA, USA
cyberx-labs.com

Cydome
ICS Maritime
Tel Aviv, Israel
cydome.io

Cylera (19)
Medical Devices
New York, NY, USA
cylera.com

Cylus (23)
Railway
Tel Aviv, Israel
cylus.com

Cymotive (75)
Automotive
Tel Aviv, Israel
cymotive.com

Cynash (13)
ICS
Wilmington, DE, USA
cynash.com

Cynerio (19)
Medical Device Security
Ramat Gan, Israel
cynerio.co

Dellfer (8)
Automotive
Novato, CA, USA
dellfer.com

Dover Microsystems (23)
Firmware Hardening
Waltham, MA, USA
dovermicrosystems.com

Dragos (164)
ICS
Hanover, MD, USA
dragos.com

Engage Technologies
Code Automation
Kibbutz, Israel
engageiot.com

Enigmatos (5)
Automotive
Yavne, Israel
enigmatos.com

Exein (9)
IoT
Rome, Italy
exein.io

Extunda (8)
IoT Device Management
Istanbul, Turkey
extunda.com

Finite State (22)
Firmware Monitoring
Columbus, OH, USA
finitestate.io

FireDome (19)
IoT for Device Manufac-
turers
Tel Aviv, Israel
firedome.io

ForceShield (14)
Bot Protection
Taipei, Taiwan
forceshield.com

Fortiphyd Logic (7)
ICS
Norcross, GA, USA
fortiphyd.com

Genians (51)
Device Fingerprinting
Anyang-si, South Korea
genians.com

Guard Knox (26)
Automotive
Tel Aviv, Israel
guardknox.com

HENSOLDT Cyber
IoT
Taufkirchen, Germany
hensoldt-cyber.com

Hmatix (4)
IoT Network Security
San Jose, CA, USA
hmatix.com

**Icon Labs (acquired by
Sectigo)**
PKI for IoT
IA, USA
iconlabs.com

ICS2 (1)
ICS
Jerusalem, Israel
ics2.com

Indegy (60)
Visibility for ICS
New York, NY, USA
indegy.com

Intertrust Technologies
(252)
PKI for IoT
Sunnyvale, CA, USA
intertrust.com

Ioetec (4)
Device Security
Sheffield, UK
ioetec.com

IoT Defense (2)
Network, Home Firewall
for IoT Devices
Falls Church, VA, USA
iotdef.com

IoTSploit
IoT Scanning
Singapore, Singapore
iotsploit.co

Irdeto (1,169)
Entertainment Systems
Hoofddorp, Netherlands
irdeto.com

JpU (15)
IoT
Petah Tikva, Israel
jpu.io

Karamba Security (46)
Automotive Defense
Hod HaSharon, Israel
karambasecurity.com

Levl Technologies (20)
Device Identity
Palo Alto, CA, USA
levltech.com

MalCrawler (16)
Anti-malware
Washington, DC, USA
malcrawler.com

MB Connect Line (24)
ICS Firewall
Dinkelsbühl, Germany
mbconnectline.com

Medcrypt (17)
Medical Device Protection
Encinitas, CA, USA
medcrypt.co

MediGate (47)
Medical Devices
Tel Aviv, Israel
medigate.io

Minim (40)
Home Protection
Manchester, NH, USA
minim.co

Mission Secure (43)
ICS
Charlottesville, VA, USA
missionsecure.com

MTG AG (230)
ICS Key Management
Darmstadt, Germany
mtg.de

N-Dimension Solutions
(14)
ICS
Richmond Hill, Canada
n-dimension.com

Nanolock (16)
Automotive
Nitzanei Oz, Israel
nanolocksecurity.com

Nation-E (8)
Energy Security
Herzliya, Israel
nation-e.com

Naval Dome (3)
Security for Ships
Ra'anana, Israel
navaldome.com

Nelysis (17)
Monitor Physical Systems
Wilmington, DE, USA
nelysis.com

NeuroMesh (2)
Device Inoculation
Cambridge, MA, USA
neuromesh.co

NewSky Security (12)
Device Monitoring
Redmond, WA, USA
newskysecurity.com

NextNine (23)
OT security
Petah Tikva, Israel
nextnine.com

Norma
Wireless
Seoul, South Korea
norma.co.kr

Nova Leah (25)
Medical Device Vulnerability Management
Dundalk, Ireland
novaleah.com

Nozomi Security (116)
ICS
San Francisco, CA, USA
nozominetworks.com

NXM Labs (28)
Device Security
San Francisco, CA, USA
nxmlabs.com

NXT-ID (11)
Mobile Security
Sebastian, FL, USA
nxt-id.com

Ordr (61)
Device Management
Santa Clara, CA, USA
ordr.net

Note: Numbers in parentheses indicate employee count

OxCEPT
Device Authentication
London, UK
oxcept.com

Phosphorus (12)
Agentless Patch Management
Atlanta, GA, USA
phosphorus.io

RadiFlow (42)
ICS
Tel Aviv, Israel
radiflow.com

RazorSecure
Automotive
Basingstoke, UK
web.razorsecure.com

Refirm Labs (12)
Firmware Analysis and
Monitoring
Fulton, MD, USA
refirmlabs.com

Regulus (16)
Automotive
Haifa, Israel
regulus.com

Rhebo (23)
ICS
Leipzig, Germany
rhebo.com

RunSafe Security (15)
Firmware Hardening
McLean, VA, USA
runsafesecurity.com

SafeRide Technologies
(22)
Automotive
Tel Aviv-Yafo, Israel
saferide.io

ScadaFence (33)
ICS
Tel Aviv, Israel
scadafence.com

Secure Crossing R&D
ICS
Dearborn, MI, USA
securecrossing.com

Securithings (16)
Device Management
Ramat Gan, Israel
securithings.com

Senrio (15)
ICS
Portland, OR, USA
senr.io

SensorHound (6)
ICS
West Lafayette, IN, USA
sensorhound.com

Sentryo (28)
ICS
Lyon, France
sentryo.net

Sepio Systems (11)
IoT Network Security
Gaithersburg, MD, USA
sepio.systems

ShieldIOT (10)
For Service Providers
Herzliya, Israel
shieldiot.io

SIGA Cyber Alert System
(20)
ICS
Ashkelon, Israel
sigasec.com

Suavei (10)
Vulnerability Management
Las Vegas, NV, USA
suavei.com

Surance.io (5)
Home Device Protection
Ramat HaSharon, Israel
surance.io

Terafence (11)
ICS Gateway
Haifa, Israel
terafence.com

**TowerSec (a HARMAN
company)** (35)
Automotive Security
Hod HaSharon, Israel
tower-sec.com

Trapezoid (11)
Firmware Monitoring
Miami, FL, USA
trapezoid.com

Trillium Secure (20)
Automotive
Sunnyvale, CA, USA
trilliumsecure.com

Trusted Objects
IoT
Aix-en-Provence, France
trusted-objects.com

Ubirch
Encryption and Blockchain
for ICS
Berlin, Germany
ubirch.de

Upstream (34)
Automotive
Herzliya, Israel
upstream.auto

V5 Systems (78)
ICS
Fremont, CA, USA
v5systems.us

Vdoo (68)
Embedded Systems Security
Tel Aviv, Israel
vdoo.com

**Veracity Industrial
Networks** (13)
ICS
Aliso Viejo, CA, USA
veracity.io

Virta Labs (4)
Healthcare
Seattle, WA, USA
virtalabs.com

Waterfall (72)
ICS Air Gap Firewall
Rosh HaAyin, Israel
waterfall-security.com

Wisekey (124)
Root of Trust Chips
Geneva, Switzerland
wisekey.com

Wispero (2)
Anomaly Detection
San Jose, CA, USA
wispero.com

Xage Security (40)
ICS
Palo Alto, CA, USA
xage.com

**Zingbox (acquired by Palo
Alto Networks)** (83)
IoT
Mountain View, CA, USA
zingbox.com

Zymbit (2)
Device Security Modules
Santa Barbara, CA, USA
zymbit.com

MSSP

2Keys (77)
Managed Identity Platform
Ottawa, Canada
2keys.ca

AaDya Security (24)
For SMB
Plymouth, MI, USA
aadyasecurity.com

Acumera (32)
Managed Firewalls
Austin, TX, USA
acumera.net

Allgeier IT (63)
Managed Email Security
Bremen, Germany
Allgeier-it.de

Apollo Information Systems (20)
Managed Security Services
Los Gatos, CA, USA
apollo-is.com

Armor (243)
MSSP Cloud Security
Richardson, TX, USA
armor.com

Avertium (108)
Managed Services
Phoenix, AZ, USA
avertium.com

BAE Systems (150)
Managed Services
Guildford, UK
baesystems.com

Banff Cyber (1)
Website Defacement Monitoring
Singapore, Singapore
banffcyber.com

Barricade IT Security (2)
Managed Services
Islip, NY, USA
barricadeitsecurity.com

Binary Defense (55)
SOC as a service
Stow, OH, USA
binarydefense.com

BitLyft (6)
Managed SIEM
Lansing, MI, USA
bitlyft.com

Blackpoint (26)
MDR
Ellicott City, MD, USA
blackpointcyber.com

BlackStratus (57)
Security Platform for MSPs
Piscataway, NJ, USA
blackstratus.com

BlueVoyant (175)
MDR
New York, NY, USA
bluevoyant.com

Braintrace (36)
MDR
Salt Lake City, UT, USA
braintrace.com

British Telecom (300)
Managed Services
London, UK
bt.com

Bugsec Group (87)
Managed Security Services
Rishon LeZion, Israel
bugsec.com

Bulletproof (23)
Managed SIEM
Stevenage, UK
bulletproof.co.uk

CACI International Inc. (140)
Managed Services
Arlington, VA, USA
caci.com

Capgemini (250)
Identity as a Service
Paris, France
capgemini.com

CenturyLink (2,000)
Network Monitoring
Monroe, LA, USA
centurylink.com

Cerdant (48)
Managed Services
Dublin, OH, USA
cerdant.com

CI Security (68)
MDR
Seattle, WA, USA
ci.security

CIPHER Security (187)
Managed Security Services
Miami, FL, USA
cipher.com

ClearDATA (191)
HIPAA Cloud Hosting
Austin, TX, USA
cleardata.com

Clearnetwork (8)
SOC as a service
Hazlet, NJ, USA
clearnetwork.com

Clone Systems (13)
Security Monitoring
Philadelphia, PA, USA
clone-systems.com

Cloud24X7 (18)
MSSP Enablement
Fort Lauderdale, FL, USA
cloud24x7.us

ControlScan (137)
Managed Security Services
Alpharetta, GA, USA
controlscan.com

Critical Start (112)
MDR
Plano, TX, USA
criticalstart.com

Cyberhat (47)
Managed SOC
Tel Aviv, Israel
cyberhat.co.il

Cybersafe Solutions (16)
MDR
Jericho, NY, USA
cybersafesolutions.com

Cyberseer (11)
Threat Intel
London, UK
cyberseer.net

Cybriant (30)
MDR
Alpharetta, GA, USA
cybriant.com

Cygilant (110)
MDR
Boston, MA, USA
cygilant.com

DATASHIELD (38)
Managed Security Services
Salt Lake City, UT, USA
datashieldprotect.com

deepwatch (133)
MDR
Denver, CO, USA
deepwatch.com

Delta Risk (71)
MDR
San Antonio, TX, USA
deltarisk.com

Difenda Labs (37)
MDR
Oakville, Canada
difenda.com

Digital Hands (79)
Managed Security Services
Tampa, FL, USA
digitalhands.com

Emprise (35)
Managed Services
Toledo, OH, USA
emptechllc.com

Ensign Infosecurity (255)
Managed Services
Kuala Lumpur, Malaysia
ensigninfosecurity.com

eSentire (424)
MDR
Cambridge, Canada
esentire.com

EventTracker (64)
Managed Security Services
Fort Lauderdale, FL, USA
eventtracker.com

Note: Numbers in parentheses indicate employee count

Expel (124)
SOC as a Service
Herndon, VA, USA
expel.io

FCI Cyber (939)
Device Management
Bloomfield, NJ, USA
fcicyber.com

Field Effect Software (28)
MDR
Ottawa, Canada
fieldeffect.com

Fortify 24x7 (3)
Managed Security Services
Los Angeles, CA, USA
fortify24x7.com

Fox-IT (303)
MDR
Delft, Netherlands
fox-it.com

GigaNetworks (20)
Managed Security Services
Miami, FL, USA
giganetworks.com

Greenview Data, Inc. (11)
Managed Services
Ann Arbor, MI, USA
greenviewdata.com

Guidepoint Security (304)
Managed Services
Herndon, VA, USA
guidepointsecurity.com

Herjavec Group (329)
Managed Services
Toronto, Canada
herjavecgroup.com

HighCastle Cybersecurity
(3)
Managed Services
New York, NY, USA
highcastlecybersecurity.
com

I-Tracing (126)
Managed Security Services
Puteaux, France
i-tracing.com

IBM (2,000)
Managed Services
Armonk, NY, USA
ibm.com

Igloo Security (46)
Managed Security Services
Seoul, South Korea
igloosec.co.kr

Intelisecure (181)
Managed Services
Greenwood Village, CO,
USA
intelisecure.com

Invinsec (14)
Managed Security Services
Cheltenham, UK
invinsec.com

IP Infusion (331)
Managed Services
Santa Clara, CA, USA
ipinfusion.com

IPV Security (17)
Monitoring
Ra'anana, Israel
ipvsecurity.com

ITC Secure Networking
(136)
Managed Security Services
London, UK
itcsecure.com

Kernel, Inc. (1)
Managed Services
Fayetteville, AR, USA
kernelops.com

Kobalt (5)
Managed Security Services
Vancouver, Canada
kobalt.io

Mako Networks Ltd. (40)
Managed Services
Elgin, IL, USA
makonetworks.com

Masergy (594)
Managed Services
Plano, TX, USA
masergy.com

MMOX (6)
SMB Solutions
The Hague, Netherlands
mmox.co

Mnemonic (227)
MDR
Oslo, Norway
mnemonic.no

Netintelligence (5)
Managed Services
Glasgow, UK
netintelligence.com

NETprotocol Limited (8)
Firewall Management
Wakefield, UK
netprotocol.net

Netsurion (364)
Managed Security Services
Houston, TX, USA
netsurion.com

**Netswitch Technology
Management** (22)
MDR
South San Francisco, CA,
USA
netswitch.net

Network Box USA (14)
Managed Services
Houston, TX, USA
networkboxusa.com

NRI Secure Technologies
(398)
SOC as a Service
Otemachi Chiyoda-ku,
Japan
Nri-secure.com

Nuspire (117)
Managed Services
Commerce, MI, USA
nuspire.com

OnePath (547)
Managed Services
Kennesaw, GA, USA
1path.com

Open Systems (257)
Managed Services
Zürich, Switzerland
open-systems.com

Optiv (200)
Managed Services
Denver, CO, USA
optiv.com

Perch (39)
SOC
Tampa, FL, USA
perchsecurity.com

Proficio (132)
MDR
Carlsbad, CA, USA
proficio.com

R&K Cyber Solutions (11)
Managed Security Services
Manassas, VA, USA
rkcybersolutions.com

RedScan (60)
MDR
London, UK
redscan.com

Rook Security (29)
Managed Services
Carmel, IN, USA
rooksecurity.com

Seccom Global (25)
Managed Services
Sydney, Australia
seccomglobal.com

Secnap (14)
Managed Services
Fort Lauderdale, FL, USA
secnap.com

Secon Cyber (135)
MDR
Surrey, UK
seconcyber.com

Secureme2 (5)
MDR
Rijen, Netherlands
secureme2.eu/en

SecureSky (16)
Cloud MDR
Omaha, NE, USA
securesky.com

SecureWorks (2,692)
Managed Services
Atlanta, GA, USA
secureworks.com

Security On-Demand (72)
Managed Firewalls
San Diego, CA, USA
securityondemand.com

Sentinel IPS (9)
Reputation Firewall
Dallas, TX, USA
sentinelips.com

Sentor (68)
Managed SIEM
Stockholm, Sweden
sentor.se

Solutionary (NTT) (128)
Managed Services
Omaha, NE, USA
solutionary.com

Solutions-II (97)
Monitoring
Littleton, CO, USA
solutions-ii.com

Specialized Security Services Inc. (43)
Managed Services
Plano, TX, USA
s3security.com

Tata Communications (1200)
Managed Services
Mumbai, India
tatacommunications.com

Tesorion (146)
Managed Services
Leusden, Netherlands
tesorion.nl

The Cyberfort Group (17)
Managed SOC
Thatcham, UK
cyberfortgroup.com

The DigiTrust Group (23)
Managed Endpoint and WAF
Los Angeles, CA, USA
digitrustgroup.com

Tophat Security (2)
Managed SIEM
Wilmington, DE, USA
tophatsecurity.com

True Digital Security (62)
Managed SIEM
Tulsa, OK, USA
truedigitalsecurity.com

Trushield, Inc. (40)
Managed Security Services
Sterling, VA, USA
trushieldinc.com

TrustWave (a Singtel Company) (1,417)
Managed Security Services
Chicago, IL, USA
trustwave.com

US Interactive (1)
Managed Services
Santa Clara, CA, USA
usinteractive.com

Vario Secure Networks (15)
Managed Security Services
Tokyo, Japan
variosecure.net/en

Verisign (1,323)
Managed Services
Reston, VA, USA
verisign.com

Verizon Business Security Solutions (1,000)
Managed Services
Basking Ridge, NJ, USA
verizonenterprise.com/
solutions/security

Vijilan Security (27)
Security for MSPs
Ft. Lauderdale, FL, USA
vijilan.com

VirtualArmour (50)
Managed Services
Centennial, CO, USA
virtualarmour.com

Zen Internet (464)
Managed Services
Rochdale, UK
zen.co.uk

Zyston (41)
Managed Security Services
Dallas, TX, USA
zyston.com

NETWORK

1H (8)
Security for Webhosting
Sofia, Bulgaria
1h.com

6WIND (76)
IPSec VPN Router
Montigny-le-Bretonneux, France
6wind.com

8e14 Networks (5)
Microsegmentation
San Francisco, CA, USA
8e14.net

A10 Networks (821)
DDoS Defense Appliance
San Jose, CA, USA
a10networks.com

Accolade Technology (10)
Network Appliance Security
Franklin, MA, USA
accoladetechnology.com

Adtran Inc. (200)
Firewalls
Huntsville, AL, USA
adtran.com

ADVA Optical Networking (2,241)
Secure Switching
Munich, Germany
advaoptical.com

Advenica (50)
Air Gap
Malmö, Sweden
advenica.com

Aerobyte (10)
Zero-Trust Networking
Boca Raton, FL, USA
aerobyte.com

Agat Software (29)
Security for Unified Comms
Jerusalem, Israel
agatsoftware.com

Akamai Technologies (500)
DDoS Defense
Cambridge, MA, USA
akamai.com

Aker (72)
Web Filtering
Brasilia, Brazil
aker.com.br

Akheros (4)
NBAD
Paris, France
akheros.fr

Note: Numbers in parentheses indicate employee count

Allot (926)
Content URL Filtering
Hod HaSharon, Israel
allot.com

Alsid (31)
AD Defense
Paris, France
alsid.com

Amgine Securus (2)
Network and Endpoint
Monitoring
South Korea
amgine.co.kr

Anchiva (10)
UTM
Beijing, China
en.anchiva.com

Apcon (249)
Packet Capture and Analysis
Wilsonville, OR, USA
apcon.com

Applicure (7)
Web Application Firewall
Ramat Gan, Israel
applicure.com

Arbor Networks (554)
DDoS Defense
Burlington, MA, USA
netscout.com

ArQit (13)
Post-quantum Defense
London, UK
arqit.io

Array Networks (OSS Corp.) (193)
SSL VPN
Milpitas, CA, USA
arraynetworks.com

Aruba Networks, an HP Company (150)
UEBA
Santa Clara, CA, USA
arubanetworks.com

Arxceo Corporation (3)
Intrusion Prevention
Ponte Vedra Beach, FL,
USA
arxceo.com

Aunigma Network Solutions (5)
Cloud Browser Proxy
Atlanta, GA, USA
aunigma.com

Authentic8, Inc. (75)
Cloud Browser Isolation
Redwood City, CA, USA
authentic8.com

Avaya (150)
SSL VPN
Santa Clara, CA, USA
avaya.com

Avi Networks (330)
Web Application Firewall
Santa Clara, CA, USA
avinetworks.com

Aviatrix (90)
Firewall Enablement in the
Cloud
Palo Alto, CA, USA
aviatrix.com

Awake Security (51)
Network Monitoring
Sunnyvale, CA, USA
awakesecurity.com

AwareHQ (43)
Monitor Social Networks
Columbus, OH, USA
awarehq.com

Baffin Bay Networking (34)
Threat Detection & Network Forensics
Stockholm, Sweden
baffinbaynetworks.com

Bandura Cyber (36)
Reputation Firewall
Columbia, MD, USA
banduracyber.com

Banyan Security (19)
Zero-Trust Networking
San Francisco, CA, USA
banyansecurity.io

Barac (11)
NBAD
London, UK
barac.io

Barracuda Networks
(1,427)
Anti-spam
Campbell, CA, USA
barracuda.com

Barrier1 (2)
UTM
Minneapolis, MN, USA
thebarriergroup.com

Bastille (1)
Wireless Security
Atlanta, GA, USA
bastille.net

Bettercloud (256)
Cloud Activity Monitoring
New York, NY, USA
bettercloud.com

Big Switch Networks (218)
DDoS Defense
Santa Clara, CA, USA
bigswitch.com

Bivio Networks (36)
Gateway Security Platform
Pleasanton, CA, USA
bivio.net

Blacksands (13)
Software Defined Perimeter
Ann Arbor, MI, USA
blacksandsinc.com

BlastWave (16)
Microsegmentation
Mountain View, CA, USA
blastwaveinc.com

Block Armour (6)
Zero-Trust Networking
Mumbai, India
blockarmour.com

Blue Ridge Networks (34)
Microsegmentation via
Tokens
Chantilly, VA, USA
blueridgenetworks.com

Bluecat Networks (10)
DNS Security
Bracknell, UK
bluecatnetworks.com

BluVector (Part of Comcast) (44)
IDS
Arlington, VA, USA
bluvector.io

BOSaNOVA (19)
Secure Terminal Emulation
Phoenix, AZ, USA
bosanova.net

Bricata (34)
IPS
Columbia, MD, USA
bricata.com

Broadcom (2,000)
Security Hardware
San Jose, CA, USA
broadcom.com

Caligare (1)
Network Monitoring
Netflow
Prague, Czech Republic
caligare.com

Calyptix Security Corporation (9)
UTM
Charlotte, NC, USA
calyptix.com

Cato Networks (118)
Cloud Security Layer
Tel Aviv, Israel
catonetworks.com

CD Networks (322)
DDoS Defense
Diamond Bar, CA, USA
cdnetworks.com

CensorNet (78)
Content URL Filtering
Basingstoke, UK
censornet.com

Centripetal (39)
Reputation Firewall
Herndon, VA, USA
centripetalnetworks.com

Certes Networks (49)
VPN
Pittsburgh, PA, USA
certesnetworks.com

CGS Tower Networks (12)
Network Taps
Rosh HaAyin, Israel
cgstowernetworks.com

Check Point Software
(5,604)
UTM
Tel Aviv, Israel
checkpoint.com

Cigent (16)
Network Monitoring
Fort Myers, FL, USA
cigent.com

Cisco (5,000)
Firewall
San Jose, CA, USA
cisco.com

Citrix Systems, Inc. (1,000)
Secure Remote Access
Fort Lauderdale, FL, USA
citrix.com

Clavister (142)
UTM
Örnsköldsvik, Sweden
clavister.com

Cloudflare (951)
CDN and DDoS Defense
San Francisco, CA, USA
cloudflare.com

Cloudmark Inc. (94)
DNS Security
San Francisco, CA, USA
cloudmark.com/en

Cloudpurge (1)
Virtualized Remote
Browsing
Sydney, Australia
cloudpurge.info

Cloudsploit (8)
AWS Config Testing and
Monitoring
Silver Spring, MD, USA
cloudsploit.com

Cohesive Networks (17)
Cloud Tunnels over IPSec
Chicago, IL, USA
cohesive.net

ColorTokens (230)
Zero-Trust Networking
Santa Clara, CA, USA
colortokens.com

Columbitech (12)
Mobile VPN
Stockholm, Sweden
columbitech.com

ContentKeeper (37)
Content URL Filtering
Braddon, Australia
contentkeeper.com

Corelight (80)
Traffic Analysis
San Francisco, CA, USA
corelight.com

Corero Network Security
(90)
DDoS Defense
Marlborough, MA, USA
corero.com

Coronet (85)
Endpoint Radio Protection
Tel Aviv-Yafo, Israel
coro.net

Corsa (32)
Zero-Trust Networking
Ottawa, Canada
corsa.com

CoSoSys (63)
DLP
Cluj-Napoca, Romania
endpointprotector.com

CounterFlow AI (14)
Forensics
Crozet, VA, USA
counterflow.ai

Countersnipe Systems (11)
IPS
Boston, MA, USA
countersnipe.com

cPacket (60)
Packet Capture
San Jose, CA, USA
cpacket.com

**Critical Research
Corporation** (1)
Endpoint Discovery
Austin, TX, USA
rumble.run

Crusoe Security (6)
Web Browsing Isolation
Neve Yarak, Israel
crusoesecurity.com

Cryptonite (6)
Segmentation
Rockville, MD, USA
cryptonitenxt.com

CSPi (143)
Packet Capture
Lowell, MA, USA
cspi.com

Cubro (64)
Packet Capture
Vienna, Austria
cubro.com

Cujo AI (150)
Home Security for Carriers
El Segundo, CA, USA
getcujo.com

CYAN Network Security
(2)
Secure Web Gateway
Vienna, Austria
cyannetworks.com

**Cyber Advanced
Technology**
IPS
Berkeley, CA, USA
www2.unhackablecloud.
com

Cyber Driveware
Network Malware Defense
Herzliya, Israel
cyberdriveware.com

Cybera (168)
SDN Application & Net-
work Security
Franklin, TN, USA
cybera.net

CyberGhost (67)
VPN
Bucharest, Romania
cyberghostvpn.com

Cyberhaven (26)
Network Data Flow Mon-
itoring
Boston, MA, USA
cyberhaven.io

Cyberinc (43)
Browser Isolation
San Ramon, CA, USA
cyberinc.com

CyberSeal (3)
SIGINT Offensive
Yehud, Israel
cyber-seal.net

Note: Numbers in parentheses indicate employee count

CyberSecure IPS (11)
IPS
Upper Marlboro, MD, USA
cybersecureips.com

cyel (5)
IP Address Morphing
Bern, Switzerland
cyel.ch

Cyren (266)
Web, Email & Mobile
Security
McLean, VA, USA
cyren.com

Cyxtera Technologies
(982)
Zero-Trust Networking
Coral Gables, FL, USA
cyxtera.com

D-Link Systems, Inc.
(1,000)
UTM
Taipei City, Taiwan
us.dlink.com

Dark3 (20)
SaaS Network Monitoring
Alexandria, VA, USA
darkcubed.com

Deep-Secure (48)
Air Gap (Data Diodes)
Malvern, UK
deep-secure.com

Deepfence (8)
IPS
Milpitas, CA, USA
deepfence.io

DH2i (8)
Zero-Trust Networking
Fort Collins, CO, USA
dh2i.com

DigiPortal, Inc. (1)
Anti-spam
Altamonte Springs, FL,
USA
digiportal.com

DigitalShark (3)
Web Defense
New York, NY, USA
digitalshark.org

Disconnect (16)
Consumer VPN
San Francisco, CA, USA
disconnect.me

Dispersive Networks, Inc.
(69)
VPN
Alpharetta, GA, USA
dispersive.io

Distil Networks (109)
Bot Detection
San Francisco, CA, USA
distilnetworks.com

Ditno (6)
Cloud Firewall Manage-
ment and WAF
Sydney, Australia
ditno.com

Dojo by BullGuard (1)
Home Wifi Security
Ra'anana, Israel
dojo.bullguard.com

**Dome9 (acquired by
Check Point in 2018)** (82)
Cloud Firewall Policy
Management
Tel Aviv, Israel
dome9.com

DOSarrest (26)
DDoS Defense
Richmond, Canada
dosarrest.com

Eastwind (5)
Network Monitoring for
Cloud
Salt Lake City, UT, USA
eastwindnetworks.com

Edgewise Networks (34)
Zero-Trust Networking
Burlington, MA, USA
edgewise.net

EfficientIP (106)
DNS Management
West Chester, PA, USA
efficientip.com

Endace (136)
IDS
Ellerslie, New Zealand
endace.com

Endian (26)
UTM
Bolzano, Italy
endian.com

Equiinet (18)
Firewall UTM for Voice
Las Vegas, NV, USA
equiinet.com

Ericom (93)
Browser Isolation
Closter, NJ, USA
ericomshield.com

ESCOM (1)
Anti-spam
Oakton, VA, USA
escom.com

ExpressVPN (12)
VPN
Tortola, British Virgin
Islands
expressvpn.com

F5 Networks (2,000)
DDoS and Firewall
Seattle, WA, USA
f5.com

Fastly (567)
DDoS Defense
San Francisco, CA, USA
fastly.com

FireEye (3,086)
Malware Sandbox
Milpitas, CA, USA
fireeye.com

Flowmon Networks (122)
Network Monitoring
San Diego, CA, USA
flowmon.com

FlowTraq (3)
Netflow Analysis
Manchester, NH, USA
flowtraq.com

ForeScout Technologies
(1,133)
Network Access Control
San Jose, CA, USA
forescout.com

Fortinet (5,735)
UTM
Sunnyvale, CA, USA
fortinet.com

FortyCloud (2)
Cloud VPN
Overland Park, KS, USA
40cloud.com

ForumSystems (28)
XML Firewall
Needham, MA, USA
forumsys.com

Full Armor Systems (6)
Content URL Filtering
Conroe, TX, USA
fullarmorsys.com

FullArmor (24)
Policy Management
Boston, MA, USA
fullarmor.com

GajShield (37)
Firewall
Mumbai, India
gajshield.com

Gama Operations (7)
Secure PBX
Petah Tikva, Israel
gamaoperations.com

Garrison (159)
Browser Isolation
London, UK
garrison.com

GateWatcher (39)
Threat Detection
Paris, France
gatewatcher.com

Gigamon (866)
Span Port Mirroring
Santa Clara, CA, USA
gigamon.com

Gita Technologies (42)
SIGINT Offensive
Tel Aviv, Israel
gitatechnologies.com

Gladius.io (8)
DDoS Defense
Washington, DC, USA
gladius.io

GlobalSCAPE, Inc. (128)
Secure File Transfer
San Antonio, TX, USA
globalscape.com

GOCOM Systems and Solutions Corporation (23)
Firewall
Mandaluyong City, Philippines
gocomsystems.net

GreeNet (16)
DPI for Carriers
Beijing, China
greenet.net.cn

GreenTeam Internet (1)
Cloud URL Filtering
Tel Aviv-Yafo, Israel
greentm.co.uk

Grey Wizard (17)
Network Web Protection
Poznań, Poland
greywizard.com

GreyCortex (34)
Traffic Analysis
Brno, Czech Republic
greycortex.com

H3C (2,806)
Secure Gateway
Beijing, China
h3c.com

Haltdos (12)
DDoS Defense
Noida, India
haltdos.com

HDN (17)
Security Switches
Guro-gu, South Korea
handream.net

Hermetric Software Services
Web Security
Kiryat Tiv'on, Israel
hermetric.com

Hillstone Networks (267)
Data Analytics Firewall Protection
Santa Clara, CA, USA
hillstonenet.com

HOB Networking (1)
VPN
Cadolzburg, Germany
hob.de

Hopzero (14)
Hop Minimization
Austin, TX, USA
hopzero.com

Horangi (71)
AWS Vulnerability Scanning
Singapore, Singapore
horangi.com

Huawei (4,000)
Firewalls
Shenzhen, China
www1.huawei.com/en/products/data-communication/network-security/index.htm

Human Presence (10)
Network Bot Detection
Greenville, SC, USA
humanpresence.io

Hyperion Gray (9)
Open Source Web Security
Concord, NC, USA
hyperiongray.com

Hypersonica (6)
Web Safety
London, UK
hypersonica.com

I-Trap Internet Security Services (1)
Intrusion Detection System
Doylestown, OH, USA
i-trap.net

iboss (249)
Secure Web Gateway
Boston, MA, USA
iboss.com

idappcom (8)
Packet Capture and Analysis
Ludlow, UK
idappcom.com

Imperva (1,185)
Web Application Firewall
Redwood Shores, CA, USA
imperva.com

Imvision Technologies (17)
Network Behavior Analysis
Ramat Gan, Israel
imvisiontech.com

Indusface (57)
Cloud WAF
Vodadora, India
indusface.com

Infoblox, Inc. (1,255)
DNS Security
Santa Clara, CA, USA
infoblox.com

Infobyte (47)
Intrusion Detection Platform
Miami, FL, USA
infobytesec.com

InGate (23)
Firewall
Sundbyberg, Sweden
ingate.com

Innefu Labs Pvt Ltd. (90)
Internet Surveillance for Law Enforcement
New Delhi, India
innefu.com

Inpixon (67)
Rogue Wifi AP Location
Palo Alto, CA, USA
inpixon.com

Instasafe (27)
Cloud VPN Gateway
Bangalore, India
instasafe.com

Intego Inc. (18)
Personal Firewall
Seattle, WA, USA
intego.com

Interface Masters Technologies (63)
Intrusion Prevention
San Jose, CA, USA
interfacemasters.com

Introspective Networks (7)
VPN
Broomfield, CO, USA
introspectivenetworks.com

Intrusion Inc. (27)
IDS/IPS
Richardson, TX, USA
intrusion.com

Note: Numbers in parentheses indicate employee count

InvizBox (6)
Portable VPN hardware
Dublin, Ireland
invizbox.com

Ipswitch (325)
Secure File Transfer
Burlington, MA, USA
ipswitch.com

IPV Tec (1)
Website Monitoring
Ra'anana, Israel
ipvtec.com

IPVanish (8)
VPN
Dallas, TX, USA
ipvanish.com

Iris Network Systems (23)
Netflow Analysis
Alpharetta, GA, USA
irisns.com

IronNet Cybersecurity
(245)
Traffic Analysis
Fulton, MD, USA
ironnet.com

IT Security, Inc. (1)
Application, Cloud & Network Security
Pittsburgh, PA, USA
it-security-inc.com

Ixia (1,271)
Network Visibility
Calabasas, CA, USA
ixiacom.com

Juniper Networks (2,000)
Firewall
Sunnyvale, CA, USA
juniper.net

Kasada (22)
Web Defense
Sydney, Australia
kasada.io

Keezel (11)
Wifi Firewall
Amsterdam, Netherlands
keezel.co

L7 Defense (7)
Network API Security
Be'er Sheva, Israel
l7defense.com

Light Point Security (6)
Secure Web Gateway Proxy
Baltimore, MD, USA
lightpointsecurity.com

Link11 (28)
DDoS Defense
Frankfurt, Germany
link11.de

Loki (6)
UTM
Izmir, Turkey
getloki.com

Lumeta (48)
Network Discovery
Somerset, NJ, USA
lumeta.com

Macmon (37)
Network Access Control
Berlin, Germany
macmon.eu

Magen (1)
Surveillance
Tel Aviv, Israel
ma-gen.com

Mancala Networks (5)
Network Monitoring
Meylan, France
mancalanetworks.com

Mantis Networks (8)
Visibility
Reston, VA, USA
mantisnet.com

Menlo Security (150)
Browser Isolation
Palo Alto, CA, USA
menlosecurity.com

**Meta Networks
(Proofpoint)** (22)
Zero-Trust Networking
Tel Aviv-Yafo, Israel
metanetworks.com

MetaFlows (1)
Network Monitoring
San Diego, CA, USA
metaflows.com

**Militus Cybersecurity
Solutions** (2)
NBAD
Newport Beach, CA, USA
milituscyber.com

Milton Security Group (41)
Network Access Control
Inline
Fullerton, CA, USA
miltonsecurity.com

Mimir Networks (3)
DDoS Defense
Sydney, Canada
mimirnetworks.com

MindoLife (11)
IDS and Network Management
Haifa, Israel
mindolife.com

Monarx (10)
Webshell Detection and
Blocking
Cottonwood Heights, UT,
USA
monarx.com

Myra Security (18)
Web Defense
Munich, Germany
myracloud.com

NCP Engineering (47)
VPN
Mountain View, CA, USA
Ncp-e.com

Netecs Evohop (1)
Gateway Security Platform
Norco, CA, USA
evohop.com

NetFlow Auditor (9)
Network Monitoring
Sydney, Australia
netflowauditor.com

NetFlow Logic (5)
Netflow Concentrator
Atherton, CA, USA
netflowlogic.com

**NetFort (acquired by
Rapid7, April 2019)** (13)
Network Traffic Capture
and Analysis
Galway, Ireland
netfort.com

NETGEAR (300)
Firewall
San Jose, CA, USA
netgear.com

NetLinkz (1)
Zero-Trust Networking
Sydney, Australia
netlinkz.com

NetMotion Wireless (153)
Wireless Security
Seattle, WA, USA
netmotionwireless.com

NetNinja (1)
Wifi Hot Spot Encryption
San Francisco, CA, USA
getnetninja.com

Netography (10)
DDoS Defense
San Francisco, CA, USA
netography.com

NetPilot (2)
UTM
Bristol, UK
netpilot.com

NetScout (3,018)
Situational Awareness &
Incident Response
Westford, MA, USA
netscout.com

Netshield (16)
Gateway Vulnerability
Scanning Appliance
Nashua, NH, USA
netshieldcorp.com

NetSTAR, Inc. (28)
Secure Web Gateway
Bellevue, WA, USA
NetSTAR-inc.com

Netsweeper (57)
Web Filtering
Waterloo, Canada
netsweeper.com

Network Critical (24)
Intrusion Prevention
Caversham, UK
networkcritical.com

Neustar (300)
DDoS Defense
Sterling, VA, USA
neustar.biz

Nexcom (1)
Network Security Appli-
ances
New Taipei City, Taiwan
nexcom.com

Nexusguard (180)
DDoS Defense
Tsuen Wan, Hong Kong
nexusguard.com

Niagra Networks (49)
Network Monitoring
San Jose, CA, USA
niagranetworks.com

NIKSUN (281)
NBAD
Princeton, NJ, USA
niksun.com

Noble (14)
Anomaly Detection
London, UK
noblecss.io

Nominet (250)
DNS Threat Detection
Oxford, UK
nominet.com

NordVPN
VPN Consumer
Panama City, Panama
nordvpn.com

Novetta Solutions (810)
Network Traffic Monitor-
ing
McLean, VA, USA
novetta.com

NoviFlow (44)
SDN
Montreal, Canada
noviflow.com

NS1 (113)
DNS Security
New York, NY, USA
ns1.com

NSFocus (468)
DDoS Defense
Santa Clara, CA, USA
nsfocus.com

Obsidian Security (55)
Cloud Monitoring
Newport Beach, CA, USA
obsidiansecurity.com

Odo Security (18)
Zero-Trust Networking
Tel Aviv, Israel
odo.io

One Identity (461)
Firewall
Aliso Viejo, CA, USA
oneidentity.com

OnlyMyEmail (12)
Anti-spam
Brighton, MI, USA
onlymyemail.com

OPAC (104)
Zero-Trust Networking
Herndon, VA, USA
opaq.com

OpenVPN (63)
VPN
Pleasanton, CA, USA
openvpn.net

Owl Cyber Defense (62)
Air Gap
Danbury, CT, USA
owlcyberdefense.com

P-X Systems (2)
IDS
Amsterdam, Netherlands
p-x.systems

Palo Alto Networks (6,488)
UTM
Santa Clara, CA, USA
paloaltonetworks.com

Pearl Software Inc. (14)
Web Filtering
Exton, PA, USA
pearlsoftware.com

Penta Security (114)
Web Application Firewall
Seoul, South Korea
pentasecurity.com

Perimeter 81 (38)
Secure Web Gateway
Tel Aviv, Israel
perimeter81.com

PerimeterX (146)
Website Defense
Tel Aviv-Yafo, Israel
perimeterx.com

Perytons (3)
IoT Defense
Ness Ziona, Israel
perytons.com

Plixer (94)
Netflow Analysis
Kennebunk, ME, USA
plixer.com

Positive Technologies
(483)
Web Application Firewall
Framingham, MA, USA
ptsecurity.com

PresiNET Systems Corp.
(8)
Network Monitoring
Victoria, Canada
presinet.com

Prismo Systems (16)
Zero-Trust Networking
San Francisco, CA, USA
prismosystems.com

Profitap (31)
Traffic Capture
Eindhoven, Netherlands
profitap.com

Protected Media (28)
Advertising Security
Petah Tikva, Israel
protected.media

**ProtectWise (acquired by
Verizon, March 2019)** (70)
Network Data Capture
Denver, CO, USA
protectwise.com

Protocol 46 (20)
Firewall
Saint Paul, MN, USA
protocol46.com

Proxim (155)
Wireless Security
San Jose, CA, USA
proxim.com

Pyramid Computer GmbH
(64)
Firewall
Freiburg, Germany
pyramid.de

Note: Numbers in parentheses indicate employee count

Q-Branch Labs (3)
VPN Device
Wilmington, DE, USA
q-branch-labs.com

Qgroup, GmbH (8)
Firewall
Frankfurt am Main, Germany
qgroup.de

QoSient (1)
Network Monitoring
New York, NY, USA
qosient.com

Qosmos, Division of ENEA (79)
DPI Technology
Paris, France
qosmos.com

Qrator (32)
DDoS Defense
Prague, Czech Republic
qrator.net

Quttera (5)
Malware Scanning of Websites
Herzliya Pituach, Israel
quttera.com

Radware (1,196)
Load Balancing, DDoS Defense, IPS, Firewall
Tel Aviv, Israel
radware.com

Rawstream (3)
DNS-Based Security
London, UK
rawstream.com

RealVNC (67)
Remote Access
Cambridge, UK
realvnc.com/en

Reblaze Technologies Ltd. (34)
Web Proxy Defense
Tel Aviv, Israel
reblaze.com

Red Button (3)
DDoS Defense
Tel Aviv, Israel
red-button.net

Red Piranha (41)
UTM
Melbourne, Australia
redpiranha.net

Redborder
IDS Based on SNORT
Sevilla, Spain
redborder.com

RedJack (31)
Network Monitoring
Silver Spring, MD, USA
redjack.com

RedShield Security (36)
Web Application Defense
Wellington, New Zealand
redshield.co

RedShift Networks (24)
VoIP Security
San Ramon, CA, USA
redshiftnetworks.com

Redstout (5)
UTM
Lisbon, Portugal
redstout.com

RelateData (3)
Network Monitoring
London, UK
relatedata.com

remote.it (6)
Zero-Trust Networking
Palo Alto, CA, USA
remote.it

Reprivata (3)
Microsegmentation
Palo Alto, CA, USA
reprivata.com

Responsight (8)
UEBA
Melbourne, Australia
responsight.com

RioRey (17)
DDoS Defense
Bethesda, MD, USA
riorey.com

Rocket Software, Inc. (1,211)
Secure Terminal Emulation
Waltham, MA, USA
rocketsoftware.com

Rubica (27)
VPN
San Francisco, CA, USA
rubica.com

SafeDNS (34)
DNS Filtering
Alexandria, VA, USA
safedns.com/en

Safehouse Technologies (7)
Network Cloud Proxy
Scottsdale, AZ, USA
safehousetechnologies.com

SaferVPN (26)
Consumer VPN
New York, NY, USA
safervpn.com

Sage Data Security (32)
Firewall
Portland, ME, USA
sagedatasecurity.com

Salt Security (19)
API Attack Detection
Palo Alto, CA, USA
salt.security

SAM (51)
Home Gateway Defense
Tel Aviv, Israel
securingsam.com

Sangfor (1444)
UTM
Shenzhen, China
sangfor.com

Secucloud (70)
Cloud Proxy Security
Hamburg, Germany
secucloud.com

Secui (1)
Firewall
Seoul, South Korea
secui.com

Secure64 (36)
DNS Security
Fort Collins, CO, USA
secure64.com

SecureLogix Corporation (72)
VoIP Security
San Antonio, TX, USA
securelogix.com

SecureSwitch (1)
Air Gap Switches
Pittsburgh, PA, USA
secureswitch.com

SecurityCTRL
Intrusion Detection
Edinburgh, UK
securityctrl.com

SecurityDAM (27)
DDoS Defense
Ramat HaHayal, Israel
securitydam.com

SEGURO (1)
Secure PBX
Petah Tikva, Israel
seguro-com.com

Sentrix (9)
Web App Security and DDoS Sefense
Waltham, MA, USA
sentrix.com

Septier Communication (79)
SIGINT Offensive
Petah Tikva, Israel
septier.com

Shaka Technologies (5)
DLP
Witham, UK
shakatechnologies.com

Shape Security (333)
Web Application Firewall
Mountain View, CA, USA
shapesecurity.com

Sharktech (13)
DDoS Defense
Las Vegas, NV, USA
sharktech.net

**Shield Square (acquired
by Radware, 2019)** (61)
Anti-bot, Anti-scraping
Bangalore, India
shieldsquare.com

ShieldX (57)
Cloud Microsegmentation
San Jose, CA, USA
shieldx.com

Signal Science (142)
WAF
Culver City, CA, USA
signalsciences.com

SiteLock (200)
Website Security
Scottsdale, AZ, USA
sitelock.com

SkyFormation (8)
CASB
Giv'at Shmuel, Israel
skyformation.com

Smoothwall (116)
UTM
Leeds, UK
smoothwall.com

Solarflare (210)
Network Security Moni-
toring
Irvine, CA, USA
solarflare.com

SonicWall (1,907)
UTM
Milpitas, CA, USA
sonicwall.com

Source Defense (32)
Client-Side Protection
against Third Party Attacks
Be'er Sheva, Israel
sourcedefense.com

StackPath (305)
WAF and DDoS at the
Edge
Dallas, TX, USA
stackpath.com

**StormShield (was NetASQ
and Arcoon)** (276)
UTM
Issy-les-Moulineaux,
France
stormshield.com

Stridepoint (5)
Secure Network Fabric
Tampa, FL, USA
stridepoint.com

SubpicoCat (2)
IPS
Sydney, Australia
subpicocat.com

Sucuri (63)
Website Defense
Menifee, CA, USA
sucuri.net

SynerComm (55)
Network & Security Infra-
structure
Brookdfield, WI, USA
synercomm.com

TamosSoft (1)
Network Monitoring
Christchurch, New Zea-
land
tamos.com

Tavve Software (15)
Packet Routing
Morrisville, NC, USA
tavve.com

Tehama (39)
Secure Virtual Desktops
Ottawa, Canada
tehama.io

Telesoft Technologies (86)
Netflow Monitoring Tools
Annapolis Junction, MD,
USA
Telesoft-technologies.com

Tempered Networks (65)
Zero-Trust Networking
Seattle, WA, USA
temperednetworks.com

Tenzir (4)
Network Forensics
Hamburg, Germany
tenzir.com

Teskalabs (9)
Secure Mobile Gateway
London, UK
teskalabs.com

The Email Laundry (11)
Managed Services
Naas, Ireland
theemaillaundry.com

Threat Stack (136)
Cloud Security Monitoring
Boston, MA, USA
threatstack.com

ThreatSTOP, Inc (30)
Cloud Reputation Service
Carlsbad, CA, USA
threatstop.com

ThreatWarrior (5)
Network Monitoring and
Defense
Austin, TX, USA
threatwarrior.com

ThreatX (20)
Web Application Firewall
Louisville, CO, USA
threatx.com

Titan IC (22)
IDS
Belfast, UK
Titan-ic.com

TitanHQ (52)
DNS Filtering
Galway, Ireland
titanhq.com

Todyl (5)
Remote Access Protection
New York, NY, USA
todyl.com

Total Digital Security (4)
Consumer VPN
West Palm Beach, FL, USA
totaldigitalsecurity.com

TransientX (1)
Zero-Trust Networking
San Francisco, CA, USA
transientx.com

Traversal Networks
IDS
Brazil
traversalnetworks.com

TunnelBear (47)
VPN
Toronto, Canada
tunnelbear.com

Unisys Stealth (500)
Network Cloaking
Blue Bell, PA, USA
unisys.com

United Security Providers
(57)
Web Application Firewall
Bern, Switzerland
united-security-providers.
com

Note: Numbers in parentheses indicate employee count

Untangle (68)
UTM
San Jose, CA, USA
untangle.com

VADO Security (3)
Air Gap
Giv'atayim, Israel
vadosecurity.com

Variti (7)
DDoS Defense
Lucerne, Switzerland
variti.com

Venustech (260)
UTM
China
venusense.com

Versa (304)
SDN
San Jose, CA, USA
versa-networks.com

Votiro (33)
File Scrubbing
Tel Aviv, Israel
votiro.com

Wallarm (71)
Cloud WAF
San Francisco, CA, USA
wallarm.com

Wandera (177)
Secure Mobile Gateway
San Francisco, CA, USA
wandera.com

**WatchGuard
Technologies, Inc.** (720)
UTM
Seattle, WA, USA
watchguard.com

Wavecrest Computing (15)
Secure Web Gateway
Melbourne, FL, USA
wavecrest.net

WebARX (4)
Web Application Firewall
London, UK
webarxsecurity.com

Webgap (3)
Remote Browser Isolation
Walnut, CA, USA
webgap.io

webScurity Inc. (1)
Web Application Firewall
Minneapolis, MN, USA
webscurity.com

WebTitan (TitanHQ) (53)
Content and Email Fil-
tering
Salthill, Ireland
webtitan.com

Wedge Networks (40)
Cloud Proxy Security
Calgary, Canada
wedgenetworks.com

Westgate Cyber Security
(4)
Zero-Trust Networking
Cwmbran, UK
westgatecyber.com

WifiWall (2)
Wifi Firewall
Kfar Haim, Israel
wifiwall.com

WinGate (Qbik) (1)
Gateway Security, VPN
Auckland, New Zealand
wingate.com

Winston Privacy (12)
Private Browsing
Chicago, IL, USA
winstonprivacy.com

Wintego (10)
Wifi Offensive
Yokne'am Illit, Israel
wintego.com

WiTopia (9)
VPN
Reston, VA, USA
witopia.com

wolfSSL (26)
Open Source Internet
Security
Edmonds, WA, USA
wolfssl.com

Xabyss
Traffic Capture and Anal-
ysis
Seoul, South Korea
xabyss.com

YAXA (2)
UEBA
Concord, MA, USA
yaxa.io

Yottaa (83)
DDoS Defense
Waltham, MA, USA
yottaa.com

ZenMate (13)
VPN
Berlin, Germany
zenmate.com

Zentera Systems (27)
Zero-Trust Networking
San Jose, CA, USA
zentera.net

Zorus (11)
Cloud Proxy
Monroe, CT, USA
zorustech.com

Zscaler (1,504)
Cloud Security Layer
San Jose, CA, USA
zscaler.com

Zvelo (41)
URL Categorization
Greenwood VillageCO,
CO, USA
zvelo.com

**ZyXEL Communications
Corp.** (33)
Firewall
Anaheim, CA, USA
zyxel.com/us/en/homep-
age.shtml

OPERATIONS

5Nine Software (46)
Hyper-V Security
West Palm Beach, FL, USA
5nine.com

Accudata Systems, Inc.
(195)
Security Management
Houston, TX, USA
accudatasystems.com

Algosec (395)
Firewall Policy Manage-
ment
Petah Tikva, Israel
algosec.com

Atar Labs (32)
Security Orchestration
London, UK
atarlabs.io

Augur Systems (1)
SNMP Traps
Wakefield, MA, USA
augur.com

Avanan (55)
Security Tool Deployment
New York, NY, USA
avanan.com

Awareness Technologies
(25)
Employee Monitoring
Westport, CT, USA
awarenesstechnologies.com

Axonius (33)
Orchestration
New York, NY, USA
axonius.com

Ayehu (55)
Orchestration
San Jose, CA, USA
ayehu.com

Basil Security (4)
Policy Enforcement
Atlanta, GA, USA
basilsecurity.com

Basis Technology (131)
Forensics (Text Analysis)
Cambridge, MA, USA
basistech.com

Belkasoft (19)
Mobile Device Forensics
Palo Alto, CA, USA
belkasoft.com

BinaryEdge (5)
Internet Scanning
Zürich, Switzerland
binaryedge.io

Bugcrowd (581)
Bug Reporting Platform
San Francisco, CA, USA
bugcrowd.com

Buglab (10)
Pen Testing Network
Casablanca, Morocco
buglab.io

CESPPA (13)
Bug Bounty
Manhattan Beach, CA,
USA
cesppa.com

Cloudera (247)
Cloud Security
Palo Alto, CA, USA
cloudera.com

Code 42 Software (505)
Secure Backup and Re-
covery
Minneapolis, MN, USA
code42.com

**Communication Devices,
Inc.** (7)
Secure Remote Manage-
ment
Boonton, NJ, USA
commdevices.com

CommVault (2,532)
Backup and Recovery
Tinton Falls, NJ, USA
commvault.com

Cyan Forensics (9)
Endpoint Forensics
Edinburgh, UK
cyanforensics.com

Cybeats (12)
Incident Response
Aurora, Canada
cybeats.com

Cyber 20/20 (11)
Behavior-Based Malware
Detection
Herndon, VA, USA
cyber2020.com

Cyber Operations, LLC (1)
ACL Management
Pelham, AL, USA
cyberoperations.com

Cyber Triage
Incident Response Man-
agement
Herndon, VA, USA
cybertriage.com

CyberCPR (1)
Secure Incident Response
Management
Cheltenham, UK
cybercpr.com

CyberObserver (22)
Manager of Managers
Caesarea, Israel
cyber-observer.com

CyberSponse (67)
Incident Response & Secu-
rity Operations
Arlington, VA, USA
cybersponse.com

Cybric (19)
Security Orchestration
Boston, MA, USA
cybric.io

Cydarm (4)
Incident Response Case
Management
Docklands, Australia
cydarm.com

Cymulate (57)
Breach and Attack Simu-
lation
Rishon LeZion, Israel
cymulate.com

Cynet (97)
APT Discovery via Agent-
less Scan
Rishon LeZion, Israel
cynet.com

Cyware (89)
Alert Management
New York, NY, USA
cyware.com

D3 Security (101)
Incident Management
Vancouver, Canada
d3security.com

Defence Intelligence (23)
Malware Protection
Kanata, Canada
defintel.com

**Demisto (Palo Alto
Networks)** (158)
Incident Response
Cupertino, CA, USA
demisto.com

Detexian (7)
Monitor Cloud Configu-
rations
San Diego, CA, USA
detexian.com

DFLabs (56)
Automated Incident &
Breach Response
Milan, Italy
dflabs.com

DisruptOps (15)
Monitor and Fix Cloud
Deployments
Kansas City, MO, USA
disruptops.com

Elcomsoft (16)
Forensics
Moscow, Russia
elcomsoft.com

Faraday (82)
Manager of Managers
Miami, FL, USA
faradaysec.com

Fenror7 (6)
Lateral Movement Detec-
tion
Herzliya, Israel
fenror7.com

FireMon (224)
Firewall Policy Manage-
ment
Overland Park, KS, USA
firemon.com

Flexible IR (1)
Incident Response
Singapore, Singapore
flexibleir.com

Fractal Industries (121)
Incident Response
Reston, VA, USA
fractalindustries.com

Glasswall Solutions (63)
Document Scrubbing
West End, UK
glasswallsolutions.com

HackerOne (813)
Operations / Zero Day
Research and Bounties
San Francisco, CA, USA
hackerone.com

Note: Numbers in parentheses indicate employee count

HALOCK Security Labs (35)
Incident Response
Schaumburg, IL, USA
halock.com

HoloNet Security (11)
Incident Investigation
Sunnyvale, CA, USA
holonetsecurity.com

Huntress Labs (10)
SaaS Malware Discovery
Baltimore, MD, USA
huntresslabs.com

HyTrust (147)
Cloud Security Automation
Mountain View, CA, USA
hytrust.com

InCyber (5)
Employee Monitoring
Cherry Hill Township, DE, USA
incyber1.com

Indeni (70)
Security Automation
San Francisco, CA, USA
indeni.com

Insider Spyder (2)
Employee Monitoring
Chantilly, VA, USA
insiderspyder.com

Interfocus Technologies (4)
User Behavior Monitoring
Costa Mesa, CA, USA
interfocus.us

Interguard (8)
Employee Monitoring
Westport, CT, USA
interguardsoftware.com

Intezer (30)
Malware Analysis
New York, NY, USA
intezer.com

Invincea (27)
Incident Response
Fairfax, VA, USA
invincea.com

Jemurai (5)
Security Program Dashboard
Chicago, IL, USA
jemurai.com

JOESecurity (8)
Malware Analysis
Reinach, Switzerland
joesecurity.org

KEYW (1,061)
Forensics
Hanover, MD, USA
keywcorp.com

Kroll (200)
Risk Mitigation & Response
New York, NY, USA
kroll.com

Loggly (18)
Log Aggregation
Austin, TX, USA
loggly.com

LogicHub (35)
Automated Incident Response
Mountain View, CA, USA
logichub.com

Loom Systems (28)
Incident Response
San Francisco, CA, USA
loomsystems.com

Magnet Forensics (240)
Forensics
Waterloo, Canada
magnetforensics.com

MistNet (17)
Cloud-Based Threat Hunting
Mountain View, CA, USA
mistnet.ai

MixMode (17)
Network Forensics
San Diego, CA, USA
mixmode.ai

Napatech (97)
Network Acceleration Cards
Soeborg, Denmark
napatech.com

Network Intelligence (567)
Firewall Policy Management
Mumbai, India
niiconsulting.com

Neuralys (16)
Risk Mitigation
Bethesda, MD, USA
neuralys.io

NIMIS Cybersecurity (2)
Automated Pen Testing
Melbourne, Australia
nimis.ai

NNT (47)
Workflow Automation
Naples, FL, USA
newnettechnologies.com

NTrepid (222)
Forensics and Linkage
Herndon, VA, USA
ntrepidcorp.com

Orca Security (25)
Cloud Vulnerability Scanning
Tel Aviv, Israel
orca.security

Paterva (4)
Maltego Enhancement
Pretoria, South Africa
paterva.com

PatternEx (20)
Security Automation
San Jose, CA, USA
patternex.com

Pcysys (30)
Automated Pen Testing
Petah Tikva, Israel
pcysys.com

Polarity (39)
Onscreen Data Augmentation
Farmington, CT, USA
polarity.io

Qingteng (15)
Asset Discovery and Protection
Beijing, China
qingteng.cn/en/index.html

QuoScient GmbH (36)
Security Operations Platform
Frankfurt am Main, Germany
quoscient.io

R-Vision (44)
Incident Response Platform
Moscow, Russia
rvision.pro

RangeForce (26)
Training
White Plains, NY, USA
rangeforce.com

Reposify (15)
Asset Discovery
Bnei Brak, Israel
reposify.com

Reversing Labs (152)
Malware Analysis
Cambridge, MA, USA
reversinglabs.com

SafeBreach (56)
Automated Pen Testing
Tel Aviv, Israel
safebreach.com

SaltStack (94)
Orchestration
Lehi, UT, USA
saltstack.com

SaltyCloud (6)
Workflow Automation
Austin, TX, USA
saltycloud.com

SearchInform (97)
Employee Monitoring
Moscow, Russia
searchinform.com

SecuLetter (3)
Malware Analysis
Seongnam-si, South Korea
seculetter.com

ServiceNow (500)
Orchestration
Santa Clara, CA, USA
servicenow.com

Seworks (221)
Automated Pen Testing
San Francisco, CA, USA
se.works

Shevirah (3)
Mobile Testing
Herndon, VA, USA
shevirah.com

Silicon Forensics (9)
Forensic Hardware
Pomona, CA, USA
siliconforensics.com

Skybox Security (352)
Security Management
San Jose, CA, USA
skyboxsecurity.com

SocView (7)
Alert Management
London, UK
socview.com

SolSoft (24)
Policy Management
Bristol, UK
solsoft.co.uk

StackStorm (1)
Orchestration
San Jose, CA, USA
stackstorm.com

Swimlane (75)
Incident Response
Louisville, CO, USA
swimlane.com

Syncurity Networks (20)
Incident Response Work-
flow
Bethesda, MD, USA
syncurity.net

Teramind (64)
Employee Monitoring
Aventura, FL, USA
teramind.co

TNT Software (5)
Security Management
Vancouver, WA, USA
tntsoftware.com

ToothPic (22)
Forensics Cameras
Turin, Italy
toothpic.eu

TriagingX (8)
Malware Sandbox
San Jose, CA, USA
triagingx.com

Tufin (442)
Firewall Policy Manage-
ment
Boston, MA, USA
tufin.com

**Twistlock (acquired by
Palo Alto Networks)** (121)
Container Security
Portland, OR, USA
twistlock.com

Uplevel Security (13)
Incident Response
New York, NY, USA
uplevelsecurity.com

Verint (3,132)
Data Mining
Melville, NY, USA
verint.com

VMRay (50)
Malware Analysis
Boston, MA, USA
vmray.com

Wetstone (15)
Forensics
Cortland, NY, USA
wetstonetech.com

Whistic (35)
Vendor Management
Pleasant Grove, UT, USA
whistic.com

WireX (20)
Network Forensics
Sunnyvale, CA, USA
wirexsystems.com

WiseSec (10)
Microgeolocation
Yokne'am Illit, Israel
wisesec.com

WitFoo (10)
Security Operations
Platform
Dunwoody, GA, USA
witfoo.com

Workspot (80)
Secure Remote Access
Campbell, CA, USA
workspot.com

X-Ways (8)
Forensics
Delhi, India
x-ways.net

XM Cyber (60)
Breach and Attack Simu-
lation
Herzliya, Israel
xmcyber.com

YesWeHack (49)
Bug Bounty
Paris, France
yeswehack.com

Yogosha (28)
Bug Bounty Platform
Paris, France
yogosha.com

ZecOps (19)
Automated Defense
San Francisco, CA, USA
zecops.com

Zyudly Labs (23)
Cloud Security for AWS
Palo Alto, CA, USA
zyudlylabs.com

SECURITY ANALYTICS

Acsia (372)
UEBA
Dublin, Ireland
acsia.io

Active Countermeasures
(16)
Threat Hunting
Spearfish, SD, USA
activecountermeasures.
com

Arc4dia (5)
Breach Detection and
Response
Montreal, Canada
arc4dia.com

Arctic Wolf Networks (236)
SIEM
Sunnyvale, CA, USA
arcticwolf.com

Assuria (20)
SIEM
Reading, UK
assuria.com

AT&T Cybersecurity (297)
SIEM
San Mateo, CA, USA
alienvault.com

Note: Numbers in parentheses indicate employee count

BitGlass (123)
Breach Discovery
Campbell, CA, USA
bitglass.com

Blue Hexagon (32)
Breach Detection
Sunnyvale, CA, USA
bluehexagon.ai

Blumira (10)
Threat Detection and
Response
Ann Arbor, MI, USA
blumira.com

BMC Software (200)
SIEM
Houston, TX, USA
bmc.com

BroadBridge Networks (3)
Network Monitoring
Fremont, CA, USA
broadbridgenetworks.com

Cambridge Intelligence
(35)
Data Visualization
Cambridge, UK
cambridge-intelligence.
com

Cequence Security (47)
NBAD
Sunnyvale, CA, USA
cequence.ai

Chronicle (part of Google)
(133)
SIEM
Mountain View, CA, USA
chronicle.security

Cienaga Systems (4)
Cyber Threat Management
Lakewood Ranch, FL, USA
cienagasystems.net

Confluera (19)
Autonomous Detection
and Response
Palo Alto, CA, USA
confluera.com

Cortex Insight (4)
Vulnerability Measurement
London, UK
cortexinsight.com

CounterTack (57)
Real-Time Attack Intelligence
Waltham, MA, USA
countertack.com

CTM360 (34)
Breach Detection
Seef, Bahrain
ctm360.com

Custodio Technologies (13)
Breach Detection and
Response
Ubi, Singapore
custodio.com.sg

Cyber adAPT (28)
Network Traffic Monitoring
Dallas, TX, USA
cyberadapt.com

Cyber Crucible (6)
Breach Detection
Severna Park, MD, USA
cybercrucible.com

Cybereason (459)
Breach Detection
Boston, MA, USA
cybereason.com

Cybraics (38)
Security Analytics
Atlanta, GA, USA
cybraics.com

Cycurity (45)
Security Analytics
Tel Aviv, Israel
cycurity.com

CyGlass (27)
Cloud SIEM
Littleton, MA, USA
cyglass.com

Cymatic (15)
UEBA
Raleigh, NC, USA
cymatic.io

Dark Cubed (20)
Network Monitoring
Charlottesville, VA, USA
darkcubed.com

DarkLight.ai (20)
Security Analytics
Bellevue, WA, USA
darklight.ai

Darktrace (889)
Breach Detection
San Francisco, CA, USA
darktrace.com

DataResolve (82)
UEBA
Noida, India
dataresolve.com

Datavisor (105)
Security Analytics
Mountain View, CA, USA
datavisor.com

DeUmbra (3)
Visualization
Austin, TX, USA
deumbra.com

Devo (184)
Cloud SIEM
Cambridge, MA, USA
devo.com

DNIF (6)
SIEM
Mumbai, India
dnif.it

Elastic (200)
SIEM
Amsterdam, Netherlands
elastic.co

Empow (34)
SIEM
Ramat Gan, Israel
empow.co

Encode (98)
Security Analytics
London, UK
encodegroup.com

Endgame, Inc. (153)
Security Intelligence and
Analytics
Arlington, VA, USA
endgame.com

**Ensilo (acquired by
Fortinet, 2019)** (86)
Breach Detection
San Francisco, CA, USA
ensilo.com

EventSentry (6)
SIEM
Chicago, IL, USA
eventsentry.com

Exabeam (358)
User Behavior Analytics
San Mateo, CA, USA
exabeam.com

Exeon Analytics (10)
Network Monitoring
Zürich, Switzerland
exeon.ch

ExtraHop Networks (451)
Network Detection and
Response
Seattle, WA, USA
extrahop.com

Fast Orientation (5)
UEBA
Washington, DC, USA
fastorientation.com

Fidelis Cybersecurity (282)
Security Analytics
Bethesda, MD, USA
fidelissecurity.com

Fluency Corp. (5)
Network Traffic
College Park, MD, USA
fluencysecurity.com

GuruCul (129)
Security Analytics
El Segundo, CA, USA
gurucul.com

Hawk Network Defense (5)
Security Analytics
Dallas, TX, USA
hawkdefense.com

Haystax (62)
Threat Analytics
McLean, VA, USA
haystax.com

Humio (37)
Log Analysis
London, UK
humio.com

Hunters.AI (22)
Breach Detection and
Response
Tel Aviv, Israel
hunters.ai

Huntsman (21)
SIEM
Chatswood, Australia
huntsmansecurity.com

IntelliGO Networks (30)
Breach Detection
Toronto, Canada
intelligonetworks.com

Interset (86)
Security Analytics
Ottawa, Canada
interset.com

**JASK (acquired by Sumo
Logic, 2019)** (121)
SIEM
Austin, TX, USA
jask.com

Jazz Networks (74)
UEBA
Uxbridge, UK
jazznetworks.com

LogDNA (79)
Security Analytics
Mountain View, CA, USA
logdna.com

LogPoint (199)
SIEM
Copenhagen, Denmark
logpoint.com

Logsign (52)
SIEM
Istanbul, Turkey
logsign.com

Logz.io (157)
Cloud Log Collection and
Analysis
Boston, MA, USA
logz.io

Mantix4 (5)
Threat Hunting
Englewood, CO, USA
mantix4.com

Micro Focus (239)
SIEM
Newbury, UK
microfocus.com

Nuix (468)
Analytics for Digital Investigations
Sydney, Australia
nuix.com

Palantir Technologies
(2,339)
Link Analysis
Palo Alto, CA, USA
palantir.com

pixlcloud (1)
Visualization
San Francisco, CA, USA
pixlcloud.com

Preempt Security (58)
UEBA
Ramat Gan, Israel
preemptsecurity.com

ProactEye (2)
CASB and UEBA
Pune, India
proacteye.com

Qomplx (94)
Monitoring and Response
Reston, VA, USA
qomplx.com/cyber

**Quadrant Information
Security** (29)
SIEM
Jacksonville, FL, USA
quadrantsec.com

RANK Software, Inc. (20)
Threat Hunting
Toronto, Canada
ranksoftwareinc.com

Reliaquest (380)
Threat Hunting
Tampa, FL, USA
reliaquest.com

Reservoir Labs (28)
Real-Time Threat Visibility
New York, NY, USA
reservoir.com

Respond Software (53)
Automated Incident Iden-
tification
Mountain View, CA, USA
respond-software.com

root9B (29)
Threat Hunting Platform
Colorado Springs, CO,
USA
root9b.com

Sapian Cyber (28)
Breach Detection
Joondalup, Australia
sapiencyber.com.au

SecBI (25)
Security Analytics
Tel Aviv, Israel
secbi.com

Seceon (56)
SIEM
Westford, MA, USA
seceon.com

Seclytics (10)
Threat Intelligence
San Diego, CA, USA
seclytics.com

SECNOLOGY (25)
Big Data Mining & Secu-
rity
El Granada, CA, USA
secnology.com

Secure Decisions (4)
Security Visualization for
Cyber Defense
Northport, NY, USA
securedecisions.com

Securonix (368)
UEBA
Addison, TX, USA
securonix.com

Senseon (38)
Breach Detection and
Response
London, UK
senseon.io

SIEMonster (9)
Security Analytics
New York, NY, USA
siemonster.com

Siemplify (79)
Threat Detection and
Response
New York, NY, USA
siemplify.co

Sift Security (3)
Cloud Monitoring
Palo Alto, CA, USA
siftsecurity.com

Skout Cybersecurity (76)
Streaming Data Analysis
New York, NY, USA
getskout.com

Note: Numbers in parentheses indicate employee count

Solarwinds (400)
SIEM
Austin, TX, USA
solarwinds.com

Splunk (1,000)
SIEM
San Francisco, CA, USA
splunk.com

SS8 (125)
Security Analytics
Milpitas, CA, USA
ss8.com

**STEALTHbits
Technologies, Inc.** (202)
Threat Prevention
Hawthorne, NJ, USA
stealthbits.com

Stellar Cyber (31)
Threat Detection & Network Forensics
Santa Clara, CA, USA
stellarcyber.ai

Sumo Logic (629)
SIEM
Redwood City, CA, USA
sumologic.com

Telemate Software (22)
SIEM
Norcross, GA, USA
telemate.net

ThetaRay (87)
Security Analytics
Hod HaSharon, Israel
thetaray.com

Threshing Floor (3)
SIEM Enrichment
Washington, DC, USA
threshingfloor.io

Trovares (8)
Graph Analytics
Seattle, WA, USA
trovares.com

Uptycs, Inc. (45)
OSQuery
Waltham, MA, USA
uptycs.com

Vectra Networks (246)
Cyber-Attack Detection & Management
San Jose, CA, USA
vectra.ai

VuNet Systems (30)
Log Analysis
Bangalore, India
vunetsystems.com

Zerho (2)
Machine Learning
Crestview, VA, USA
zerho.info

TESTING

achelos GmbH (33)
TLS Testing
Paderborn, Germany
achelos.de

AttackIQ, Inc. (61)
Security Instrumentation
San Diego, CA, USA
attackiq.com

Cronus (17)
Attacker Simulation
Haifa, Israel
cronus-cyber.com

MazeBolt Technologies
Testing for DDoS
Ramat Gan, Israel
mazebolt.com

NSS Labs (101)
Product Testing
Austin, TX, USA
nsslabs.com

Paladion (960)
Cybersecurity Testing & Monitoring
Reston, VA, USA
paladion.net

PeachTech (3)
Fuzzing
Seattle, WA, USA
peach.tech

Pwnie Express (17)
Wireless Scanning
Boston, MA, USA
pwnieexpress.com

Riscure (109)
Security Product Test Labs
Delft, Netherlands
riscure.com

SCYTHE (22)
Attack Simulation and Automated Pen Testing
Arlington, VA, USA
scythe.io

Spirent Communications
(200)
Security Instrumentation
Crawley, UK
spirent.com

Synack (155)
Testing
Redwood City, CA, USA
synack.com

**Verodin (acquired by
FireEye, 2019)** (93)
Security Instrumentation
McLean, VA, USA
verodin.com

THREAT
INTELLIGENCE

418 Intelligence (4)
Threat Intelligence Gamification
Reston, VA, USA
418intelligence.com

4iQ (100)
Stolen Identities
Los Altos, CA, USA
4iQ.com

Abusix (19)
Threat Intelligence
San Jose, CA, USA
abusix.com

ACID Technologies (2)
Threat Intel
Tel Aviv-Yafo, Israel
acid-tech.co

Alpha Recon (14)
Threat Intelligence Platform
Colorado Springs, CO, USA
alpharecon.com

Analyst Platform (8)
Threat Intelligence Platform
Reston, VA, USA
analystplatform.com

Anomali (301)
Threat Intelligence Platform
Redwood City, CA, USA
anomali.com

AppDetex (102)
Brand Monitoring
Boise, ID, USA
appdetex.com

Arctic Security (20)
Threat Intelligence
Oulu, Finland
arcticsecurity.com

BI.ZONE (81)
Threat Intel Aggregator
Moscow, Russia
bi.zone

Blueliv (67)
Threat Intel
Barcelona, Spain
blueliv.com

CriticalStack (12)
Threat Intel Aggregator
Cambridge, MA, USA
criticalstack.com

Crypteia Networks (PCCW) (15)
Threat Intelligence Platform and Analytics
Neo Psychiko, Greece
crypteianetworks.com

Cyabra (11)
Fake News Defense
Tel Aviv, Israel
cyabra.com

Cyberint (87)
Threat Intelligence
Petah Tikva, Israel
cyberint.com

CYFIRMA (23)
Threat Intelligence
Oak Park, IL, USA
cyfirma.com

CYFORT Security (2)
Threat Intel
Herzliya, Israel
cyfort.com

Cyjax (10)
Threat Intelligence
London, UK
cyjax.com

Darkbeam (5)
Threat Intelligence
London, UK
darkbeam.com

DarkOwl (25)
Dark Web Collection
Denver, CO, USA
darkowl.com

Darkscope (2)
Threat Intelligence
Wellington, New Zealand
darkscope.com

Digital Shadows (180)
OSINT Dark Web
San Francisco, CA, USA
digitalshadows.com

DigitalStakeout (5)
Threat Intel Web
Alpharetta, GA, USA
digitalstakeout.com

DomainTools (102)
Threat Intel from DNS
Seattle, WA, USA
domaintools.com

Echosec (22)
Intel Gathering Tool
Victoria, Canada
echosec.net

EclecticIQ (110)
Threat Intelligence Platform
Amsterdam, Netherlands
eclecticiq.com

Elemendar (4)
Threat Intelligence Analysis
Stourbridge, UK
elemendar.com

Farsight Security (54)
Threat Intel Enrichment from DNS
San Mateo, CA, USA
farsightsecurity.com

Flashpoint (140)
Dark Web Intel
New York, NY, USA
flashpoint-intel.com

GitGuardian (24)
Github Credential Monitoring
Paris, France
gitguardian.com

GreyNoise (7)
Dark Web Collection
Washington, DC, USA
greynoise.io

GroupSense (23)
Dark Web Collection
Arlington, VA, USA
groupsense.io

Hyas (18)
Attribution Intelligence
Victoria, Canada
hyas.com

Intel 471 (50)
Threat Actor Intelligence
Amsterdam, Netherlands
intel471.com

Inteller (3)
Threat Intelligence Platform
Israel
inteller.com

Intelliagg (5)
Threat Intelligence
London, UK
intelliagg.com

Intsights (150)
Deep & Dark Web
New York, NY, USA
intsights.com

iZOOlogic (10)
Threat Intelligence
London, UK
izoologic.com

LastLine (143)
Honeynet Malware IOCs
Redwood City, CA, USA
lastline.com

LifeRaft (35)
OSINT Monitoring
Halifax, Canada
liferaftinc.com

Lookingglass Cyber Solutions (308)
Threat Intelligence
Reston, VA, USA
lookingglasscyber.com

Malware Patrol (1)
Threat Intel Feed
São Paulo, Brazil
malwarepatrol.net

MarkMonitor (504)
Brand Monitoring
San Francisco, CA, USA
markmonitor.com

MXTools
Threat Intelligence
Brossard, Canada
mxtools.com

Nucleon Cyber (3)
Aggregation
Tampa, FL, USA
nucleon.sh

Prevailion (26)
Threat Intelligence
Fulton, MD, USA
prevailion.com

Q6 Cyber (40)
Dark Web Mining
Miami, FL, USA
q6cyber.com

Recorded Future (acquired by FireEye, 2019) (392)
Threat Intelligence
Somerville, MA, USA
recordedfuture.com

RepKnight (22)
Dark Web Breach Alert
Belfast, UK
repknight.com

Searchlight Security (2)
Dark Web Intel
Portsmouth, UK
slcyber.io

SecurityZONES (6)
Spamhaus
London, UK
securityzones.net

SenseCy (9)
Deep Web OSINT
Poleg Netanya, Israel
sensecy.com

Note: Numbers in parentheses indicate employee count

Silobreaker (36)
Threat Intel Management
London, UK
silobreaker.com

Sixgill (28)
Dark Web Intel
Netanya, Israel
cybersixgill.com

Skurio (26)
Brand Monitoring
Belfast, UK
skurio.com

SOC Prime (64)
Threat Intelligence Platform
Kiev, Ukraine
socprime.com

SpyCloud (44)
Dark Web Collection
Austin, TX, USA
spycloud.com

Sweepatic (7)
Brand Monitoring
Leuven, Belgium
sweepatic.com

Team Cymru (46)
Threat Intel IoCs Malware
Lake Mary, FL, USA
team-cymru.org

The Barrier Group (2)
Threat Intelligence Platform
Minneapolis, MN, USA
thebarriergroup.com

ThreatConnect (117)
Threat Intelligence
Arlington, VA, USA
threatconnect.com

ThreatLandscape (24)
Threat Intelligence
San Jose, CA, USA
threatlandscape.com

ThreatQuotient (104)
Threat Intelligence Platform
Reston, VA, USA
threatquotient.com

Thred Tech (45)
Threat Intelligence Platform
London, Canada
thredtech.com

TruSTAR (65)
Threat Intelligence Platform
San Francisco, CA, USA
trustar.co

Vigilante ATI (9)
Dark Web Research
Phoenix, AZ, USA
vigilante.io

Wapack Labs (17)
Hacker Account Takeover
New Boston, NH, USA
cms.wapacklabs.com

ZeroFOX (187)
Threat Intelligence / Social Media Monitoring
Baltimore, MD, USA
zerofox.com

TRAINING

Aries Security (12)
Cyber Range
Wilmington, DE, USA
ariessecurity.com

Be Strategic Solutions (7)
Crisis Simulation
Tel Aviv, Israel
best.be-strategic.solutions

BlueKaizen (5)
Training
Egypt
bluekaizen.org

BSI Group (50)
Standards Certification
London, UK
bsigroup.com

Circadence (175)
Cyber Range
Boulder, CO, USA
circadence.com

CTF365 (8)
Capture the Flag Exercise
Cluj-Napoca, Romania
ctf365.com

Cyber Skyline (5)
Continuous Training for Cybersecurity
College Park, MD, USA
cyberskyline.com

Cyberbit (334)
Cyber Range
Ra'anana, Israel
cyberbit.com

Cybergym (47)
Cyber Range
Hadera, Israel
cybergym.com

Cympire (12)
Cyber Range
Tel Aviv, Israel
cympire.com

Gyomo (3)
Anti-phishing
Herndon, VA, USA
gyomo.com

Hack the Box (115)
Cyber Range
Kent, UK
hackthebox.eu

Hueya (6)
Phishing Simulation
Bend, OR, USA
hueya.io

Immersive Labs (94)
Cyber Range
Bristol, UK
immersivelabs.com

Kernelios (10)
Simulation and Training
Rishon LeZion, Israel
kernelios.com

Protect2020 (2)
SaaS Platform
Camberley, UK
p2020academy.com

SecureSight Technologies (6)
Collaborative Learning
Ulhasnagar, India
securesighttech.in

SimSpace (57)
Cyber Range
Boston, MA, USA
simspace.com

Terranova Security (55)
Security Training
Laval, Canada
terranovasecurity.com

Cybexer (12)
Cyber Range
Tallinn, Estonia
cybexer.com

Defentry (10)
Web Scanning
Stockholm, Sweden
defentry.com